Praise for Laurence Rees's

HITLER'S CHARISMA

"[Rees] vividly illustrates the bonds of Germany's elites with Hitler—bonds which led to world war and genocide, and ensured that the dictator's power remained unbroken until the end." —Sir Ian Kershaw, author of *Hitler*: *A Biography*

"So how did Hitler convince his generals to invade Russia and his subjects to ignore the genocide around them? This readable, fascinating book, a worthy addition to the vast literature surrounding Hitler, has plausible answers." —*Kirkus Reviews*

"Rees moves easily from the broad themes of German politics and economics to the individual voices of those who supported and opposed Hitler. Incorporating most of the latest scholarship on Hitler, Rees provides valuable insights here into a topic that is not new." —*Library Journal*

"Rees's spotlight on charisma forces us to think hard about what it means to persuade, to argue, to reason—or simply to assert one's will." —*The Chronicle of Higher Education*

LAURENCE REES

HITLER'S CHARISMA

Laurence Rees is the writer, director, and producer of the BBC
TV series *The Dark Charisma of Adolf Hitler*. The former head
of BBC Television History programs, he has specialized for the
last twenty years in writing books and making television docu-
mentaries about the Nazis and World War II. Previous projects
that were both series and books include *Auschwitz: The Nazis
and the "Final Solution"* and *World War II: Behind Closed Doors*.
In 2006 Rees won the British Book Award for History Book of
the Year for *Auschwitz*. Educated at Oxford University, he was
appointed in 2009 a senior visiting fellow in the International
History Department of the London School of Economics and
Political Science. In 2010 he launched the multimedia website
WW2History.com, which won best in class awards in the education and reference categories at the 2011 Interactive Media
Awards. He lives in London.

HITLER'S CHARISMA

LEADING MILLIONS INTO THE ABYSS

LAURENCE REES

VINTAGE BOOKS
A DIVISION OF RANDOM HOUSE LLC
NEW YORK

FIRST VINTAGE BOOKS EDITION, JANUARY 2014

Copyright © 2012 by Laurence Rees

All rights reserved. Published in the United States by Vintage Books, a division of
Random House LLC, New York, and in Canada by Random House of Canada
Limited, Toronto, Penguin Random House Companies. Originally published in the
United Kingdom as *The Charisma of Adolf Hitler* by Ebury Press, an imprint of Ebury
Publishing, a division of the Random House Group Limited, London, in 2012, and
subsequently published in the United States in hardcover by Pantheon Books,
a division of Random House LLC, New York, in 2013.

Vintage and colophon are registered trademarks of Random House LLC.

The Library of Congress has cataloged the Pantheon edition as follows:
Rees, Laurence, [date]
Hitler's charisma : leading millions into the abyss / Laurence Rees.
p. cm.
Includes bibliographical references and index.
1. Hitler, Adolf, 1889–1945—Psychology.
2. Hitler, Adolf, 1889–1945—Public opinion.
3. Hitler, Adolf, 1889–1945—Influence.
4. Charisma (Personality trait)—Germany—History—20th century.
5. Hate—Political aspects—Germany—History—20th century.
6. Self-confidence—Political aspects—Germany—History—20th century.
7. National socialism—History.
8. Germany—Politics and government—1933–1945.
9. Germany—Social conditions—1933–1945. I. Title.
DD247.H5R386 2013 943.086092—dc23 [B] 2012033948

Vintage Trade Paperback ISBN: 978-0-307-38958-9
eBook ISBN: 978-0-307-90813-1

www.vintagebooks.com

Author photograph © Martin Patmore
Book design by Soonyoung Kwon

Printed in the United States of America
10 9 8 7 6 5 4 3 2 1

To the memory of my mother and father

Margaret Julia Rees (1927–1977)
and
Alan William Rees (1924–1973)

My whole life can be summed up as this ceaseless effort of mine to persuade other people.[1]

—ADOLF HITLER

That such a man could go so far toward realizing his ambitions and—above all—could find millions of willing tools and helpers; that is a phenomenon the world will ponder for centuries to come.[2]

—KONRAD HEIDEN

CONTENTS

HITLER'S CHARISMA

INTRODUCTION

My parents had very firm views about Adolf Hitler. Having both experienced the war—with my father's brother killed on the Atlantic convoys—they thought Hitler was the embodiment of all evil. But even as a child I can remember thinking if Hitler was the Devil in human form how did he get so many people to do his bidding? In a way, that's a question I have been thinking about ever since, and one that I attempt to answer in this work.

Adolf Hitler was, at first sight, the most unlikely leader of a sophisticated state at the heart of Europe. He was incapable of normal human friendships, unable to debate intellectually, filled with hatred and prejudice, bereft of any real capacity to love, and "lonely."[1] He was, undoubtedly, "as a human figure, lamentable."[2] Yet he played the most important part in three of the most devastating decisions ever taken: the decision to invade Poland that led to the Second World War, the decision to invade the Soviet Union, and the decision to murder the Jews.

But Hitler did not create all this horror on his own, and alongside his many personal inadequacies he undoubtedly possessed great powers of persuasion. "My whole life," he said memorably in 1942, "can be summed up as this ceaseless effort of mine to persuade other people."[3] And I've met many people who lived through this period who confirmed that judgement. When pressed on the reason why they found such a strange figure so persuasive they pointed to a myriad of factors, like the circumstances of the time, their fears, their hopes and so on. But many also described simply the powerful sense of attraction they felt for Hitler—something that a number of people ascribed to his "charisma."

But what exactly is "charisma"? The word has Greek roots meaning a grace or favour divinely bestowed, but charisma, as we use the term today, is not a "divine" gift but "value neutral"[4]—nasty people can possess it just as much as nice ones. The original meaning also implies that charisma is an absolute quality that exists—or does not exist—in a particular individual. But Adolf Hitler's charismatic appeal was not universal. It was present only in the space between him and the emotions of his audience. Two people could meet Hitler at the same time and one might find him charismatic and the other might think he was a fool.

Our modern understanding of the concept of "charisma" begins with the work of the German social theorist Max Weber, who famously wrote about "charismatic leadership"[5] at the turn of the last century. Even though he was writing long before Hitler became Chancellor of Germany, his work is still full of relevance for anyone interested in the study of Nazism in general and Hitler in particular. Crucially, what Weber did was to examine "charismatic leadership" as a particular type of rule—rather than a personal quality that a pop star can possess as much as a politician. For Weber, the "charismatic" leader must possess a strong "missionary" element and is almost a quasi-religious figure. Followers of such a leader are looking for more than just lower taxes or better health care, but seek broader, almost spiritual, goals of redemption and salvation. The charismatic leader cannot exist easily within normal bureaucratic structures and is driven forward by a sense of personal destiny. Hitler, in these terms, is the archetypal "charismatic leader."

In particular, I think it is hard to underestimate the importance of understanding that charisma is created in an interaction between individuals. And in this context my ability to meet and question people who lived through this extraordinary period has been of enormous benefit. In writing this book I've been fortunate to have access to a unique primary source—the hundreds of interviews with eyewitnesses and perpetrators conducted for my work as a historical filmmaker over the last twenty years. Only a small fraction of this material has ever been published before, and so the vast majority of the testimony that is quoted in this book appears here in print for the first time.

I was hugely privileged to be able to travel the world and meet these people—from those who worked closely with Hitler to those who committed murders in pursuit of his aims, from those who suffered at his hands to those who finally helped destroy him. I was also lucky, after the fall of the Berlin Wall, to be one of the first to travel into the former Communist countries of Eastern Europe and record open and honest interviews about Nazism with people who had lived behind the Iron Curtain. What they said was often both shocking and surprising.

I've also benefited from the lengthy discussions I've held with many of the world's greatest academic historians—material I gathered for my educational website WW2History.com—as well as studying information from archival and other more traditional research sources. But it was meeting and questioning people who met Hitler and who lived under his rule that offered me the greatest clues into the nature of his appeal. (One must treat eyewitness testimony with considerable care and I've written elsewhere of the many tests and safeguards we used when gathering this material.[6])

I've also learnt a great deal from studying reel upon reel of archive footage from the period—particularly footage of Hitler's speeches. I had thought, when I started my work on Nazism twenty years ago, that the "charisma" of Hitler might somehow be visible in the footage. However, it soon became clear—at least for me—that Hitler is decidedly uncharismatic on film today. But, of course, this is precisely the point. I felt nothing because I am not a person of that time—a person, moreover, already predisposed to accept Hitler's charismatic appeal. I was not hungry; humiliated after the loss of a war; unemployed; frightened of widespread violence on the streets; feeling betrayed by the broken promises of the democratic system I lived in; terrified of my savings vanishing in a bank crash; and wanting to be told that all of this mess was the fault of someone else.

It's also important to state emphatically that people who accept the "charisma" of a leader are most definitely not "hypnotised." They know exactly what is going on and remain completely responsible for their actions. The fact that someone chooses to follow a charismatic leader cannot subsequently be used as an alibi or excuse.

Yet Hitler was not, it has to be said, only a leader with charisma. He also used threat, murder and terror to get his way, and I attempt to show how these aspects fitted into the history of his rise to power and his subsequent rule. There were certainly some people who carried out Hitler's desires only out of fear, just as there were others who never found Hitler charismatic at all.

Finally, whilst this work is entirely about Hitler, I do believe that it has relevance today. The desire to be led by a strong personality in a crisis, the craving for our existence to have some kind of purpose, the quasi worship of "heroes" and "celebrities," the longing for salvation and redemption: none of this has changed in the world since the death of Hitler in April 1945.

Human beings are social animals. We want to belong. Life, otherwise, can be a very cold experience indeed. And only by understanding how those who seek power try to influence us, and how we often actively participate in our own manipulation, can we finally understand the dangers we face if we leave rationality and scepticism aside and, instead, put our faith in a leader with charisma.

PART ONE

THE ROAD TO POWER

1

DISCOVERING A MISSION

In 1913, when Adolf Hitler was twenty-four years old, nothing about his life marked him out as a future charismatic leader of Germany. Not his profession; he eked out a living as a painter of pictures for tourists in Munich. Not his home; he lived in a small room, rented from Josef Popp, a tailor, on the third floor of a house at 34 Schleissheimer Strasse, north of Munich's main station. Not the clothes he wore; he dressed conservatively, if shabbily, in the conventional bourgeois apparel of the day—black coat and trousers. Not his physical appearance; he was distinctly unprepossessing in looks, with sunken cheeks, discoloured teeth, a straggly moustache, and black hair lying limply across his forehead. Not his emotional life; he found it impossible to sustain any lasting friendship and had never had a girl friend.

His chief distinguishing characteristic was his capacity to hate. "He was at odds with the world," wrote August Kubizek who had lodged with him in Austria several years before. "Wherever he looked, he saw injustice, hate and enmity. Nothing was free from his criticism, nothing found favour in his eyes . . . Choking with his catalogue of hates, he would pour his fury over everything, against mankind in general who did not understand him, who did not appreciate him and by whom he was persecuted."[1]

How was it possible for this man, so undistinguished at the age of twenty-four, to become one of the most powerful and infamous figures in the history of the world—a leader, moreover, known for his "charisma"?

Circumstances, of course, would play a large part in this transformation. But one of the many remarkable aspects of this story is how a number of the key personality traits which Hitler possessed as an oddball painter, trudging the streets of Munich in 1913—aspects of his character which contributed to his lack of professional and personal success at the time—would not only remain consistently with him for the rest of his life, but subsequently be perceived not as weaknesses but as strengths. Hitler's monumental intolerance, for instance, meant that he found it impossible to debate any issue. He would state his views and then lose his temper if he was systematically questioned or criticised. But what was perceived as ignorant slogan shouting in 1913 would later be seen as certainty of vision. Then there was his massive over-confidence in his own abilities. Back in Vienna, a few years before, he had announced to his mystified roommate that he had decided to write an opera—and the fact he could neither read nor write music properly was no handicap. In years to come, this over-confidence would be perceived as a mark of genius.

By the time he arrived in Munich, Hitler had already experienced years of disappointment. Born on 20 April 1889, at Braunau am Inn in Austria, on the border with Germany, Hitler did not get on with his elderly father, a customs official, who beat him. His father died in January 1903 at the age of sixty-five and his mother succumbed to cancer four years later in December 1907 when she was just forty-seven years old. An orphan at the age of eighteen, Hitler drifted between Linz in Austria and the capital, Vienna, and for some months in 1909 he experienced real destitution before a small financial gift from an aunt allowed him to set up as a painter. He disliked Vienna, believing it to be a seedy, impure city awash with prostitution and corruption. It wasn't until his twenty-fourth birthday, when he received a delayed legacy of just over 800 Kronen from his father's will, that he was able to leave Austria and seek lodgings in Munich, this "German" city, a place which he later said he was "more attached" to "than to any other spot of earth in this world."[2]

But even though he was living, at last, in a city he loved, Hitler seemed en route to absolute obscurity. Despite the impression he later wanted the world to have—in his autobiography, *Mein Kampf,* written eleven years later, Hitler tried to convince his readers that during this time he had functioned almost as an embryonic politician[3]—in 1913 Hitler was a socially and emotionally inadequate individual drifting through life without direction. Crucially, what he lacked at twenty-four—and what many other historical figures perceived as charismatic leaders already possessed by this age—was a sense of personal mission. He only discovered what he passionately believed was his "mission" in life as a result of the First World War and the manner in which it ended. Without these epic events he would almost certainly have remained in Munich and be unknown to history.

Instead, he began his journey into the consciousness of the world on 3 August 1914 when he petitioned—as an Austrian—to join the Bavarian Army. Just two days before, on the first of August, Germany had declared war on Russia. Hitler now passionately wanted to serve the German state he so admired, and his wish was granted when in September 1914 he was sent as an ordinary soldier to the 16th Bavarian Reserve Regiment (also known as the "List" Regiment). The following month he saw action for the first time close to Ypres. He wrote to an acquaintance back in Munich describing the scene, "To the left and right the shrapnel were bursting, and in between the English bullets sang. But we paid no attention . . . Over us the shells were howling and whistling, splintered tree-trunks and branches flew around us. And then again grenades crashed into the wood, hurling up clouds of stones, earth, and stifling everything in a yellowish-green, stinking, sickening vapour . . . I often think of Munich, and every man of us has the single wish that the gang out here will have their hash settled once and for all. We want an all-out fight, at any cost . . . "[4]

These are the words of a man who has found something. Not just—for the first time—a sense of purpose in a communal enterprise with other human beings, but a real insight into the dramatic possibilities of existence. And this conflict would have a similar effect not just on Hitler, but also on many others. "War, the father of all things, is also our father," wrote Ernst Jünger, another veteran of the war. "He hammered us and chiselled us, hardened us into that which we now are. And forever, as long as the wheel of life still turns in us, war will be the axis on which it revolves. He trained us for war, and warriors we will remain as long as we draw the breath of life."[5]

What Hitler, Jünger, and millions of others experienced on the Western Front was a war unlike any other before. A war in which the power of defensive weapons like the machine gun and barbed wire confined the conflict to narrow, bloody killing grounds. A war in which flamethrowers, high explosives and poison gas wreaked havoc. As a result, for Hitler, the "romance" of battle was soon "replaced by horror."[6]

It's not surprising that Hitler formed the view that life was a constant and brutal struggle. Life for an ordinary soldier in the First World War was exactly that. But it was not only that. There was also—especially for Adolf Hitler—a sense in which the experience of this war was also a test, offering the possibility of acts of heroism. And still, despite recent scholarly work that confirms that Hitler did not live in the trenches but served as dispatch runner based at regimental headquarters just behind the front line,[7] there is no disputing that Adolf Hitler was a courageous soldier. He was wounded in October 1916 at the Battle of the Somme and then, two years later, won the Iron Cross, First Class. He was put forward for this award by a Jewish officer, Hugo Gutmann, and the official recommendation, by the commander of the regiment, Emmerich von Godin, stated that "as a dispatch runner he [i.e., Hitler] was a model in sangfroid and grit both in static and mobile warfare," and that he was "always prepared to volunteer to deliver messages in the most difficult of situations under great risk to his own life."[8]

However, despite his bravery, Hitler remained just as unusual a character to his regimental comrades as he had to his acquaintances before the war. As one of his fellow soldiers, Balthasar Brandmayer, later recalled, "there was something peculiar about Hitler."[9] Hitler's comrades thought it odd that he never wanted to get drunk or have sex with a prostitute; that he spent what leisure time he had reading or drawing, or occasionally haranguing those around him about any subject that took his fancy; that he seemed to have no friends or family and, as a consequence, was a man resolutely alone.[10] As for "charisma"—Hitler seemed to possess none whatsoever.

But he was absolutely committed to the war, and he extrapolated from his own bravery and commitment the belief that almost everyone else at the front line felt the same. It was behind the lines, back in Germany, he wrote in *Mein Kampf,* that the troops were "betrayed" by those who wanted to profit from the sacrifice of the soldiers in combat. This idea of a *Frontgemeinschaft,* a united comradeship of front-line soldiers let down by others away from the battlefield, is a myth—but it was a popular one. By the time Hitler was injured for the last time in battle, in October 1918 close to Ypres, Germany had lost the war for a variety of reasons, none of which was "betrayal" behind the lines. The reality was that the Germans were crushed by the sheer weight of forces ranged against them—not least the Americans whose entry into the war in April 1917 guaranteed the arrival of hundreds of thousands of fresh troops. In addition, a blockade of Germany by Allied naval vessels had caused widespread food shortages—a bad situation that was made worse by a mass outbreak of influenza in spring 1918.

By that autumn there were plenty of members of the German armed forces who had decided the war was lost. In October, Admiral Franz von Hipper's sailors refused to leave port to fight in one last doomed action against the Allies. A mutiny soon followed in the naval city of Kiel, and spread to Lübeck, Bremen and eventually Hamburg. A widespread German revolution seemed a possibility—one inspired by the successful Bolshevik revolution in Russia the previous year. It was obvious to leading German politicians that an end needed to be made to the war as quickly as possible, and just as obvious—given the demands of the Allies—that whatever Germany's future was, it did not include one in which the Kaiser, the man most closely associated with the decision to go to war in the first place, remained as head of state. General Wilhelm Groener gave the Kaiser this unwelcome news, and on 9 November 1918 Germany became a Republic.

This sudden departure of the head of state caused immense dismay to many German officers. "At the worst moment of the war we have been stabbed in the back," wrote Ludwig Beck, then serving with the Army High Command, and later to be Chief of Staff of the German Army. "Never in my life have I been so upset about something I have personally witnessed as I was on the 9 and 10 November. Such an abyss of meanness, cowardice, lack of character, all of which I had until then considered impossible. In a few hours 500 years of history have been shattered; like a thief the Emperor was deported to Dutch territory. It could not happen fast enough—this to a distinguished, noble and morally upstanding man."[11]

Among a number of the ordinary soldiers at the front, who were unaware that Germany could scarcely continue to wage this war, there was a similar sense of bewilderment, not only at the swift removal of the Kaiser but at the immediate declaration of an armistice, which came into effect on 11 November 1918. "The front-line troops didn't feel themselves beaten," says Herbert Richter, who fought on the Western Front, "and we were wondering why the armistice was happening so quickly, and why we had to vacate all our positions in such a hurry, because we were still standing on enemy territory, and we thought all this was strange . . . we were angry, because we did not feel that we had come to the end of our strength."[12]

Germany seemed to be splitting apart—between those like Beck and Richter who believed that the army had somehow been betrayed and those like the mutinous German sailors who had accepted defeat and now wanted the whole social order to be overturned. In Berlin, in January 1919, a General Strike developed into a socialist uprising. Fridolin von Spaun, then a teenager from Bavaria, travelled to the capital to witness these historic events. "I was so excited by what was taking place. Because I read in the papers about the revolution in Berlin. And I just had to see for myself how such a revolution is done. I was driven to Berlin by curiosity. And once there I threw myself into the tumult, the city was absolutely mad. Hundreds of thousands of people ran through the streets and were shouting: first on one side, then on the other. There was a very Left-wing faction. And this very Left-wing faction was decisively influenced by one man, called Karl Liebknecht. And fortune, which sometimes does smile on me, granted me seeing him in the flesh . . . I was in the crowd. And suddenly I heard a shout. And then a truck arrived, the people had left some space for it, like an alley. It drove up, and everyone shouted, 'Liebknecht, Liebknecht!' They cheered. I hadn't even seen him. Because he was so surrounded by a mass of people, by a bodyguard with loaded rifles, all kinds . . . And [then] this legendary man, Karl Liebknecht, appeared at the upstairs window and made a rousing speech. It wasn't very long, a quarter of an hour or half an hour, I can't remember any longer. And this speech made such an impression on me, that from that hour onward I was a sworn anti-Bolshevist. Because all the silly phrases which he chucked to the people, and the inflammatory, incredibly inflammatory statements . . . I noticed that he is not at all interested in creating a paradise for the workers. In fact, it's only a lust for power. And so, completely immune to all temptations from the Left, I left the square an anti-Bolshevist. Fourteen days later this Mr. Liebknecht was no longer alive. His opponents had caught him and his accomplice—a woman from Poland, Rosa Luxemburg. They simply killed the both of them. Perhaps it sounds very callous, but I couldn't shed any tears for them. They got their just deserts."[13]

Fridolin von Spaun was so appalled at what he perceived as Karl Liebknecht's "lust for power" in Berlin in January 1919 that he subsequently joined a *Freikorps* unit in order to fight back against the Communist revolutionaries. In the wake of the destruction of order at the end of the war, a number of these paramilitary *Freikorps* had been formed in an attempt to suppress the Left-wing revolution. These groups consisted mostly of ex-soldiers who had responded to the call of their old commander. And it was *Freikorps* units—rather than the established German army or police—who played the most important role in suppressing the revolution in Berlin in January 1919 and who then became the initial guarantors of the new German Republic. Many of the figures who were later to become infamous as Nazis—Heinrich Himmler, Rudolf Höss and Gregor Strasser among them—were active in the *Freikorps* around this time. But, significantly, Adolf Hitler was not.

In *Mein Kampf,* Hitler wrote that as he lay in bed in hospital in Pasewalk in November 1918, temporarily blinded[14] after a gas attack, he was overwhelmed with the feeling that the circumstances of the end of the war represented "the greatest villainy of the century."[15] As he saw it, an alliance of Marxists and Jews had come together in an attempt to topple the Fatherland. It was this moment, he wrote, that was decisive in his decision to "go into politics."

The attractions of such a dramatic story in the formation of a myth are obvious. The noble soldier from the front line, betrayed by corrupt and self-serving politicians, now decides to devote his life to saving his country. Everything fits. But whilst fictional tales can work like this, life seldom does. And the evidence is that Hitler's great "mission" was not formed here at all.

Hitler left hospital on 17 November 1918 and returned to Munich.

He found the city in the midst of seismic change. Ten days before, on 7 November, a demonstration in Munich's Theresienwiese park organised by the Socialist politician, Erhard Auer, had led to revolution. The spark had been lit by a journalist and anti-war campaigner called Kurt Eisner. He had incited soldiers who were attending the demonstration to mutiny against their officers and take control of their own barracks. "Workers councils" and "Soldiers councils" were formed to bring order to the revolution, and the hereditary monarchy of Bavaria, the house of Wittelsbach, was deposed. Munich now became a Socialist Republic under the leadership of Kurt Eisner.

Hitler later expressed in *Mein Kampf* his repulsion for the way events had transpired in his beloved Munich; hardly surprising, since Kurt Eisner was both Jewish and a Socialist. However, his actions at the time were very different. Unlike thousands of other Germans like Fridolin von Spaun, who joined paramilitary *Freikorps* units to fight the Communist revolution, Hitler decided to remain in the army. Then, after a brief spell out of Munich guarding a prisoner-of-war camp, he is to be found in early 1919 back in the city serving in his unit at a time when Munich was still under the control of Kurt Eisner.[16] And when the ill-fated "Soviet Republic" of Bavaria was declared a few weeks later, led by fanatical Communists like Eugen Levine (who, like Eisner, was Jewish), documents show that Hitler was elected as a representative of his battalion[17]—something that would scarcely have been possible if he had opposed the Communist revolution.

There were clear alternative actions available to Hitler at this time—he could have tried to leave the army and join a *Freikorps* or, at the very least, decided to have as little to do with the Communist regime in Munich as possible. Hitler's failure to do any of this casts severe doubts on his subsequent protestations in *Mein Kampf* that he possessed a fanatical political "mission" in early 1919. Yet only a few months later, in the autumn of that year, when Hitler wrote his first political statement, it dripped with hatred against the Jews and fitted consistently with views that he was to express for the rest of his life.

What changed, between Hitler's apparent acceptance of the Communist revolution in Munich in April 1919 and the expression of his hatred against the Jews in September, was the political situation. *Freikorps* units entered Munich on 1 May 1919 in order to retake the city. The "Soviet Republic" of Bavaria soon crumbled—but not before the Communists had murdered around twenty hostages. The *Freikorps'* revenge was bloody and extensive, and at least one-thousand people were killed. The city was traumatised by this experience with Left-wing revolution and would now swiftly embrace the forces of the Right. As did Adolf Hitler. Shortly after the fall of the Communist government in Bavaria, Hitler was part of a new soldiers' committee investigating if members of his regiment had given practical support to the regime. Hitler's brief flirtation with the institutions of the Left was over for good.

The relatively recent discovery of this evidence about Hitler's unlikely relationship with Munich's Left-wing revolution has resulted, under-standably, in a number of different attempts to explain his actions. Perhaps Hitler was subsequently a "turncoat,"[18] and his actions a sign of an "extremely confused and uncertain"[19] situation, one which served to illustrate that Hitler's life could still "have developed in different directions."[20]

So how can we best understand Hitler's actions during this period? Is it possible that his tacit support for the Socialist revolution in Bavaria was a con? That Hitler was in his heart consistent to previously held extreme Right wing beliefs, but was just going along with events, perhaps acting as a spy in order to best learn about his opponents? This, no doubt, is the explanation Hitler himself would have given, had he been forced to. He would have felt extremely vulnerable to the charge that this history demonstrates that he was merely like most other human beings, blown about by what happened to happen.

However, there is no persuasive evidence to support the view that Hitler was pursuing some kind of Machiavellian strategy in these months immediately after the end of the war—quite the contrary. Captain Karl Mayr, head of the army's "Information" department in Munich (tasked with "re-educating" soldiers in the wake of the Socialist revolution), met Hitler in the spring of 1919, and his later recollection was clear: "At this time Hitler was ready to throw in his lot with anyone who would show him kindness. He never had that 'Death or Germany' martyr spirit which later was so much used as a propaganda slogan to boost him. He would have worked for a Jewish or a French employer just as readily as for an Aryan. When I first met him he was like a tired stray dog looking for a master."[21]

Mayr was an unusual character. He later swung from the extreme Right wing of German politics to become a Social Democrat and a fierce opponent of Hitler. He was eventually to die in a Nazi concentration camp in 1945. And while some of his later attacks on Hitler seem exaggerated to the point of fancifulness—he claimed, for instance, that Hitler was so stupid he could not write his own speeches—there seems little reason to doubt his impressions on first meeting Hitler in May 1919. In fact, they offer the most convincing explanation of Hitler's conduct at the time.

So, Hitler, it appears, was not a cunning political operator in early 1919. He was simply an ordinary soldier, dispirited by a lost war, confused and uncertain as to what fate now had in store for him, and content to stay on as long as he could in the army, the only home and employment he had. Which is not to say that he was a blank canvas. Hitler did already believe in certain political principles—like Pan-Germanism—and his time in pre-war Vienna in particular had exposed him to a variety of virulent anti-Semitic influences. But it was the next few months of tuition as one of Mayr's agents of "re-education" that would allow him to crystallise his thinking.

Hitler's task was to speak to other soldiers about the dangers of Communism and the benefits of nationalism. And in order to be trained to do this Hitler attended a special course at the University of Munich between 5 and 12 June 1919. Here he listened to a variety of lectures, including those on the "Political History of the War" and "Our economic situation"[22] all positioned in the "correct" anti-Bolshevik way. By all accounts Hitler lapped up all this eagerly and then regurgitated it to other German soldiers at a camp near Augsburg in August.

In particular, Hitler gave vent to vicious anti-Semitic views in his speeches, linking the Jews with Bolshevism and the Munich revolution. This was scarcely an original thought—it was common among Rightwing extremists in Germany at the time—and it was this grossly simplistic equation of Judaism with Communism that was the wellspring for much of the anti-Semitic prejudice in the wake of the First World War. "The people sent to Bavaria to set up a [Communist] councils' regime," says Fridolin von Spaun, also a convinced anti-Semite, "were almost all Jewish. If you look at the names of the people who played a part there. Naturally we also knew from Russia, that the Jews there were in a very influential position . . . the Marxist theory also originated with a Jew [i.e., Karl Marx], on which Lenin supposedly built."[23]

Hitler had previously been exposed to harsh anti-Semitic rhetoric, for instance from the mayor of Vienna, Karl Lueger, but contrary to the view Hitler expressed in *Mein Kampf,* there is no compelling contemporary evidence that proves he was a committed anti-Semite before the end of the war. That he was undoubtedly expressing strong anti-Semitic views by August 1919 is clear, but by then, of course, he had attended the lectures organised by Mayr and witnessed the mood of many in Munich in response to the short-lived Soviet republic which had been established in the city.

Nonetheless, there is no sign that Hitler was now play-acting with regard to his anti-Semitism. The power and force with which he expressed his views were those of a full-fledged believer.

Hitler was thirty years old. And it is only at this point, in the summer of 1919, that one can detect in the historical record the first reference to any "charismatic" quality that he might possess. At the army camp at Augsburg a number of soldiers remarked positively on Hitler's ability as a lecturer. One of them, a gunner called Hans Knoden, wrote that Hitler "turned out to be a brilliant and spirited speaker who compels the whole audience to follow his exposition. On one occasion he was unable to finish a longer speech [in the time available] and asked the audience if they were interested in listening to his talk after their daily service—immediately everyone agreed. It was obvious that the men's interest was aroused."[24]

Hitler had always despised debate and only wanted to lecture. However, before the war there had not been a willing audience for his harangues about opera or architecture. But now there were people who were prepared to listen to his opinions about Germany's immediate post-war predicament. Hitler had always been certain in his judgements and unwilling to listen to argument. And in this crisis many were predisposed to welcome such inflexibility.

Many of Hitler's views were now recognisably those of the future Führer of the German people. On 16 September 1919, for example, Hitler wrote, at the request of Captain Mayr, an anti-Semitic statement that was uncompromisingly nasty. He said that Jews "produce a racial tuberculosis among nations" and that the aim must be the "removal of the Jews altogether" from Germany.[25]

Four days before writing this letter, Hitler had attended a political meeting in the Leiber Room of the Sterneckerbräu beer hall in Munich.

As part of his work for Captain Mayr, Hitler had been told to observe and report on fringe political parties—and they didn't come much more "fringe" than this one: the "German Workers' party." It was little more than a discussion club, formed in January 1919 by a thirty-five-year-old locksmith called Anton Drexler and a journalist called Karl Harrer. They had decided that they both wanted to push an anti-Semitic, anti-Bolshevik, pro-worker agenda of the kind which was already commonplace on the Right. Drexler had previously been a member of the "Fatherland Party" which had been established by Wolfgang von Kapp two years before, one of countless other similar Right-wing groups around at the time—like the "German Nationalist Protection and Defiance Federation" and the "Thule Society."

Only a couple of dozen people were in the Leiber Room that night, and when Hitler spoke out against the call for Bavaria to declare independence from the rest of Germany he made an immediate impression. Drexler spotted Hitler's rhetorical talents and urged him to join the tiny party. It was the moment when Adolf Hitler and what was to become the Nazi party came together.

Over the next few weeks, Hitler revealed that he was possessed of a "mission": to proclaim the ways in which Germany could be rebuilt from the ruins of defeat. But he did not yet announce that he himself was the great leader who would personally accomplish this task. Though already, in his 16 September letter attacking the Jews, he had pointed to the need for Germany to become an autocratic state ruled by autocratic individuals: "This rebirth will be set in motion not by the political leadership of irresponsible majorities under the influence of party dogmas or of an irresponsible press, nor by catchwords and slogans of international coinage, but only through the ruthless action of personalities with a capacity for national leadership and an inner sense of responsibility."[26] The man, it seems, had found his mission—but it was not a mission he had been pre-ordained to have.

After his arrival in the Sterneckerbräu, Hitler's life changed. He had been tossed around tempestuous seas and now he had found a harbour. For the rest of his life he would pretend that he had always been destined to arrive in this place.

2

MAKING A CONNECTION

Hitler's successful rise to power—and his entire charismatic leadership—was based on his rhetorical skill. "Threatening and beseeching with pleading hands and flaming, steel-blue eyes, he had the look of a fanatic," wrote Kurt Lüdecke, who heard Hitler speak in 1922. "His words were like a scourge. When he spoke of Germany's disgrace I felt ready to spring on an enemy. His appeal to German manhood was like a call to arms, the gospel he preached a sacred truth. He seemed another Luther. I forgot everything but the man. Glancing around, I saw that his magnetism was holding these thousands as one."[1] In the years just after the First World War there were many small extremist political groups in Munich, but none possessed a speaker who could inspire an audience like this.

Hitler had already gained a great deal of practice as a didactic speaker—though without previously convincing anyone that he was "another Luther." Despite impressing August Kubizek in pre-war Vienna, for example, with his ability to "fluently"[2] express himself, Hitler could also rant on so much that he appeared "unbalanced."[3] But times had changed, and Germany now was an altogether different place from comfortable pre-war Vienna. Germans had to deal with the trauma of a lost war, the destruction of the old political system based on the Kaiser, the fear of a Communist Revolution, a humiliating peace treaty which called on them to accept "guilt" for starting the war in the first place, and castigatory reparations which at the January 1921 Paris conference called for over 220 thousand million gold marks to be paid to the victors.

Hitler was thus preaching to people who were desperate. So bad was the economic situation that it seemed as if the whole financial infrastructure of the nation might collapse as hyperinflation hit in 1923. "They [the Allies] wanted to keep Germany down economically, industrially, for generations," says Bruno Hähnel who grew up during the immediate post–First World War years. "There was inflation—you paid billions [of marks] for a loaf of bread."[4] And for returning soldiers, like Herbert Richter, it was all but heartbreaking to witness the economic hardship on top of the suffering of the war. "My parents had only capital," he says. "They didn't own any land. And they didn't own a house. And their fortune melted away like snow in the sunshine—it disappeared. Beforehand we had been quite wealthy. And then suddenly we were without resources—we were poor."[5]

Germans were experiencing a crisis that was not just economic but also political and, in many cases, spiritual. In such circumstances it is easy to understand why Germans asked themselves: who was to blame for this horror? Why were they forced to suffer so much? And these were questions that Adolf Hitler said he could answer, telling his growing audience how they should feel about the life they were experiencing and what they could do to make things better.

Hitler structured his early speeches not only to control the mood of the audience but—most importantly—to provoke an emotional response. He would often begin, as he did in his speech on 12 April 1922, by outlining the terrible situation in which Germany found herself. "Practically," said Hitler, "we have no longer a politically independent German Reich, we are already a colony of the outside world."[6]

He would then ask who was responsible for this nightmare—and here, for the audience, there would be good news. Because it turned out, as Hitler saw it, that the bulk of the German population were not to blame for their misfortune. It was all, he claimed, the fault of the Jews: they had been responsible for the outbreak of the First World War, for the abuses of capitalism and the new revolutionary creed of Communism, and they had been behind the "November criminals" who had signed the armistice in 1918 that had ended the war. The Jews, Hitler argued, owed no allegiance to any nation state, but only an allegiance to other Jews across national boundaries. He created a fantasy world in which Jews even pretended to be on both sides of an industrial dispute in order to disrupt society—the side of the workers and the side of the employers. "They [i.e., the Jews] both pursue one common policy and a single aim. Moses Kohn on the one side encourages his association to refuse the workers' demands, while his brother Isaac in the factory incites the masses and shouts, 'Look at them! They only want to oppress you! Shake off your fetters . . . ' His brother takes care that the fetters are well and truly forged."[7]

Hitler was also conscious that he was speaking to an audience in the heart of Catholic Bavaria and so was even prepared, in the context of the fight against the Jews, to compare the nascent Nazi movement to Jesus and his disciples. "My feeling as a Christian points me to my Lord and Saviour as a fighter," Hitler said in April 1922. "It points me to the man who, once in loneliness, surrounded by a few followers, recognised these Jews for what they were and summoned men to fight against them and who—God's truth!—was greatest not as a sufferer but as a fighter. In boundless love as a Christian and as a man I read the passage [in the Bible] which tells us how the Lord at last rose in His might and seized the scourge to drive out of the Temple the brood of vipers and adders."[8]

It is extremely unlikely that Hitler was, even at this stage, a Christian as he claimed. But large numbers of his audience certainly were. And it was possible for them to make other personal—and blasphemous—comparisons between Jesus and Hitler. For example, that both leaders had waited until they were thirty years old before beginning their "mission," and that both promised redemption from the suffering of the moment. In order to support such views the Nazis—not surprisingly—ignored the historical record and claimed that Jesus was not Jewish.

Hitler was doing nothing out of the ordinary in attempting to paint the Jews as responsible for Germany's misfortune. At the time, they were a convenient and popular scapegoat for many on the extreme Right. As Professor Christopher Browning explains, "Just about every ailment in Germany can be tied to the Jews: reparations, predatory Jews as financiers, and national humiliation. The Jews were also [portrayed as] the weakness behind the home front, the profiteers who didn't fight in the war. Liberalism—considered to be a Jewish product—emancipation, equality before the law, Soviets and Judeo-Bolshevism, all make viable a far more radical and far more widespread anti-Semitism that has political clout . . . So no warning signals go up and no alarm bells go off when Hitler becomes obsessed about the Jews, because he's making in an extreme form arguments that are, one might say, already in a kind of form. So, Hitler's certainly appealing to Germans to end economic distress, to end political gridlock, to make Germany strong and proud internationally and to end the disintegration of German culture, and for him this is all tied together with anti-Semitism."[9]

Hitler, from the very beginning, was also contemptuous of democracy, ridiculing the notion that "the people governs."[10] What was needed, he said, was not democracy, but one determined individual who would arise and restore strong leadership to Germany. And he was explicit about the central political idea that this strong leader ought to pursue in order to rescue Germany—a national renewal based on classlessness and race. Hitler demanded that all but "Aryans" should be excluded from German citizenship. (Again, the idea that there was a distinct "Aryan" subset of Caucasian people, or that this Nordic-type group was somehow a "superior race," was not original, but had been proselytised by a number of racial theorisers before the First World War.) Once Germany consisted only of these "Aryan" people—and the vast majority of the current population of Germany were already "Aryan," according to Hitler—then Germany could become a nation of one "race," and in the process, all class distinctions could be eliminated. "And then we said to ourselves: there are no such things as classes: they cannot be. Class means caste and caste means race."[11]

This call for "all true Germans" to work together to make a new Germany was particularly attractive to young Bavarians like Emil Klein. "This party wanted to eradicate class differences," he says. "[The existing order was] the working class here, the bourgeoisie here and the middle-classes here. These were deeply ingrained concepts that split the nation. So that was an important point for me, one that I liked—'the nation has to be united!' That was already clear to me as a young man—it was self-evident that there wasn't a working class here and a middle class there."[12] And linked to this idea was the notion that "international high finance, the financial power of Jewry," had to be eliminated. Believing in the fantasy Hitler peddled, Klein was convinced that this power stemmed in part from New York. "Wall Street was always being mentioned."

What Emil Klein and others who heard these early speeches discovered was that to listen to a Hitler speech was to be taken on a journey, from an initial sense of despair as Hitler outlined the terrible problems the country faced, through a realisation that the audience were not to blame for the current troubles, to a vision of how all this could be corrected in a better, classless world once one strong leader, who had emerged from the German people, was able to gain power at the head of a national revolution. For people who were struggling under the impact of an economic crisis, this could be enthralling.

Hitler has often been accused of being an "actor," but a vital part of his early appeal was that his supporters in the beer halls, like Emil Klein, thought he was "genuine" through and through. "When I first saw him address a meeting at the Hofbräuhaus [a large beer hall in Munich]," says Emil Klein, "the man gave off such a charisma that people believed whatever he said. And when someone today says that he was an actor, then I have to say that the German nation must have been complete idiots to have granted a man like that such belief, to the extent that the entire German nation held out to the last day of the war . . . I still believe to this day that Hitler believed that he would be able to fulfil what he preached. That he believed it in all honesty, believed it himself . . . And ultimately all those I was together with, the many people at the party conferences everywhere, the people believed him, and they could only believe him because it was evident that he did [believe it] too, that he spoke with conviction, and that was something lacking in those days."[13]

The emotional sincerity that many thought they detected in Hitler as an orator was a necessary precondition of his charismatic appeal. Hans Frank, who would later become the ruler of much of Nazi-occupied Poland during the Second World War, was hugely influenced by what he perceived as Hitler's lack of artifice when he heard him speak in January 1920: "The first [thing] that one felt was: the speaker is somehow honest, he does not want to convince you of something that he himself does not fully believe in . . . And in the pauses of his speech his blue eyes were shining passionately, while he brushed back his hair with his right hand . . . Everything came from the heart, and he struck a chord with all of us . . . He uttered what was in the consciousness of all those present and linked general experiences to clear understanding and the common wishes of those who were suffering and wishing for a programme . . . But not only that. He showed a way, the only way left to all ruined peoples in history, that of the grim new beginning from the most profound depths through courage, faith, readiness for action, hard work, and devotion, a great, shining, common goal . . . From this evening onwards, though not a party member, I was convinced that if one man could do it, Hitler alone would be capable of mastering Germany's fate."[14]

Hans Frank was just nineteen years old when he heard Hitler speak, and perhaps it's not so surprising that a young, impressionable man like him was so affected by Hitler's words during these desperate times for Germany. What's less immediately explicable is why Hermann Göring, a much-decorated air force veteran, and commander of the famous Richthofen squadron during the First World War, pledged himself to Hitler, a former ordinary soldier, after they met for the first time in the autumn of 1922.

Göring was nearly thirty years old when he encountered Hitler, and was an individual used to impressing others himself. His daring exploits as one of the pioneering members of the German air force had gained him not only an Iron Cross but many other decorations including the Pour Le Mérite, one of the highest awards possible in the German Empire. He had been outraged by the decision to end the war on 11 November 1918, and had told the men in his squadron just eight days after the armistice, "The new fight for freedom, principles, morals and the Fatherland has begun. We have a long and difficult way to go, but the truth will be our light. We must be proud of this truth and of what we have done. We must think of this. Our time will come again."[15]

By the autumn of 1922 Göring had returned to Germany after spending time working in Scandinavia, first as a stunt pilot and then as a commercial pilot for the Swedish airline, Svensk-Lufttrafik. He would shortly marry the soon-to-be divorced Baroness Carin von Kantzow. Now a mature political science student at Munich University, Göring was a worldly, hard-bitten man of immense personal confidence. Yet he was immediately impressed when he first saw Adolf Hitler. "One day, on a Sunday in November or October of 1922, I went to this protest demonstration as a spectator," Göring said during his war crimes trial at Nuremberg in 1946. "At the end Hitler too was called for. I had heard his name briefly mentioned once before and wanted to hear what he had to say. He declined to speak, and it was pure coincidence that I stood nearby and heard the reasons for his refusal . . . He considered it senseless to launch protests with no weight behind them. This made a deep impression on me. I was of the same opinion."[16]

Intrigued by Hitler, Göring went to hear him speak a few days later. "Hitler spoke about Versailles. He said that . . . a protest is successful only if backed by power to give it weight. The conviction was spoken word for word as if from my own soul." As a result, Göring sought a personal encounter with Hitler. "I just wanted to speak to him at first to see if I could assist him in any way. He received me at once and after I had introduced myself he said it was an extraordinary turn of fate that we should meet. We spoke at once about the things which were close to our hearts—the defeat of our Fatherland . . . Versailles. I told him that I myself, to the fullest extent, and all I was and possessed were completely at his disposal for this, in my opinion, most essential and decisive matter: the fight against the Treaty of Versailles."

What Göring's testimony reveals, above all else, is that Hitler did not need to convince him of anything—they both already shared the same sense of what was wrong with Germany. This is a vital insight into the nature of how Hitler's "charisma" functioned in those early days, because what Hitler chiefly offered Göring (and many others) was a profound sense of re-enforcement—a confirmation that what he already thought about the world was correct.[17]

In this respect Hitler was helped by one other important quality that he exuded in his speeches—a sense of absolute certainty. Hitler's analysis left no room for any doubt. He never appeared remotely undecided between possible options. Hitler had used this technique in his monologues for years. He would read a book, for example, and then declaim loudly what the "correct" conclusion about it should be. "He was not interested in 'another opinion,'" said August Kubizek, "nor in any discussion of the book."[18]

Hitler also specialised in presenting life as "either—or" by which he meant that either "the enemy" (by which he most often meant "the Jews") "or" everyone else would be destroyed. The world was profoundly black or white in Hitler's mind. Life was a perpetual struggle—and to opt out of the struggle was not an option. "They [people who didn't play an active part in politics] have never yet understood that it is not necessary to be an enemy of the Jew for him to drag you one day on the Russian model to the scaffold," he said in April 1922.[19] "They do not see that it is quite enough to have a head on your shoulders and not to be a Jew: that will secure the scaffold for you."

For his early supporters Hitler demonstrably possessed "charisma," but these supporters had to be predisposed by virtue of their own existing personality and political outlook to believe in this "charisma" in the first place.[20] "One scarcely need ask with what arts he conquered the masses," wrote Konrad Heiden, who heard Hitler speak many times. "His speeches are day dreams of this mass soul . . . The speeches begin always with deep pessimism and end in overjoyed redemption, a triumphant happy ending; often they can be refuted by reason, but they follow the far mightier logic of the subconscious, which no refutation can touch . . . Hitler has given speech to the speechless terror of the modern mass . . . "[21]

This was a view shared by Otto Strasser, brother of the early Nazi supporter Gregor Strasser: "I can only attribute it [the success of Hitler as a speaker] to his uncanny intuition, which infallibly diagnosed the ills from which his audience is suffering . . . speaking as the spirit moves him . . . he is promptly transformed into one of the greatest speakers of the century . . . His words go like an arrow to their target, he touches each private wound on the raw, liberating the mass unconscious, expressing its innermost aspirations, telling it what it most wants to hear."[22]

It was an analysis that Sir Nevile Henderson, British Ambassador to Germany in the late 1930s, also endorsed, "He [i.e., Hitler] owed his success in the struggle for power to the fact that he was the reflection of their [i.e., his supporters'] subconscious mind, and his ability to express in words what that subconscious mind felt that it wanted."[23]

If those who encountered Hitler were not already predisposed to have their "innermost aspirations" touched by his words then they detected no "charisma" in him at all. Josef Felder, for example, was completely unconvinced by Hitler when he heard him speak at the Hofbräuhaus in Munich in the early 1920s. As a committed supporter of the Social Democratic Party, he found Hitler's arguments repulsive. "I listened very carefully to that speech of Hitler's and noticed that he was working in an extraordinarily demagogic fashion. He always used to sort of throw sentences at the audience. The speech was partly devoted to talking about the Social

Democrats' betrayal in 1919, signing the Treaty of Versailles. He started by talking about the November Revolution and the November humiliation. And then, of course, he brought out his theories against Versailles. And then he emphasised further, with a number of particularly aggressive statements, about all of that only being possible as a result of the activities of the Jews. And this is where he made the anti-Semitic problem the basis of his speech . . . He put forward certain claims that were in no way valid. When I left that meeting, we would get together and talk in groups. And I said to my friend, 'After that speech, my impression is that this man, Hitler, will hopefully never come to political power.' We were agreed on that then."[24]

Herbert Richter, a veteran of the First World War, felt an even greater antipathy to Hitler when he came across him in a Munich café in 1921. He "immediately disliked him," because of his "scratchy voice" and his tendency to "shout" out "really, really simple" political ideas. Richter also found Hitler's appearance "rather comical, with his funny little moustache" and came to the conclusion that he was "creepy" and "wasn't quite normal."[25]

The testimony of people like Herbert Richter and Josef Felder reminds us that Hitler's appearance on the Munich political scene did not, at the time, mark a watershed moment. Even though he gradually attracted a following, it represented only a small proportion of potential voters. Indeed, a recent study[26] has revealed that in 1919 the vast majority (more than 70 per cent) of soldiers still in military accommodation in Munich voted not for Right-wing groups but for the Social Democratic party.

But within the splinter parties on the right—the so-called "völkisch" groups—Hitler undoubtedly made an impression. He quickly dominated the tiny German Workers' Party and became not just its star speaker but also the propaganda chief. He worked with Anton Drexler on a "party programme" and then presented the resulting "twenty-five points" to a meeting on 24 February 1920. Shortly afterwards the name of the party was changed to "National Socialist German Workers Party" (NSDAP)—hence their opponents using "Nazis" as a shorthand form.

The "twenty-five points" of the party programme reflected the familiar themes which Hitler repeatedly focused on in his speeches: a demand that the peace treaties of Versailles and Saint-Germain be set aside; that Jews be stripped of German citizenship; that no more foreigners be allowed to immigrate into Germany; that only those of "German blood" should be considered true citizens. There were also a number of measures directed against capitalism—a call for profit sharing and the destruction of large department stores so that small traders could flourish.

How any future Nazi government might be able in practical terms to implement these "twenty-five points" was not mentioned. The whole "programme" was deliberately vague on detail. This vagueness was to prove advantageous to Hitler in a number of ways. It offered maximum flexibility for him to interpret Nazi policy as he liked once he became leader, and it allowed the Nazis to position themselves as a "movement" rather than a run-of-the-mill political party tied down in formulating and agreeing detailed policy. It also permitted a broad range of people to profess support for the Nazis, since the proposal, for example, to "remove the Jews" could be interpreted in a large number of different ways—from legislation to prevent Jews entering certain professions to the forced expulsion of Jews from Germany to something worse altogether.

This idea that the Nazis should stand for a "vision" of Germany rather than a collection of detailed policies was not unique. The *Freikorps Oberland*, for example, also wanted to see the establishment of a "Third Reich" in Germany (in succession to the "first" Reich of the Holy Roman Empire and the "second" German Reich established by Bismarck in 1871 which ended in 1918). And its members despised detailed definitions. "Nothing is more characteristic of the associative spirit of the *Oberlander* than their Idea of the Third Reich," said one supporter, " . . . the men dreamed deep dreams of this Mystery—a mystery which would have been debased in a concreted political programme as soon as one attempted to define it precisely."[27] And, just like the Nazis, the *Oberland* called for "the subordination of the individual . . . to the needs of the whole nation."[28]

By August 1921, Hitler had gained dictatorial power over the fledgling Nazi party. The old days of Anton Drexler's committee meetings and discussion papers were gone for good. But Hitler was still not claiming that he himself was the saviour of Germany—merely that Germany needed a saviour.

"In the very early years we didn't say '*Heil Hitler*,' that was never said, and nobody would ever have thought of it," says Bruno Hähnel who was active in the party in the 1920s. "Hitler hadn't moved to centre stage so much then, the way it happened later. He was simply the chairman of the NSDAP."[29]

It was also obvious, from the beginning of Hitler's involvement with the German Workers' Party, that much of the strength and certainty that flowed through him when he was speaking to a crowd seemed to desert him when he was talking to two or three other people. As he later said to the photographer, Heinrich Hoffmann, "In a small intimate circle I never know what to say . . . as a speaker at a small family gathering or a funeral, I'm no use at all."[30]

Others also noticed this odd inconsistency in Hitler—this yawning gap between the public performance and the private reality. Captain Mayr, who had "discovered" Hitler as a speaker in the first place, remarked how Hitler was "shy and self conscious"[31] amongst other soldiers in the barracks and yet was able to inspire large audiences in the beer hall. Mayr later argued that this allowed subsequent, more intelligent, figures on the extreme Right to manipulate Hitler for their own ends. "As a leader," wrote Mayr, "Hitler is probably the greatest hoax ever played on the world."[32]

But whilst it is true that more obviously politically astute figures like Hermann Göring and Ernst Röhm, who had been a captain in the German army during the war, did attach themselves to the Nazi party in these early days, it simply isn't the case that somehow Hitler was subordinate to them. Clearly, Hitler did take most of his ideas from others—like Gottfried Feder, the political economist who called for an end to "interest slavery"—but by the summer of 1921 he was the undisputed leader of the Nazi party. In a way, Hitler's very weirdness—in particular, the fact that he found "normal" social intercourse difficult and yet could inspire a crowd—contributed to the growing sense that here was a very different type of political leader. "There was always a certain element in his personality into which he would allow nobody to penetrate," remembered an early acquaintance. "He had his inscrutable secrets, and in many respects always remained a riddle to me."[33]

It was this extraordinary combination—Hitler's ability to connect with a large audience of supporters, often by reinforcing and then heightening their existing beliefs, together with his inability to interact in a normal everyday way with individuals—that was at the centre of the creation of Hitler's "charisma" as an orator. Hitler, almost incredibly, could be both intimate with an audience and distant with an individual.

The need for a political leader to create "distance" is something which Charles de Gaulle, a contemporary of Hitler's, recognised as of vital importance. "First and foremost," wrote de Gaulle, "there can be no prestige without mystery, for familiarity breeds contempt. All religions have their holy of holies, and no man is a hero to his valet. In the designs, the demeanor, and the mental operations of a leader there must always be a 'something' which others cannot altogether fathom, which puzzles them, stirs them, and rivets their attention . . . [34] Aloofness, character and the personification of quietness, it is these qualities that surround with prestige those who are prepared to carry a burden that is too heavy for lesser mortals . . . He [the leader] must accept the loneliness which, according to Faguet, is the 'wretchedness of superior beings.' "[35]

But one of the many differences between de Gaulle and Hitler—who were born within a few months of each other—is that de Gaulle recognised the value of creating "distance" from those he led and consciously acted to create it. Hitler was not acting in this way out of choice. He had always found it hard to connect with other individual human beings—a "normal" friendship was impossible for him. It was just that now this characteristic worked to his advantage. Many of Hitler's followers witnessed his apparent lack of need for personal intimacy and thought it the mark of a man of charisma. Indeed, the mark of a hero.

3

SEARCHING FOR A HERO

Heroism and charisma are intertwined. So much so that Max Weber maintained that "personal heroism" was one of the most important indicators of "genuine charisma."[1] It was therefore no accident that Adolf Hitler claimed that his leadership of the Nazi party was justified, to a large extent, because of his "heroic" past.

In Germany after the First World War, there were many who longed for a hero to emerge—a "strong man"[2] as Nazi supporter Emil Klein puts it—to lead them into a new and brighter world. Steadily, between 1919 and 1923, Adolf Hitler evolved into that heroic leader for them, and in doing so he was able to build on a powerful tradition of individual heroism—one that had been fanned by the creation of the modern German state in the nineteenth century. More than two hundred *Bismarcktürme* (Bismarck towers), for example, had been erected throughout Germany to commemorate the "heroic" leadership of Bismarck, the Chancellor who had united the country. German philosophers like Arthur Schopenhauer also revered the rule of individuals rather than governments, whilst Friedrich Nietzsche was a passionate advocate of the importance of the hero in what he announced was a Godless world. Nietzsche hero-worshipped Napoleon as the "embodiment of the noble ideal."[3]

Germans were now inspired to look further back into their own history for examples of individual heroes. One of the most popular tourist attractions in Germany was the *Hermannsdenkmal* (Hermann monument) completed in 1875 in the Teutoburg Forest, which commemorated the victory of the German tribes led by Arminius (or Hermann, leader of the Cherusci) over the Roman General Varus and his three legions nearly two thousand years before.

Before the war, many members of the *Wandervogel,* a popular youth movement, called for a heroic leader to rescue Germans from the increasing industrialisation of the country and lead a return to nature. "Their eager, tense, young faces light up," wrote Peter Viereck of one group of *Wandervogel,* "as, in the light of the campfire, someone reads from his favorite writer: Nietzsche or perhaps Stefan George who, as early as 1907, had pleaded, 'The Man! The Deed! Volk and high counsel yearn for The Man! The Deed! . . . Perhaps someone who sat for years among your murderers and slept in your prisons, will stand up and do the deed.' "[4]

Founded in 1901, and inspired by the ideals of a young diplomat, Herman Hoffmann Fölkersamb, the *Wandervogel* grew into the most popular youth movement in pre-war Germany. Subsequently, a number of members of the *Wandervogel,* like Bruno Hähnel, joined the Nazi party and took their youthful idealism with them. "We would sit there [in the countryside] in the evening, and these were big occasions for us, and my wife also took part later; we met when we were very young. And in later life we always thought back to it because for us it was a beautiful time in our lives. Often there was singing, we had singing groups, we had folk dancing groups, both of us, my wife and I both come from the folk dance movement. There was a real feeling of belonging based on the philosophy of the *Wandervogel.* We were something like a protest against the bourgeois world."[5]

"It was a reaction against the Emperor Wilhelm era, which was all about industry and commerce," confirms Fridolin von Spaun, another member of the *Wandervogel* who was to grow into a committed believer in Adolf Hitler. "They were young people, they simply got bored stiff with it and went out into nature and searched in natural surroundings for something which they couldn't get in their own environment. I joined quite by chance an association in Elberfeld—this was still during World War One. We went on rambles . . . we could sing our songs, cook, play, also do sports . . . It was a spiritual movement."[6]

Richard Wagner, another supporter of "spiritual movements" and a protester "against the bourgeois world," was a hero to many of these *Wandervogel*—just as he was to Adolf Hitler. Wagner's operas, like *The Ring of the Nibelung* (*Der Ring des Nibelungen*), which contains such epic works as "The Twilight of the Gods" (*Götterdämmerung*), harked back to the great Norse and German saga myths. Hitler was so obsessed with the "heroic" nature of Wagner's work that he saw the opera *Lohengrin,* featuring a Knight of the Holy Grail, "at least ten times"[7] in pre-war Vienna. He even tried—unsuccessfully—to write his own heroic opera called *Wieland the Blacksmith.*

Hitler's favourite reading in Vienna was *The Sagas of German Heroes* (*Die Deutschen Heldensagen*) and, according to his flatmate, August Kubizek, Hitler "identified himself with the great men of this vanished epoch. Nothing appeared more worthy of the struggle than a life like theirs, full of brave acts of great consequence, the most heroic life possible . . . "[8]

More recently, during the First World War, individual leaders had stamped their own names on their units in a demonstration of the importance of the individual "hero." Hitler himself, for example, joined the 16th Bavarian Reserve Infantry Regiment, but his unit was actually known as the "List" regiment after Colonel Julius von List who commanded the regiment at the start of the war. This tendency to name units after individual commanders grew even stronger with the formation of the paramilitary *Freikorps* units in the immediate aftermath of the end of the First World War. One of the most powerful, for instance, was known as the "Rossbach *Freikorps*" after its commander Gerhard Rossbach, another was the "Ehrhardt Brigade" led by a former captain in the Imperial Navy called Hermann Ehrhardt. Units like these, says Fridolin von Spaun, himself a *Freikorps* member, "depended entirely on their leader's personality and skills."[9] Moreover, wrote Ludwig Gengler, "The individual commander [of the *Freikorps*] was often called the Führer. He is idolised as the concrete embodiment of all those qualities that the Volunteer wanted to possess in himself. And the Führer is also an abstraction. The Man who will come."[10]

As well as this historical predisposition towards a belief in the individual "hero," there was for Hitler and the Nazi party in the early 1920s concrete evidence of just how a heroic "Man who will come" could influence an entire country. In Italy, Benito Mussolini, who like Hitler had been wounded during the First World War and had then become active in violent extreme nationalistic politics, had formed a Fascist party in 1919 to fight the influence of Socialists and Communists. Here was proof of how a "heroic" leader could fight his way out of obscurity.

In those early years, it was a drunken writer called Dietrich Eckart who most helped Adolf Hitler develop into someone who could be Germany's answer to Benito Mussolini. Hitler first met Eckart at the second meeting of the German Workers' party he attended in the autumn of 1919. Irascible, bald and looking older than a man in his early fifties, Eckart was a virulent anti-Semite who, like Hitler, felt that Germany had been betrayed by the way the war ended and the peace treaty of Versailles. His hatred of the Jews was such that he remarked that he would like "to load all Jews into a railway train and drive into the Red Sea with it."[11] But, unlike Hitler, Eckart was well connected in sophisticated Munich social circles and comparatively wealthy—his plays, particularly his version of Ibsen's *Peer Gynt,* had made him a considerable amount of money. And Eckart had been waiting for a man like Hitler. In 1919 Eckart had said that Germany needed a leader who was a "fellow who can stand the rattle of a machine gun. The rabble has to be scared shitless. I can't use an officer; the people no longer have any respect for them. Best of all would be a worker who's got his mouth in the right place . . . He doesn't need much intelligence; politics is the stupidest business in the world."[12] So, not surprisingly, Eckart immediately saw the potential Hitler possessed. Here was a simple soldier—the defiant voice of the dispossessed and defeated. A simple soldier, moreover, who had been decorated for heroism and received the Iron Cross. After his first meeting with Hitler, Eckart remarked: "This is the coming man of Germany, one day the world will speak of him."[13]

Eckart introduced Hitler to wealthy potential patrons in Munich, and he became a particular hit with women of a certain age—one widow fussed around him so much that she became known as *Hitler-Mutti* ("Hitler's mum"). Eckart, before his death from a heart attack in 1923, also helped Hitler and the fledgling Nazi party financially, raising the money to buy a newspaper to propagate the Nazi viewpoint, the *Völkischer Beobachter.*

But perhaps the greatest practical assistance that Eckart gave to Adolf Hitler was to support him when his dominant role in the Nazi party came under threat in the summer of 1921. Anton Drexler had been flirting with the idea of merging the Nazi party with other similar groups like the German Socialist Party (the DSP). Drexler saw this as an obvious way to grow the party swiftly. Then, in the summer of 1921, he became impressed with the work of a philosophy professor at the University of Augsburg called Otto Dickel. Professor Dickel had written *Resurgence of the West,* a book which contained similar ideas to those expressed in the twenty-five points of the Nazi programme agreed the previous year, although Dickel expressed his own views with greater intellectual weight. When Drexler heard Dickel speak he—and others in the Nazi party—were keen that some form of alliance be struck with him and his own party, the *Abend-ländischer Bund* (Western League).

All this manoeuvring occurred when Hitler was out of Munich, and he was subsequently outraged to discover what had been discussed in his absence. Hitler walked out of a meeting with Dickel in fury and quit the Nazi party altogether. Once again he had shown that he was both unwilling and unable to participate in intellectual debate.

Initially, Eckart had been interested in what Dickel could add to the party—not least intellectual respectability—but once Hitler resigned he did his best to convince him to return. And return Hitler did, but on his own terms as the unquestioned dictator of the Nazi party. Eckart then splashed his own support for Hitler across the front page of the *Völkischer Beobachter.*[14]

It was a significant moment on Hitler's journey: he was no longer just drumming up support for an as-yet-unknown future leader of Germany, he was now positioning himself as potentially that leader. Hitler had demonstrated that he was not prepared to share power—and would take whatever consequences might come from his refusal to collaborate. And what is just as significant is that others began to accept Hitler's own valuation of himself. Dietrich Eckart, for example, would have preferred to have involved Professor Dickel in the Nazi party, but once Hitler refused, then Eckart was forced to choose, and in the process accept, that Hitler be given undisputed power within the Nazi movement. Hitler was now able to portray himself as a "hero" partly because others could see his intransigence as in part "heroic." Hitler could often be a very difficult character to deal with, but in that difficulty lay—potentially—a powerful appeal. After all, who expects "heroes" to be reasonable people?

The following year—1922—the Nazi party began growing by acquisition. In October 1922 Hitler managed to convince the supporters of the *Deutsche Werkgemeinschaft* in Nuremberg to subordinate themselves within the Nazi party—not in a loose alliance as had been proposed the year before, but recognising that Hitler was now their leader. Hitler was always to be grateful to the leader of the *Deutsche Werkgemeinschaft* in Nuremberg for arranging this—a man called Julius Streicher.

Streicher had heard Hitler speak the year before, and had been transfixed. "I had never seen the man before," he said in evidence at his trial after the war. "And there I sat, an unknown among unknowns. I saw this man shortly before midnight, after he had spoken for three hours, drenched in perspiration, radiant. My neighbour said he thought he saw a halo around his head, and I experienced something which transcended the commonplace."[15]

Streicher was an appalling character. In 1923 he would start publishing *Der Stürmer,* a sadistic semi-pornographic newspaper committed to the most disgusting anti-Semitic pictures and stories. But Streicher was not untypical of the kind of people who were now linking themselves with Hitler. Other influential figures in the Nazi party now included Christian Weber, a former nightclub bouncer, Hermann Esser, an aggressive Jew-baiter, and Ernst Röhm, a dissolute captain in the German Army who later wrote that "I wanted to serve a *Volk* of fighters, not a people of poets and dreamers."[16] All of these men would go on to hold senior positions in the Nazi party—and all of them were disreputable thugs. These kind of violent low-life characters would no doubt have agreed with the view Hermann Göring expressed at his war crimes trial, when he said that he joined the Nazi party in the early 1920s because he was a "revolutionary." Otto Strasser's view was that—simply put—"Hitler enjoys their company, for they confirm his profound conviction that man is essentially vile."[17]

Ernst Röhm, in particular, was a crucial figure in those early days of the Nazis, in part because he helped organise weapons for the fledgling paramilitary wing of the Nazi party, the SA—the *Sturmabteilung* or stormtroopers. The SA was officially established in November 1921, but almost from the first days of the party a number of Nazi thugs—many former soldiers—had "protected" party meetings in beer halls by chucking out anyone who heckled Hitler, and it was from this group of bouncers that the SA developed.[18]

It was into this violent and seedy mix that news came in October 1922 that Benito Mussolini had become Prime Minister of Italy, a moment that energised the revolutionaries in the Nazi party. For if an ultra-nationalist leader could suddenly gain power in Italy, then why not in Germany? On 3 November 1922, just days after Mussolini's success in Italy, Hermann Esser stated to a crowd at the Nazi haunt of the Hofbräuhaus Beer Hall in Munich that "Germany's Mussolini is called Adolf Hitler."[19] The following month, December 1922, the *Völkischer Beobachter* published an article that proclaimed that Adolf Hitler was no mere "drummer" but the leader who would rescue Germany.[20]

The following year, 1923, Hitler seized the opportunity to demonstrate his credentials as a heroic revolutionary. But—and this is a recurring theme of his rise to power—in order to do so he needed to exploit a crisis in the German state. Fortunately for Hitler, in 1923 Germany faced just such a crisis when the French occupied the Ruhr, the industrial region in the west of Germany. Under the terms of the Versailles treaty the Germans were forbidden from stationing troops in this area, so the French faced little concerted opposition when they moved on to German territory on 11 January 1923. The French Prime Minister, Raymond Poincaré, had taken this drastic course of action because the Germans had defaulted on deliveries of coal and timber due to France as part of reparations payments.

Not surprisingly, the French occupation was wildly unpopular. "That was when we did find out that the French ruled with an iron hand," says Jutta Rüdiger,[21] a teenager at the time. "If there was something that was not to their liking, if you were walking on the pavement, for instance, they came along with their riding crop and you had to step down onto the street . . . There was quite a bit of harassment." And as well as coping with the French in the Ruhr, the population of Germany had to somehow carry on functioning under the pressure of hyperinflation. "In 1923," recalls Rüdiger, "an exercise book cost about three billion marks, I think."

Hitler did not call on his supporters to take part in the passive resistance that some Germans were mounting against the French in the Ruhr. His focus remained on building on the inspiration of Mussolini's example in Italy. But he realised that he needed at least the tacit support of the *Reichswehr*, the German Armed Forces, in his quest to overthrow the government in Berlin. Yet in May 1923, when as a first step towards national revolution the Nazis attempted to stir up soldiers of the *Reichswehr* who were parading on the Oberwiesenfeld in Munich, their approaches were comprehensively rejected. Nonetheless, Hitler believed he had to act. Who knew how long the crisis would last? And so in November 1923 he launched the Beer Hall Putsch—an event that was to gain Hitler national publicity for the first time, though not in the way he had anticipated.

It wasn't obvious to anyone involved in the planning of the putsch whether or not Hitler really was the "heroic" equivalent of Mussolini. Hitler was in discussion with General Erich Ludendorff, hero of the German victory at Tannenberg in the First World War, about his potential involvement in a Nazi-inspired revolution, but it was never made explicit exactly what Ludendorff's role would be. Was Ludendorff to be just the military leader, with Hitler the political head of the revolution, or was Ludendorff the real "hero" for whom Hitler had merely been preparing the way?

What was clear, however, was that by the end of 1923 Hitler had decided to seize the initiative. The plan was simple—force the leaders of the authoritarian government of Bavaria to declare their support for a Nazi-led "march on Berlin" to overthrow the "November criminals" who were in power. Since it was obvious that the Nazis needed the assistance—or at the very least the acquiescence—of the Bavarian state security forces as well as Bavarian political leaders, Hitler decided that the coup should be attempted whilst the "state commissioner" of Bavaria, Gustav von Kahr, was speaking at a meeting at the Bürgerbräukeller in Munich. Kahr was effectively the dictator of Bavaria, and had been appointed in September 1923 in response to a crisis in government in Berlin caused by the threat once again of revolution.

There were some signs that perhaps Hitler's strategy might succeed—the Bavarian Government, for example, seemed more sympathetic to the Nazis than the authorities in other German states. The Nazis had been banned in much of the rest of Germany after the murder of Walther Rathenau, the Jewish Foreign Minister of Germany, the year before. But in Bavaria the Nazis were still able to function and Kahr shared Hitler's contempt for the government in Berlin.

It was to the Nazis' advantage to make their move at Kahr's meeting since both the Head of the Bavarian Police, Hans von Seisser, and the commander of the German Army in Bavaria, General Otto von Lossow, would also be present. Hitler's gamble was that, presented with a fait accompli, all of these leading figures would go along with his planned revolution.

So, at around 8:20 p.m. on 8 November 1923, Hitler and more than a dozen supporters, including Hermann Göring, Rudolf Hess and Alfred Rosenberg, forced their way into the Bürgerbräukeller whilst Kahr was speaking to an audience of several thousand. Outside the beer hall, units of the SA guarded the exits. After a shot had been fired into the ceiling of the beer hall, Hitler announced that the revolution had begun. He and his comrades then hustled the key figures of the triumvirate—Kahr, von Seisser and von Lossow—into an adjoining room.

But then Hitler faced a problem—none of the three men was enthusiastic about supporting the Nazi cause. It took the arrival of Ludendorff at the beer hall to make them finally offer their lukewarm consent. Hitler, who had announced melodramatically to Kahr and his colleagues that he would kill himself if the coup did not succeed, left to try and shore up support for the putsch elsewhere in Munich, leaving Ludendorff in control at the Bürgerbräukeller. However, Ludendorff—old-fashioned officer as he was—then decided to release Kahr, von Seisser and von Lossow on their word of honour to support the revolution. It was a catastrophic mistake, as Hitler realised when he returned to the Bürgerbräukeller later that night and found the three men had disappeared. All of them now disavowed their support for Hitler and actively worked against the Nazi-inspired putsch.

No strategy for the revolution had been thought through, so a march through Munich was swiftly improvised for the next day, after a group of Nazis had robbed a factory where billion-Mark notes were being printed. Emil Klein took part in the march, and remembers how shots rang out when the Nazi supporters reached the war memorial at the Feldherrnhalle in central Munich and were confronted by Bavarian security forces. "The first thing: is Hitler wounded?" says Emil Klein. "Is Ludendorff wounded? And everyone split up. Of course, if there are shots you have to take cover. We, of course, were well-trained SA men who knew what to do when there were shots . . . And people got up and started looking about to see what was happening. There was a real ballyhoo, partly because the masses who were all there—all in uniform—didn't know what was going on. But one thing we did know. Kahr had betrayed the whole deal. They did not keep their word. They shook hands on it, and this handshake was broken by Kahr and his colleagues leaving Hitler apparently standing alone."[22]

In the midst of the shooting at the Feldherrnhalle—and no one knows exactly who started the gun battle—the man standing next to Hitler, Erwin von Scheubner-Richter, was shot dead. Hitler dropped to the ground—with his critics subsequently suggesting this was evidence of his cowardice.[23] But Emil Klein vehemently disagrees, saying that Hitler "always" showed that he was brave and courageous. "I was always amazed that Hitler only had a couple of bodyguards who accompanied him on his journeys, [and] when he drove around it was always in an open car."

Ludendorff demonstrated his own bravery by carrying on marching through the police lines and out the other side unscathed. But sixteen of Hitler's supporters were killed that day, as well as four members of the Bavarian security forces. Many more were wounded—including Hermann Göring. Shot in the groin, he was helped away from the Feldherrnhalle, patched up and smuggled across the Austrian border to hospital in Innsbruck.

Hitler was arrested just two days after the firefight. He had appallingly mismanaged the whole operation, from his failure to ensure that Kahr, von Seisser and von Lossow were securely held by the plotters once the Bürgerbräukeller had been stormed, to his lack of any coherent plan as to what to do if the Bavarian leadership seemed less than enthusiastic about the putsch. Moreover, Hitler had demonstrably not lived up to his promise to kill himself if the revolution failed, since he was now in the custody of the Bavarian authorities awaiting trial. It was scarcely the behaviour of a "charismatic hero."

Hitler's trial began on 26 February 1924 in Munich. And from the start Hitler pursued what appeared to outsiders to be a high-risk strategy—he not only admitted what he had done, but he gloried in it. Not just that, he openly stated in court what he saw as his own role in the fight ahead. "I have resolved to be the destroyer of Marxism," he said. And whilst he said he had at one time been a "drummer," he now "demanded for myself the leadership in political struggle." As a consequence, he announced that he was the "hero" who would save Germany: "I demanded that the leadership of the organisation for which we all longed and for which you inwardly long just as much, should go to the hero who, in the eyes of the whole of German youth, is called to it."[24]

Hitler's supporters in Bavaria saw his conduct at the trial as evidence of their leader's strength of character. "I said to myself that he's come out of it well and behaved decently before the court," says Emil Klein. "It's important that a man stand up for himself, even if he is doing something wrong, and I had the impression that Hitler stood up for himself at this trial."[25] The court case was widely reported and Hitler became known to large numbers of people across Germany for the first time. Many of them now judged, as Emil Klein had done, that he was a man of integrity, bravery and courage—a "charismatic hero" in fact. This transformation took place largely because of Hitler's defiant conduct at his trial for high treason, and in the face of compelling evidence that the coup itself had been badly misjudged.

But Hitler knew before he spoke at the trial that it was likely that the judges would go easy on him. The presiding judge, Georg Neithardt, had already shown in a previous case[26] that he was sympathetic to Hitler and the Nazi cause, and Hitler was also aware that he was sitting on potentially embarrassing revelations about Kahr and the Bavarian authorities. Hadn't Kahr himself agreed to participate in this act of "high treason" in front of an audience at the Bürgerbräukeller?

For those privy to this knowledge, the lenient verdict of the court could not have come as a surprise. The London *Times* reported that "Munich is chuckling over the verdict" which proved "that to plot against the constitution of the Reich is not considered a serious crime in Bavaria."[27]

Hitler received the minimum sentence possible—five years—and was likely to be back on the streets of Munich much earlier than that, released on probation. Meanwhile, he would benefit from his time in prison. For whilst incarcerated he would spend his days plotting how to portray himself—unequivocally—as a charismatic "hero" with the "mission" to save Germany.

4

DEVELOPING A VISION

In order to be perceived as truly charismatic, a political leader must possess a coherent vision of the future—a picture of how the world ought to be, based on a special insight into the nature of reality. For as Max Weber said, a charismatic leader needs to be not just a "hero" but a "prophet."[1] In 1924 Hitler attempted to outline his own credentials in this regard in *Mein Kampf* ("My Struggle") and despite the crudity of the work, despite the appalling writing style, *Mein Kampf* is of paramount importance in understanding the development of Hitler as a charismatic leader.

Hitler had faced problems three years before when senior figures in the Nazi party had flirted with the idea of a partnership with Professor Dickel, author of *Resurgence of the West*. And though Hitler had seen off that challenge and emerged with his authority enhanced, the memory of how this "intellectual" had shown up the paucity of Hitler's political thinking must still have been raw. *Mein Kampf* was designed to show that Hitler was no mere beer-hall agitator, but a political thinker with a wide-ranging vision.

The book certainly does present a coherent vision of the world, albeit a horrifying one. To Hitler, we live in a cold universe where the only constant is struggle. And if you cannot win in this struggle then you deserve to die. There is no moral structure beyond the harsh reality of the fight between different people for supremacy. "Those who want to live," said Hitler, "let them fight, and those who do not want to fight in this world of eternal struggle do not deserve to live."[2]

What's missing from *Mein Kampf*—and this is a fact which has not received the acknowledgement it should—is any emphasis on Christianity. Germany had been a Christian society for more than a thousand years, and the belief in a Christian God and Christian redemption after death had been central to millions of German lives. But Hitler offers little of this comfort in *Mein Kampf*. He was later to alter his rhetoric about religion according to the time and situation, but his core belief is expressed here. And whilst he does say in just one sentence in *Mein Kampf* that "a religion in the Aryan sense cannot be imagined which lacks the conviction of a survival after death in some form"[3] the thrust of the work is one of bleak nihilism. Hitler never elaborates on what possible "form" any life after death might take—nor whether he as an individual believes in it. As a consequence, the most coherent reading of *Mein Kampf* is that whilst Hitler was prepared to believe in an initial creator God, he did not accept the conventional Christian vision of heaven and hell, nor the survival of an individual "soul"—an analysis that, as we shall see, is borne out by many of his later private statements on the subject.[4] For Hitler, there is little for the individual personality beyond the experience of here and now. We are animals, and just like animals we face the choice of destroying or being destroyed.

Hitler emphasises the animal nature of human life in graphic and desolate detail. Ernest Becker would explore the consequences of this kind of belief fifty years later in his Pulitzer prize-winning *The Denial of Death*, asking, "What are we to make of a creation in which the routine activity is for organisms to be tearing others apart with teeth of all types—biting, grinding flesh, plant stalks, bones between molars, pushing the pulp greedily down the gullet with delight, incorporating its essence into one's own organisation, and then excreting with foul stench and gases the residue. Everyone reaching out to incorporate others who are edible to him."[5]

The vision Becker expresses here is one that Hitler would most certainly have supported. Hitler concluded that life *is* about the strong "tearing apart" the weak, though he would have disagreed with Becker's conclusion about where this realisation leads us. For Becker, to ask the human consciousness to conceive of a world in which the individual must inevitably be extinguished after a life of animalistic struggle was simply too much to bear, " . . . you can realise what an impossible situation it is for an animal to be in. I believe that those who speculate that a full apprehension of a man's condition would drive him insane are right, quite literally right."[6] By contrast, for Hitler, the belief that life was essentially about the strong destroying the weak was enormously invigorating. This was because he allied his quasi-Darwinian vision to the idea of race. It wasn't just that one strong individual ought to destroy one weak individual, but whole racial groups should band together to eliminate other races. The "Aryan" race, wrote Hitler, was a "superior" race responsible for "all the human culture."[7] The core of Hitler's message was that individual life had meaning because the individual was part of a "race." Individuals that subordinated themselves for the good of the racial "community" led the best lives. Your life thus did have a kind of meaning—you may not live on as an individual but if you lived the correct life then the racial community to which you belonged would flourish after your death.

For Hitler, the key opponent in this fight for racial supremacy was the Jew. *Mein Kampf* exudes animosity in almost every paragraph, but the overwhelming volume of hatred is directed at the Jews. "He [i.e., the Jew] remains the typical parasite," writes Hitler, "a sponger who like a noxious bacillus keeps spreading as soon as a favourable medium invites him."[8] And whilst Hitler does not call for all the Jews to be killed, he made it clear that the "sacrifice" of German soldiers on the front line during the First World War "would not have been in vain" if "twelve or fifteen thousand of these Hebrew corrupters of the people had been held under poison gas . . . "[9] Hitler also linked Judaism to Marxism and said that "Fate" was calling the German people to colonise land in "Russia and her vassal border states."[10] He called on his readers to "never forget that the rulers of present day Russia are common blood stained criminals."[11]

Hitler had arrived at this bleak and violent vision having been influenced by many different sources. From Social Darwinists he took the idea that the essence of life was struggle; from Arthur de Gobineau, author of *The Inequality of Human Races,* and his followers, he took the notion of the superiority of the Aryan Race; from events on the Eastern Front towards the end of the First World War—when Germany had snatched agricultural land from the nascent Soviet Union (land which had been lost to Germany at the end of the conflict)—he took the idea of creating an empire in the east; and from Alfred Rosenberg, a Nazi born in the Baltic States, he took the idea of a linkage between Judaism and Bolshevism. He then mixed these noxious elements into a uniquely potent and deadly philosophy of his own. His ideas were now fixed.

Hitler's argument was this: life was a struggle between races for living space; the greatest danger to the Ayran race in pursuit of victory in this struggle was the Jews; the Soviet Union was run by Jews; and the Soviet Union contained prime agricultural land which the Aryan Germans needed. Ergo: creating an Aryan German Empire in the agriculturally rich territories of the western Soviet Union would solve three problems in one—destroy the threat from Bolshevism, the threat from the Jews and gain Germany *Lebensraum,* valuable "living space."

Each element in this specious argument supported the other—something that made Hitler's vision enormously robust. If you disagreed that Jews were a threat, or that Jews controlled the Soviet Union, or any other aspect of Hitler's political thinking, then he would simply dismiss you as "wrong" and incapable of seeing what was in front of you. But once you accepted one element then you were embarked on a carousel where one idea led to another.

Wrapped around this central vision of hate, struggle and conquest, Hitler tried to create a coherent story out of his autobiography, demonstrating the consistency of his views over his lifetime. But as we have already seen, and as historical research over the last twenty years has demonstrated, many of these auto-biographical sections were simply a crude attempt to rewrite history. Hitler was never as certain in his views prior to 1919 as he pretends to have been in *Mein Kampf.*

Nonetheless, *Mein Kampf* remains an extraordinary piece of work, not least because there is no evidence that the vast majority of Germans agreed with the twin pillars which underpinned Hitler's vision—the desire to systematically persecute the Jews and the need to capture and colonise land in the western territories of the Soviet Union. After all, the idea of "colonising" parts of the Soviet Union would most certainly mean another war.

So what kind of politician espouses policies that appear to render him unelectable? A *conviction* politician, one might argue—someone who seeks first to state policies that appear unattractive and then persuade the general public to support them. But that is not what happened here. By the time the Nazi party had a chance of political breakthrough—from 1929 onwards—Hitler was careful not to push either of these two policies to any great degree. He remained an anti-Semite, of course, and still hated the Soviet Union, and he never publicly renounced these views, but he sought to emphasise other ideas that were much more popular—like the rejection of the peace treaties made at the end of the First World War and a call for a new united Germany of brotherhood and fellow feeling.

But even if Hitler subsequently didn't press the core agenda in *Mein Kampf* as much as his own beliefs might warrant, the book still existed and anyone interested in the views of Adolf Hitler could read it. Not surprisingly, many Nazi supporters say they didn't think Hitler "literally" meant what he said. Johannes Zahn, an economist who supported aspects of Nazi policy, says "reading *Mein Kampf* was exactly like belief in the demands of the Bible. These are demands, but nobody believed they would be fulfilled one hundred per cent."[12] For diplomat Manfred von Schröder, *Mein Kampf* was a book that was easy to dismiss. "Nobody believed that *Mein Kampf* was of any importance, you know. That a young man has written a book—what would politicians think today of what they had written 20 years ago! So nobody took it really seriously. I have read it probably as a student once and didn't think it was very interesting and then never opened the book again. One should have but we didn't."[13] Herbert Richter, who fought in the First World War and then later joined the German Foreign Office, says that he started to read the book and found it too crazy to continue. "This was the case for most educated people."[14]

Such comments, made after the war, might appear self-serving. But it is also true that many people at the time found *Mein Kampf* difficult, if not impossible to read. Benito Mussolini, for example, found it so boring that he was unable to get through it.[15] Equally, one must be careful to take the one section of the book where Hitler talks of "poison gas" in relation to the Jews in the context of many other pages of more generalised hatred, which call for Jews to be persecuted and stripped of their citizenship but not to be murdered en masse.

However, whilst there is no evidence that most Germans would have supported in the 1920s the seemingly wild beliefs Hitler expresses in *Mein Kampf*, there is plenty of evidence that many Germans, like Johannes Zahn, thought that Jewish influence had "gone too far" in Germany, and, like Herbert Richter, that the settlement at the end of the First World War had been too harsh on Germany and that the territory lost—particularly in the East—should be returned. So in calling for the persecution of the Jews and land to be seized in the Soviet Union, Hitler was once again voicing in extreme form beliefs that existed amongst many Germans in more moderate form.[16]

Yet it is still hard to read *Mein Kampf* without thinking that it is the work of an obsessive, almost unhinged, mind. That's partly because of the sense of violence that pervades the work. "The fact that all of his schemes, even his friendships, mean bloodshed," wrote Konrad Heiden, "that is what gives this foreign policy its sinister significance. Whether he speaks of art, of education, of economics, he always sees blood."[17] But of equal importance in *Mein Kampf* is its enormous ambition and conceit. Hitler was a thirty-five-year-old convicted terrorist who had just led a small band of supporters in a hopeless attempt at revolution in Bavaria. Yet here he attempts a book that deals in large part with a proposed foreign policy for Germany, one of the most important states in Europe. Significantly, Hitler gives virtually no one else any credit for the development of the Nazi party. He positions himself not just at the centre of events but as effectively their sole creator. "The combination of theoretician, organiser and leader in one person is the rarest thing that can be found on this earth," writes Hitler in *Mein Kampf.* "This combination marks the great man."[18] And there is no doubt that Hitler now wanted the world to think that he himself was just such a "great man."

Published in two volumes, the first in 1925 and the second the following year, *Mein Kampf* was not a best-seller—at least initially. By 1929, for example, less than 15,000 copies of the second volume had been sold. Only Hitler's subsequent electoral success propelled the book into the publishing stratosphere with ten million copies sold in Germany alone by 1945.[19]

Hitler was discharged from Landsberg prison shortly after midday on 20 December 1924. He had served only a fraction of his five-year sentence. The Bavarian state prosecutor had opposed his early parole, but the Bavarian Supreme Court had disagreed and ordered his release.

In Hitler's brief absence the Nazi party had begun to fall apart. Alfred Rosenberg, chosen by Hitler to oversee the Nazi movement whilst he was incarcerated, had been unable to control the various factions. Hitler's appointment of the weak and academic-minded Rosenberg to act as his replacement was one of the first examples of his desire never to allow anyone to grow into a serious threat to his authority—even if it meant that his appointee was unsuited to the task in hand.

Hitler emerged from Landsberg as the leader not just of the Nazi party but of much of the *Völkisch* Right. He also now believed the Nazis should attempt a new way of gaining power—through the ballot box.[20] As he famously remarked, "If outvoting them takes longer than outshooting them, at least the results will be guaranteed by their own Constitution!"

However, though he was allowed to refound the Nazi Party on his release from prison, Hitler himself was banned from speaking publicly in almost all of Germany. But nonetheless his political rivals appeared to be fading away. In March 1925, his erstwhile senior partner in the Beer Hall Putsch, Erich Ludendorff, stood—disastrously—in the German Presidential election, gaining little more than 1 per cent of the vote. Ludendorff was destroyed as a political force. No one would speak of Hitler as Ludendorff's inferior again.

Hitler worked to consolidate his own position as leader. And in that respect the greatest challenge he had to surmount in those immediate months after his release came from Gregor Strasser. At Hitler's request, Strasser had moved from his chemist's shop in Bavaria to northern Germany to help organise the Nazi party. Strasser took the opportunity to open a debate within this northern satellite about the precise content of Nazi policy. Included in the discussions was a young follower of Strasser's called Joseph Goebbels. He was a relatively new member of the party—he had joined only at the end of 1924—and held a doctorate in German Literature.

Strasser wasn't trying to overthrow Hitler as leader of the Nazi party, but his attempt to suggest changes to party policy was perceived by Hitler as almost as dangerous. At stake was not the detail of whether or not the Nazis should be more socialist in approach—which was ostensibly the point which divided Strasser and Hitler—but the broader issue of whether this was a "normal" political party that allowed internal debate or a "movement" led by a single charismatic leader.

One other problem Hitler faced was that it seemed as if Strasser and the other leaders of the Nazi party in northern Germany were as much at odds with the leadership in Munich—excluding Hitler—as anything else. And Hitler's way of dealing with this aspect of the dispute is an early example of his preferred method of resolving disputes between senior members of the party. His technique—as far as he felt able—was to do nothing. He intuitively realised that to come down on one side or another would only serve to alienate the disappointed faction. Such a leadership style went against his profound belief that people should be left to fight things out amongst themselves. Such inaction also suited his somewhat indolent character. Ultimately, he must have felt, what did it matter that Gregor Strasser and some northern Nazis couldn't stand Julius Streicher and Hermann Esser in Bavaria?

But that relaxed attitude would change in an instant if Hitler felt that his personal authority as absolute dictator of the Nazi party was questioned. And that was what happened in November 1925 when the northern group of Nazi leaders asked Gregor Strasser to suggest amendments to the programme of policy that Hitler and Drexler had devised in 1920. Strasser was happy to oblige, but some of his new proposed policies—like the redistribution of land—threatened Hitler's desire to make the Nazi party more attractive to the business community. So Hitler called a special party conference to meet on 14 February 1926 at Bamberg in the north of Bavaria. Strasser and Goebbels attended, along with Hitler's dedicated Munich supporters, including Esser, Streicher and Feder.

Hitler, typically, did not debate with Strasser. He spoke for two hours in didactic terms, stating his—and thus the Nazi party's—unalterable opposition on all of the policy issues that Strasser and his supporters wished to revisit. Goebbels was distraught. He was upset not just at Hitler's view that the task of Nazism was to destroy Bolshevism—Goebbels wanted to work with the Soviets against, as he saw it, Jewish power in the West—but at the way the meeting was conducted. Hitler spoke, his supporters nodded, there was a short exchange of views, Strasser spoke briefly and that was it. The party programme stood word for word as it was written in 1920.

Goebbels wrote that he felt that he and Strasser were "a poor match" for "those pigs down there" and that he could "not entirely believe in Hitler any more."[21] He was in "despair." But he also had the sense that Hitler was somehow being constrained by those who were in leading positions in the party in Munich and that the only way forward for Strasser and his supporters was to talk to Hitler directly.

Goebbels' belief that matters could be sorted out if only Hitler could be detached from his "rogue" advisors is an example of an attitude which would become commonplace within the Nazi state. This sense that "if only Hitler really knew" then everything could be sorted out would become a vital safety valve for the regime to deflect criticism away from the leader. But what is intriguing is that Goebbels expresses this attitude not only this early in the development of the Nazi party, but directly in the face of compelling evidence to the contrary. It had not been "rogues" in the party who had lectured Strasser and Goebbels about the error of their ways in Bamberg, but Hitler himself. So why would Goebbels think that a potential way forward was to talk to Hitler? Adolf Hitler, even by this stage, was the least likely person in the world to change his mind on any issue he felt was important.

The answer, surely, is that Goebbels was projecting onto the figure of Adolf Hitler what he wanted to see. Goebbels understood that he was part of a political structure that granted the leader complete authority, so the only way to change party policy was to believe that it was possible to change the mind of the party leader.

Hitler understood all this. And he was keen to repair any damage done to his relationship with Goebbels, obviously recognising the potential value to the Nazi party of this twenty-eight-year-old intellectual radical. So Hitler wrote to Goebbels and asked him to come to Munich and give a speech in April 1926. As a result, Goebbels' attitude to Hitler completely turned around. Goebbels made no effort to convince Hitler to change his mind on the key issues of policy that had been the cause of so much upset at the Bamberg meeting. Instead, he basked in what he felt was the charisma of Adolf Hitler. "I love him," he wrote in his diary. "He has thought through all of this. Such a sparkling mind can be my leader. I bow to the greater—the political genius."[22] Shortly afterwards he wrote, "Adolf Hitler, I love you because you are great and simple at the same time. This is what one calls a genius."[23]

Goebbels' critics[24] argued that the reason that he had now changed his mind about Hitler was that he had been seduced by the sense of privilege and power that the Nazi party in Munich—and particularly Hitler—exuded compared to the Strasser group in the north. But Goebbels' diaries and his actions at the time strongly suggest an alternative interpretation, one that focuses on his wholehearted acceptance of the belief that the Nazi party was not a political party but a "movement," and that Hitler was less a political leader and more a quasi-religious prophet. What Goebbels had decided to do was to abandon the Strasser debate about detail of policy, and instead put his faith in Hitler's judgement on all matters of significance.

The importance of "faith" in understanding the actions of members of the Nazi party around this time is crucial—as Hitler himself stated. He said in 1927, "Be assured, we too put faith in the first place and not cognition. One has to believe in a cause. Only faith creates a state. What motivates people to go and do battle for religious ideas? Not cognition, but blind faith."[25] In emphasising the vital importance of "faith" Hitler was echoing the views of Benito Mussolini who had written in 1912: "We want to believe, we have to believe; mankind needs a credo. Faith moves mountains because it gives us the illusion that mountains do move. This illusion is perhaps the only real thing in life."[26]

Rudolf Hess, at this time one of those closest to Hitler, also wrote about how important it was to create a sense of commitment in Nazi followers that went beyond that normally expected in a traditional political party. "The great popular leader," he said in 1927, "is similar to the great founder of a religion. He must communicate to his listeners an apodictic faith. Only then can the mass of followers be led where they should be led. They will then also follow the leader if setbacks are encountered; but only then if they have communicated to them unconditional belief in the absolute rightness of their own people." He also remarked that Hitler "must not weigh up the pros and cons like an academic, he must never leave his listeners the freedom to think something else is right."[27]

By the time Hess voiced these views Hitler had long been acting on them. Hitler was naturally inclined to demonstrate a great number of the qualities that Hess demanded of "a great popular leader." Chief amongst those, as Hitler had shown to Goebbels at Bamberg, was his certainty in the correctness of his own judgements. But he allied this to an equal certainty that events would one day work in the Nazis' favour. Essentially, the single most important message he wanted to convey to his followers was the necessity of "keeping the faith."

Demonstrably, not all of Hitler's followers accepted this. Gregor and Otto Strasser certainly did not. And Gregor's insistence on treating Hitler as a "normal" political leader and openly questioning his judgement would lead to further conflict. But the majority of supporters who joined the Nazi party around this time would have had little choice but to follow the same line as Goebbels did after spending time with Hitler in the wake of the Bamberg meeting. The structure and systems of the party were now set in concrete—and they all pointed one way, to Hitler as a leader who would "never leave his listeners the freedom to think something else is right." What Nazi supporters got in exchange for accepting Hitler's omnipotence was—to borrow Ernest Becker's phrase—a "secure communal ideology of redemption."[28]

Hitler—largely because he seemed no longer to be a threat—had seen his speaking ban gradually lifted across Germany, starting with Saxony in January 1927, then Bavaria in March 1927 and finally Prussia in September 1928. However, even though Hitler could speak openly, and even though Nazi membership stood at around 100,000 in 1928, there seemed little objective chance of a breakthrough for the party. The lowest point was the election of May 1928 when the Nazis polled just 2.6 per cent of the vote. More than 97 per cent of the German electorate still rejected Adolf Hitler and his policies.

In the election of 1928 two of the twelve seats in the Reichstag that the Nazis won went to Goebbels and Göring. Goebbels was clear how he perceived his own parliamentary responsibilities in this democratic Germany, "We enter parliament in order to supply ourselves, in the arsenal of democracy, with its own weapons . . . If democracy is so stupid as to give us free [railway] tickets and salaries for this work, that is its affair . . . We flout cooperating in a stinking dung heap. We come to clear away the dung . . . We do not come as friends, nor even as neutrals. We come as enemies. As the wolf bursts into the flock, so we come."[29]

Goebbels was not alone in his hatred of democracy—it was an attitude that was common on the extreme Right. Colonel von Epp, for example, also ran for the Reichstag in 1928. He had commanded one of the most notorious *Freikorps* and now announced, "I am supposed to be a parliamentarian. You will doubt that I have the requisite qualities for that position. I do not have those qualities. I will never have them; for nothing depends on those qualities."[30] After his election, he noted in his diary that the Reichstag was "an attempt of the slime to govern. Church slime, bourgeois slime, military slime."

But, as far as the Nazis were concerned, in 1928 the evidence was that the democratic "slime" were winning. Indeed, the Nazis were so short of money in 1928 that they had trouble financing their party rally in Nuremberg.[31] However, there were stirrings in German society that offered some hope to a Nazi party that so clearly needed a crisis to be able to progress. German agricultural workers were suffering as the price of food on the world market began to drop. Since the relative prosperity of the Weimar government had been built on using loans from America to pay the British and French their reparations, this was a fragile economy, and it already showed signs of cracking.

Working hard to stabilise Germany's position was Gustav Stresemann, the German Foreign Secretary. He had convinced the German government to sign the Kellogg-Briand Pact in August 1928 that committed Germany to a peaceful resolution of international problems. Stresemann then built on the subsequent goodwill by negotiating the Young Plan in February 1929, by which the burden of German reparations would be reduced.

Stresemann was unusual at this point in the history in that he was a senior political figure who was intensely concerned about Hitler and the Nazis. As Theodor Eschenburg recalls, "I was often together with Stresemann, the foreign minister at the time. A liberal, a Right-wing liberal. I remember very well. It was Whitsun 1929. One evening Stresemann started talking about Hitler and said, 'He is the most dangerous man in Germany. He possesses a devilish rhetoric. He has an instinct for mass psychology like no-one else. When I retire, I will travel through Germany and get rid of this man.' There were also a few men from the foreign office there. We didn't understand Stresemann. We said, 'This little party? Let the guy shout.'"[32]

Gustav Stresemann suffered a stroke and died on 3 October 1929, just days before the Wall Street Crash. And amidst this new economic crisis, millions of Germans would be responsive to Hitler's charismatic offer of leadership for the very first time. Now when Hitler shouted, people would listen.

5

OFFERING HOPE IN A CRISIS

Between 1929 and 1933 millions of Germans turned their back on their previous party allegiances and decided to support Adolf Hitler and the Nazis—and they did this knowing that Hitler intended to destroy the German democratic system and supported acts of criminal violence.

Two events from 1932 illustrate the extraordinary nature of what was now happening in this cultured nation at the heart of Europe. In an election speech[1]—one of the very first to be filmed with synchronised sound—Hitler mocked German multi-party democracy and the thirty or so parties that were standing against the Nazis. He announced that he had "one goal" which was to "drive the thirty parties out of Germany." He proudly boasted that the Nazis were "intolerant" and that "there is more at stake [in this election] than just deciding on a new coalition." He could scarcely have been more explicit about his intention to create a totalitarian state. Then, in August, Hitler offered his "unbounded loyalty"[2] and support to five Nazi stormtroopers who had just been sentenced to death for the murder of a Communist supporter in Potempa in Silesia. Hitler did not deny that the murder had taken place, nor that these five Nazis had committed it—he simply said that the verdict against them had been "monstrous." Hitler, who aspired to be Chancellor of Germany, thus publicly allied himself with extrajudicial killings.

In the light of all that, how could so many Germans possibly have decided that Hitler should be voted into power, and what role did Hitler's perceived "charisma" play in the Nazis' undoubted electoral success?

The most important precondition for Hitler's rise in popularity was the apparent failure of democracy in the face of economic crisis. In March 1930 the coalition of the Social Democrats and the Liberal People's Party that had previously governed Germany collapsed when they couldn't agree how best the crisis should be handled. For many, like Nazi supporter Bruno Hähnel, this was evidence of the need for radical change. The Reichstag was known as the "chattering circle" to Hähnel and his friends because they believed that all of the different political parties—many of whom represented particular interest groups—did little but talk. Thus "it was our aim that a strong man should have the say, and we had such a strong man . . . Today people talk a lot about the Weimar Republic. But that was a disaster, at least it was to us . . . From 1929 onwards, I was willing to bet anybody, even my own father, that we National Socialists would come to power."[3]

Then there was the sense that under the rule of a "strong man" the country could unite at last. It was the belief that this "difficult [economic] situation" needed to be controlled through "solidarity" that was instrumental in leading Fritz Arlt, an eighteen-year-old student in 1930, to the Nazi party. Under the influence of his older brother he had previously flirted with the idea of Marxism, but now he felt that the "solidarity of socialism" across national boundaries, as preached by Marx, was impossible since individual countries were now pursuing their own national self-interest. "The Socialists abroad dropped us," says Fritz Arlt. "So, I thought this other solution [i.e., Nazism] is better. What also needs to be added is that the people who represented this idea were actually more credible. They were former soldiers. They were workers. They were people of whom you said, 'They live in accordance with their beliefs.' It may look like propaganda now. But it isn't propaganda. That's how I felt about it then . . . In our one group there was a bricklayer. There was a factory owner. There was an aristocrat. There they were, all in it together. We were quite simply a unit and supported one another. A second feature of it was that you said, 'We have to share with each other.'

In other words—national community. The rich man gives to the poorer. And there was a great deal of poverty in those days."[4]

Fritz Arlt paints a "positive" vision of Nazism that Adolf Hitler could have spoken word for word himself. But Arlt also knew that one of the core beliefs of Nazism was the racist belief that this new "National Community" would be defined by excluding other Germans—most notably German Jews. "Racist is not the right word in my opinion," says Arlt, who ten years later as a member of the SS was to play a leading role in the Nazis' ethnic cleansing of Poland. He prefers to say that the Nazis held a "belief in natural orders" that was against "multi-culturalism." "There was no theory of [racial] mingling," he says. "That did not exist."

By January 1930, just four months after the Wall Street crash, there were more than three million Germans unemployed—perhaps, taking into account part-time workers, as many as four million. In this atmosphere of crisis, many Germans willingly heard Hitler's message of "solidarity" and national unity. So much so that the Nazis achieved a remarkable breakthrough in the general election of September 1930. Their share of the vote leapt from 2.6 per cent to 18.3 per cent and they were now the second largest party in the Reichstag with more than a hundred seats. Perhaps more significantly, this exceptional result was gained without putting a detailed programme of policies before the electorate. It was almost as if the German population were voting for an emotional idea, one which was physically manifested in the charismatic person of Adolf Hitler.

That's certainly the impression which Albert Speer gained when he heard Hitler speak to a gathering of students in a beer hall. "I was carried away on the wave of the enthusiasm which, one could almost feel this physically, bore the speaker along from sentence to sentence . . . Finally, Hitler no longer seemed to be speaking to convince; rather, he seemed to feel that he was expressing what the audience, by now transformed into a single mass, expected of him."[5]

Speer was so affected by listening to Hitler speak that after the meeting he went for a long walk in a pine forest and thought about what he had heard. "Here, it seemed to me," he concluded, "was hope."[6] In his autobiography, Speer emphasises that he decided to become a "follower of Hitler" rather than a member of the Nazi party (though he joined the party in 1931) and that this had been an emotional rather than an intellectual decision. "Today, in retrospect, I often have the feeling that something swooped me up off the ground at the time, wrenched me from all my roots, and beamed a host of alien forces upon me."[7]

But Speer—like many of those who were moved by hearing Hitler speak—was already predisposed to be receptive to his message. His own teacher, Professor Heinrich Tessenow, whom he hero-worshipped, had previously spoken of the importance of recovering the simple "peasant" virtues of previous years in the face of rampant urbanisation, and also longed for a "simple" figure to emerge to lead Germany—words which seemed to Speer to "herald Hitler."[8]

Of course, Speer based his defence at Nuremberg on the notion that he was intoxicated with Hitler, rather than coldly supportive of the racist and anti-Semitic aims of the party. But whilst Speer almost certainly knew about the Holocaust and was involved with the later atrocities of the regime—something he denied after the war—this early testimony seems sincere. Not just because Speer was an architect in 1931, rather than the Minister for Armaments he subsequently became, but also because many other Germans expressed similar views, both at the time and later. For these Germans—including Speer—the key component of Hitler's charismatic appeal in the early 1930s was a sense of connection. Hitler was speaking explicitly to their needs and they responded with gratitude.

Between 1930 and 1932 the economic crisis grew still worse—by the start of 1932 more than six million Germans were unemployed. "It was really depressing to see how many people were on the streets," says Herbert Richter, "looking for any kind of little job to do. When you came in by the train, they would take your suitcase from your hands just to earn a few coins."[9]

"Six million unemployed, what did that mean?" says Johannes Zahn, then a young economist. "Six million unemployed means, with three people in one family, six times three equals 18 million without food! And when a man was unemployed at that time, then there was only one thing left: either he became a Communist or he became an SA man [i.e., a Nazi stormtrooper]."[10] By the start of 1932 there were more than a quarter of a million members of the SA—three times as many as just a year before. Wearing brown shirts and carrying Nazi banners, they were a common sight, not just marching through German towns and villages, but also fighting with Communist youth groups. Economic desperation was leading to violent confrontation on the streets. It seemed as if German society

was politically splitting apart as support not just for the Nazis but also for
the Communists increased.

Alois Pfaller was one of many young Communists who took part
in the fight against the Nazis. As an apprentice painter and decorator in
the early 1930s, he had joined the German Communist Party in Bavaria
because he both despised the anti-Semitic policies of the Nazis and felt
they were not concerned with the welfare of each and every German.
"When they marched, you didn't notice anything about representing the
interests of the workers, of the people, that they should have work and
so on, they only spoke in support of their Führer, and about what a great
Reich and such that they wanted to build."[11]

Just how prepared the SA were to take the fight to the Communists
became clear to Pfaller when he hired a room in the Bürgerbräukeller
in Munich for a meeting. He arrived, early, to find that SA men already
occupied two tables. "The SA all had a *stein* [a large beer glass] in front
of them, practically a missile, you could already see it, how it would start,
they wanted to stop the meeting . . . So I was gobsmacked, hell! And then
I sent my people on bicycles to go and get help . . . reinforcements."

Once more of his comrades had arrived, Pfaller tried to start the
meeting, but as soon as the first speaker stepped forward to the rostrum
the fighting began. The Nazi stormtroopers brawled with the Communist
supporters, and chairs, bottles and glasses were used as weapons. Alois
Pfaller was hit and retreated from the battle. "So I got into the toilets and
I had a head wound, I was bleeding; [so] in order to get out of the way
of the police, I got out through the toilet window and on all fours along
the gutter, jumped on to a shed and then down. And then I disappeared,
my face was bloody and I had to go onto the street and into the tram, but
there were SA people in there as well, so I thought it was too risky, and
I tried to make my way home [by walking]. Well, the battle was pretty
fierce, several people were hospitalised, some SA people too, they had face
wounds, and some of ours of course too, many people were wounded."

Amidst this civil discontent—trouble which the Nazis themselves
were helping to create—Hitler tried to position himself as the political
messiah who would guide Germans out of the chaos. And in that context he emphasised themes of national renewal. He talked of removing
a democratic system that had—he claimed—failed Germany; and the
"righting" of the "wrongs" of the Versailles treaty. His obsession with anti-

Semitism—something that had pervaded the pages of *Mein Kampf*—was not highlighted. And so, whilst still maintaining that there was a "Jewish problem" in Germany that had to be resolved, he went as far as to say, on 15 October 1930, "We have nothing against decent Jews; however, as soon as they conspire with Bolshevism we look on them as an enemy."[12]

In July 1931 the huge German Danat-Bank crashed.[13] As a result, it wasn't just the millions of unemployed who were now suffering in Germany, but swathes of the middle class as well. Jutta Rüdiger's family was amongst those affected, with her father forced to accept a cut in his salary. She was now predisposed to be influenced by the charismatic appeal of Adolf Hitler, and when she heard him speak at an election rally in 1932 she became convinced that he was her saviour. "It was dead quiet, and then he started to speak extremely calmly, very calmly, he spoke slowly with a sonorous voice and ever so slowly got caught up in his own enthusiasm. He described how the German people could be helped, how they could be led out of this misery. And when the rally was over I myself had the feeling that here was a man who did not think about himself and his own advantage, but solely about the good of the German people."[14]

Increasingly, Hitler had been promoting a special bond of powerful idealism that had supposedly linked the German troops serving on the front line in the First World War,[15] and he called for a return to that "comradeship" of the trenches and for all "true" Germans to work together. As Jutta Rüdiger says, "I was told that this front-line soldier had said, 'In a case of real need neither an aristocratic background nor money is going to be of any help. The only thing that matters is comradeship, the willingness to help and stand by one another. And if we find ourselves in trouble in Germany today, we have to all stand together and jointly—as the saying goes—all pull on the same rope in the same direction.'"[16]

It served Hitler's purposes to make a direct link between his "heroic" service during the war, the "mission" he adopted afterwards in response to the "betrayal" of these noble soldiers, and the current misery in German society which he attributed to the legacy of a Jewish-inspired democratic "talking shop" in thrall to those countries benefitting from Germany's defeat. So it came as a considerable threat to Hitler's developing reputation when a Hamburg newspaper, *Echo der Woche,* published an article on 29 February 1932 that said that Hitler had made up chunks of his personal history during the war.[17] The article, which was written by an officer from Hitler's regiment but which was published anonymously, alleged that Hitler hadn't really been a front-line soldier at all, but had lived behind the trenches as a messenger, and that his Iron Cross had been awarded because he knew the officers who put soldiers forward for such decorations. Hitler realised how potentially damaging any such attack on his "heroism" could be. He instinctively knew—as Professor Nathaniel Shaler put it, back in 1902—that "valiant self-sacrifice for faith" is "at least to the truly civilised man, the type of highest valour."[18] Hitler's charismatic appeal was built on the foundation of his personal "valour" and he could not afford to have it challenged.

So Hitler quickly moved to sue *Echo der Woche* for libel. Only one officer—not the person who had written the article—came forward to give evidence in support of the newspaper, whilst the Nazis collected a host of witnesses prepared to defend Hitler's honour. And since the article had been written anonymously and did contain one obvious mistake—alleging that Hitler had been a deserter from the Austrian army—the newspaper lost the case. Hitler thus turned this potential damage to his charismatic image into a plus. He had "proven" in court that he had been a "hero" in the First World War.

But Hitler had not just faced accusations about his wartime record. The previous year, 1931, had seen rumours about his personal life. And since Germans were deciding whether or not to vote for the Nazis in large part based on the charismatic appeal of Adolf Hitler, it followed that it mattered a great deal to the Nazis' chances of electoral success that Hitler's private life was as beyond reproach as his war record appeared to be in the light of the *Echo der Woche* verdict.

But the questions Hitler faced about his sexuality were a good deal less straightforward than those asked about his wartime exploits. On 19 September 1931 Hitler's niece, Geli Raubal, had been found dead in his flat on the second floor of 16 Prinzregentenplatz in Munich. She had shot herself with Hitler's own pistol. Newspapers, including the *Münchener Post* (Munich Post) which had been a vociferous critic of Hitler and the Nazis for years, began to ask a series of awkward questions about Hitler's possible involvement in the affair—questions which threatened to damage the careful positioning of Hitler as a man "alone," a charismatic bachelor hero who had sacrificed his own personal happiness for the good of Germany.

Hitler had been obsessed with Geli, the daughter of his half-sister, Angela, who acted as his housekeeper. Geli had revolted against the suffocating attentions of her uncle and formed a friendship—perhaps a sexual relationship—with Hitler's own chauffeur, Emil Maurice. Hitler had been beside himself when he found out, and Maurice had been frightened that Hitler might even try to kill him.[19]

But the key question—if not directly asked, then implied—was what exactly had been Hitler's relationship with Geli? Various second-hand sources, chiefly people with a grudge against Hitler, subsequently came forward to state that Hitler had engaged in a sexual relationship with Geli, and that it had been conducted at such a level of perversion that it contributed to her decision to end her own life.

But whilst there was no direct evidence linking Hitler to any sexually improper relationship with his niece—and had there been, it might well have destroyed Hitler's chances in the early 1930s of attaining power—what was obvious was the devastating effect that her death had on him. In her memoirs, Leni Riefenstahl describes an encounter with Hitler in his flat in Munich at Christmas 1935 during which he opened a locked room and revealed a bust of Geli "decked out with flowers."[20] Hitler then told her that he had "loved" Geli "very much" and that "she was the only woman" he could ever have married. Immediately after Geli's death in 1931 Hitler had been in such an emotional state that he had relied on Gregor Strasser to help him through the crisis—ironically so, since it was Strasser's brother who was subsequently to make sexual allegations of impropriety against Hitler.

Hitler's obsession with Geli did not demonstrate that he had suddenly become in need of a close relationship between equals. He did not seek a friendship or emotional partnership with Geli. Instead, he sought to dominate her utterly. Far from showing any tender side to Hitler's character, the Geli episode is further evidence of his inability to connect intimately with another human being in any normal way.

Just as he had with the *Echo der Woche* case, Hitler managed to protect his image—even despite the suicide of his niece in his own flat. The rumours about a sexual relationship between Hitler and Geli remained only unproven gossip. And Hitler did recover his composure after Geli's death, but—as Riefenstahl discovered—he turned her room in his flat into a shrine to her. He resolved to continue his very occasional flirting with a young, empty-headed blonde woman called Eva Braun whom he had met at Heinrich Hoffmann's photo shop, and focus most of his time—as he had for years—on political matters.

The political question Hitler now needed to answer urgently was whether or not he should challenge Paul von Hindenburg for the Presidency in 1932. It was not that there was a serious possibility that Hitler would win—even given the Nazis' recent electoral success, Hindenburg offered the broad German population a much more unifying alternative as head of state. But a noisy, intense campaign could potentially help Hitler's public profile—though a poor showing at the polls would be humiliating. It was a tough choice, and for weeks Hitler could not decide what to do.

Vacillation is not a quality that is normally associated with charismatic leadership; but Hitler undoubtedly possessed it. Goebbels, for example, had railed against Hitler's delay in making up his mind about whether or not to expel Otto Strasser from the Nazi party in 1930. "That's so typically Hitler," he wrote in his diary on 25 June 1930, "today he pulls back again . . . he makes promises, and doesn't keep them."[21] But, as we have seen, Hitler's hesitancy was not to be confused with a lack of fundamental resolve. About the big issues and ultimate goals, Hitler was always clear. About tactics along the way he was often more equivocal. By delaying making up his own mind he could wait and see how events transpired, something that—from his perspective—made an eventual decision more likely to be the right one. That was certainly the case with the expulsion of Otto Strasser from the party in the summer of 1930. By vacillating, Hitler flushed out what other senior figures in the party thought and allowed Strasser to make his own opposition all the clearer.

Similarly, the decision whether or not to run for the Presidency was a finely balanced tactical one, with Hitler ultimately deciding that he had more to gain by running against Hindenburg than by avoiding the contest. It was a battle that Joseph Goebbels, in particular, relished. Goebbels had been appointed to run the Nazi propaganda machine in April 1930, and now, two years later, he was to show that he had evolved into a formidable political operator. Hitler's campaign for the presidency was to become famous because of the use of aircraft to ferry him between meetings—the image of the Führer arriving from the skies like a quasi-God, that was later to be utilised by Leni Riefenstahl as the opening of

her own propaganda film *Triumph des Willens* ("Triumph of the Will")
in 1934, had its origins in this presidential campaign. But there was much
more to Goebbels' work in 1932 than simply the employment of air
travel. The coordination of press stories across Germany; the stage management of meetings; and the use of a revolutionary poster—showing
Hitler's head, stark against a black background—were some of the other
propaganda techniques which the Nazis pioneered. Virtually all of these
innovations were an attempt to create a charismatic mystique around the
figure of Adolf Hitler.

Johann-Adolf Graf von Kielmansegg, an army officer in his early
twenties, was one of those who heard Hitler speak during the campaign.
"At the time Hitler was the first and only politician to use all the modern
means of transport. The other politicians, you only saw them in newsreels
or read about them in the newspapers. Hitler was present everywhere, he
flew from place to place, from meeting to meeting.

"And so there was a meeting in Kassel. At the time I was in the Kassel
garrison, and simply out of interest and curiosity, so to speak, I drove over,
with another comrade. I wanted to look at him and listen to him. And it
was in a big tent, apparently there were 7,000 people there . . . and the
thing that impressed me at first was that Hitler was absent. That was part
of—you didn't realise it [at the time], we know it today—his tactics, his
method. He kept people waiting, deliberately waiting. And so we waited
two or three hours, I think. Usually, though, when you have to wait like this
you become impatient. Waiting for this man made people peaceful. I was
impressed by that."[22] When Hitler arrived and spoke, Kielmansegg—who
was standing towards the back of the audience—didn't think he was hearing anything special. It was, he says, "what you had read in the newspaper." But what did make a lasting impression on him was the behaviour
of the enormous crowd who had waited so patiently for Hitler's arrival. It
was clear, he felt, that they "hoped for a saviour."

Hitler's appeal to officers of the German army was more direct than
the vague promises of national redemption that he addressed to the general population. Hitler offered members of the armed forces salvation
from the "shame" of defeat and the reduction in their prestige suffered in
the aftermath of the First World War. "I was born in 1912," says Ulrich
de Maizière, then a young army officer, "so my consciousness developed
in the Twenties, with all the economic problems of the Weimar Repub-

lic and burdened with the Treaty of Versailles, which the whole German
nation considered a disgrace. We had lost territories, we had to pay reparations, above all else we were burdened with the blame for war which the
German people did not accept—the war guilt of 1914 . . . And now here
comes a man proclaiming a national revolution."[23]

It was around this same time that Theodor Eschenburg also attended
his first Hitler meeting. As we have seen, back in 1929 Eschenburg had
dismissed Hitler as a political threat. But he now took a different view:
"I never experienced it again—how a man could dominate a mass meeting in such a captivating way—as he did at the Sportpalast [in Berlin]. It
impressed me enormously and frightened me at the same time. I sat there,
and left and right of me and behind me, the National Socialists were
screeching enthusiastically. This happened when he [i.e., Hitler] came in,
like a God. A messianic man. It was simply impressive and frightening at
the same time."[24]

Eschenburg felt that the audience was responding to Hitler in this
passionate way for two reasons: "on the one hand it was the despair [at the
economic crisis] and on the other, Hitler's genius for mass-psychology."
Crucially, Eschenburg—a sophisticated political critic—recognised that
"Hitler didn't promise anything. It was always: 'only for the German
people.' And 'we have to free the people from Marxism.' But he didn't
make any concrete promises. I could very easily see through this . . . I only
admired the technique."

Hitler's decision to challenge Hindenburg for the presidency paid off.
As expected, he didn't win, but he gained 30 per cent of the popular vote
in the first round of the election held on 13 March 1932, and then nearly
37 per cent of the vote in the direct run-off against Hindenburg which
took place the following month. Hitler was now centre-stage in German
politics—after President Hindenburg, the most important single individual in the political life of the state. But the problem he now faced was
seemingly insurmountable. Hindenburg did not think that Hitler was a
fit person to become Chancellor of Germany. It didn't matter that three
months after challenging for the presidency, Hitler led the Nazis to an
astonishing victory in the general election of July 1932—the Nazis became
the largest party in the Reichstag with 230 seats and a share in the vote
of nearly 38 per cent. Hindenburg was not about to ask Hitler to form a
government.

Hindenburg didn't reject Hitler because as Reich President he was committed to democracy in Germany. For two years now the Reichstag had been all but an irrelevance, with Germany ruled by presidential decree under the Weimar Constitution's Article 48. And many powerful people around Hindenburg, like the state secretary Otto Meissner, and the aristocratic Franz von Papen, who had succeeded Brüning as Chancellor at the end of May 1932, were also no friends of democracy. All favoured some kind of authoritarian solution to Germany's current problems—one that would both deal with the economic crisis and thwart the growth of the Communist party. They weren't against removing democracy, it was just that Hitler was not the kind of person they wanted as Chancellor of Germany.

State Secretary Otto Meissner reported that Hindenburg said to Hitler on 13 August, "He [i.e., Hindenburg] could not justify before God, before his conscience or before the Fatherland, the transfer of the whole authority of government to a single party, especially to a party that was biased against people who had different views from their own."[25]

Hitler's chances of success now seemed to have vanished. How he surmounted Hindenburg's devastating judgement, and became Chancellor of Germany five months later, is one of the most intriguing political stories of the last hundred years.

6

BEING CERTAIN

The history of how Hitler overcame President Hindenburg's initial rejection and became Chancellor of Germany is not, as some Nazis believed, evidence of their leader's "destiny." Instead, it illustrates two different perceptions of Hitler's charisma. One shows the effect of Hitler's charisma on his committed followers, and the other—paradoxically—reminds us once again that many other people were completely immune to his powers of attraction.

The first reason for Hitler's success was the power of his intransigence. He refused to accept anything less than the chancellorship, even when success looked impossible. His certainty that all would come right was an inspiration to his followers. After his disastrous meeting with President Hindenburg on 13 August 1932, Hitler discussed the consequences with his Nazi colleagues. "Hitler holds his nerve," recorded Goebbels in his diary. "He stands above the machinations. So I love him."[1]

Hitler may have been calm about the knock-back from Hindenburg, but plenty around him were anything but. What had been the point, they asked, of eschewing violent revolution and embracing the ballot box if Hindenburg could still frustrate the Nazis even though they were now the biggest single party in the Reichstag? One senior figure in the Nazi party, Gregor Strasser, in particular, wanted to find a pragmatic way around the president.

But Hitler would not compromise on his most important demand—that he himself should be appointed Chancellor of Germany. As the existing chancellor, Franz von Papen, recognised in a statement he made in Munich in October 1932, Hitler was not a "normal" politician, and the Nazi movement not a "normal" political party. He referred to the Nazi party as "a political religion"[2] whose followers professed a "mystical messiah faith" in Hitler.

Whilst von Papen acknowledged that millions of Germans now recognised Hitler as a "mystical messiah," he himself was immune to Hitler's charisma. When he first met Hitler, in the summer of 1932, he found him "curiously unimpressive."[3] Although von Papen "had heard much about the magnetic quality" of Hitler's eyes, they had no effect on him. Papen wrote that he "could detect no inner quality which might explain his extraordinary hold on the masses."

Papen's own aristocratic background and individual character made him feel superior to the shabby rabble rouser who stood in front of him in June 1932. Papen's own writings on the subject—composed after the war—are still laced through with condescension and smugness, even though these were some of the very qualities in his own personality that helped bring Hitler to power. He writes like a headmaster giving marks to the various personalities he encountered. Here, for example, is his verdict on Mussolini: "I found the Italian dictator a man of very different calibre to Hitler. Short in stature, but with an air of great authority, his massive head conveyed an impression of great strength of character." Unlike Hitler, Mussolini was a man of "immense charm" whilst Hitler "always had a slight air of uncertainty." Mussolini, thought Papen, "would be a good influence on Hitler."[4]

This was a monumental misjudgement about the personal and leadership qualities of Adolf Hitler—and is the second crucial reason why Hitler was able to become chancellor. Von Papen, like many in the German elite, grossly overestimated his ability to control Hitler. A former army officer and diplomat, he fancied he knew how Hitler and the Nazis could be manipulated to serve the needs of those within the German upper strata who sought to remove democracy and create a new authoritarian regime based on popular support. Hitler and the Nazis, von Papen reasoned, had the popular support, whilst he and his friends had the intelligence to manage them. He believed that the best way of using Hitler was to get him into the government in some subordinate capacity—perhaps as vice-chancellor. Since Hitler positioned himself as a "mystical messiah" he would quickly be compromised as he did von Papen's bidding. Unfortunately for von Papen, the Nazis were not quite as stupid as he thought.

As Hermann Göring recalled at his trial after the war, "There was some talk [when] von Papen's name had been given to the president as a nominee for Reich Chancellor, that Hitler should become the vice-chancellor in this Cabinet. I remember that I told Herr von Papen at that time that Hitler could become any number of things, but never vice. If he were to be made anything, he would naturally have to be in the highest position and it would be completely unbearable and unthinkable to place our Führer in any sort of second position."[5]

So the intriguing situation by the autumn of 1932 was that whilst Hitler was perceived as a charismatic leader by large numbers of ordinary Germans, key members of the German elite were almost scornful of him. Equally instructive is the fact that von Papen and his cronies found it easy to belittle Hitler's qualities because he was not of their class. He was not an officer, not formally educated and seemed to von Papen to be the "complete petit bourgeois" with his "little moustache and curious hair style."[6] Equally dismissive was President Hindenburg, who referred to Hitler as a "Bohemian corporal."[7]

The trouble for von Papen was that he and his Cabinet had no electoral authority from the people to continue to govern. The lack of support for his government was illustrated in dramatic terms on 12 September 1932 when Göring—now elected as President of the Reichstag (a similar role to that of speaker of the House of Commons)—helped orchestrate a successful vote of no confidence in the von Papen regime. In a breathtakingly cynical piece of tactical politics, the Nazis and the Communists—sworn enemies—voted together in order to humiliate von Papen.

New elections were called for November, and Hitler set to work once again to travel across Germany and gather votes for the Nazi cause. But it was soon apparent that the high point of Nazi support had been reached. The committed were still enthusiastic—more than 100,000 young supporters attended a rally in Potsdam—but other venues showed acres of empty space. Part of the problem for the Nazi party was that by refusing to join the von Papen government Hitler had shown himself to be intransigent in this national crisis. And whilst that uncompromising attitude played well with the core Nazi support, it didn't impress those who were wavering. Nor were Hitler's attacks on the von Papen regime calculated to make the Nazis look like supporters of the middle class—and without middle-class support the Nazi vote was fragile. Nazi support before the November election, for instance, for a transport strike in Berlin, was almost certainly a tactical error.

The 6 November 1932 election was a battle lost for Hitler and the Nazis. Whilst the German Communist party gained nearly 3 per cent more share of the vote, the Nazis polled two million votes less than in the election earlier in the year and their overall share dropped by 4 per cent to 33 per cent. Yet despite the fall in the Nazi vote, the fundamental difficulty faced by the von Papen government still remained—lack of popular support. Von Papen now toyed with a straightforward, if radical, solution: replacing the Weimar constitution with some kind of dictatorship. But this was a risky way forward, not least because senior figures in the German army were concerned about civil war breaking out between the Nazis and the Communists if both these popular movements were excluded from government.

Von Papen's cabinet resigned on 17 November 1932 and in the machinations over the next few weeks the figure of Kurt von Schleicher emerged from the shadows. Schleicher was a General with a penchant for political intrigue and had been appointed Minister of Defence six months earlier. Schleicher remembered the revolutionary turmoil immediately after the First World War and was all too well aware of the dangers of turning German soldiers against demonstrators on the street. His preferred solution to the current impasse was to try and convince elements from both the political right and left to join a Cabinet under his leadership. In the hope that such a compromise government could be created, Hindenburg had reluctantly let von Papen resign and appointed Schleicher as chancellor.

Schleicher knew that Hitler would not accept a post in his government and so on 3 December 1932 he met with Gregor Strasser. He offered Strasser both the vice-chancellorship and the key post of Minister President of Prussia. The next day, 4 December, the Nazis saw a drop of 40 per cent in their vote in local elections in Thuringia in central Germany.

Hitler had good cause to panic. But he held firm, meeting Strasser at the
Kaiserhof Hotel in Berlin, first on 5 December and then 7 December, to
expressly forbid him from accepting Schleicher's offer.

Hitler now faced a potential crisis. If Strasser joined Schleicher's Cabinet then Hitler's prestige as leader of the Nazis would be considerably
damaged. However, Strasser, after hearing Hitler's outrage at Schleicher's
offer, decided to resign from the Nazi party and remove himself altogether from politics. He would serve neither Hitler nor Schleicher. On
the morning of 8 December, the day after his meeting with Hitler, Strasser
spoke to a group of senior Nazi leaders at the Reichstag. One of them,
Hinrich Lohse, recorded after the war what Strasser had said.

Strasser emphasised that ever since the formation of the von Papen
government in the summer, he felt Hitler had been clear only "about one
thing—he wishes to be Reich Chancellor."[8] But in Strasser's view Hitler
"should, however, have become aware of the fact that he is being consistently refused the post by everybody and that in the foreseeable future
there is no prospect of achieving this goal." Strasser said he refused "to
wait until the Führer is made Reich Chancellor, for by then the collapse
[of the Nazi movement] will have occurred." Hitler's mistake, according
to Strasser, had been in refusing to accept von Papen's offer of the post of
vice-chancellor. Strasser didn't mention in this speech that he himself had
just been offered the vice-chancellorship, but the implication that he had
decided to act because Hitler was behaving in an irrational way is clear.

Then Strasser went on to mention another complaint, one that is
especially intriguing in any investigation into Hitler's charismatic leadership. Strasser revealed that he was upset because of a "personal aspect of
the problem." He complained that there were those "within the entourage
of the Führer" who made "insults" about him. Moreover, he claimed that
Göring, Goebbels, Röhm and others received invitations to meet with
Hitler that he didn't. He said he regarded this "as a slight, as a personal
humiliation which I have not deserved and which I am no longer prepared to tolerate. Apart from this, I am at the end of my strength and
nerves. I have resigned from the party and I am now going to the mountains to recuperate."

It was an extraordinary statement to make at a time of national emer-
gency, more reminiscent of an emotional outburst caused by a lover's
rebuff than a series of reasoned arguments about political strategy. And

Gregor Strasser was no weakling. He'd won an Iron Cross for bravery in
the First World War, taken part in the Beer Hall Putsch and then forced
his way into the highest echelons of the Nazi party. He'd previously
admitted that politics was "a rough business . . . especially in a strongly
activist-orientated movement like ours."[9]

Yet here was Strasser walking away from not just the Nazi party, but
also from the chance of obtaining one of the most important public positions in the German state, partly because he felt Hitler was not inviting
him to functions and taking enough notice of him. And this from someone who, out of all of the senior Nazis (with the possible exception of
Ernst Rohm) had seemed the most resistant to the personal charisma of
Adolf Hitler. Strasser, for instance, was the only senior Nazi privately to
call Hitler the "Chief" or "PG" (*Parteigenosse,* or party comrade) rather
than "Führer."[10]

As one historian who has made a special study of Gregor Strasser
writes, "The irony is that, while Strasser had consistently and overtly
repudiated the quasi-mystical Führer cult, it would appear that for all his
bluff assertiveness the innately sensitive Strasser really was captivated by
Hitler's charismatic personality. He thus became the most unsuspecting
victim of the Führer myth."[11]

As soon as Hitler heard that Strasser had spoken to this collection
of senior Nazis he immediately called his own meeting for noon at the
Kaiserhof hotel. Here he addressed all of those who had listened to Strasser just a few hours before. In a calm and rational response to Strasser's
objections, he pointed out that if he had accepted the offer of the vice-
chancellorship then he would have had "serious differences"[12] with von
Papen "within the first week." He then would have had to resign and
his position would have been seriously weakened. He also said that the
option of another putsch was simply impossible, revealing that Colonel
von Reichenau, a German Army officer sympathetic to the Nazis, had
told him how the army would have little choice but to open fire on the
stormtroopers if the Nazis attempted an armed insurrection. Reichenau
had "urged" Hitler "to keep within the law" since "one day power will
inevitably fall into your lap." As for Strasser's claim that he wasn't invited
to meet with Hitler as often as he wanted, Hitler said that he was always
available to "anyone who wishes to speak with me."

Hitler exuded confidence that all would come right, saying that he

still intended to wait until he was offered the chancellorship. He promised, "that day will come—it is probably nearer than we think." Success depended on "our unity and on our unshakeable faith in victory; it
depends on our leadership." Hitler ended his remarks—as he often did in
moments of potential crisis—with a personal appeal for loyalty.

Hitler had managed to avert a crisis within senior Nazi ranks. And,
significantly, he had achieved this by making a speech that contained no
logical explanation of how he was going to achieve the desired goal of the
chancellorship. It was enough to have "unshakeable faith." It was enough
to make an emotional commitment.

However, what Hitler also knew was that without Strasser as part of
his government, General Schleicher's position as chancellor was no more
tenable than von Papen's had been. Schleicher had managed to oust von
Papen by saying to Hindenburg that he could deliver a broader-based
regime—and he couldn't. Moreover, he had now earned the enmity of
von Papen. (In German, Schleicher means "sneak," which many at the
time thought was an apt name for the general.)

Von Papen now opened negotiations with Hitler about the formation
of a new government, and met Hitler at the house of Kurt von Schröder
in Cologne on 4 January 1933 for preliminary discussions. True to form,
Hitler insisted that the price to be paid for his active participation in any
new administration remained the chancellorship—but he would be flex-
ible on the composition of the Cabinet and would be prepared to include
within it a majority of non-Nazis.

Hitler, understanding the crucial element of timing in all political decisions, now ordered the Nazis to commit a vast—seemingly
disproportionate—effort in state elections to be held in the tiny district
of Lippe-Detmold on 15 January. The tactic worked. When the results
were announced the Nazi share of the vote had increased by 20 per
cent—from 33,000 to 39,000. The message to the German political elite
was clear—the Nazi party was not going away. Von Papen now decided
that he could accept Hitler as chancellor, as long as he—von Papen—was
vice-chancellor. The problem they faced now was to convince Hindenburg that this was the right solution to Germany's political crisis.

Hindenburg remained unimpressed by Hitler. But, nonetheless, now
he too began to consider the possibility of a Hitler chancellorship. There
were a number of reasons why he was prepared to change his mind—all

pragmatic, and none of which related to any new-found belief in Hitler's "charisma." First, there was the presence of von Papen. Hindenburg had grown personally fond of von Papen when they had been working closely together in the summer and autumn of 1932. So much so that he had presented von Papen, on his departure as chancellor, with a portrait of himself on which he had inscribed *"Ich hatt einen Kameraden"*[13] ("I had a comrade")—the words from a poignant soldiers' song. Now, here was von Papen, a man he trusted, saying that the best way forward was for Hitler to be chancellor, and that he could successfully be constrained by other members of the German elite.

Then there was the issue of Schleicher's support for potential land reform in eastern Germany, where a number of German aristocrats (including Hindenburg himself) held vast tracts of land. A Hitler/von Papen government would make this contentious issue disappear. In addition, Hindenburg hadn't forgotten the results of an army war game that had been presented to him early in December 1932, which had demonstrated that the armed forces of the state couldn't suppress an uprising by the Nazis and the Communists and protect the borders of Germany at the same time.[14]

Finally, there was the sudden presence on the scene of General Werner von Blomberg. Von Papen suggested to Hindenburg that Blomberg become Minister for the Armed Forces in the proposed Hitler cabinet. This post was, not surprisingly, vital to Hindenburg, and had previously been held as a power base by Schleicher. Blomberg seemed to be everything Schleicher was not—upright, honest and not the least bit "sneaky." But Blomberg had also recently been converted to the merits of Nazism. Naturally enthusiastic, he had formed the view during his most recent posting in East Prussia that the Nazis were attempting a national revival. He had also fallen under the influence of a leading army chaplain called Ludwig Müller who was himself a Nazi. So Blomberg was a character that von Papen, Hindenburg and Hitler could all support. Although, as events were to turn out, it was Hitler who benefited by far the most from Blomberg's presence in the forthcoming government.

But still, up until almost the last moment, Hindenburg wavered. Instinctively, he must have felt that Hitler was the wrong man to lead Germany. But Hindenburg was by now an old man of eighty-five, and with people he trusted—including his own son Oskar—saying that Hitler should be appointed chancellor, his resistance collapsed. The only immediate alternative would have been to allow Schleicher to form an authoritarian dictatorship, and that was worse, in Hindenburg's mind, than seeing Hitler as chancellor.

"He [Hindenburg] felt his age," says Josef Felder, who was elected as a Socialist member of the Reichstag in 1932. "And he realised that he was becoming physically weaker, very much weaker. He could barely carry his marshal's baton any more. One of the officers who marched with him once said that Hindenburg, the older he got, and the more difficult the situation became, the more afraid he became [that] he could no longer get Germany to go back to being an empire, that he would die before the old constitution was reinstalled in place of the German parliament—parliament being turned back into the monarchy. He wanted to see a new monarchy before he died."[15]

Hindenburg held out until the afternoon of Sunday, 29 January. It was only then that he finally told von Papen that he was prepared to accept Hitler as chancellor. At eleven o'clock the next morning Hitler achieved the goal he had been striving for—he was Chancellor of Germany.

To Hitler's supporters his success in gaining the chancellorship was a further demonstration of his legitimacy as a charismatic leader. At key points in the future, whenever doubts arose and they felt that Hitler was pursuing an apparently damaging policy, they could hark back to this moment and remember that in the end Hitler had been right and they had been wrong.

However, Hitler's appointment as chancellor wasn't necessarily seen by everyone as a watershed in the history of Germany. "At first we didn't take him seriously," says Herbert Richter, a veteran of the First World War and someone who had so far been immune to Hitler's charisma, "because in the first Hitler government, the Nazis weren't even in the majority." Richter felt that since Hitler was surrounded by "quite reasonable people" then "he couldn't do much harm."[16] As for the Socialist politician, Josef Felder, he remembers that "we believed we could still control him [i.e., Hitler] through parliament—total lunacy!"[17] And even after he had witnessed the abyss into which Hitler had led Germany, von Papen still refused to accept full responsibility for his catastrophic misjudgement in pushing for a Hitler chancellorship. Hitler, he wrote, became chancellor "by the normal interplay of democratic processes" and that "it still seemed reasonable to suppose that the responsible head of a government would adopt a different attitude" than that of "an irresponsible party chief."[18]

But for those who believed in the charismatic leadership of Adolf Hitler, this moment was of obvious and immense significance. Hitler had said openly in his election speeches that he despised democracy and wanted to sweep it away. Therefore for Nazi supporters this was not just a change in government, but the beginning of a change in political systems. "I have never myself been a democrat," says Reinhard Spitzy, at the time a committed Nazi. "I believe a country should be ruled like a big company. That means a certain council of specialists and so on, but I didn't believe in the role of parliament. When we had such a terrible crisis, like an economic crisis, and hunger and unemployment, and in such a moment, we were longing for a new general director, like what happens in a big company. You find a man, and he has to bring the whole thing in order."[19]

As for President Hindenburg, he would see the beginnings of a "new monarchy" installed before he died—just not the kind of monarchy he had been expecting.

PART TWO

JOURNEY TO WAR

7

THE MAN WHO WILL COME

Adolf Hitler looked out from the window of the Reich Chancellery in Berlin on the evening of 30 January 1933 as row upon row of Nazi storm-troopers paraded past him in celebration. But despite witnessing this image of strength, he knew he was not yet secure in power as chancellor. Less than half the population of Germany had voted for him and his Nazi party. There were only three Nazis in the Cabinet and he had to rule, as had the recent failed chancellors, with the consent of President Hindenburg via the constitutional device of Article 48.

Hitler had been explicit in the election campaign that he wanted to sweep democracy out of Germany. But a truly charismatic leader needs the support of the masses—even in a one party state. Without that support Hitler could perhaps cling on to power as a straightforward dictator, but he would never become what he aspired to be—a statesman who ruled by acclamation.

As a consequence he had to try and transcend the support for the party he led. The more he was associated with the actions of individual Nazis or connected himself with the detailed implementation of policies, the more he risked the German public perceiving him as a politician like all the others. So what Hitler attempted, during the first eighteen months of his chancellorship, was not just to force through measures which released him from the burden of Article 48 and the Weimar constitution, but to demonstrate in dramatic ways that he was not just the leader of the Nazi party but the ruler of all Germany. In pursuit of this aim he would order the murder of many of his old party comrades.

At the start of his chancellorship, Hitler acted predictably enough. He had always supported the use of violence against his opponents, and he moved to suppress opposition from the first moment he came to power. In this respect the actions of Hermann Göring were of most help to him. Göring, as Prussian Minister of the Interior, had direct control of the police force in the greater part of Germany. And he soon made his wishes clear in a directive of 17 February 1933: "Police officers who fire their revolvers in the execution of their duty will be protected by me without regard to the consequences of using their weapons."[1] He then summed up his attitude to human rights in a speech at Dortmund a few days later: "A bullet fired from the barrel of a police pistol is my bullet. If you say that is murder then I am a murderer . . . I know two sorts of law because I know two sorts of men: those who are with us and those who are against us."[2]

Göring was a devoted creature of Hitler's. Ernst Röhm and the stormtroopers, however, were a less straightforward proposition. Many of them saw in the elevation of Hitler to the chancellorship a chance to take rewards for themselves and practise unlimited revenge on their ideological enemies. Rudi Bamber's father, for example, was one of their victims in those early days of Nazi rule. Nazi stormtroopers took him, along with a group of other Jews, to a sports stadium in Nuremberg and made them cut the grass with their teeth. "It's very traumatic," says Rudi Bamber, "to feel that whatever you have done is of no consequence and you're just a Jew and that's all there is to it."[3]

But though there were a number of attacks on Jews in the immediate aftermath of Hitler's appointment as chancellor, it was the political enemies of the Nazis who were particularly targeted. "Right at the beginning," says Maria Mauth, then a schoolgirl in northern Germany, "the first Communists and Social Democrats were carted off. I even saw it myself—the lorries—but it did not make us think. They were only Communists after all . . . they were enemies of the people."[4]

Initially these "enemies of the people" were imprisoned in makeshift jails where they were often cruelly mistreated. They were held without charge, without due legal process, and at the whim of their captors. But Hitler, whilst he approved of violently suppressing any opposition, did not necessarily approve of all the SA's actions. He was concerned, as he said in a speech on 10 March 1933, that the "molesting of individuals, the obstruction of business life, must cease on principle."[5] Two days later, on 12 March, he called on his "party comrades" to "exercise the strictest and blindest discipline from now on. There must be no more isolated operations . . ."[6]

Significantly, just over a week later on 21 March 1933, the first "official" concentration camp opened at Dachau, outside Munich. Dachau was under the control of Heinrich Himmler, head of the SS. Even though Himmler nominally reported to Röhm, it was obvious that he had grander ambitions. Himmler was not a buccaneering thug like his direct boss, but an altogether colder character who would terrorise the Nazis' enemies systematically and to order. Dachau, administered by a reliable secret policeman like Himmler, fitted into Hitler's vision of the new Germany in a way that Röhm's stormtroopers did not.

Not that those caught up in the horror of Nazi oppression would have seen much difference in the way Himmler's SS, as opposed to Röhm's SA, treated them. Under Himmler's control, conditions inside Dachau were still appalling. The socialist politician Josef Felder was imprisoned in the notorious "bunker" a collection of isolation cells away from the main prison huts. Here he was tied up with chains and taunted with threats of his imminent execution. He was also starved—given only water to drink and the occasional piece of stale bread to eat.

Nonetheless, many of those who had welcomed Hitler's promise to restore "order" to Germany were not unhappy to see concentration camps established—and consequently they put an inaccurate gloss on events. "In Dachau he [i.e., Hitler] collected all the people—really the professional criminals," says Karl Boehm-Tettelbach, then a young air force officer. "And they were there in Dachau, in that working camp, and people didn't object too much at this."[7] Others rationalised the suffering as a necessary consequence of a "revolution." "At the moment we thought it [the establishment of camps like Dachau] was necessary," says Reinhard Spitzy. "We knew this was revolution. But look here, I studied the French Revolution. How many people have been killed by guillotine—40,000 have been killed by guillotine in France . . . That means that in all revolutions—and we thought we had a revolution—blood is running . . . That the Nazi revolution killed some people, I think that's normal, there was never a revolution in the world without killing."[8]

Hitler was careful to demonise the Communists as the biggest and most immediate threat to the new "national community" which the Nazi revolution wished to establish. And in this respect he was helped by a Dutch Communist called Marinus van der Lubbe, who set fire to the German parliament—the Reichstag—on 27 February 1933. The destruction of this iconic building increased the fear amongst the German population of a possible Communist revolution and thus served to justify the Nazis' oppression of their political opponents. The convenient timing of van der Lubbe's actions—a week before elections called by Hitler—has led a number of historians to believe that the Nazis conspired to create the fire themselves and that van der Lubbe did not act alone, but there is no conclusive evidence for this conspiracy theory. Certainly the unsystematic actions of the Nazis after the fire do not suggest that they knew about it beforehand.

However, the Reichstag fire did lead—the very next day—to the hurried adoption of one of the most restrictive legislative measures the Nazi state ever imposed: the decree of the Reich President for the Protection of People and State. Article 1 of the decree suspended basic human rights—such as the right to a free press and peaceful assembly—whilst Article 2 allowed the Reich Government, via the Nazi Interior Minister Wilhelm Frick, to take over the police powers of the individual German states in order to "restore security."

Five days later, on 5 March 1933, the Germans voted in the last general election to be held for more than a dozen years. Despite a massive propaganda effort, despite fear of a Communist uprising, despite Hitler's "appeal to the nation," despite all of this and more, the Nazis did not manage to gain the support of a majority of the German electorate. Fifty-six per cent of the German people voted for other political parties.

The fact that most Germans still did not want the Nazis represented a huge challenge for Adolf Hitler. He had already privately announced that the election would not make him change the composition of his Cabinet, nor would it remove him from power. Instead, he pushed forward with an attempt to pass an Enabling Law in the new Reichstag. This would allow him to issue decrees without referral to President Hindenburg under Article 48—but he needed a two-thirds vote in the Reichstag in order to pass the necessary legislation.

In particular, the Nazis needed the support of the Catholic Centre Party, and in his speech to the new Reichstag representatives on 23 March 1933—with the meeting held in the Kroll Opera House as a result of the Reichstag fire—Hitler was deliberately conciliatory to them, saying that his government "regards Christianity as the unshakeable foundation of the morals and moral code of the nation."[9] Hitler believed no such thing, but he recognised that for purely political reasons he had to make this assertion. He had acted in a similar way before. After his release from Landsberg prison he had demonstrated his understanding of the power of Christianity in German politics when he had expelled the Gauleiter of Thuringia, Artur Dinter, from the Nazi party. Against Hitler's wishes, Dinter had wanted to promote his own Aryan religion *Geistchristentum*—a heretical version of Christianity that excluded the Old Testament from the Bible and violently attacked the Jews. But, at the time, Hitler needed the support of the Minister President of Bavaria, a member of a Catholic party—so Dinter had to go.[10]

In 1933, just as it had years before, Hitler's ploy of telling the German Catholics what they wanted to hear worked. Members of the Catholic Centre party—who were also all too well aware of the fate awaiting those who opposed the Nazis—decided to support the Enabling Law.

Hitler's first, carefully prepared, statement to parliament on 23 March was in marked contrast to his hurriedly constructed response later in the same debate when the Enabling Act was attacked by Otto Wels of the Social Democrats. In his first speech Hitler attempted to portray himself as a statesman and as the leader of the whole of Germany: "We want to restore the unity of spirit and will to the German nation. We want to preserve the everlasting foundations of our life . . . "[11] In the second he returned to his beer hall origins and ridiculed Wels, pouring contempt upon both him and the party he led. "You are sissies [*wehleidig*—literally "snivelling"], gentlemen," said Hitler, "and not worthy of this age, if you start talking about persecution at this stage of the game." He also announced that the Nazis were "restraining" themselves from "turning against those who tortured and humiliated us for 14 years."[12] After telling the Social Democrats that he didn't even want them to vote for the Enabling Law and that "Germany will be liberated but not by you!" Hitler sat down to a rapturous reception from the Nazi members of parliament.

It was a telling moment. In his speech attacking the Social Democrats, Hitler had shown all of the rhetorical attributes that had made him undisputed dictatorial leader of the Nazi party. But he had also demonstrated many of the qualities that frightened large numbers of ordinary German voters—intolerance, aggression and wild partisanship.

Still, the Nazis won the vote. With the support of the Centre party the Enabling Law received 444 votes against the 94 votes cast by the Social Democrats. It was the moment all pretence of democracy left Germany. As a consequence, within four months, every political party in the country other than the Nazis was either banned or broke up voluntarily.

However, even with this milestone reached, Hitler still could not act exactly as he wanted. One of the most serious restraints on him was that the two policies that were central to his world view—the desire to remove all the Jews from Germany and the longing to acquire a Nazi empire in Eastern Europe—had not been trumpeted during the various election campaigns of the previous three years. There was little evidence that a majority of Germans supported either of them. This left Hitler in an unusual position for a leader just voted into office—he didn't yet feel able to implement his most important "visionary" ideas.

It wasn't that Hitler pretended not to believe in these policies—just that he was careful how he expressed this belief. The delicate line that Hitler trod was demonstrated by his action over the Jewish boycott in April 1933. Hitler was angry at the reception that measures like the Enabling Law and the mistreatment of German Jews by Nazi stormtroopers—as well as the start of the removal of Jews from the civil service and universities—had received in the foreign press. He saw in this criticism evidence of one of his most cherished fantasies—a worldwide "Jewish conspiracy." This belief in Jewish influence crossing national boundaries was certainly shared by much of the core Nazi support. "We looked at it [anti-Semitism] in terms of global Jewry which wanted to gain power, which wanted to rule the world," says Bruno Hähnel, one of the earliest Nazi supporters. "So it was global Jewry that we were—I don't want to say afraid of, perhaps we were afraid of it—well, standing up to."[13]

In order to "stand up" to "global Jewry," a Jewish boycott was organised by the Nazis to start on 1 April 1933. Significantly, Hitler chose not to put his name to the document dated 28 March that called for this action against German Jews. It was signed only "Leadership of the National

Socialist German Workers Party." Further evidence of Hitler's sensitiv-
ity on this issue was a report in the Nazi paper, the *Völkischer Beobachter*
on 29 March, which quoted Hitler as saying that it had been necessary
to organise these "defensive measures" because "otherwise it [i.e., action
against the Jews] would have come from the people [*Volk*] themselves
and might have taken on undesirable forms."[14] Hitler—already revealed
in *Mein Kampf* as an anti-Semite of the most venomous sort—now
sought to portray himself as somehow judicious in his action against the
Jews.

The boycott was called off after only one day. Hitler judged that the
time was not right for such visible "official" actions against the Jewish
population of Germany to be sustained over days and weeks. His attempts
to balance his own violent anti-Semitism with the prevailing mood of the
German public would be one of the recurring features of Nazi rule during
the 1930s.

Hitler's reticence to advertise his desire for Germany to obtain an
empire in Eastern Europe—specifically at the expense of the Soviet
Union—was also evident. Despite having openly acknowledged this goal
in *Mein Kampf,* and despite the fact that Germany was about to embark
on the biggest rearmament programme ever conducted in peacetime,
Hitler stuck to the mantra, expressed in an interview with Sir John Fos-
ter Fraser of *The Daily Telegraph,* that "no one in Germany who went
through the War wants to repeat the experience."[15] However, he also said
in the same interview that "the fate of Germany was dependent not on
colonies or dominions, but on its Eastern borders"—a phrase which was
interpreted as a desire to gain back the territory lost as a result of the peace
treaties at the end of the First World War.

It was clear that it would be entirely Hitler's decision as to how and
when fundamental Nazi policy would be introduced to the German people. Goebbels wrote that there would be no more voting, and that now
the "Führer's personality" was what counted.[16] Just two days before he
wrote those words Goebbels had helped organise mass public celebrations
on the occasion of Hitler's forty-fourth birthday—a physical manifesta-
tion of the way in which the personality of the new chancellor would
now drive German politics. From now on, until Hitler's fifty-sixth birthday party in 1945 at the Reich Chancellery of Berlin, 20 April would be
treated as a sacred date in the German calendar.

As a consequence of all the attention that had been focused on Hitler, beginning with his attempt to unseat Hindenburg as president the year before, an interesting phenomenon was taking place. Some of those who had thought Hitler was unimpressive in the past were now beginning to see him as charismatic. Fridolin von Spaun, for example, a sympathiser of the Nazis since the early 1920s, had first witnessed Hitler at a rally in 1923. "There stood Ludendorff, a mighty figure in uniform with his decorations," he says. "And a small figure stood next to him—nowhere near as imposing, in quite a shabby coat. And I paid no attention to him. Then I asked later, 'Who was that who stood nearby [to Ludendorff]?' Well, that was Hitler, the leader of the National Socialists."[17]

But now nearly ten years later, von Spaun encountered Hitler once again and formed an entirely different opinion. At a dinner, attended by a large number of Nazi sympathisers, Spaun saw Hitler looking at him. He felt Hitler's eyes bore into him and as a result became immediately convinced of his sincerity. Then Hitler got up to talk to someone and held on to the back of Spaun's chair. "And then I felt a trembling from his fingers penetrating me. I actually felt it. But not a nervous trembling. Rather I felt: this man, this body, is only the tool for implementing a big, all-powerful will here on earth. That's a miracle in my view."

So, as far as von Spaun was concerned, Hitler had been transformed from an insignificant man in a shabby coat to a "tool for implementing a big, all-powerful will." Of course, much had changed in the ten years or so between Spaun's two encounters with Hitler. But chiefly what had altered was Spaun's own personal perception of the man. By the time he was moved by Hitler's touch, Spaun knew that he was in the presence of the most famous man in Germany. Moreover, Spaun had always been predisposed to believe in the Right-wing, *völkisch* politics that Hitler espoused. Hitler himself hadn't altered that much. It was just that people like Spaun were now ready to believe in his charisma.

However, Hitler's charisma had obvious limits. There were still those who worked closely with him—even served in his Cabinet—who remained immune to it. Von Papen, of course, was one such person, and another was the media tycoon Alfred Hugenberg. Both of them would cause Hitler problems as they gradually realised that their hope of "taming" the Nazis and using them for their own ends had been hopelessly naïve. Hugenberg in particular had anticipated that he would possess immense power in Hitler's government as Minister of Economics, Food and Agriculture. Unlike Hitler, Hugenberg possessed impressive academic and business qualifications—he held a doctorate in economics and had been chairman of one of the most important German industrial concerns, Krupp steel. But Hitler still out-manoeuvred him. Once the Enabling Law was passed the Cabinet ceased to have any real power. Hitler wanted it to continue to function, but only in a ceremonial way. Hugenberg finally realised how Hitler would sideline him when his subordinate, the State Secretary in the Ministry of Economics, a committed Nazi called Fritz Reinhardt, put forward a proposal to create new jobs that Hugenberg was against. Hitler chose to support Reinhardt and there was nothing that Hugenberg could do about it.[18] Dealing directly with subordinates in order to unsettle and destabilise ostensibly powerful figures in the regime was a tactic that Hitler would employ many times in the future.

Hugenberg was not prepared to endure this kind of treatment and told Hitler that he wanted to resign from the Cabinet. Hitler met Hugenberg on 27 June 1933 and attempted to persuade him to stay. Hitler realised that it would be potentially embarrassing if, just five months into his tenure as chancellor, he appeared to break the promise he had given not to change the composition of his Cabinet. But Hugenberg was impervious to Hitler's blandishments. Even Hitler's threats had no effect. Hitler was forced to tell President Hindenburg that Hugenberg wanted to leave the government. Hindenburg, who had never warmed to Hugenberg and was relieved to have shaken off the burden of regular involvement in government policy that Article 48 had forced on him, was relaxed about this new development.

But what is significant is what happened next to Hugenberg—which was nothing. There was no persecution, no imprisonment, no revenge. He retained his seat in the Reichstag, and though he had to relinquish control of his media empire, he struck an advantageous financial bargain that allowed him to invest heavily in German industry. He died peacefully at the age of eighty-five in 1951. Whilst Hitler undoubtedly possessed what the historian David Cesarani describes as a "murderous personality,"[19] nonetheless, as long as he believed those who chose to leave his government had not betrayed him, then they could carry on living safely in Germany after they had left his service, as Hugenberg did.

However, Ernst Röhm would not be as amenable as Hugenberg, and

he was not prepared to let himself be sidelined. "A victory on the road of
the German revolution has been won," Röhm wrote in an article in June
1933. "But not absolute victory!"[20] The "goal," he said, of "a new Germany,
reborn in a spiritual revolution of nationalist and socialist spirit" was still
far from being accomplished. "And as long as the real National Socialist
Germany still awaits fulfilment, the fierce and passionate struggle of the
SA and SS will not stop. Germany becomes national socialist or it dies.
And that is why the German revolution continues, until the swastika on
our flags and emblems will not be an external symbol of honest confes-
sion or of conformity, but the sacred possession of the whole people."
This was a code calling for a greater role for Röhm and his stormtroopers
in the new Germany. Not just in terms of jobs and financial reward, but
in retaining the spirit and comradeship of the SA in some kind of unification with—or takeover of—the German army.

These ambitions were intensified by the belief that the stormtroopers
were the true revolutionaries. Wolfgang Teubert, for example, joined the
SA in 1928 and he now wanted to see fundamental change in Germany.
In the first place that meant the removal of the Jews: "My parents' factory
in Görlitz had already been liquidated under Jewish influence, you might
say, because one of my uncles had a Jewish agent, who had cheated him
of tens of thousands Marks . . . We wanted to stop the increasing 'Jew-
ification' of Germany . . . I could just say to the Jews, 'You are no longer
wanted here. Please leave this country.'"[21]

Wolfgang Teubert wasn't just anti-Semitic—and prepared to condemn all German Jews for the alleged misconduct of one of them—he
also had a broader desire for change in Germany. He believed passionately in the concept of the *Volksgemeinschaft,* the "people's community,"
in which all ethnically "pure" Germans treated each other as equals. More
than that—and the single most important factor for him—was his conviction that the Nazis would "break the *Zinsknechtschaft,*" the "interest
slavery" that Gottfried Feder had so opposed back in the earliest days of
the Nazi party. Essentially it was the belief that workers who owned farms
or shops had to pay disproportionate amounts of their income back in
interest to the people who had loaned them the money. It was the kind
of outright "socialist" policy that Hitler had backtracked from during the
various election campaigns of the early 1930s.

However, it was Röhm's desire for the SA to become the dominant

The Man Who Will Come   91

military force in the new Germany that was to cause the greatest friction. Hitler, initially at least, was careful in his treatment of his old comrade. Not only were there three times as many stormtroopers as soldiers in the German army in 1933, but he must have seen in the potential conflict between the SA and the army a means to benefit himself as a charismatic leader—as long as he handled the situation deftly.

On 1 December 1933, Röhm was appointed to the Cabinet, and from this base of institutional—if symbolic—power, two months later on 1 February 1934 he put a proposal before Blomberg, the Minster of Defence, that the SA should be recognised as the pre-eminent military force in Germany. He thus called for the German armed forces, the *Reichswehr*, to be subordinated to the SA. It was almost a declaration of war on the traditional armed forces of Germany.

Not surprisingly, officers in the German army like Johann-Adolf Graf von Kielmansegg did not take kindly to this. "One rejected the SA because of their behaviour, the way they looked, they way they were. Well, the SA were gradually, at the end they were, well, one can almost say, they were hated by most soldiers. On top of this, on top of the rejection of the SA, I would say, was the fact that it became ever more clear, not just in the army, that Röhm, the highest commander of the SA, was trying in some way to take over the Reichswehr."[22]

Blomberg and the rest of the army leadership were equally opposed to this attempt to sideline them. And since they recognised that the final decision on this crucial question would rest with one man—Adolf Hitler—they moved to introduce changes to the *Reichswehr* that they knew would make him happy. One such change was the immediate instruction, just days after Röhm's proposal, that the Nazi emblem of an eagle holding a swastika be incorporated on all uniforms. The fact that every member of the German armed forces would now carry a swastika on their uniform was a symbolic step towards the politicisation of the *Reichswehr*. This was coupled with the decision to enforce an "Aryan" clause which meant that members of the *Reichswehr* had to prove that they were of "Aryan" descent or risk expulsion.

Hitler made his own position clear at a conference on 28 February 1934, attended by the leaders of the SA and the *Reichswehr*, when he rejected Röhm's proposal. The SA was not to take over the army, but be subordinate to it in matters of national defence. He also outlined in general terms the future tasks that he wanted the new *Reichswehr* to perform. Since "living space" needed to be created and "the Western Powers would not let us do this" as a consequence "short decisive blows to the West and then to the East could be necessary."[23]

This was an astonishing admission for Hitler to make openly at such a conference and, as Field Marshal Weichs later wrote, "it is almost miraculous that this prophecy of 1934 has never become known."[24] But Weichs believed that since "the soldier was accustomed never to take the words of politicians too seriously" these "warlike prophecies" were not taken at "face value" at the time.

There is, of course, another possible interpretation of the army's quiescence at the 28 February conference—which is that Hitler's coupling of his decision to curb the SA's ambitions with the announcement of his broader military ambitions was a deliberate attempt to stifle any potential opposition within the army to his long-term goals. For the leaders of the German army would find it hard to object to Hitler's vague future plans for expansion at the same time as they welcomed his suppression of the SA.

Röhm, predictably, was extremely unhappy with Hitler's decision to place the SA under the control of the army in the event of future conflict. And over the next few months there were rumours that the SA might even be planning to take matters into their own hands—perhaps via a coup. After a meeting with Hitler on 7 June 1934 Röhm announced that he was taking sick leave and that the stormtroopers should take a holiday as well, ready to return to service on 1 August. He ended the missive with the words "The SA is and remains Germany's destiny."[25]

This was most certainly not a view that Adolf Hitler shared. The SA was by now a divisive force and one that wasn't helping Hitler in his attempt to leap from mere leadership of the Nazi party to capturing the hearts of all "true" Germans as the leader of the whole nation. And for Hitler there was a particular urgency to the Röhm problem, since it was clear that President Hindenburg did not have long to live. On Hindenburg's death Hitler wanted to combine the offices of Reich Chancellor and president and so become both the political leader of Germany and the head of state, but opposition from the traditional German elite—especially the *Reichswehr*—might well prevent that transition happening smoothly.

This danger was all too apparent from a public statement in June 1934 made by Franz von Papen. In a speech at Marburg University he said that "the government must represent the people as a whole, and must on no account be the exponent only of particular groups; otherwise it would fail in its attempt to construct the national community."[26] He warned against a "second wave" of revolution and stated that "The government is well aware of the selfishness, the lack of principle, the insincerity, the unchivalrous behaviour, the arrogance which is on the increase under the guise of the German revolution." He said that people would follow the Führer but not if "every word of criticism" was "immediately interpreted as malicious."

Hitler's reaction to Papen's speech was predictable. The distribution of the speech was banned, and the co-author of Papen's words of warning and criticism, Edgar Jung, was later arrested and killed. But Hitler knew that von Papen was also vocalising the concerns of a large segment of the German population. Almost more importantly, he was expressing the concerns of two people whose opinion mattered a great deal to Hitler—President Hindenburg and General Blomberg. They told Hitler on 21 June that he should bring "the revolutionary troublemakers . . . to reason"[27] or else the "Hitler experiment" would cease.

Heinrich Himmler, and his ambitious subordinate Reinhard Heydrich, now seized the chance to gain more influence and power for themselves as they briefed senior figures in the army that Röhm was planning a coup. Soon a spiral of rumour upon rumour developed as German army units moved to an increased state of alert, and SA leaders did the same once they heard about the actions of the army. This culminated on 26 June, when an "order" was found by the military intelligence organisation, the *Abwehr*, which purported to come from Röhm, calling for the SA to prepare themselves for an attack on the Army.[28] It was almost certainly a forgery—Röhm and his comrades had not been planning a coup. Yes, they were dissatisfied about the pace of the "revolution" and wanted a good deal more power for themselves, but they remained loyal to Hitler. Still, Röhm had made a serious misjudgement. He had grossly underestimated the scale and nature of the enemies ranged against him. From the leadership of the SS to the leadership of the German Army; from the traditional German elite to the local businessmen who were bullied by the stormtroopers: all of them would be happy to see Röhm disappear.

Hitler decided to confront the leaders of the SA at their holiday resort in Bad Wiessee in Bavaria. It was a decision that was a long time coming. As far back as January he had asked the Gestapo to monitor the actions of the SA and report back to him examples of their bad behaviour.[29] Now, in the early morning of 30 June 1934, he finally acted. He led a group of his close comrades into Röhm's hotel room on the first floor of the Hotel Hanselbauer. Röhm, still in bed, looked up at Hitler and said "sleepily"[30] *"Heil, mein Führer."* Hitler shouted that he was under arrest, turned and left. SA Obergruppenführer Heines, in a room nearby, was found in bed with an eighteen-year-old stormtrooper. Others thought to be implicated in "Röhm's schemes" were arrested and held temporarily in the laundry room of the hotel before being taken to Stadelheim prison in Munich.

Simultaneously, in Berlin, Göring organised not just the round-up of key SA figures but also the murder of other opponents of the regime. Old scores were brutally settled. General Schleicher and his wife were shot, as was Gregor Strasser and a host of others. No one knows the exact number of dead, but the figure is at least 150—including Ernst Röhm who, having declined the opportunity to commit suicide, was shot in his cell by two SS men.

"The Night of the Long Knives," as the episode came to be known, was a breathtaking example of the total breakdown of the rule of law in Germany. None of those who suffered was tried in court. None of the alleged evidence against them was tested. None of them was given a chance to speak in their own defence. And yet Hitler's decision to order the murder of so many of his old comrades was widely welcomed. General Blomberg, in a statement on 1 July, said, "The Führer with military decision and outstanding courage has himself attacked and destroyed the traitors and murderers."[31] President Hindenburg said that he was grateful that the "treasonable intrigues" had been "nipped in the bud" and that Hitler had "saved the German nation from serious danger."[32] Much lower down the command structure the views of air force officer Karl Boehm-Tettelbach were typical: "It was described as a revolt against Hitler . . . As a young officer you read the reports and you listened to the stories written in the paper and it [the attack on the SA] sounded reasonable. If somebody starts a revolution and is killed right at the beginning, then that's good."[33]

It was the most telling example yet of a paradox at the heart of Hitler's rule. Many people were frightened of the violence that abounded in

German society—perpetrated both by the Communists and the SA. The majority longed for peace and stability. Now Hitler appeared to be about to deliver that peace and stability—but only by the use of more violence. Thus many who decried violence, came to support it—even welcome it.

Because of his control of the media, Hitler was able to spin the events of 30 June 1934 in a way that was extremely advantageous for him. The fact that he had acted against elements of the Nazi party enabled him to position himself as the protector of all Germany, rather than the protector of just his own narrow self interests. The discovery of Heines in bed with a young stormtrooper at the time of the raid on the SA's spa hotel, and the revelation of the "luxury" in which the SA had been enjoying themselves, also allowed him to speak in support of conventional morality and thrift. On 30 June, after the arrest of Röhm and the others, Hitler issued an order of the day to the new chief of staff of the SA, Lutze, which called on SA leaders to be "a model of modesty and not extravagance" and in a specific reference to the number of homosexuals previously at the top of the SA, said that he would "particularly want every mother to be able to give her son to the SA, to the party or the Hitler Youth without fear that he might become ethically or morally corrupt."[34]

It was a piece of jaw-dropping hypocrisy. Hitler was surrounded by Nazi leaders like Hermann Göring who were scarcely an example "of modesty and not extravagance" and the existence of homosexuals in leadership roles in the SA had been well known long before Hitler arrived at Wiessee on 30 June 1934. "We knew it [already] about Obergruppenführer Heines," says former stormtrooper Wolfgang Teubert, "his adjutant was always addressed as 'Fräulein Schmidt.' But that didn't really bother us a great deal, we had other things to think about."[35] Hitler himself had previously ignored those who had brought up the subject of Röhm's homosexuality. Emil Klein,[36] a Hitler Youth leader, for instance, had—years before—accompanied one of the commanders of the Munich SA to a meeting with Hitler at which Röhm's homosexuality had been raised, but Hitler had seemed unconcerned at the news. Yet now Hitler was posing as a model of propriety.

This all contributed to a gap opening, in the perception of many Germans, between the Nazis on the one hand and Hitler on the other. After all, they could argue, hadn't Hitler shown his loyalty to Germany by attacking the "bad" Nazis? This warped logic—warped because Hitler had demonstrably acted outside of the established law, having previously tolerated many of the "abuses" he now condemned—was especially found in the minds of a number of army officers, like Johann-Adolf Graf Kielmansegg. "For the army you have to make a clear distinction, and this goes for the whole of the Third Reich, between Hitler . . . and the behaviour and programme of the Nazis. This [the behaviour and programme of the Nazis] was rejected, even before the war . . . But not Hitler."[37]

The practical benefits for Hitler of his action against the SA were immediate and substantial. When President Hindenburg died on 2 August 1934, little more than a month after the murder of Röhm and the others, Hitler was confirmed by acclamation as both chancellor and head of state with the post of Reich President abolished. Then, on 20 August, every member of the armed forces and all public officials swore an oath of loyalty to Hitler personally as "Führer of the German Reich."

As Karl Boehm-Tettelbach, who swore the oath as an air force officer, remembers, this was a serious business; his oath "accompanied me my whole life to the end. I mean oath is oath . . . I can't break the oath, otherwise I might [have to] commit suicide." Or, as Johann-Adolf Graf Kielmansegg put it simply, "A German officer does not break an oath sworn before God."

Once Hitler was the undisputed supreme commander of the armed forces and head of state, a truly remarkable phenomenon occurred in Germany. Between 1934 and 1938, despite spending money on rearmament on an unprecedented scale, despite a variety of economic and political difficulties, despite the Nazi party often conducting a series of quarrelsome and distracting battles in government over who was responsible for what, despite the creation of concentration camps and the persecution of minorities, despite all of that and more, Adolf Hitler grew in power and prestige until he received a level of adulation without parallel in modern European history.

One crucial reason for this transformation was the creation of a charismatic aura around Hitler—one whose legitimacy was purportedly based both on scientific and quasi-religious sources. This mingling of an ancient justification for charismatic leadership—spiritual endorsement—and a modern justification—science—was new.[38] And it was hugely successful.

Joseph Goebbels, the Nazi propaganda minister, considered the conscious manufacture of Hitler's "image" as one of his greatest achievements.

He remarked in December 1941 that via the "creation of the Führer myth Hitler had been given the halo of infallibility, with the result that many people who looked askance at the party after 1933 now had complete confidence in Hitler."[39]

Goebbels certainly did not underestimate his own abilities. He told his wartime press adjutant, Wilfred von Oven, that he worked "almost 20 hours a day; he claimed that he could survive on four hours' sleep [a night] as could Frederick the Great and other great men."[40] Goebbels also, according to von Oven, "had a huge need for recognition . . . But I always say there is nothing wrong with having a need for recognition, providing that you are sufficiently gifted."

But by claiming credit for the "creation of the Führer myth," Goebbels was exaggerating his own contribution to Hitler's success, because Hitler himself played the most important part in the creation of his own myth. Hitler had always understood the importance of propaganda and believed he knew better than anyone else how he and the party should be portrayed—it's significant that his first job in the German Workers' Party was propaganda chief. It was Hitler, as much as Goebbels, who understood that as a charismatic leader he must have distance from the ordinary workaday world, that he must appear to be without the ordinary human need for close relationships and that he must present himself as "infallible." More than all of that, Hitler realised that this portrayal of himself as outside of the normal mainstream of humanity allowed space for others to project their own needs and desires on to him. It was in this interaction that a transference occurred of great consequence. Hitler's followers became confident and gained self-worth because of their faith in him. Their belief in Hitler gave special meaning to their own lives. That's one explanation for the kind of fawning praise Göring spewed out in 1934: "There is something mystical, inexpressible, almost incomprehensible about this one man . . . We love Adolf Hitler because we believe, deeply and steadfastly, that he was sent to us by God to save Germany . . . There is no quality that he does not possess to the highest degree . . . For us the Führer is simply infallible in all matters political and all other issues concerning the national and social interest of the people."[41]

Did Göring really believe that Hitler possessed every human quality "to the highest degree"? He was certainly cynical and tough enough to recognise that it was in his own interests to say that he did. But Göring—

who loathed the concept of democracy—was also deeply predisposed to believe in the value of one single "infallible" leader, and he realised that this belief absolved him from the burden of ultimate responsibility for his own actions.

This idea of the Führer as a quasi-mystical liberating force pervades the most infamous and influential propaganda film ever made about Hitler—Leni Riefenstahl's *Triumph des Willens* (*Triumph of the Will*). Filmed at the 1934 Nazi Party rally in Nuremberg the work purported to be a "documentary"—but in fact it was as conceived and structured as any work of fiction. Significantly, *Triumph of the Will* was not controlled by Goebbels. Unusually, Riefenstahl worked directly with Hitler on the composition of the film. It was even Hitler who suggested the title.[42]

Riefenstahl was no neutral observer of Hitler—in fact, she was captivated by him. "I had an almost apocalyptic vision that I was never able to forget," she wrote after she had seen him speak at an election rally a few years before. "It seemed as if the Earth's surface were spreading out in front of me, like a hemisphere that suddenly splits apart in the middle, spewing out an enormous jet of water, so powerful that it touched the sky and shook the earth."[43]

Riefenstahl now attempted to transmit this same "apocalyptic vision" to a mass audience. And from the opening shots of the film, showing Hitler's plane flying above Nuremberg and his arrival as a quasi messiah from the sky, the intention of the work is obvious—to demonstrate the Führer's perceived special nature. He is portrayed as a man alone, separate from the crowds of his supporters. The images of the swastika, the use of fire in rituals, the repeated incantations—all are designed to trigger associations with a religious service. But the images of *Triumph of the Will* were not simply pseudo-religious, they carried a powerful modern appeal as well. This wasn't a religious service that admitted everyone to worship—the sick and the old were absent—but a demonstration of the raw power of nature, with only vigorous adults and youths on view. Nazism was thus presented here as rooted in a combination of pseudo-religion and pseudo-Darwinian science.

Events like the party rally featured in *Triumph of the Will* allowed thousands to bask in Hitler's presence. As the American journalist William Shirer, who attended the 1934 rally, wrote, "And there, in the flood-lit night, jammed together like sardines, in one mass formation, the little men of Germany who have made Nazism possible achieved the highest state of being the Germanic man knows: the shedding of their individual souls and mind—with the personal responsibilities and doubts and problems—until under the mystic lights and at the sound of the magic words of the Austrian they were merged completely in the Germanic herd."[44]

Shirer's belief that "the highest state of being the Germanic man knows" was to shed "their individual souls and mind" was a commonplace belief at the time (and is not unknown today). That there were historical and cultural reasons why Germans at that time were perhaps particularly susceptible to the idea of leadership by an individual "hero" has already been discussed. But the danger with pursuing this notion too far is that it minimises the unique personality of Hitler. Yes, the stage management and direction of the 1934 rally played a part, but most important was the personality of the leader. This was a point that George Orwell—a dedicated anti-Nazi—recognised better than anyone. In his brilliant review of *Mein Kampf*, he wrote of the "attraction" of Hitler's personality, which he felt was "no doubt overwhelming when one hears his speeches."[45] Orwell maintained, "The fact is that there is something deeply appealing about him. One feels it again when one sees his photographs—it is a pathetic, dog-like face, the face of a man suffering under intolerable wrongs. In a rather more manly way it reproduces the expression of innumerable pictures of Christ crucified, and there is little doubt that that is how Hitler sees himself."

Orwell rightly emphasised this aspect of the "suffering" Hitler portrayed, for an important part of Hitler's appeal was his claim that Germany had "suffered" and that he was destined to right this terrible wrong. Moreover, rallies like the one at Nuremberg in 1934 appealed to large numbers of Germans because they went against many of the comfortable assumptions of the time, as Orwell explains: "Hitler, because in his own joyless mind he feels it with exceptional strength, knows that human beings don't only want comfort, safety, short working-hours, hygiene, birth-control and, in general, common sense; they also, at least intermittently, want struggle and self-sacrifice, not to mention drums, flags and loyalty-parades."[46]

Above all, what Hitler offered to his audience was redemption. In his speeches he talked less about policy and more about destiny. It was a privilege, he said, to live at such a decisive time in history. The Nazis were on a "splendid crusade" that would "go down as one of the most miraculous and remarkable phenomena in world history."[47] There might be a tough road ahead, Hitler implied, but the forthcoming journey offered every German a chance to find meaning in their lives. Thus, Hitler suggested, Germans were special not just because they were racially superior but because they had been born at such a time and had great tasks before them.

"How deeply we feel once more in this hour the miracle that has brought us together!"[48] Hitler said to a gathering of National Socialist leaders in Nuremberg in September 1936. "You have come to this city from your small village, from your market towns, from your cities, from mines and factories, from behind the plough. You have come from your daily routine and from your labours for Germany to share this feeling: We are together . . . and we are now Germany!" Earlier that day, in an extraordinary speech to a gathering of women of the *NS Frauenschaft* (the Nazis' "Women's League"), Hitler had claimed that not only did German children "belong to their mothers" they also belonged "to me." There was an almost mystical connection, implied Hitler, between him and these German children.

Jutta Rüdiger, who was to become Reich Leader of the League of German Girls just a year after Hitler gave this speech, says that she is "still utterly amazed" by Hitler's achievement in drawing Germans (or at least those Germans the Nazis considered "Aryan") into one community: "If you look at the German people throughout the ages—how they quarrelled with one another and are quarrelling again—the fact is that Hitler managed to get all of them, almost all of them, under the one roof, so to speak, to pull them together. People said that Hitler had the effect of a magnet that was being passed over the heads of the German people." And that "magnet" seemed to have a particular effect on women, as William Shirer observed in Nuremberg in 1934 when he came across a group of women outside Hitler's hotel. He thought that, "They looked up at him as if he were a messiah, their faces transformed into something positively inhuman."[49]

Hitler had always used religious terms in his speeches, talking of the "resurrection" of the German people and, as we have seen, emphasising his commitment to the Christian church in Germany to the Centre party in 1933. He had also ensured that the original Nazi programme of 1920, in point 24, stated that the party "represents the standpoint of positive Christianity." And, as discussed earlier, he had made positive comments about Jesus as a "fighter" against the Jews.[50] But the most persuasive explanation of these statements is that Hitler, as a politician, simply recognised the practical reality of the world he inhabited. In conversation with Ludendorff years before he had said, "I need Bavarian Catholics as well as Prussian Protestants to build up a great political movement. The rest comes later."[51] Had Hitler distanced himself or his movement too much from Christianity it is all but impossible to see how he could ever have been successful in a free election. Thus his relationship in public to Christianity—indeed his relationship to "religion" in general—was opportunistic.

There is no evidence that Hitler himself, in his personal life, ever expressed any individual belief in the basic tenets of the Christian church. He once said to Albert Speer, "You see, it's been our misfortune to have the wrong religion. Why didn't we have the religion of the Japanese, who regard sacrifice for the Fatherland as the highest good? The Mohammedan religion too would have been much more compatible to us than Christianity. Why did it have to be Christianity with its meekness and flabbiness?"[52]

All of which makes the increasingly quasi-religious role of Hitler in the Nazi state particularly intriguing. The hordes of Germans who travelled—almost as pilgrims—to pay homage to Hitler at his home above Berchtesgaden; the thousands of personal petitions sent to Hitler at the Reich Chancellery; the pseudo-religious iconography of the Nuremberg rallies; the fact that German children were taught that Hitler was "sent from God" and was their "faith" and "light"[53]; all this spoke to the fact that Hitler was seen less as a normal politician and more as a prophet touched by the divine. For Wilhelm Roes, growing up in the early years of Nazi rule, Hitler "was God himself. All the media sort of glorified him. And we young people believed all of that; you know we were stupid. If I look at my grandchildren, we were so stupid."[54]

Adolf Hitler became an object of veneration for millions. And the evidence is that in his public pronouncements during these first few years in power he gradually shifted the emphasis he placed on traditional notions of Christianity towards a less precise idea of "Providence." Memorably,

in a speech in 1936, he remarked that "Neither threats nor warnings will
prevent me from going my way. I follow the path assigned to me by
Providence with the instinctive sureness of a sleepwalker."[55]

Just who or what did Hitler think was this "Providence" who had
"assigned" him his "path"? Almost certainly not the Christian God. As
Hitler said to a group of Nazi leaders in 1937, "there is no universal agreement as to the specific nature of God"[56] but "belief in God is one of the
most ingenious and noblest presentiments of man which lifts us above the
animals." So, most likely, Hitler was using what he saw as the "ingenious"
device of a supernatural being in order to justify his own actions. If he
was following "Providence" then his actions could only be questioned by
that "Providence"—certainly never by mere mortals. And since he was
the only route to this "Providence" then he could do whatever he liked
and claim divine support. Moreover, the increasing ambiguity in Hitler's
public speeches about whether or not his idea of "Providence" bore any
relationship to Christianity prevented any Catholic or Protestant clergy
claiming that they had any special ability to interpret his claim of a direct
link to a supernatural being.

The result was that the established Christian church in Germany did
not know quite what to make of Adolf Hitler, or how exactly to respond
to his government. The Nazis never banned the church—indeed, a number of key Nazis were Christian believers. For example, Erich Koch, the
hard-line Nazi Gauleiter of East Prussia, said after the war, "I held the
view that the Nazi idea had to develop from a basic Prussian–Protestant
attitude and from Luther's unfinished Reformation."[57]

On gaining power, Hitler, whilst most certainly not sharing Koch's
belief, seems to have been concerned most of all about the potential
power of the church in Germany—Catholic and Protestant—as an
oppositional power-bloc to his ambitions rather than as a spiritual force.
For some years Hitler encouraged the placement of clergy who were out-
and-out Nazis in senior positions within the Protestant church in Germany. But by 1937 it was obvious to Hitler that the German Protestant
church would never be as acquiescent as he desired, and his rhetoric—in
private—grew more overtly anti-Christian. And whilst in public Hitler
was still ambiguous about where he stood in his relationship to a Christian God, a number of other leading Nazis were outspoken in their dislike
of Christianity. Martin Bormann, who would become Hitler's secretary,

Alfred Rosenberg, a leading party ideologue, and Heinrich Himmler, would all openly condemn Christianity. Members of Himmler's SS were not allowed to say they did not believe in God, but equally they were not encouraged to say they worshipped a Christian God. The preferred option was for them to proclaim that they were *"gottgläubig"* or "God believers"—without the need to specify the exact nature of the God they believed in.

As time went on, Hitler's true feelings about Christianity became ever more apparent within the Nazi elite. "The Führer is a man totally attuned to antiquity," wrote Goebbels in his diary on 8 April 1941. "He hates Christianity, because it has crippled all that is noble in humanity."[58] That same year, chatting to five of his cronies—including Ribbentrop and Rosenberg—Hitler said, "The war will be over one day. I shall then consider that my life's final task will be to solve the religious problem." Declaring that "Christianity is an invention of sick brains," he said that "the concrete image of the Beyond that religion forces on me does not stand up to examination." Instead Hitler said, he dreamt "of a state of affairs in which every man would know that he lives and dies for the preservation of the species."[59]

However, since Hitler knew that if he openly expressed such antireligious views his own popularity might suffer, what he did was to mingle two justifications for his authority—a religious one and a scientific one—together. On the one hand Hitler claimed legitimacy from "Providence," which millions of German Christians could take to be their God, but on the other he also claimed that the fundamental laws of nature supported his beliefs—hence the dual views presented in *Triumph of the Will* of pseudo-religious iconography and the raw animal power of healthy young Nazis.

Revealingly, Goebbels had anxieties about the commissioning of *Triumph of the Will*. In part this concern was motivated by jealousy of the director, Leni Riefenstahl. As Fritz Hippler, who worked closely with Goebbels, puts it, "Riefenstahl angered Goebbels because it was made possible for her to be creative in films by Hitler personally, and Goebbels had no say over her whatsoever."[60] But there was more to his reluctance to embrace the idea of *Triumph of the Will* than simple resentment. Goebbels was always concerned about the effect of overtly National Socialist propaganda on film. Wilfred von Oven recalls that Goebbels thought films like *Hitlerjunge Quex,* about a heroic Hitler Youth boy who sees a vision of Nazi banners flying in heaven as he lies dying, were "dreadful."[61] As Goebbels announced in the *Völkischer Beobachter* in February 1934, "If I believe that there is an honest artistic attitude behind a film, then I will protect it . . . I do not demand that a film begins and ends with National Socialist parades. The Nazi parades should be left to us, we better understand them."[62]

Fritz Hippler explains that his boss, Goebbels, believed that "articles in the papers or what was said, influenced the brain, the consciousness, the intelligence, the imagination, while the real primary forces of men are moved by the unconscious, that which he doesn't raise into his consciousness, but which drives him on from beyond his consciousness. On these primary sources, the moving picture works in a particularly intensive manner, and this medium he therefore wanted to use in a particularly pointed way."[63] Goebbels believed that in order to work effectively propaganda had to possess two qualities—it must not look like crude propaganda and it must be entertaining. As he said to a gathering of senior figures from German radio in March 1933, "First principle: at all costs avoid being boring. I put that before everything."[64]

All of which meant that Goebbels was predisposed to be suspicious of a propaganda effort like *Triumph of the Will.* But once he had seen the film and—more importantly—seen Hitler's positive reaction to it, he praised it, calling *Triumph of the Will* "a magnificent cinematic vision of the Führer" and remarking that "the film has successfully avoided the danger of merely a politically slanted film . . . it is an epic, forging the tempo of marching formations, steel-like in its conviction and fired by passionate artistry."[65]

Significantly, however, the experiment of portraying Hitler in a feature-length documentary was never repeated. Goebbels preferred an altogether more understated approach to embedding Hitler in the German psyche. His preference, in feature films, was not to mention Hitler explicitly at all. Instead, he wanted the audience themselves to make the connection between the film they were watching and their Führer. This led to the later commissioning of a series of historical films featuring heroes from Germany's past, like Friedrich Schiller, Bismarck and Frederick the Great. The scripts were carefully constructed so that parallels could be drawn between these historical figures and Hitler, but the analogies were never blatantly spelt out. Instead, history was twisted so that, for example, Bismarck was shown acting very much like Hitler in dissolving parliamentary democracy.[66] Whilst, according to Fritz Hippler, in *Der Grosse König* ("The Great King") about Frederick the Great, "the German who watched it was supposed to think that here was a similar situation to the present . . . Frederick the Great was supposed to symbolise Hitler."[67]

Goebbels sought to demonstrate that all of these great historical figures—especially Hitler—were linked by certain key charismatic components. None of them sought legitimacy by democratic means; instead, either explicitly or implicitly, they relied on a mystical concept of "Providence" to justify their actions. None were motivated by conventional goals—in particular, none of them sought personal financial gain and all served the interest of the German people above all else. Goebbels emphasised in these films, as Max Weber had written years before, that these charismatic figures stood "outside the ties of this world."[68]

Moreover, Goebbels wanted members of the audience to feel, after watching the films, that they themselves had independently reached the conclusion he desired. On occasion he disagreed with Hitler, who demanded a less subtle approach. "A few disagreements over the newsreel," Goebbels wrote in his diary. "The Führer wants more polemical material in the script. I would rather have the pictures speak for themselves and confine the script to explaining what the audience would not otherwise understand. I consider this to be more effective, because then the viewer does not see the art in it."[69]

But there was no disagreement between Goebbels and Hitler about the truth of another of Weber's theories—that "charismatic authority is specifically unstable."[70] They knew that there was little point in encouraging the German population to treat Hitler as a quasi-religious figure if the life of the average German did not improve under his rule. Hitler required people to have "faith" and "belief" in him. But if over a period of years all of his interventions and initiatives fell flat then, inevitably, that faith and belief would die.

It is no accident that this period in the growth in Hitler's popularity—between 1933 and the end of 1937—coincided with a series of foreign policy triumphs, all of which Hitler took the credit for. In swift succession Germany withdrew from the League of Nations (1933), agreed a ten-year non-aggression pact with Poland (1934), and signed a naval agreement with Great Britain (1935). The last action by the British significantly undermined the League of Nations and the previous notion of a collective European response to German rearmament. Then, in 1936, Hitler ordered German troops to reoccupy the Rhineland, an area of Germany that the *Wehrmacht* (as the *Reichswehr* was renamed in 1935) had been forbidden to enter under the terms of the Versailles treaty. There was, as a consequence, an outpouring of national pride.

On the domestic front, alongside a vast expenditure on armaments—all built in German factories—the Nazis managed to reduce unemployment from a high of six million in January 1933 to one million in September 1936 and just 34,000 by the time of the outbreak of the war in September 1939. As recent research has shown, this achievement was less to do with much-hyped public work schemes like the autobahn building programme, and more to do with a recovery in the private sector of the economy.[71]

In parallel with the fall in unemployment came the rise of *Volksgemeinschaft* (the idea of a "people's community") that manifested itself not just in events like the Nuremberg rally but also in movements like the *Kraft durch Freude* ("Strength through Joy") and *Schönheit der Arbeit* ("Beauty of Labour") initiatives instigated by Robert Ley, head of the German Labour Front. The former was directed at the leisure time of workers, with the organisation of a whole range of different community activities, and the latter was an attempt to convince employers to offer better facilities in the workplace.

What this all meant, as Professor Christopher Browning puts it, is that, "Much of what Hitler brings in the 1930s in a sense can be offered as beneficial to the vast majority at extreme cost to vulnerable and isolated minorities. So if you're an asocial, or if you're a gypsy, or if you're Jewish, or if you're Communist, you're going to suffer greatly. But the vast majority of Germans benefit and don't feel threatened in any way by these things."[72]

For someone like Erna Krantz, then a schoolgirl in Munich, this was a "positive" time in her life. "An elite race was being promoted," she says. "Well, I have to say it was somewhat contagious. You used to say that if you tell a young person every day, 'You are someone special,' then in the end they will believe you."[73]

But the only way that an "elite race" could be "promoted," of course, was by the exclusion of others. And the way in which Hitler set about persecuting those Germans he did not want in his Nazi state reveals another key aspect of his charismatic leadership. Because, as Hitler understood, an enemy can be a leader's greatest asset.

8

THE IMPORTANCE OF ENEMIES

It is almost impossible to overestimate the importance of enemies to Adolf Hitler. Enemies did not just feed the hatred he had felt at much of the world since his earliest years, but provided a much-needed bonding element for the first supporters of the Nazi party. As Hitler discovered, it is much easier for charismatic leaders to define themselves by who they hate rather than by what they believe in.

Hitler also realised the value of focusing hatred on one single enemy. As he wrote in *Mein Kampf*, "It belongs to the genius of a great leader to make even adversaries far removed from one another seem to belong to a single category . . . a multiplicity of different adversaries must always be combined so that in the eyes of the masses of one's own supporters the struggle is directed against only one enemy. This strengthens their faith in their own right and enhances their bitterness against those who attack it."[1]

Deep in his psyche Hitler possessed just such a clearly defined enemy—the Jews. But a number of other political constraints prevented him from acting on this passionately held hatred as drastically as he might have wished. As a result, when legislation was passed in 1933 to "legally" exclude Jews from employment in the public sector—like the civil service and the army—it contained a number of conditions which specifically exempted some Jews, like those who had fought in the First World War or who had lost a son in the conflict.

The advantage for Hitler of such legislation was that it was capable of receiving wider support than more extreme measures, and its success indicated a strong latent anti-Semitism in Germany (even though, when the Nazis came to power, less than 1 per cent of the German population was Jewish). For example, Johannes Zahn, an economist, admits that the "general" opinion in Germany was that the Jews were disproportionately represented in key professions like the law and medicine. (What he didn't do was to contextualise this statistic, since the reason why this had occurred was because for centuries German Jews had been denied access to many other means of employment.)

This feeling that the Jewish population of Germany represented a kind of "danger" was even to be found amongst some devout Christians. For example, Paul Althaus, a Protestant theologian, said in a lecture in 1927 that whilst he rejected the anti-Semitism of the Nazis, he did think that Germany was under "threat" from a "demoralised and demoralising urban intellectual class which is represented primarily by the Jewish race."[2]

Diehard Nazi supporters, of course, went much further in their hatred of the Jews. They believed that these early attempts to legislate Jews out of positions of influence were ineffective against a people they described as their "World Enemy Number One." As a result, spontaneous acts of persecution against German Jews continued to occur. Lucille Eichengreen was one of those who suffered. She grew up in a Jewish family in Hamburg during the 1930s, and as soon as Hitler came to power the other children in her apartment block stopped speaking to her and her sister. On the way to school they threw stones at them. "That was an ongoing fear," she says. And as well as the physical threat came the psychological damage caused by ostracism and abuse. "It was very unpleasant being ridiculed, being called names; seeing the kids that used to play with us [now] in brown and white [i.e., Hitler Youth] uniforms. There was no 'Good morning,' there was no 'Good night,' there was '*Heil Hitler!*' To a child it was really frightening. It was not something that you could comprehend, because you kept asking why? It didn't make sense."[3] Lucille's experience was not uncommon. German Jews could even be physically or verbally attacked by Nazi hardliners if they tried to swim in a public swimming pool or visit a public ice rink.

These uncontrolled attacks on Jews were a matter of concern for the Nazi Finance Minister, Hjalmar Schacht, and in the summer of 1935 he declared that this "drift into lawlessness" was putting "the economic basis of rearmament at risk."[4] Johannes Zahn, who knew Schacht, concedes that whilst the Nazi finance minister never "exerted pressure" against the Nazis' basic principle of removing Jewish people from public life and professions like banking, he did "exert a lot of pressure in favour of having regulated procedures and laws and regulations, not allowing wild extremes."[5]

At the Nuremberg party rally in September 1935 Hitler announced two pieces of hurried legislation: the "Law for the Protection of German Blood and German Honour," which outlawed sexual contact and marriage between Jews and non-Jews, and the "Reich Citizenship Law," which excluded Jews from German citizenship. However, Hitler neglected to specify how a "Jew" would be defined. Subsequently, since a "racial" definition of Jewishness was impossible to establish, the Nazis used a religious definition; a "full Jew" was held to be someone who had three grandparents who had belonged to the Jewish religious community.

This definition went against Hitler's passionate belief that the Jews were a "race." But, still, the time spent by the Nazis on defining who was a Jew and who wasn't, which was subsequently to be vital in determining who would live and who would die, demonstrated once more the fanaticism of Hitler's approach. It didn't matter if a German Jew was of enormous economic value to the state—the most brilliant theoretical scientist or practical inventor—he or she would still be excluded from German citizenship and a host of other rights if "Jewishness" was established. This also illustrates how—from Hitler's perspective—the Jews were an extremely useful enemy. The vast majority of Germans knew they were not Jews and so were relatively safe from persecution. For a charismatic leader like Hitler, the more there is one single enemy for propaganda to focus upon and the more that enemy is a clearly defined minority from which the vast bulk of the population know they are excluded, the better.

Hitler then managed to take this idea of a "single enemy" and give it a twist—he interwove his hatred of the Jews with his hatred of Stalin's regime in the Soviet Union in an attempt to create one gigantic enemy. In a speech at Nuremberg on 13 September 1937 he explicitly said that what the world faced was an "all-encompassing general attack"[6] on an epic scale, one which was led by the "rulers of Jewish Bolshevism in Moscow." These "rulers" were, according to Hitler "an uncivilised Jewish–Bolshevik international guild of criminals" who had attempted, amongst other abuses, to cause a revolution in Spain. He reminded his audience that the leaders of the revolution in Berlin and Munich after the First World War had been Jewish.

There was, in fact, no evidence that Stalin was operating alongside any Jewish group—but Hitler's rhetoric was so certain, so persuasive, that it influenced many who heard it. For Hitler, one of the many advantages of claiming that there was a secret, worldwide "conspiracy" amongst the Jews was that any inconsistencies in his vision could be explained away by saying that the Jews sought to confuse and conceal "the truth." For a young man like Johannes Hassebroek, this kind of thinking offered an easy way of understanding the world. He said he was "full of gratitude"[7] for "the intellectual guidance" given to him. Before joining the Nazis and then the SS he and his comrades had been "bewildered." They "did not understand" what was happening around them as "everything was so mixed up." But now they had been offered "a series of simple ideas" that they could understand and believe in.

Jutta Rüdiger, by 1937 leader of the Nazi League of German Girls (the BDM), says that Hitler "spoke to the young people so simply and so understandably—and I suppose that was his gift—that they could follow him perfectly and even a very simple person could understand what he was saying."[8] And in expressing himself in this easily comprehensible way, Hitler could always be relied upon to be true to his racist world view. "Once, for instance," explains Jutta Rüdiger, "he said, 'Well, in Africa people can just lie down underneath a banana tree'—that might have been a bit of an exaggeration, but nevertheless—'and the bananas grow into their mouths. But here in Germany we have to make provisions for the winter. We have to make sure that we have coal and potatoes stored in the cellar and we have to work for that.'"

Each year that Hitler remained in power and pushed for ever-greater rearmament, he focused more and more on the goal that he had expressed in *Mein Kampf* of seizing territory from the Soviet Union to create a vast Nazi empire in the east. For those at the time who observed Hitler at work and at leisure, like Herbert Döhring who was the SS manager of Hitler's house, the Berghof in Bavaria, it was obvious how the Führer perceived himself. "He saw himself as the saviour of the Western world, because at that time, under Stalin, Communism was very strong. And he felt he had been called to do something to save the Western world."[9]

In 1936, a year before his speech at Nuremberg in which he spoke of the dangers which stemmed from the "Jewish–Bolshevik" leadership in Moscow, Hitler had laid out a similarly apocalyptic vision in a secret memo—only this time he had openly stated that he believed Germany's destiny was to confront the Soviet Union militarily. Even in this memo he linked the Soviet leadership to a Jewish conspiracy—demonstrating, if anyone still doubted it, that he genuinely believed this crackpot idea. "Since the outbreak of the French Revolution," he wrote, showing once again that history had been his favourite subject at school, "the world has been moving with ever increasing speed towards a new conflict," one which would be caused by the necessity to prevent "Bolshevism" from attempting to replace the current leaders of society with members of "world-wide Jewry."[10]

This memo went much further than the speech he gave in public the following year at Nuremberg. Hitler, like Goebbels, understood that public opinion had to be manipulated slowly over time. "Propaganda is like a convoy in war," Goebbels told his press adjutant Wilfred von Oven, "which has to make its way to the target under heavy military protection. It has to adjust its marching speed to suit the slowest of the unit."[11]

During one of their increasingly rare meetings, the contents of Hitler's memo were shared with the Cabinet on 4 September 1936. Göring, with his penchant for pugnacious summary, announced that Hitler's memo "starts from the basic premise that the showdown with Russia is inevitable"[12] and that Germany must continue to prepare wholeheartedly for war. Göring's tone was one of breezy confidence, the basis of which was a supreme faith in Hitler's charismatic leadership. All these plans could be accomplished, Göring said, because "through the genius of the Führer things which were apparently impossible have very quickly become reality."[13]

This was the kind of "can-do" attitude that was typical of Göring— the archetypal adventurer. "Of all the big Nazi leaders, Hermann Göring was for me by far the most sympathetic," wrote Sir Nevile Henderson, British ambassador to Berlin from May 1937. "In any crisis, as in war, he would be quite ruthless. He once said to me that the British whom he really admired were those whom he described as the pirates, such as Francis Drake, and he reproached us for having become too 'debrutalised.' He was, in fact, himself a typical and brutal buccaneer, but he had certain attractive qualities, and I must frankly say that I had a real personal liking for him."[14]

Göring was appointed in October 1936 to head a Four Year Plan designed to ready Germany for war by increasing spending on armaments, decreasing Germany's reliance on raw materials from abroad, and achieving all this whilst keeping the standard of living of the general population at an acceptable level. It was a task that would have been beyond the ability of the most talented economist, let alone a former fighter pilot who happily confessed that he knew nothing about economics but had an "unbridled will."[15]

Despite his obvious intellectual deficiencies, Göring was of enormous value to Hitler. From the very first moment that he met Hitler back in 1922, Göring had accepted Hitler's charismatic leadership. As a result, he was admitted to the coterie of people around Hitler who knew that their Führer intended to provoke a future conflict. Another who was aware of the magnitude of the events ahead of them was Walther Darré—like Göring, a hard-line committed Nazi—who had announced earlier in 1936 to officials from the *Reichsnährstand*, the National Food Estate, that "The natural area for settlement by the German people is the territory to the east of the Reich's boundaries up to the Urals, bordered in the south by the Caucasus, Caspian Sea, Black Sea and the watershed which divides the Mediterranean basin from the Baltic and the North Sea. We will settle this space, according to the law that a superior people always has the right to conquer and to own the land of an inferior people."[16]

Hitler knew that there were those in his government who, unlike Göring and Darré, did not share a belief in his charismatic genius—the finance minister Hjamlar Schacht, for instance, who had already seen his power shrink as a result of squabbles over jurisdiction with officials working for the Four Year Plan. He resigned as Minister of Economics in 1937 and was eventually replaced by the malleable Nazi, Walther Funk. However, in any attempt to confront his twin enemies (or as he saw it, his one single, combined enemy) of Judaism and Bolshevism, Hitler realised that the most important power group he had to deal with was the army. He had already gained the trust and admiration of Werner von Blomberg, the Minister of Defence, in the wake of the suppression of Röhm and the SA. Indeed, Blomberg almost came to hero worship Hitler. Karl Boehm-Tettelbach, who was Blomberg's adjutant during the 1930s, remembers how his boss would return energised from meetings with Hitler, praising all the Führer's ideas—big and small. "For instance,"[17] recalls Boehm-Tettelbach, "Hitler was thinking of his career as a soldier in the First World War . . . [and how] there was a captain on a horse ahead of 100–110 people who carried a heavy rucksack. 'That's not the way to conduct a modern war,' [said Hitler]. 'He [the captain] should walk and his horse should pull a cart and the heavy rucksacks should be pulled by the horse.'" Blomberg was in awe of this and virtually all of Hitler's various other suggestions.

The fundamental anti-Semitism of Hitler and the Nazis was not of much consequence to Blomberg and the rest of the army leadership. Ludwig Beck, for example, the Chief of Staff of the German Army, wrote to a friend saying that the decision whether or not Jews should be expelled from army veterans' associations "should primarily be left to the respective member's tact."[18] He also remarked that "I am also aware that in several cases, former Officers of the Reserve, who are non-Aryans, have voluntarily resigned from associations in order to not expose themselves or others to any inconvenience." Beck thus tried to turn the anti-Semitism of the Nazis into a test of good manners.

"A certain anti-Semitic feeling still exists today, in England and France and Italy and Germany," says Johann-Adolf Kielmansegg, then a young Army officer. "But that has nothing to do with the fundamental concept of the extermination of the Jews . . . And these gradual tightening measures against the Jews [during the 1930s] didn't allow one in any way to see what would come out of it."[19] However, the actions of the army leadership in support of the Nazi regime during this period went much further than the "traditional" anti-Semitism that Kielmansegg mentions. Senior commanders like Ludwig Beck accepted that officers should receive instruction on "racial hygiene" and "racial biology"[20] in line with Nazi ideological thinking.

But whilst, in principle, officers like Blomberg and Beck may have agreed with Hitler about the threat from Bolshevism, and also that Germany should strive to become more self sufficient—even to the extent that, one day, it might be necessary to try and expand east in search of an empire—that was a long way from setting a specific timetable to accomplish such a goal. In this respect, Hitler was able to use his long-expressed desire to "right the wrongs of Versailles" as a smokescreen to conceal the timescale of his desire to fight Bolshevism on Soviet soil. For whilst the practical consequences of an invasion of the Soviet Union within the next few years might have frightened many German officers, an attempt to revoke the terms of the Versailles settlement was a good deal less terrifying. Ludwig Beck, for example, in a speech in Hitler's presence in October 1935 at the *Kriegsakademie,* said he hoped that German officers would realise the "obligation" which they owed to the "patron of the German Wehrmacht [i.e., Adolf Hitler]" because of his efforts to break "the shackles of Versailles."[21]

Beck also came to the conclusion, after he had spent time with Hitler over dinner, that he felt no personal bond with the Führer. As far as he was concerned—and in sharp contrast to the feelings of his superior, Werner Blomberg—Hitler possessed no charisma at all. But that did not matter. Hitler was supporting the army in every way possible. Rearmament was proceeding apace, universal military conscription was reintroduced in March 1935 and the Rhineland had been reoccupied by the German army in 1936. For Beck, whether the man who had made all this possible possessed charisma or not was irrelevant.

But, demonstrably, there still remained much to be done to break the "shackles of Versailles" completely. One of the most glaring legacies of the treaty, for instance, remained the continued separation of East Prussia from the rest of Germany. The Poles now controlled a corridor of land between these two parts of Germany, and the port of Danzig, within the corridor, was under the sovereignty of the League of Nations. "As a young man I visited Danzig myself," says Ulrich de Maizière, then an army officer, "because I had an aunt there, and I regarded Danzig as an absolutely German city. Everyone had hoped it could be solved through negotiations. And if Poland had been willing to negotiate in this question perhaps there would not even have been a war with Poland, I might dare to assert." The fact that de Maizière, interviewed long after the end of the Second World War, could still believe that "negotiations" could have solved the issue of Danzig and the Polish corridor demonstrates how entrenched the belief was in some quarters that rearmament was designed simply to return Germany peacefully to its 1914 borders.

As 1937 came to an end there was thus a split in those who served Hitler. All of them knew of the power of his anti-Semitic and anti-Bolshevik beliefs—and many of them shared these views to a greater or lesser extent. But they divided into those—like Schacht and a number of senior figures in the army—who followed Hitler largely because of rational considerations, and those—like Göring and many other committed Nazis—who did their Führer's bidding not just because they ideologically supported him, but because they accepted his charismatic leadership. They believed in faith rather than crude facts. And they, not surprisingly, were the people Hitler increasingly wanted to have around him.

9

THE LURE OF THE RADICAL

The charismatic leader is not an ordinary politician who seeks to rule only after extensive consultation. There is an element of personal conviction, bordering on the magical, associated with the decision-making process of a person with charisma—a magic that the committee room destroys. And Hitler, who possessed a fanatical hatred of committee meetings, took this idea of only making important decisions in isolation to extremes.

It's hard to think of another politician, for example, who could maintain that it was important *not* to read briefing notes and memos from close colleagues—but that was Hitler's position. When, for example, in 1935 Martin Bormann sent a paper on youth issues to Hitler, he received a reply on 5 June from Fritz Wiedemann, Hitler's adjutant, which said, "I am returning to you the enclosed memorandum. The Führer received it but then gave it back to me at once unread. He himself wishes to deal with this question in his major speech at the next Party Rally and thus does not want his thinking to be influenced in any way from any quarter."[1] It was this attitude that was behind Göring's remark to the British Ambassador, Sir Nevile Henderson, "When a decision has to be taken, none of us count more than the stones on which we are standing. It is the Führer alone who decides."[2]

All this was in large part an illusion, of course. Hitler obviously received intellectual input from others—for instance, he had taken a great deal in the early years of the Nazi party from the views of Dietrich Eckart and Gottfried Feder. But he never gave anyone else credit for helping to form his opinions, and instead of talking with other people in an attempt to understand different points of view Hitler preferred to work on his ideas on his own.

Herbert Döhring, as manager of the Berghof, was familiar with Hitler's routine. "Hitler was a night owl, a night worker,"[3] he says. "He would go to bed very late. If at all possible he would read a fat book in one night . . . [In the morning] he would get the newspapers brought to his room, but he would remain there until 12:30, 1:00, 1:30 . . . He would never relax. He always had plans for something, and then he would read the whole night through."

The staff at the Berghof came to recognise the signs of how well or how badly Hitler's solitary musing in his bedroom had gone. "When he came downstairs," says Döhring, "if you heard him whistle to himself, that was the most serious alarm signal, don't talk to him, let him go, hardly say hello, let him pass . . . But if he came downstairs humming a tune, and going from painting to painting, looking at them, if you were clever you would just busy yourself with one of the paintings, and when he saw this he wouldn't be unhappy about it at all, and he would get into a conversation with you."

Karl Wilhelm Krause,[4] Hitler's valet from 1934 to 1939, confirms that Hitler liked to spend large amounts of each day alone in his bedroom, and that he would not leave his room in the Reich Chancellery much before lunchtime. Indeed, Krause paints a portrait of a man obsessive about privacy. Hitler demanded that Krause not enter his bedroom in the morning, but leave newspapers and a summary of world news prepared by Otto Dietrich, his press officer, on a chair immediately outside his bedroom door. When Hitler awoke he would open his door, snatch up the material left on the chair and then shut himself back in the room for several hours more. But, notwithstanding this strange routine, Krause, like Döhring, was not scared of his boss. "I got on well with him. He wasn't a tyrant. He was angry sometimes, but who isn't?"

Hitler's desire to work through problems in his own mind and then simply present the results to an audience was an aspect of his character that had been present since his youth. But this particular trait was most dramatically on show at the Reich Chancellery in Berlin on 5 November 1937, in one of the most important meetings held during the Third Reich. The meeting had originally been called to sort out the allocation of resources between the three military services. Admiral Raeder, head of the German Navy, felt his battleship building programme was under threat because of a lack of steel. There was also tension caused by Göring's conflicting roles within the Nazi state, since he was in charge of both the Four Year Plan and the German air force. But, in the event, the 5 November meeting took on far greater significance, because Hitler decided to use it as an opportunity to present what he called "the fruit of thorough deliberation and the experiences of his four and a half years of power" to an audience of Hermann Göring, Konstantin von Neurath (Foreign Minister), Werner Blomberg (Minister of War), Erich Raeder (head of the navy) and Werner von Fritsch (head of the army).

Whilst the participants in the meeting all supported Nazi policy in general terms, they were by no means all committed believers in the charisma of Adolf Hitler. Göring and Blomberg certainly did have faith in the "special" powers of the Führer, as—to a lesser extent—did Raeder, a career naval officer. But Neurath was still at root a traditional Foreign Office official, and Fritsch was an archetypical Prussian officer, not predisposed to falling emotionally for a former ordinary soldier like Hitler.

Hitler began the meeting by reading out a long memorandum he had written. This was an unusual way for a statesman to announce important policy, not least because there had been no prior consultation with any of those present about the issues he was about to raise. Hitler emphasised both the vital nature of his role in the German state and the importance of this meeting, and said that "in the interest of a long-term German policy, his exposition should be regarded, in the event of his death, as his last will and testament." He then reiterated his familiar view that Germany's problem was how to "solve the need for space." What was new—and shocking to a number of those present—was Hitler's opinion on how and when this "problem" should be solved. In his exploration of a number of possible "contingencies" which might occur in the future, Hitler made it clear that he was resolved to force a union with Austria and eliminate

Czechoslovakia at the latest by 1943–45. This would also involve, of course, potential conflict not just with France but with Great Britain as well.

The response, particularly from Fritsch, the head of the Army, was not the one Hitler had desired. Fritsch made a series of objections to Hitler's plan—chiefly that Germany could not win a war against both Britain and France. Blomberg agreed, and also mentioned the strength and power of Czech defences along the border with Germany. Neurath, for his part, openly disagreed with Hitler's assumption that war would break out in the future between Italy on the one hand and Britain and France on the other, and that this conflict would be to Germany's advantage.[5] It was obvious, as Hossbach, Hitler's military adjutant later put it, that the Führer's grand political vision had not gained "applause and approval" from his military leaders but "sober criticism."[6]

Hitler argued with them, and in doing so demonstrated a side to his charismatic leadership that differentiated him from a fellow dictator like Stalin—for it would have been potentially fatal to have dared to argue so overtly and so vociferously with the Soviet leader. But despite the objections from those present at the meeting, Hitler remained resolved to stick to the timetable he had announced—perhaps to act even more quickly if circumstances allowed. What was believed by some to be a strength of his leadership—his certainty—was here perceived as a weakness. Any facts that were inconvenient to his analysis Hitler simply disputed or denied. He had decided that any advantage the Germans possessed in armaments would shortly be lost as other European powers stepped up their own rearmament programmes. So the time to act was now. It was immaterial to him what any other person thought.

Less than three months after the November meeting, two of the key military participants—Blomberg and Fritsch—were no longer in office. But this was not as a result of some master plan devised by Hitler, but instead a consequence of circumstance. On 12 January 1938, Blomberg married Margarethe Gruhn, a woman more than thirty years his junior. But a few days later police discovered that Ms. Gruhn had a colourful past—six years before she had posed for pornographic pictures. Blomberg had known nothing of this—in fact, he had not known his new bride long at all. She worked as a typist and he had only recently become infatuated with her. He had been a widower since 1932 and now, demonstrating perhaps the same type of impetuous emotional enthusiasm which was behind his attachment to the charisma of Hitler, he had fallen for the charms of Fräulein Gruhn.

In the light of Blomberg's controversial marriage, Hitler asked Heinrich Himmler to reopen an investigation into Fritsch, Head of the Army. Himmler had previously presented evidence to Hitler that Fritsch was homosexual—evidence Hitler had dismissed. But after Blomberg's actions, Hitler wanted to be reassured that there was no substance to the allegation.

Events now moved quickly. Blomberg was prevailed on to resign and Fritsch was confronted with a witness in the presence of Hitler who claimed to have had homosexual relations with him. Fritsch said, on his word of honour, that the charges were false. But he was still subsequently removed from office, though Hitler agreed that the evidence against him could, in due course, be tested in a military court.

Then something surprising happened. Blomberg, in his final meeting to say farewell to Hitler, suggested that Hitler himself—rather than one of Blomberg's own colleagues—should become Minister of War. It was an idea that was calculated to appeal to the Führer. Hitler had always understood the value of holding multiple jobs in the hierarchy of power. For example, he was not only Führer of the German people and Chancellor of Germany, but also remained head of the SA. But this new proposed appointment would create a strange hierarchical structure in which Hitler as war minister was responsible to himself as Chancellor. Hitler subsequently amended Blomberg's suggestion and became commander-in-chief of the armed forces rather than War Minister, a post that disappeared. The consequences of Hitler taking this role were far reaching, especially when the weak-willed Wilhelm Keitel—an officer Blomberg did not rate—was appointed head of the staff of the combined armed forces reporting directly to Hitler. At a stroke, Hitler no longer needed to act—as he saw it—through a maze of restrictive senior figures in the military in order to get what he wanted done.

Why did Blomberg suggest Hitler should become head of the armed forces and then not protest about the appointment of the toadying Keitel to assist him? One scholar who has closely studied the history suggests that Blomberg was full of "rancour against his colleagues"[7] for believing he had disgraced the honour of the officer corps by his recent marriage, but perhaps more likely, Blomberg wanted to ensure that Göring did not get the job. For Hitler still remained the "acceptable" face of Nazism to many in the elite of the armed forces.

Hitler also took advantage of the departure of Fritsch. Not just because he could now consider appointing a more amenable head of the army, but also because Hitler coupled this change with the retirement of more than a dozen other senior officers and the removal of Neurath as Foreign Minister. Neurath was made the president of a committee of the Privy Council that never met, and was replaced as Foreign Minister by Joachim von Ribbentrop—a man whose chief objective was to please Adolf Hitler in any way he could.

At first sight, this swift reorganisation appears similar to Stalin's purging of army officers in the Soviet Union during the 1930s—both involve dictators removing obstructive influences within the army hierarchy—but there are significant differences. Unlike Stalin, Hitler did not move pro-actively to change these personnel. Instead he reacted to Blomberg's predicament. Stalin, on the other hand, instigated the Great Terror of the 1930s himself—a series of mass killings in which around 700,000 people died. The fate of the generals that the dictators removed from office was also very different. When Marshal Mikhail Tukhachevsky, for example, was arrested by the Soviet Secret Police in 1937, he was the most brilliant military thinker in the Red Army, responsible for the innovative theory of "deep operations" whereby armoured units would strike far into enemy territory. But Stalin was suspicious of him—based on no coherent evidence—and had him tortured and then shot in the head. In contrast, when Field Marshal Blomberg fell from grace in February 1938, he wasn't tortured or arrested, but given a 50,000 Mark golden "goodbye"[8] plus a munificent pension. Then Blomberg and his wife left for a tour around the world. After their luxurious year-long vacation they settled peacefully in Blomberg's home in the holiday resort of Bad Wiessee.

Of course, both leaders—ultimately—were mass murderers, but Hitler employed techniques of charismatic leadership that Stalin did not. Hitler, as the 5 November meeting demonstrates, felt compelled to try and persuade his military leaders to accept his vision, whilst Stalin preferred to terrify his generals into acquiescence. Hitler knew that within a few years he needed his armed forces to act aggressively in wars of conquest, whereas Stalin had no such grandiose plan. His prime objective was to keep his generals from plotting against him and attempting to overthrow him in revolution. And Stalin, like Hitler a keen reader of history, always remembered how Napoleon, a French general, had supplanted the leaders of the French Revolution (he even referred to Tukhachevsky as "Napoleonchik"[9]). More recently he had been surprised how simple it had been for General Franco to foment an uprising against the Spanish Republic in 1936.[10]

In Germany, fearing neither torture nor murder at the hands of the Nazi state, Ludwig Beck, the chief of staff of the army, had been adding his voice to those protesting at the ideas Hitler had put forward at the 5 November meeting. Beck, who unlike Hitler was fond of putting his thoughts on paper, penned a devastating critique of his supreme commander's thinking, even going so far as to question the core policy which underpinned everything else—*Lebensraum*. Whilst acknowledging that nations which were integrated into a network of foreign trade were not "independent," he argued that "to conclude from this fact that the only way forward is the production of a larger living space [*Lebensraum*] seems to me to be little thought through."[11]

However, when the crisis engulfing Blomberg and Fritsch broke, Beck still found it hard to believe that Hitler was not a man of honour. General Keitel had deliberately kept Beck in the dark about Hitler's plan to appoint a new head of the army to replace Fritsch—even though the case against Fritsch had not yet been tested in an army court. Keitel confidentially asked General Walther von Brauchitsch if he would be prepared to become head of the army—but only on condition that he endorsed the structural changes Hitler was making and made the army even more sympathetic to the Nazi state.

When he found out, Beck enlisted the help of the distinguished General Gerd von Rundstedt in an attempt to intervene with Hitler and modify the proposed changes, but it was useless. Hitler had made up his mind. The whole of the organisation at the top of the Wehrmacht would be restructured. Hitler would be commander-in-chief of all the armed forces with General Keitel as his slavish assistant. General Brauchitsch—a much more amenable figure to the Nazis than Fritsch had ever been—would become head of the army. So Hitler got what he wanted. But in their own way Generals Keitel and Brauchitsch got what they wanted too. Keitel was elevated to a position of power that he could not otherwise have expected to gain (Blomberg had spoken to Hitler in derogatory terms about Keitel, saying that he merely "ran his office" for him[12]) and Brauchitsch leap-frogged over several rivals to replace Fritsch. Personal ambition, rather than deep commitment to Hitler, was the most important motivation for them. Hitler, however, would have been aware that both of these German generals were more susceptible to his charismatic leadership than Fritsch had been. Brauchitsch, in particular, was in awe of Hitler and often tongue-tied in his presence. "Please do not hold it against me," he was later to say to General Halder. "I know you are dissatisfied with me. When I confront this man, I feel as if someone was choking me and I cannot find another word."[13] Brauchitsch would also—literally—be in Hitler's debt as he was given 250,000 Reichsmarks shortly after his appointment as head of the army to enable him to get a divorce from his wife and marry his mistress, a fanatical Nazi.

Ludwig Beck, chief of staff of the German army, remained outraged over the treatment of Fritsch, but still confused about Hitler's role in the crisis. Not susceptible to Hitler's charismatic leadership, Beck had dutifully obeyed him as head of state—though not without reserving the right to question his decisions. However, in the wake of the dismissal of Fritsch, Beck gradually came to the view that Hitler was not to be trusted. After a conference on 5 February 1938 he told a senior colleague that Hitler had broken his promise to him. Hitler had said that he would consult him on any proposed military restructure and yet he had failed to do so. Beck's colleague called him a "fool" for believing Hitler's promise and asked "How long will you continue to be taken in by Hitler's tricks?"[14]

The Fritsch affair was thus an important turning point in the history of Hitler's leadership, the moment at which traditionalists like Beck finally had their eyes opened about the character and personality of their head of state. For soldiers like Beck, their "word of honour" was a sacred promise. And not only had Hitler broken his promise to Beck about consulting him over senior personnel changes in the army, but he had also refused to accept Fritsch's word of honour when he had said that the charges against him of homosexuality were false. And Fritsch was no ordinary officer, but the head of an officer corps which valued honour above all else.

"I knew him [i.e., Fritsch] very well," says Johann-Adolf Kielman-segg. "He was the godfather of one of my sons, and so there's a human relationship there. Fritsch was a conservative Prussian officer from a good background and not just a good background, but [a background] in the best sense . . . there are very many good Prussian qualities and Fritsch had them." Moreover, as far as Kielmansegg was concerned, "Fritsch was the last dam against Hitler, and the army were the only ones who could do anything [against Nazi rule]."[15]

Beck now helped prepare Fritsch's defence against the homosexuality charge at a forthcoming army court. Beck still believed in the old-fashioned, "honourable" way of doing things. And it seemed as if this course of action might be the right one, when Beck's colleagues investigating the case discovered that a junior army officer, Captain von Frisch, had been sexually involved with the man who now accused Fritsch. It was not only evidence of the innocence of the head of the army but a possible explanation for the whole episode. Perhaps the incident had been a case of simple mistaken identity. Beck now looked forward to Fritsch's rehabilitation.

But events had moved on for Hitler. At the same moment as the army's formal investigation into the Fritsch case opened, a long-running foreign policy sore reached a moment of crisis. On 10 March 1938 Beck and his assistant, von Manstein, were called to a meeting with Hitler and were told that the army must be readied immediately for a move into Austria.

Ever since his youth Hitler had longed for *Anschluss* (union) between Germany and Austria, and Austrian Nazis had been agitating for just such a merger for years. What made matters so urgent was the decision of the Austrian Chancellor, Kurt Schuschnigg, to hold a referendum on 13 March on the issue of unification with Germany.

Hitler was determined that the Austrian public would never get a chance to vote in Schuschnigg's referendum. But in response to Hitler's demand for military action against Austria, Beck expressed considerable anxiety. He worried principally about foreign reaction to any invasion. Eventually, only after Hitler had made clear his absolute determination to invade Austria did Beck leave to make plans—reluctantly—for the army to do his Führer's bidding.

Beck was not alone in his anxiety about the political consequences of any German incursion into Austria. General Keitel, now working in his new role of cross-service coordination at the headquarters of all the armed forces, the OKW, described the night of 10–11 March 1938 as a "martyrdom."[16] He received several telephone calls from senior army figures—even including Brauchitsch—almost begging him to make Hitler "renounce" his plans to invade Austria. Keitel, who was already well aware of the sensitivities of his new boss, didn't mention anything about these calls to Hitler. He knew Hitler would be outraged at the caution of his army chiefs, and he "wanted to spare" all concerned "that experience."

In the face of Hitler's threats, Schuschnigg called off the referendum and resigned. But Hitler still ordered the invasion to go ahead on 12 March. And contrary to the anxieties of the German generals, the move into Austria was an overwhelming success. German troops were pelted with flowers by welcoming Austrians amidst scenes of near ecstasy. "The Austrian *Anschluss* was like a ripe apple, it was at the moment to fall,"[17] says Reinhard Spitzy, an Austrian-born Nazi who returned to his homeland with Hitler.

Weakened by an economic depression not dissimilar to the one Germany had suffered six years before, millions of Austrians embraced the German troops. "I got the feeling that we really had to belong to Germany,"[18] says Susi Seitz, then a teenager. She had been taught that Austrians had been denied the right to join with Germany after the First World War, and had personally witnessed the effects of the economic depression in the 1930s. "We saw the needs of the people, and I was terribly depressed when I walked on our main street and I saw at each corner someone who lifted his hands up or had a little plate to ask for some money . . . Children were there and they looked starved . . . At the end of '37, people used to come to the doors of apartments and flats and ask for food. And I saw lots of people coming, and I always had to take out a plate of soup or some bread, a crust of bread."

As they entered Austria, Germans like Foreign Office official Herbert Richter were astonished at the scale of the welcome they received. "On the day of the *Anschluss,* I was driving with my wife in my open-top car through the Austrian Tyrol. And we found that our Berlin licence plates were already provoking enthusiasm amongst the Austrians. And we ate lunch in a restaurant in Schwaz, which is a little town before you get to Innsbruck, and there was a Tyrolean farmer leading his oxen, and he had put little flags with swastikas between their horns . . . I remember it very clearly. That is the extent of the enthusiasm. Austria was in a very poor economic situation at the time. And they were hoping for an improvement in their economic situation. But anyway, the enthusiasm was immense."[19]

For a committed Nazi like Bruno Hähnel this was a moment of intense joy: "During my 10 years at party conferences or at rallies with Adolf Hitler, I had certainly witnessed my share of enthusiasm, but the degree of enthusiasm that was prevalent in Austria at that time was not only surprising to us, but also quite unbelievable. That was the impression we had from the first day to the last one. When I was telling people how I'd witnessed it, I used to say that the Austrians were climbing up the front of their houses to the third floor out of sheer enthusiasm!"[20]

It was a dramatic success for Hitler, especially since none of the foreign problems that Beck and his colleagues had feared ever transpired. Hitler had received Mussolini's blessing for the invasion just before it was launched, and Britain and France never looked as if they would go to war over the *Anschluss*. The attitude in Britain was summed up by Sir Frank Roberts, a British diplomat: "I suppose a lot of people in England would say 'well, they are Germans [in Austria] after all, and if that's what they really want . . . ' "[21] And this view was set against a broader feeling that perhaps Germany had previously been badly treated. "The general view in Britain," says Sir Frank, "was that the French had imposed, and we had obviously been connected with it, too harsh a settlement on Germany in 1918, and that this should be rectified. And to that extent there was a slight feeling of 'we ought to have done better.' If you call that a sentiment of guilt, all right. I'm not sure we felt it as guilt, quite."

Hitler drove in triumph into his homeland of Austria at just before four o'clock on 12 March 1938. He passed through his birthplace of Braunau am Inn and then drove slowly on to Linz, acknowledging the vast cheering crowds along the way. Speaking that night from the balcony of Linz town hall to the rapturous crowd below in the main square he said, "The fact that Providence once summoned me forth from this city to the leadership of the Reich, must have meant it was giving me a special assignment, and it can only have been the assignment of restoring my cherished home to the German Reich!"[22] The next day he signed a proclamation announcing that Austria was now united with Germany, and on 15 March he declared in a speech in Vienna that "this land is German" and that it had "understood its mission."[23]

This was a watershed moment in the evolution of Hitler's charismatic attraction. It was by far his biggest foreign policy triumph to date—and one made all the sweeter for him by the emotional connection to his homeland. Almost more importantly, he had pushed on with his plans to invade Austria despite the fact that many senior officers had expressed grave misgivings at the idea. "The result," Franz von Papen wrote, "was that Hitler became impervious to the advice of all those who wished him to exercise moderation in his foreign policy."[24]

Hitler received the direct adulation of the hundreds of thousands of Austrians who welcomed him as a hero. The scenes in Vienna, in particular, were monumental in scale. It is scarcely possible that witnessing a crowd of almost a quarter of a million people shouting *"Sieg Heil!"* and *"Ein Volk, Ein Führer!"* did not reinforce Hitler's belief in his own "mission" and his own charismatic powers. His was, indeed, a remarkable journey. He had left Vienna twenty-five years before without qualifications, without prospects, seemingly without hope, and had now returned as the leader who had united Germany and Austria.

As for those who stood in the town squares of Linz or Vienna and listened to Hitler speak, many would never forget the emotions they experienced. "I think we cried, most of us at that time," says Susi Seitz who was part of the crowd in Linz on the evening of 12 March. "Tears were running down our cheeks, and when we looked to the neighbours it was the same."

Seitz managed to present Hitler with some flowers and basked in the glow she felt in his presence. She claims she was inspired by this encounter to become a better person. "And I promised in my heart I will try everything to be good, help others, and never do anything which was dishonest. All my free time, besides school, I gave to the work because he had called us 'You all,' and he had said that to us, 'You all shall help me build up my empire to be a good empire with happy people who are thinking and promising to be good people.'"[25] She was able to embrace her new life in the German Reich with joy: "Everything before the war, of course, and even the first years of the war, it was the best time of my life. With many others who were enthusiastic, we were happy to help . . . All the aims for the future that we were taught about: healthy family, healthy people, a healthy country, and people who work with pleasure and enthusiasm; that was something we thought worthwhile. And so, of course, we thought of that time as a good one."

People today often ask "why did so many Germans and Austrians go along with Hitler and the Nazis in the 1930s?" But Susi Seitz's testimony is a reminder that this can be the wrong question to ask. A better question is "why did so many Germans and Austrians *embrace* Hitler and Nazism in the 1930s?" And in this respect Seitz's testimony offers many clues. Not only in the emotional quality it displays but also in the connection she experienced between the audience and Hitler. She felt that Hitler almost became a vessel that enthusiastic Austrians could fill with their own longings. In the contemporary parlance of political consultants, Hitler successfully "spoke to the needs" of his audience.

All the component elements of Hitler's charisma we have examined so far in this history were present—either overtly or behind the scenes—during his triumphal progress through Austria: his mission, to unite all Germans under his rule; his ability through his oratory to establish a connection and express what his audience were wanting and feeling; his "heroic" homecoming as an Austrian; his vision of a "classless" society; the hope he offered Austrians in their economic crisis; his certainty that all would come well for the two nations now they were united; his statement of his own place in these great events, not as an ordinary leader but as one chosen by "Providence" for a special task; and his ability to act entirely on his own intuition, given that the decision to move on Austria had been his and his alone.

The part of Hitler's charisma that appealed to many of his most dedicated supporters was also on show—his desire to isolate vulnerable groups and persecute them as enemies of the state. Large numbers of Jews were brutally treated immediately after the Nazis' takeover of Austria, and many political opponents of the Nazis were imprisoned in concentration camps—former chancellor Schuschnigg, for example, was arrested moments after the Nazis entered the country. But to the majority of Austrians all this was unimportant in the face of the "national revival" which Hitler offered.

The contrast between the near hysteria in Austria and the reaction of a number of still sober German generals like Ludwig Beck could scarcely have been greater. Beck was disgusted by the behaviour of Nazis in Austria, revolted by "the carrion-vultures of the party who follow behind the untarnished shield of the army."[26] He was also appalled at the resolution to the Fritsch case. On 18 March, when the focus of the vast majority of Germans was on events in Austria, Fritsch was finally cleared of any wrongdoing—the case of the Gestapo against him was shown to be fabricated. But it did him little good. Hitler, fresh from his Austrian triumph, would not reinstate Fritsch now that the more compliant Brauchitsch was in the job.

Fritsch and many of the other senior officers who had just been forcibly retired paid the penalty for having embraced the rule of Hitler. They had collaborated with Hitler's regime to a considerable extent—they had sworn an oath to their Führer, adopted the swastika on their uniforms, removed their Jewish colleagues from their ranks, attended lectures on "racial hygiene," but it was not enough to protect them.

10

THE THRILL OF RELEASE

The single most important precondition for the creation of Hitler's charisma was his ability to connect with the feelings, hopes and desires of millions of his fellow Germans. It was in the nature of this connection that the power of his charisma resided. And after several years in office Hitler was increasingly able, through this link, to offer his followers a powerful sense of release. Not just release from the traumatic loss of the First World War and the humiliation of Versailles, as he had in the early years of his chancellorship, but release from the limitation of all conventional restraint.

Hitler, for example, said to Albert Speer's wife in the 1930s, "Your husband is going to erect buildings for me such as have not been created for four thousand years."[1] It's not hard to imagine the sense of liberation that this kind of remark must have created in Speer—already a ferociously ambitious architect. Hitler offered Speer a chance not just to become famous in Germany, not just famous throughout the world, but famous in history. Just as the Pyramids had been remembered, so would Speer's buildings. Speer even later remarked, contemptuous of the suffering of Jews made to work as forced labourers in concentration camps, "After all, the Jews were already making bricks under the Pharaohs."[2]

But it was the German medical profession in the 1930s that most experienced a sense of release because of the presence of Adolf Hitler. Nearly half of all German doctors were members of the Nazi party and so, not surprisingly, many of them approved of Hitler's racial policies. In particular, they supported his desire to introduce compulsory sterilisation of those the Nazis considered "undesirable." Germany was not the first country to introduce such legislation. Switzerland had passed a law permitting forced sterilisation in 1928[3] and by the mid-1930s around thirty American States allowed compulsory sterilisation of some categories of the mentally ill. But it was to be the Nazis who were to embrace forced sterilisation on a scale that dwarfed everyone else.

In July 1933, just five months after becoming chancellor, Hitler pushed through the "Law for the Prevention of Hereditarily Diseased Offspring." This allowed "Genetic Health Courts" to order the forcible sterilisation of those suffering not only from a variety of mental illnesses such as schizophrenia, but also people who were deaf or blind as a result of a hereditary gene and even those who were chronic alcoholics.

The fundamental inhumanity of this practice is demonstrated by the case of Paul Eggert of Dortmund. He was the eldest of twelve children born to a father who had served in the First World War and was now "hitting the bottle . . . and well, he used to beat my mother, and there was nothing to eat."[4] As the eldest he was sent out to beg for food from the local farmers. "And if I brought something back then it was OK, if not I would get beaten." Eventually, "people had enough of it . . . so they told the social services and they sent us away. One in one direction, others in another direction."

Paul was sent to a children's hospital in Bielefeld where, unbeknownst to him at the time, he was classed as "delinquent." Then, at the age of eleven, he was told that he had to have a hernia operation. It was only years later that he discovered that he had not been operated on for a hernia, but sterilised. The sense of personal violation he felt when he first heard the news remains as strong as ever: "I experience the same thing, every year, Christmas, Christmas Eve, my sister-in-law . . . they all have children, they run about downstairs, and I sit upstairs with my wife, I have no children running about, that's not a nice thing."

German doctors were not forced to sterilise children like Paul Eggert. They didn't need to be since many medical professionals embraced the opportunities the Nazi state offered them. As Professor Richard Evans says, "In German culture as a whole medicine had achieved enormous fame and prestige in the late 19th century with men like Robert Koch discovering the cause of tuberculosis, cholera and a whole range of other diseases. He was the Louis Pasteur of Germany, not as well known as Pasteur but I think he probably should be. Medicine had made huge strides in Germany and the prestige of the medical profession was just vast. Added to that there's the Nazi racist notion of racial hygiene, that medicine had to take a lead in purging the German race of its degenerate elements and so medicine becomes by far the leading profession in the 1930s. More than half of all German university students by 1939 are studying medicine. It's extraordinary. There are vast numbers of jobs in the army, the armed forces, in the SS, for medical people. Institutes of racial hygiene are set up everywhere and there's a kind of arrogance about the belief that they can experiment on what they view as racially sub-human people or people who are inferior in some way or another, like criminals or concentration camp inmates. They believe that they're entitled to do that for the future of the German race."[5]

It was against this background that more than 200,000 people were forcibly sterilised in the Nazi state (some estimates say as many as 350,000).[6] This huge number was only possible because of the interaction between willing—often enthusiastic—members of the medical profession and the well-publicised views of a head of state who embraced racial selection and brutal social control as the cornerstones of existence. In *Mein Kampf* Hitler had said explicitly that "a state which in this age of racial poisoning dedicates itself to the care of its best racial elements must some day become lord of the earth."[7] As a consequence doctors realised that their profession—always important—had become still more vital. Racism was an ersatz religion for Hitler, and so doctors were almost priests.

Because of the central place that race held in his world view, gaining the enthusiastic support of the medical profession was almost as much of a priority to Hitler as ensuring the backing of the army. And it is significant that Hitler had none of the problems with senior members of the medical profession that he had with prominent army officers like Fritsch or Beck. There were, of course, a number of individual doctors who objected to this Nazi interpretation of medical ethics, but the majority certainly went along with the introduction of forced sterilisation[8] and the supervision of their profession by the "Reich Physicians Chamber." It was, of course, in the economic interest of "Aryan" German doctors to embrace Nazi ideology, in part because further opportunities for advancement opened up for them as the Nazis progressively banned Jewish doctors from practising in Germany, a process that was finally completed in 1939 after a string of restrictive measures had been imposed from 1933 onwards.

This is not to say that the majority of German doctors necessarily supported the move from preventing racial "undesirables" from having children to eliminating them altogether. However, this was the policy that Hitler wanted to pursue. Astonishingly, he had made no secret of his commitment—in theory—to the idea of destroying the less productive members of German society. "If every year Germany had one million children," he said in a speech at the Nuremberg rally in 1929, "and eliminated 700,000 to 800,000 of the weakest, the end result would probably be an increase in national strength."[9] But Hitler knew that racial reordering on this scale was currently impractical—not least because of the massive potential opposition from the families affected and the church.

However, the basic idea that it might be legitimate to kill some people for the overall benefit of the rest of society was not new—nor was the idea of killing the mentally disabled dreamt up by the Nazis. In 1920, a book called *Die Freigabe der Vernichtung lebensunwerten Lebens* ("Allowing the Destruction of Worthless Life") was published, a collaboration between one of Germany's leading jurists, Professor Karl Binding, and one of Germany's most prominent psychiatrists, Professor Alfred Hoche. They were concerned that in the wake of the First World War large numbers of so-called "useless" people were living in Germany who were a "burden" to the state; they called such people *Ballastexistenzen,* literally those who exist only as "ballast." Both Binding and Hoche rejected the idea of killing anyone who could consciously and rationally express the desire not to be killed. But those who were in a vegetative state or who were severely mentally ill could certainly be killed without consent. "We will never cease to treat to the utmost the physically and mentally ill," wrote Professor Hoche, "as long as there is any prospect of changing their condition for the better; but we may one day mature into the view that the elimination of those who are mentally completely dead is not a crime, nor an immoral act, nor emotional cruelty, but a permissible and beneficial act."[10]

Behind this discussion about who could or could not be killed in a "beneficial act" lies a notion central to Hitler's world view—the primacy of the racial nation, or *Volk,* over the individual. As Franz Jagemann, who grew up in Germany in the 1930s, remembers, "It was hammered into us in the Hitler Youth, 'Germany must live, even if we have to die.' "[11] Thus the severely mentally ill *ought* to be killed not because they would, if they could, choose to die, but because they were useless to the nation.

The first step along this road had already been taken by the large numbers of doctors who had chosen to perform operations like forcible sterilisation that were not necessary for the medical welfare of the individual. At this point they had crossed a clear line of medical ethics. And the way they could rationalise their actions was for them to shift their responsibility of care from the individual to the nation. Just like Hitler, they now acted as if the health of the *Volk*—the racially pure German people as a whole—was of much greater importance than the health of the individual.[12]

Nonetheless, Hitler realised that he had to proceed carefully towards a policy of murdering selected disabled Germans. He needed the proactive consent of at least some doctors, and—ideally—an element of support within the general public as well. To that end, a documentary film called *Opfer der Vergangenheit* (Victims of the Past) was released in German cinemas in 1937. The film showed images of chronically sick and disabled children whilst the commentary detailed how much it cost to keep them alive. It ended by stating, "By humanely terminating their wretched and helpless lives, we shall be observing our Creator's law of natural selection and order."[13]

The Nazis had already been systematically reducing the amount of money that could be spent on disabled patients, and as a result conditions in mental hospitals grew worse and worse.[14] Local opinion-formers were now encouraged to visit the hospitals and see the disabled at close quarters—deliberately displayed in ways to make them look as much like *Ballastexistenzen* as possible. Bruno Hähnel, a committed Nazi, visited the mental hospital at Aplerbeck near Dortmund and formed this opinion: "The most shocking thing, that never left me, and which I saw in front of my eyes again and again, was the ward with the schizophrenics. It was a room in which there were, let's say, forty cots, not really beds, but simply wooden planks. And on these forty beds lay naked emaciated people . . . and the professor said that this was the final stage of schizophrenia and that the disease could attack any of us tomorrow, through some kind of mutation in the brain. This really worried me terribly, that this could really happen, and more than anything else I came away from this room with the understanding that the right thing to do was to kill people who are in such a state, not keep them alive, not like the way that the Christian Church teaches that each person is valuable . . . in my view the lives of such people were no longer worth living. That's what I took away from this ward."[15]

The Nazis, of course, had themselves created the shocking conditions in which these patients were now forced to exist. As a result, it is no surprise that many visitors found their appearance appalling. It was the result of a self-fulfilling prophecy that was a common Nazi trick. The Nazis would subsequently use a similar technique in the context of the Polish Jews. By creating crowded, dirty and disease-ridden conditions in the Polish ghettos, the Nazis were then able to point to the distressing way the Jews lived as evidence to support their own prejudice against them.

Meanwhile, despite the support of Nazis like Bruno Hähnel for the idea of killing the severely mentally ill, Hitler was wary of introducing the policy in peacetime—though he could see a way ahead. In 1935 he remarked to Dr. Gerhard Wagner, the "Reich Health Leader," that he would adopt such a policy once war began because in the context of a life and death struggle for the future of the nation such an action would be more readily accepted.[16]

It is a revealing comment, because it demonstrates how Hitler understood that there are no absolutes in politics. It was never correct to say that one particular policy was impossible to implement, merely that a policy might be impossible to implement at this moment. As the circumstances changed, so did the potential receptiveness of the population to any new measure, and radical policies could best be introduced in radical times. This understanding was further allied to two related insights that Hitler possessed. The first was that he—chiefly through the work of Joseph Goebbels—had the power to try and systematically alter the views of the German population about the acceptability of any "euthanasia" programme. The ground prepared by *Opfer der Vergangenheit,* for example, would be further developed four years later with the film *Ich klage an* (I accuse) which examined the actions of a husband who killed his wife who was suffering from incurable multiple sclerosis.

Hitler also realised that the term "public opinion" could be misleading since it masked the fact that there were different shades of opinion throughout society. Often individual opinion was not black or white on issues like euthanasia but existed in shades of grey. He could personally play an important role in encouraging individuals to move along a graduated path until they accepted his view as their own. As a charismatic leader, Hitler in this respect acted as a legitimiser, an enabler, a giver of permissions, almost as a father figure who told his followers, "Yes, pursue these dreams—forget the conventions of so-called civilised society." And now, either overtly or tacitly, many doctors were following Hitler's instruction to reject "modern sentimental humanitarianism."[17]

It needed only a spark to cause the formal introduction of a policy of killing in mental hospitals. That spark came around the end of 1938 (no one is sure of the exact date) when Philipp Bouhler, who ran the office of the Chancellery of the Führer, found amongst the myriad letters and petitions addressed to Hitler a request from the father of a severely mentally and physically disabled boy that doctors be allowed to kill his son. Hitler authorised his own doctor, Karl Brandt, to investigate the case. Brandt travelled to Leipzig to consult with the child's doctors and then told them that they could kill the boy. So began the "child euthanasia action."

Often looked on as the classic example of what Professor Sir Ian Kershaw memorably called "Working Towards the Führer"[18]—the notion that Hitler's followers initiated actions that they hoped he would like—it is also an instance of the power of Hitler's charismatic leadership. For whilst it's true that ambitious Nazi administrators acted in similar fashion to Bouhler, who seized upon this particular petition knowing it related to a subject that interested his boss, it's hard to imagine how the father of the severely disabled boy sought anything other than a desperate way out of a terrible situation. The father was not "working towards the Führer" but seeking a solution to a seemingly intractable emotional problem—and who better to offer such a solution than the father-like head of the Nazi state? The whole thrust of Goebbels' propaganda in the 1930s had been to create an atmosphere in which the Führer's judgement was thought infallible, and so this father must have thought that the one person who would know what to do about his son, and could "legitimise" his death and arguably his release from suffering, would be Adolf Hitler.

After this one child had been killed at the request of his father, Hitler authorised that other similar cases could be treated the same way. In order to administer this "will of the Führer" a whole new organisation was created—separate from the existing health administration structure—called "The Reich Committee for the Scientific Registration of Serious Hereditary and Congenital Illnesses." Midwives were ordered to report any child born with suspected congenital defects. Three different doctors then examined the forms submitted to them detailing any such defects and then separately decided if the child should live or die. Those selected to die were taken from their parents (the parents were "persuaded" to give their child over to the care of doctors at a "special clinic") and murdered at one of around thirty different centres spread throughout Germany. For example, Aplerbeck Hospital near Dortmund was one of these killing centres, and here the children were murdered by lethal injection or by being made to swallow Luminal (phenobarbital) tablets.

Hitler ordered that the child "euthanasia action" be conducted in secret. But though individual doctors could refuse to participate—and some did—there was never any shortage of medical professionals willing to take part in the murders. And, true to his word that these actions would best be conducted in the context of war, Hitler signed an authorisation for the action only in October 1939, after the war had started—and even more significantly he predated the document to 1 September, the very day the Germans invaded Poland.

There was thus a relatively smooth progression from the introduction of sterilisation to the killings of the child euthanasia scheme. Given that, it's often surprising to people new to this history to discover that, in stark contrast, Nazi anti-Semitic policy shows no such systematic progression. This wasn't because there weren't deeply anti-Semitic individuals within the Nazi party who craved to be "released" from the "shackles" of convention in order to pursue a truly radical solution to what they saw as "the Jewish problem." Nazi stormtroopers, as we have seen, moved against many German Jews in 1933, and the hurried anti-Semitic legislation of the Nuremberg Laws in 1935 was, in part, an attempt to legitimise the localised persecution of Jews that was already taking place. But, still, only a minority of German Jews had left Germany by the end of 1937. If Hitler's policy had been to expel all German Jews then five years into his chancellorship it had demonstrably failed. And yet he knew that many

Nazi hardliners—like Julius Streicher—were only waiting for the merest sign to be let off the leash and act without restraint.

In a revealing speech he gave to Nazi party officials in April 1937, Hitler laid bare how he sought to lead the party and the nation over the Jewish question. In the process he gave valuable clues as to how he managed the effect of his own charisma. Whilst asserting that the ultimate aim of Nazi policy towards the Jews was "crystal clear to all of us" he said, "My main concern is always to avoid taking a step that I might later have to retract, and not to take a step which could damage us in any way. You must understand that I always go as far as I dare—but no further. It is vital to have a sixth sense which tells you broadly, 'What can I still do, what can I not do?' "[19]

Hitler thus emphasised once again the importance for any charismatic leader of projecting an aura of certainty. So much so that he said the desire not to appear weak was "all" that concerned him. He said that, "It is not that I immediately and violently intend to challenge an enemy to fight." Instead he preferred to antagonise and goad his opponent by shouting "I want to destroy you." Only after trapping his enemy into a "corner" did Hitler "deliver the fatal thrust."

On analysis, this is a strange strategy. Hitler's long-term goal might be clear enough, but there was no coherent political mechanism linking short-term issues with that long-term goal. By simply shouting at his opponent Hitler was not offering any guidance to his followers as to how to achieve their ends. But the speech does explain why Hitler wanted, for example, his generals to be like "bull terriers on chains."[20] It was immensely useful to Hitler to have a section of support that he appeared to be "restraining" from radical action. And whilst Hitler also remarked that his generals disappointed him because he had to encourage rather than restrain them, the substantive point remains.

That "restraint" against the Jews was lifted dramatically in the wake of the *Anschluss* with Austria in March 1938. Walter Kämmerling, a fifteen-year-old Jewish schoolboy at the time, remembers the catastrophe of the arrival of the Nazis—shops were smashed, Jews violently molested and Jewish businesses expropriated. "You were completely outlawed," he says, "there was no protection from anywhere. Anyone could come up to you and do what they want and that's it."[21]

The violence and persecution in Austria in spring 1938 was on a different scale to any yet seen in Germany. There were two main reasons for this. First, there were many more Jews proportionately in Austria than Germany (about 4 per cent of the population in Austria as opposed to 0.76 per cent in Germany) and, second, Austria, though shortly to be part of the Reich, was still not quite German soil. Austria was the first example of what would become a common phenomenon in the Nazi state; the acts of greatest violence might initially take place outside the borders of the old Reich, but the consequences of the new radicalism would often then be felt in Germany.

That was certainly the case in 1938. In the wake of the violent perse-cution of Austrian Jews, the Nazis turned their attention back home. On 26 April, six weeks after the Nazis had entered Austria, Hermann Göring ordered that all German Jews must register their property, and that any property valued at more than 5,000 Reichmarks could only be sold or leased with the permission of the Nazi authorities. It was an obvious pre-liminary step towards the outright theft of Jewish assets. Other measures soon followed—Jewish doctors, lawyers, dentists and vets were prevented from working for "Aryan" clients, and Jews were forced to add certain names to their own so that they could easily be identified, like "Israel" for men and "Sarah" for women.

In the wake of the persecution of the German and Austrian Jews, the U.S. President Franklin Roosevelt decided to become more actively involved with the problem. He called for an international conference to be held to discuss what could be done, and in July 1938 representatives from more than thirty countries met at the Hotel Royal, Évian-les-Bains in France. In public, Hitler offered the delegates his cynical support: "I can only hope and expect that the other world, which has such deep sympathy for these criminals [Jews], will at least be generous enough to convert this sympathy into practical aid. We, on our part, are ready to put all these criminals at the disposal of these countries, for all I care, even on luxury ships."[22]

As it turned out, the Évian conference was the worst of all possible outcomes for the German and Austrian Jews, who had hoped that soon the rest of the world would open its doors to them. Of the thirty or so countries represented, only the Dominican Republic offered the prospect of accepting substantial numbers of Jews. The rest—for the most part—offered sympathetic words but little practical help. It seemed confirmation of the words Chaim Weizmann had said to a British newspaper two years before: "The world seemed to be divided into two parts—those places where the Jews could not live and those where they could not enter."²³

Golda Meir, who would later become Prime Minister of Israel, watched the conference proceedings. "Sitting there in that magnificent hall and listening to the delegates of 32 countries rise, each in turn, to explain how much they would have liked to take in substantial numbers of refugees and how unfortunate it was that they were not able to do so, was a terrible experience. I don't think that anyone who didn't live through it can understand what I felt at Évian—a mixture of sorrow, rage, frustration and horror. I wanted to get up and scream at them all, 'Don't you know that these "numbers" are human beings, people who may spend the rest of their lives in concentration camps, or wandering around the world like lepers, if you don't let them in?' "²⁴

The Nazi view of Évian was clear. "Nobody wants to have them" was the headline in the *Völkischer Beobachter*.²⁵ And Hitler subsequently expressed contempt for the whole approach of democratic nations to the question of Jewish emigration. In a speech at the Nuremberg rally on 12 September 1938, he ridiculed the attitude of the "democratic countries" who condemned the Germans for trying to "rid" themselves of "the Jewish element." He remarked that "not a word is heard in these democratic countries about replacing this hypocritical lamentation with a good deed and assistance. No, to the contrary, all one hears is cold reasoning, claiming that in these states there is regretfully no space either . . . Alas, no help. But morals!"²⁶

The Évian conference thus did little to deal with the practical plight of the Jews whilst feeding Hitler's fantasies about Jewish dominance, since much of the rest of the world—including the United States—was against Nazi Germany on this crucial issue. As Professor Adam Tooze says, Hitler was "fundamentally convinced, in my view, that the world Jewish conspiracy has taken on a whole new ominous character. This starts in the summer of 1938 with the Évian Conference in which America becomes involved in European affairs around the issue of the organised emigration of eastern European Jews. And this is triggered, of course, by the incredible violence that the Germans unleash in Austria after the *Anschluss*. And this, in Hitler's mind, shifts the focus of the world Jewish conspiracy, which in his view is Germany's ultimate enemy, from Moscow which has previously been aligned with Communism, to a very clear statement by early 1939 that the real centre of the world Jewish conspiracy is Washington, Wall Street and Hollywood. That, of course, fundamentally shifts your assessment of the strategic picture because behind Britain and France, as in the First World War, ultimately stands the full force of the American armaments economy."[27]

On 9 November 1938, Nazi anti-Semitic thugs were well and truly released against the Jews, and committed a series of atrocities during what became known as *Reichskristallnacht* ("night of the broken glass"). Two days before the attacks, on 7 November, Herschel Grynszpan, a seventeen-year-old Jew born in Germany of Polish parents, had walked into the German Embassy in Paris and shot a junior official called Ernst vom Rath. He had been driven to commit this crime by the plight of his parents, Sendel and Rivka. They had been amongst 12,000 or so Polish Jews living in Germany who had just been taken by the Nazis and dumped at the border with Poland. The Poles had refused to allow them into their country and so these Jews were sitting, stateless, between two regimes that wanted nothing to do with them. It was a powerful and practical illustration of the consequences of both Nazi persecution and the failure of the international community at Évian. The Nazis wanted to expel their Jews but "Nobody wants to have them."

On 9 November, vom Rath finally died of his wounds. This was already a "sacred" day for the whole Nazi movement—the anniversary of the Beer Hall Putsch fifteen years before. Hitler and the rest of the Nazi leadership had assembled in Munich for the annual commemoration, and it was here that Joseph Goebbels, always a hard-line anti-Semite, asked Hitler to allow violent action against the German Jews in revenge for the murder of vom Rath. There had already been sporadic attacks on Jewish property earlier that night, but now atrocities were committed against German Jews on a scale that was previously unparalleled under the Nazis. More than 20,000 Jewish men were imprisoned in concentration camps and over a thousand synagogues were destroyed. Several hundred Jews lost their lives. In Nuremberg, Rudi Bamber, then eighteen years old, watched in horror as stormtroopers burst down the front door of his house and destroyed everything they could find. Then a second group arrived and beat him up. Once they moved on, Rudi found his mother crying, and water from smashed pipes flooding through the floors. As he made his way through the debris of broken furniture, glass and china he came across his dying father. The stormtroopers had murdered him. Rudi was spared only because the leader of the stormtroopers had decided to go home because he had to get to work in the morning, and so the rest "were very irritated by this and they weren't going to waste any more time so they gave me a swift kick and said 'push off' or words to that effect and they walked out and left me to it."[28] Rudi sums up his own horrific experience at the hands of the Nazis by saying, "There is no sense in the whole story, really. It is absurd."

The violence of *Kristallnacht* was instigated both by initiatives from below and orchestration from above. Like the initiatives that led to the child euthanasia scheme, there was evidence of leading Nazis suggesting and then developing actions that they thought would please their boss. Philipp Bouhler wanted to grow his own power and that of the office of the Chancellery of the Führer, and Joseph Goebbels was anxious to redeem himself in Hitler's eyes after the embarrassment of his affair with the Czech actress Lida Baarová and his consequent marital difficulties.

Nazis lived in a world where, in the words of Dr. Günter Lohse of the German Foreign Office, "Everybody wanted to be close to him [i.e., Hitler]. Just to live in his favour, to be in his presence, whether for lunch or for a discussion, didn't matter. To be near him just once. That was the big event for the individual . . . I dare say that every proposal, from whatever side, that went to the Reich Chancellery, had behind it the desire to prove that one was a faithful supporter of Adolf Hitler's."[29]

But whilst that is true, it doesn't completely explain the actions of the stormtroopers who smashed their way into Rudi Bamber's house in Nuremberg and murdered his father. They were also keen to beat up and kill Jews and destroy their property out of their own deeply held beliefs. Over time these beliefs might have been supported and grown by Nazi propaganda and the structure of the Nazi state, but fundamentally they were beliefs which a number of vicious anti-Semites had held before Hitler even came on the scene. What Hitler offered them was release, and the power to act without restraint.

Even before the *Kristallnacht* violence, *Das Schwarze Korps*—the official magazine of the SS, had published articles that voiced extreme hatred against the Jews. And a week after the horrors of 9–10 November, an article entitled "This bunch is worse!" openly called for collective reprisals against the Jews, and is revealing of a mentality that would later help create the death camps: "Woe betide the Jews, if even one of them or one of their accomplices, hired and filled with hatred by them, ever lifts up their murderous hand against one German! Not one [Jew] will be held responsible for a dead or wounded German, but they all will. This is what those should know, who didn't get the message from our first moderate warning [i.e., *Kristallnacht*]. Neither will we engage in nitpicky stunts of arithmetic about the guilt or innocence of individuals. Because we are not engaged in a war according to international law with the Jews . . . Jews and Germans are not equal partners in this; we will not be mentioned in the same breath as them. There is only one right, our right, our self-defence, and we alone will decide how and when it will be redeemed."[30] Another article in December 1938 was even more explicit about the potential fate of the Jews: "The day a murder weapon that is Jewish or bought by Jews rises against one of the leading men of Germany, there will be no more Jews in Germany! We hope we made ourselves clear!"[31]

Das Schwarze Korps also insisted that persecution should be immediately intensified against German Jews. "Because it is necessary, because we no longer hear the world's clamour, and because no power on earth can stop us we will take the Jewish question to its total solution. The programme is clear: total expulsion, complete separation! What does this mean? This means not only the elimination of Jews from the German economy, which they have forfeited by their murderous attack and by their incitement to war and murder. The Jews must be removed from our homes and neighbourhoods, and be located in streets or blocks where they are amongst themselves and can be in contact with Germans as little as possible."[32]

Hitler's obsessions were now openly claimed as the shared passions of the SS. This was radical stuff, and revealed not only a powerful cocktail of hate and ambition, but demonstrated how ready the SS was for war. The bull terriers were off the leash.

11

TURNING VISION INTO REALITY

On 31 August 1939, the day before soldiers of the Wehrmacht marched into Poland and precipitated the Second World War, the American journalist William L. Shirer wrote about the mood in Germany: "Everybody against the war. People talking openly [about it]. How can a country go into a major war with a population so dead against it?"[1] Shirer's opinion, about the depth of anti-war sentiment in Germany, was shared by officials in the SD, the intelligence division of the SS. They had written in a confidential report the previous year that the mood in Germany was "often gloomy, because of the future" and that "there exists in the broadest sections of the population the most serious concern that sooner or later a war will kill off the economic prosperity and have a terrible end for Germany."[2] Another SD report stated that in the German countryside, "There was a major feeling of tension and disquiet everywhere, and one all-encompassing wish, 'Please, no war!'"[3]

Yet war was on the way nonetheless. And although, as with any major historical event, there were a myriad of causal factors, the fundamental reason why this war was about to happen was because Adolf Hitler willed it so—and his charismatic leadership helped turn that will into a reality.

Indeed, it's the presence of Hitler in this history that makes the period from the start of 1938 until the outbreak of war such an extraordinary one. Conventional politicians like the British Prime Minister, Neville Chamberlain, were working on the basis that nobody actually *wanted* war. Adolf Hitler, on the other hand, realised that in order to get what he desired war was all but inevitable. Ernst von Weizäcker, State Secretary at the German Foreign Office, tried to explain the strangeness of this situation to the British ambassador, Sir Nevile Henderson: "I have said to Henderson once again that this is not a game of chess but a rising sea. One cannot make the same kinds of assumptions as in normal times with normal reasons and normal people."[4]

But it wasn't only the British who had problems in understanding that Hitler was not a "normal" statesman. Powerful Germans were also making the mistake of thinking that their Führer would listen to reasoned argument as well. Ludwig Beck, for instance, was still clinging to the mistaken belief that Hitler could be persuaded to be sober and pragmatic in the context of his foreign policy timing and aims. Beck continued to want the "good" things that he felt Hitler's charisma and political instinct had brought Germany—in particular a resurgence of national pride and an ever-growing Army—without the "bad" things, like violent persecution of those who did not fit the Nazi image of the ideal German and the reckless pursuit of a new Nazi Empire. But Beck, like so many intelligent members of the German elite, had ultimately only himself to blame for his misjudgement. For, as Frederick Douglass, the American abolitionist, said in another context, he was the type of man who wanted "the ocean without the awful roar of its many waters."[5]

Beck, and a number of his colleagues in the senior ranks of the German army, would soon discover the extent of their error as Hitler turned his sights on the neighbouring country of Czechoslovakia. Since Czechoslovakia was both a democracy and a creation of the settlements at the end of the First World War, Hitler was already predisposed to hate it. But there were also practical reasons why Czechoslovakia was a problem for Germany. It was impossible for Hitler to contemplate moving east without somehow neutralising the Czechs—they were geographically in the way of any expansion. Moreover, within Czechoslovakia lived just over three million ethnic Germans, mostly in the border region known as the Sudetenland.

Günther Langer, twenty-four years old in 1938, was one of the Sudeten Germans who felt persecuted in Czechoslovakia: "German businesses were boycotted and that's why we actually ended up in a really dreadful state . . . " In his village, where the majority were of German ethnic origin, "we had a Czech postmaster, we had a Czech teacher, we had a Czech [local authority] chairman, and Czech street cleaners—so these posts were all lost to Germans. The Germans had all those jobs before, you see . . . That's not all they [i.e., the Czech authorities] did, because they also exploited the Germans' dire need and tempted the German children into the Czech school with promises. That was the so-called 'entrapment of German souls.' "[6]

The Nazis had for some years been supporting the Sudeten Germans in their call for greater independence within Czechoslovakia, and just days after the *Anschluss* Hitler met with Karl Frank and Konrad Henlein of the Sudeten German Party. He told them to make a series of demands on the Czech government that he knew would be unacceptable.

Initially it seemed that Hitler was in no hurry to force the Sudeten issue to a crisis. But after the British and French warned the German government not to take military action against the Czechs (ironically following a mistaken report about German intentions) Hitler called a meeting in Berlin on 28 May 1938 at which he announced that resolving this issue had become a priority. "I am utterly determined," said Hitler, "that Czechoslovakia should disappear from the map."[7] Hitler's own adjutant, Fritz Wiedemann, said he was "very shocked"[8] by these words. But it was as nothing to the effect they had on Ludwig Beck.

Beck had already sent one memo to Brauchitsch, head of the army, on 5 May, pointing out that "there is no hope of solving the Czech question by military means and not involving England and France."[9] And now, straight after Hitler revealed his intentions on 28 May, Beck returned to his desk to compose yet another warning memo. Once again he emphasised that Germany risked a "European, maybe even a world war" as a consequence of invading Czechoslovakia and that this war "will be lost by Germany."[10] But Beck's opposition to Hitler's plan was weakened by two crucial factors. In the first place Beck agreed that the very existence of Czechoslovakia was a massive problem for any future plans for German expansion. The previous September he had remarked, "As long as the Czech appendix protrudes into Germany, she will be unable to wage war."[11] The other problem Beck faced has intriguing echoes of the Strasser crisis back in 1932. Just like Gregor Srasser, Ludwig Beck professed to be immune to the charisma of Adolf Hitler. Yet—also just like Strasser—Beck now emphasised that he was upset that he could not gain access to Hitler directly. In the memo composed after the Hitler meeting on 28 May (sent to Brauchitsch on 30 May) Beck still acted as if—as he said in a memo six weeks later—"this fight is being fought for the Führer."[12] As Manfred von Schröder, who was then a diplomat in the German Foreign Office, says, "Even Weizsäcker [then Secretary of State at the Foreign Office] believed that talking alone with Hitler one could have reasonable results . . . Everybody thought that one could go on with Hitler far better if all these governors and other party people were not always around, but reasonable people, you know."[13]

Thus, despite hearing on 28 May that Hitler intended in the near future to make Czechoslovakia "disappear from the map," Beck continued to think that the solution was not the swift removal of Adolf Hitler but administrative change which would create "a clear demarcation of, and adherence to, respective responsibilities."[14] And even though Beck was not overtly affected by Hitler's charisma, one interpretation of this behaviour is that—just like Strasser—he was implicitly affected. The fact that Beck was pleased with so much that Hitler had achieved, and that he agreed with the overall objectives of Hitler's plans for future expansion, blinded him to the reality that there was no "struggle" to be had "on behalf of the Führer" at all. He was not yet ready to admit openly that the problem was not access to Hitler, but Hitler himself.

Like Strasser, Schacht and Fritsch before him, Beck couldn't fully grasp that Hitler was not susceptible to intelligent, reasoned criticism of his plans. The idea that someone could be head of the mighty and sophisticated German state—could have achieved so much already in just five years in power—and yet not be prepared to take advice from experts who were sympathetic to his goals simply did not make sense.

Then there was the question of the political and military atmosphere into which Beck launched his concerns. It was easy for someone like Beck, near the top of the military hierarchy, to underestimate the effect of five years of Nazi propaganda on the opinions of less senior officers. As Hitler himself had famously said in November 1933, "When an opponent declares, 'I will not come over to your side,' I calmly say, 'Your child belongs to us already . . . What are you? You will pass on. Your descendants, however, now stand in the new camp. In a short time they will know nothing else but this new community.' "[15]

These younger officers had all graduated from schools and a system of military training that not only emphasised the close relationship between the army and the Nazi state but trumpeted the genius of Adolf Hitler. Moreover, all these junior and middle-ranking officers knew that their own careers depended less on old-fashioned officers like Beck and more on the judgement of a new breed of politically aware military leaders who were more susceptible to Hitler's vision.

That, in part, explains the mixed reaction to Beck's attempt, at a military conference in June 1938, to explain the risks of an invasion of Czechoslovakia to his fellow officers. Edgar Röhricht, then a lieutenant colonel, later wrote that Beck simply came across as "speaking out against war amidst his own staff." He also recorded that when his comrades gathered at the Hotel Esplanade in Berlin and mulled over what they'd heard, Major Rudolf Schmundt said that Beck clearly didn't understand "the dynamism of the new regime" and if his advice had been followed "one would most likely still be a ridiculed petitioner sitting at the conference table of Geneva." Hans Jeschonnek, a Luftwaffe officer still just in his thirties, went further, saying Beck had given no credence to the power of the new German air force: "Schlieffen [the architect of Germany's invasion plan in the First World War] was [also] 20 years behind technological development—at the [battle of the] Marne we got our comeuppance. And for Beck our squadrons are nothing but an interfering add-on. But you will all get the shock of your life!"[16]

Though some officers present that day sympathised with Beck's position, it was clear to everyone that Beck's views were increasingly placing him on the periphery of power. One lieutenant colonel, who had been close to Fritsch, remarked that the events of the last few weeks had "opened his eyes" to the fact that leading figures in the German army were not a "tight knit community" but merely "public servants," and "replacements" could be found for each of them—indeed one was presumably "already available" for Beck. But this kind of cynical talk did not appeal to ambitious officers like Lieutenant Colonel Röhricht or Major Schmundt or Lieutenant Colonel Jeschonnek and, significantly, they would all go on to achieve high office. By 1945 Röhricht was an infantry general serving with the 17th Army on the Eastern Front, and the year before Schmundt—by then also a general, and head of personnel for the entire German army—had been killed on 20 July 1944 by the bomb designed to assassinate Hitler. Jeschonnek had also died at the Führer's headquarters, but in 1943 when, as chief of the Luftwaffe General Staff, he had committed suicide because he felt he had let Hitler down.

Meanwhile, Beck was still determined to convince his colleagues not to follow a plan for aggression that he was convinced would lead Germany into the abyss. And it's possible, once again, to see in the way Hitler managed to neutralise Beck during the summer of 1938 the importance of his charisma in this history—for without Hitler's ability to persuade the rest of his generals to follow his lead, often against their logical objections, it is hard to see how Germany could have been taken down such a destructive path.

Beck handed the latest in a stream of complaining memoranda to Brauchitsch on 16 July. It was his most forthright yet—almost calling for mutiny. "I consider it to be my duty this day to raise the urgent request that the Commander-in-Chief of the Wehrmacht [i.e., Hitler] be prompted to abandon the preparations for war ordered by him."[17] Shortly afterwards, when Beck met Brauchitsch, he said that the military high command should all resign together if Hitler did not change his plans. A few days later, after consulting with sympathetic colleagues, Beck told Brauchitsch that the task at hand was nothing less than altering the nature of Nazi rule. Beck still persisted in seeing the problem less as Hitler than the pernicious influence of the Gestapo and SS. "Arguably for the last time," wrote Beck, "fate offers [us] an opportunity to liberate the German people, as well as the Führer himself, from the nightmare of the secret police . . . There can and must not arise any doubt about this fight being fought for the Führer."[18] And not only did he seek to argue that any "struggle" against war should be undertaken on Hitler's behalf, he even suggested that a possible "catchword" for his proposed course of action could be, "For the Führer—Against War."

Beck must have recognised that any attempt to gain the head of the army's consent in a direct conspiracy against the head of state would be—to say the least—risky; and so he preferred to say, against direct evidence to the contrary, that Hitler was not driving events himself, but was influenced unduly by party institutions like the SS and Gestapo. Beck shared Hitler's aim of eliminating Czechoslovakia as a barrier to German expansion, only disagreeing about the timing; and he revered the old imperial system of governance and a head of state who respected the advice of the military. "Why couldn't Hitler be more like the Kaiser?" was a question that would almost certainly have been somewhere deep in Beck's mind. Most likely, Beck wanted Hitler reduced to the almost figurehead status the Kaiser had sunk to during the First World War.

But what Beck still did not yet fully understand was that Hitler was not a conventional political leader who could be swayed by closely argued memoranda. As Professor Adam Tooze[19] puts it, "He isn't a statesman in the normal sense of the word, making straightforwardly rational calculations and assuming always that there will be a high probability of ultimate success. This is a man for whom politics is drama, a tragic drama that may not have a happy end. And so he is willing to take risks that he thinks are inescapable even if the odds are very highly stacked against Germany."

Brauchitsch's exact response to Beck's pleas is not known, but he certainly did not offer immediate support for the idea of a threatened joint resignation. However, at a conference of senior officers on 4 August, Brauchitsch did ask his colleagues what they thought of the proposed plan to invade Czechoslovakia. Many supported Beck and spoke of the practical problems involved—chiefly the likelihood that Britain and France would be drawn into the conflict. Brauchitsch ended the conference by admitting openly that following Hitler's timetable for war would lead to the destruction of Germany.[20]

It was a vital moment in the history of the Third Reich. Had the generals been loyal to each other and united in their rejection of Hitler's plans then they would have precipitated a crisis in the Nazi state. But the generals were not united. Instead, General Walther von Reichenau went to Hitler and told him what had happened at the meeting. Reichenau was one of a handful of senior German generals who genuinely seems to have had complete faith in his Führer. Serving with General Blomberg in East Prussia, he first met Hitler in 1932 and from then on believed that he would prove to be the saviour of Germany. So it was no accident that it was Reichenau that tipped Hitler off about the 4 August meeting.

Hitler's immediate reaction was predictable—rage of the most intense kind. He ordered Brauchitsch to a meeting at Berchtesgaden where he screamed at the head of the German army for more than an hour. He then convened a conference on 10 August for all the generals who had been present at the original 4 August meeting. Typically, this was not to debate the merits of his proposals with his military experts, but to lecture them on why he was certain that he was right. When one general dared to question the security of the Westwall—Germany's defensive fortifications against France—Hitler shouted at him that he was wrong. During another speech five days later, after a military exercise at Jüterbog, Hitler criticised those—implicitly Beck—who had let themselves become weak, and emphasised that the decision to invade Czechoslovakia primarily involved political, not military, judgements.

It was another confident performance by Hitler in front of his generals, one that was underpinned by a familiar component of his leadership—his absolute certainty that he was right. And since Hitler's judgement had been proved right in similar circumstances in the recent past—given that Beck and others had warned that moving into Austria might result in war—Hitler now implied that little weight should be given to their latest warnings. Thus, despite all of the practical reasons why the generals were right to be so concerned about the consequences of an invasion of Czechoslovakia, many of them were prepared to support Hitler. This route of least resistance was epitomised by Lieutenant General Erich von Manstein[21] who told Beck that he should leave the politics to Hitler and concentrate on working out the practicalities of beating the Czechs in battle.

Yet there was more behind Hitler's successful appeal than merely the insistence that his generals should follow his orders. Hitler was also offering them something special—the chance of glory, of heroism, of military success that would make them famous in German history. Of course there were immense risks, but Hitler had made it clear that he would take all the responsibility for the decision to invade Czechoslovakia on himself. It was a classic example of what Dr. Fritz Redl called "the magic of the initiatory act"[22]—the notion that leaders, if they are charismatic enough, can burden themselves with the risk and potential guilt of any course of action that they initiate. As a result, they are able to create a tremendous sense of liberation in their followers.

However, in this case, not all the followers. Beck remained unconvinced, as did a number of other generals, like von Hase and von Witzleben. Admiral Canaris, head of the intelligence service, the *Abwehr,* also appeared to flirt with these figures opposed to Hitler's actions, though he was such a habitual intriguer that it is likely that he was also a double agent, with links to Heydrich and Himmler. Canaris' deputy, Hans Oster, was more committed to the opposition cause, as was Hjalmar Schacht. Via intermediaries these gentlemen, together with others, managed to approach the British Foreign Office in August 1938. "From then on Beck and that group of Germans—they didn't represent all the generals by any manner of means—kept in touch with us by underground means, and they used to come through me," says Sir Frank Roberts, then a diplomat serving on the German desk in the Foreign Office in London. "And it was the sort of thing 'if only you and the French will stand up to Hitler then we'll do something about him,' and we rather saying 'well, hadn't you better start doing something about him, then perhaps we can help you.' But of course, as Hitler went on having success after success the influence of this group of German generals became less and less."[23]

Whilst Beck, his co-conspirators and the British all dithered, Hitler made a speech in early September 1938 that passionately attacked not just the Czech government but the whole question of the way Czechoslovakia had been formed after the First World War: "The majority of its people was simply forced to submit to the structure construed at Versailles without anyone asking for their opinion. As a true democracy, this state immediately began to suppress the majority of its people, to abuse them and to rob them of their inalienable rights."[24] As for the Sudeten Germans, their situation had become "unbearable." Hitler claimed that, "In an economic context, these people are being ruined methodically and hence are subject to a slow and steady extermination. The misery of the Sudeten Germans defies description."

It was another example of Hitler's self-confessed leadership technique of shouting "louder and louder" and then observing how his opponents reacted. The British and the French had already put pressure on the Czech government to compromise with Hitler, but after his speech at Nuremberg it was clear that the situation was escalating dangerously.

Thanks to the journey to London in midsummer of Ewald von Kleist-Schmenzin, a member of Beck's opposition clique, Chamberlain was well aware that key members of the German elite felt that Hitler was trying to drive Germany into war. But when British Cabinet ministers discussed German Foreign Policy on 30 August 1938[25] they were more considered and less certain in their own view. Other intelligence—like the opinion of the British Ambassador to Berlin, Sir Nevile Henderson—argued against Hitler being determined to cause another European conflict. But what pervades the minutes of the meeting is the sense that sophisticated political operators like Neville Chamberlain and his Foreign Secretary, Lord Halifax, simply couldn't believe that a chancellor of Germany, and thus leader of a cultured European nation, could actually *want* another war.

They also felt that if the British threatened to go to war over the German occupation of the Sudetenland this might, given what they perceived as the unstable personality of Adolf Hitler, actually provoke him further. To Chamberlain and Halifax, both of whom had vivid memories of the suffering of the First World War, the prospect of another European conflict was horrific—especially given the new danger of aerial bombardment from the Luftwaffe.

It was to try and prevent this catastrophe that Chamberlain decided on a dramatic flight to meet Hitler in Germany—and, in the process, "invented modern summitry."[26] Having left London at around half-past eight on the morning of 15 September, Chamberlain arrived at Munich just after half-past twelve. By five o'clock that evening he was walking up the steps of the Berghof, Hitler's house above Berchtesgaden. During the subsequent discussion Chamberlain announced that he, personally, was quite prepared for the Sudeten Germans to leave Czechoslovakia and join the Third Reich, but he wanted assurances that Hitler had no further demands—like conquering the whole of Czechoslovakia. Hitler reassured Chamberlain that was not the case and the next day Chamberlain returned to Britain. He had spent less than four hours in Hitler's presence, but had still formed a clear opinion of him. Far from Hitler possessing any charismatic powers, he was, Chamberlain wrote, "entirely undistinguished. You would never notice him in a crowd, and would take him for the house painter he once was."[27] Moreover, as Chamberlain subsequently remarked to the British Cabinet, Hitler was the "commonest little dog I have ever seen."[28]

Chamberlain was not the first member of the British political elite to have formed the view that Hitler was most definitely not a "gentleman." A British delegation, led by Lord Halifax, had visited Hitler at the Berghof the year before and had come to a similar conclusion. One of the senior Foreign Office officials present, Ivone Kirkpatrick, thought that Hitler behaved like a "spoilt sulky child" during lunch. Worse, after they had eaten, Hitler told Halifax that the British should solve any problems they had in India by shooting Gandhi, "and if that does not suffice to reduce them [i.e., the Indians] to submission, shoot a dozen leading members of Congress; and if that does not suffice, shoot two hundred and so on until order is established." Kirkpatrick recalled that as Hitler suggested the British commit mass murder in India the beautifully mannered Lord Halifax looked at Hitler "with a mixture of astonishment, repugnance and compassion."[29]

Halifax and many others in Britain were thus immune to Hitler's charisma. They were intelligent enough to recognise that millions of Germans had succumbed to his appeal, but they still felt that, in person, Hitler was much more of a tradesman than a demi-God. He was still dangerous and possibly unbalanced, but he remained a figure almost of contempt—the antithesis of all the values that they held most precious.

The attitude of Halifax to Hitler has a huge amount in common with the initial view of Hitler held by elite German politicians like von Papen and Hindenburg. They too thought Hitler an ill-educated rabble-rouser when they met him for the first time. In fact, von Papen and Lord Halifax were strikingly similar in key aspects of their character and beliefs. Both were aristocratic and possessed an intense sense of the virtues and obligations of the patrician class to which they belonged; and both were deeply religious—Halifax was nicknamed the "Holy Fox" by Churchill because of his love of fox hunting and his piety. Whilst, of course, it's certainly not the case that every aristocratic and pious German was immune to Hitler's charisma, it is worth noting that core members of the conspiracy against Hitler that culminated in the bomb plot of July 1944 also lived by aristocratic and religious values.

However, it should be remembered that there were a number of members of the British elite who encountered Hitler during this period who *did* feel he possessed a certain charisma. Not just dizzy members of the upper class like Unity Mitford, but experienced politicians like the former Prime Minister Lloyd George, who wrote in 1936 that he believed Hitler was "a born leader of men. A magnetic and dynamic personality with a single-minded purpose, a resolute will and a dauntless heart."[30]

Still believing that Hitler did not want war, Chamberlain met on 18 September with a French delegation headed by the Prime Minister

Édouard Daladier. Together, the British and the French put pressure on the Czech government to give up the Sudetenland to Germany. Reluctantly, and recognising the hopelessness of their position if they did not agree, the Czechs succumbed. Chamberlain then flew back to Germany on 22 September and met Hitler once again, this time at Bad Godesberg just south of Bonn on the river Rhine. Chamberlain delivered what Hitler wanted, and believed he had prevented war.

But in response, Hitler demanded that matters be completely sorted out by 1 October—less than ten days away—and that the new border be agreed there and then. There would be no calm, international supervision of the handover as the British proposed. Chamberlain was dumbfounded. This was not "reasonable" behaviour. He returned to Britain on 24 September uncertain as to whether Hitler would moderate his demands or not.

Meanwhile, Chamberlain's attitude towards Hitler was beginning to trouble Duff Cooper, First Lord of the Admiralty. He had listened carefully to Chamberlain's views and had reached the conclusion that Hitler had "cast a spell"[31] over the British Prime Minister. "After all," Cooper wrote in his diary on 24 September 1938, "Hitler's achievement is not due to his intellectual attainments nor to his oratorical powers but to the extraordinary influence which he seems able to exercise over his fellow creatures. I believe that Neville is under that influence at the present time." And Cooper was not alone in thinking that Hitler had somehow suborned the British Prime Minister. Sir Alexander Cadogan, Permanent Secretary at the Foreign Office, a key official who had been excluded from Chamberlain's lightning trips to the Berghof and Bad Godesberg, wrote in his diary on 24 September: "I was completely horrified—he [i.e., Neville Chamberlain] was quite calmly for total surrender. More horrified still to find that Hitler has evidently hypnotised him to a point."[32]

Had Hitler really "hypnotised" or "cast a spell" over Chamberlain? Had the British Prime Minister fallen for Hitler's charisma? Chamberlain certainly qualified his initial negative view of Hitler, confiding to the Cabinet that "it was impossible not to be impressed with the power of the man."[33] Just as other immaculately mannered members of the German elite had discovered in the past, Chamberlain had learnt that Hitler could not be dealt with like any normal statesman, and the British Prime Minister had clearly been confused by direct exposure to Hitler's actions and personality. Hitler did not operate within the bounds of diplomatic propriety. Screams, tantrums, rapid changes of mood, sulks—all of these emotional techniques were uniquely at Hitler's disposal during these encounters. As Chamberlain said of Hitler the following year, "I shouldn't like to have him as a partner in my business."[34] So if Chamberlain was not a casualty of Hitler's charisma, he was certainly buffeted around by Hitler's moods as he desperately sought a way of coming to an arrangement with the German chancellor.

These days must have represented a torment for Chamberlain. How was it possible, he asked, that Hitler could be offered everything he said he wanted, and yet still sought to impose impossible conditions on the implementation of those demands? (Of course, Hitler never expected the British and French to be able to deliver the Sudetenland to Germany, and he was now confused about the best way forward himself, since his reason for war had been snatched away.) As Chamberlain said in his infamous radio broadcast on 27 September 1938, "How horrible, fantastic, incredible it is that we should be digging trenches and trying on gas masks here because of a quarrel in a far-away country between people of whom we know nothing. It seems still more impossible that a quarrel which has already been settled in principle should be the subject of war . . ."[35]

However, Lord Halifax was now against giving in completely to Hitler—as, naturally enough, were the Czechs. With the mood shifting, both the British and the French told the Germans that if Czechoslovakia was invaded then they would go to war. But still, Chamberlain offered to go once more to Germany to talk to Hitler and a conference to discuss the crisis was then held in Munich on 29 September. The meeting was held in Hitler's office, just yards from the two "honour temples" containing the remains of those "martyrs" killed during the Beer Hall Putsch fifteen years before.

Here a deal was brokered between the British and French on one side and the Germans on the other. Mussolini had been asked to help facilitate a way out of the impasse—one which had been entirely caused by Hitler's own uncertainty about whether or not he wished to keep upping his demands to a point that would cause war. In the event, Germany was granted the Sudetenland and the British and French managed to push through an attempt at face-saving by insisting on slightly less land being transferred to Germany over a slightly longer period than Hitler had intitially demanded (but still with the process to be completed in less than two weeks). Astonishingly to modern eyes, representatives of the one nation directly affected—the Czechs—were not asked to the talks. The deal was effectively forced on them afterwards—and how could they refuse when all the great European powers were now ranged against them? It would not be the last time that the British agreed to give away territory without representatives of the country affected present at the meeting—they were to do the same thing to the Poles at the Tehran and Yalta conferences less than seven years later.

The Munich agreement was hugely welcomed in Britain. When Chamberlain landed back from Munich at Heston airport on 30 September he was greeted by the Earl of Clarendon, the Lord Chamberlain, who invited him to travel straight to Buckingham Palace for an audience with the King. There had even been a suggestion that the King should meet Chamberlain at the airport in order to congratulate him on his achievement.[36]

A few days later Germans in the Sudetenland, like Günther Langer, watched in wonder as the Wehrmacht arrived. "They just came out of the forest," he says. "As they came by we all clamoured with joy, we were delighted, we invited them in, we gave them food, we gave them drink, we talked with them, yes, and we were happy. The joy at our redemption was very great and it was welcomed by all. I'll tell you something: when you heard how well the Germans in Germany had it compared with us then it's no wonder, is it? People said, thank God, times are changing for us now . . . Because we knew we were being freed at last from this Czech yoke. Everyone was jubilant. And the few who say the opposite, that isn't true, everyone was delighted about it. But that such a thing might result, of course, in the Second World War, nobody imagined that."[37]

Hitler still felt a sense of urgency. He had been making a number of remarks in recent months about his age. He was concerned, as Professor Richard Evans puts it, that he "didn't have that long to run."[38] And as well as these personal fears about his life expectancy, he had also made it clear at meetings back in May that it was in Germany's interest to act now, before France and Britain had completed their rearmament. However, in the course of Chamberlain's three attempts at shuttle diplomacy Hitler had also learnt that some of his key Nazi comrades were anxious about a future conflict with Britain and France. Göring, for instance, tried to talk Hitler out of war, and Goebbels realised that Chamberlain's offer to give up the Sudetenland took away the propaganda reason for any conflict. Goebbels thought that it would be tough to persuade the German population to go to war on the technicality of transfer arrangements for the Sudetenland into the Reich.[39] Goebbels had also—in the presence of several other leading figures in the regime—warned Hitler that there was a distinct lack of enthusiasm in the country as a whole for war.[40] Nor was Hitler's potential military ally, Italy, keen on conflict with the West, as evidenced by Mussolini's desire to take part in the peace talks at Munich. So Hitler waited.

By stepping back from war Hitler also—knowingly or unknowingly—stopped a potential mutiny. How serious was any plot against him is a subject that has been debated amongst historians for many years.[41] Perhaps surprisingly, given his past behaviour, Ludwig Beck was not the instigator of the conspiracy. He had resigned as Chief of the General Staff in the middle of August, though he had been asked by Hitler to keep this decision confidential for now. Beck was replaced by General Franz Halder, and it was Halder who had held discussions with sympathetic colleagues about the possibility of resisting Hitler's order to invade Czechoslovakia so that a war with France and Britain could be prevented. After the Munich conference, these plans—if formal plans they were—collapsed. However, given Hitler's hold of the SS and the rest of the Nazi infrastructure, and the number of junior soldiers in the German army who loyally supported him and trusted his judgement, it is hard to see how Halder's desire to stop Hitler could have succeeded—short of killing him, and that in 1938 would have been a step too far for many of the conspirators.

Having emerged from the immediate prospect of war with Britain and France, Hitler was faced with what appeared to democratic Western politicians as a stark choice—to follow a road to peaceful coexistence with other European countries, or to continue to pursue a policy of expansion that could only lead to conflict. For Hitler, however, this was no choice at all—he was always moving towards war.

Yet Chamberlain showed every sign of believing that Hitler was sincere when he signed the infamous "piece of paper" on the morning of 30 September in which he stated that he was keen, alongside Chamberlain, to "assure the peace of Europe." In part, of course, Chamberlain was simply hoping for the best. The idea that Hitler was mendacious was just

too horrible to contemplate. The notion that the German head of state
would publicly agree to something that was the direct opposite of his
intentions was anathema to Chamberlain. (And Chamberlain wasn't the
last British Prime Minister to be taken in by a dictator. After the conference at Yalta in February 1945, Winston Churchill returned and told his
ministers, "Poor Neville Chamberlain believed he could trust Hitler. He
was wrong. But I don't think I'm wrong about Stalin."[42] The subsequent
history demonstrated, of course, that Churchill was as wrong about Stalin
as Chamberlain had been about Hitler.)[43]

At a meeting on 14 October 1938 at the Air Ministry in Berlin—little
more than two weeks after the Munich conference—Hitler, via his loyal
servant Hermann Göring, made his real intentions abundantly clear.
Göring said that because of the "situation in the world" the Führer had
instructed him "to carry out a gigantic programme [of armaments build-
ing] compared to which previous achievements are meaningless."[44] It was
an astonishing—almost mind-boggling—expansion plan. "Very dramatically in the autumn of 1938 they plan to establish an airforce of 20,000
aircraft," says Professor Adam Tooze, "which is the size of the U.S. Army
Airforce at the end of the Second World War, the largest air arm that
anybody had seen up to that point. So it's an extraordinarily ambitious
programme for a small European state to have maintained, far bigger than
anything the RAF was able to assemble by 1945. It would have consumed
in terms of annual spending something like a third of German gross
domestic product in peacetime before the war had even started, whereas
normal military expenditure would be something like two, three, four
per cent of GDP, so tenfold what NATO, for instance, was demanding
of its members in the 1970s and 1980s."[45] Moreover, as Tooze calculated,
in order to keep this planned new air force flying, "Germany would have
needed to purchase fuel in the early 1940s at the rate of three million
cubic metres per annum, twice the current level of global production."[46]

Not surprisingly, the whole German economy was now almost breaking under the strain of Hitler's rearmament targets. "The financial situation of the Reich is catastrophic," wrote Goebbels in December 1938. "It
cannot go on like this."[47] Hitler had driven Germany into an unenviable
position. He intended war, regardless of what agreements he had signed.
But the scale of his new armaments expansion plan was ludicrous. Göring
himself came close to admitting this: "One could almost arrive at the

conclusion: *non possumus* [not possible]," he told the Defence Council. However, Göring then remarked that he had, when faced with a similar situation in the past, "never given up" and "eventually" he had "always found a way out."[48]

Hitler attempted to persuade Germans that he was not the aggressor, but that he was acting only in response to a formidable group of enemies—who were growing more dangerous by the day. In a speech to construction workers on 9 October 1938,[49] he outlined why Germany needed to rearm: "It is my opinion that it is cheaper to arm prior to certain events than to meet these unprepared and have to pay tribute afterwards . . . The minute another man rises to power in England and replaces Chamberlain—someone like Mr. Duff Cooper [who had resigned from the Cabinet over the question of Munich], Mr. Eden or Mr. Churchill—that minute we know that it would be the ambition of these men to break loose yet another world war, and that immediately. They are quite open about this, they do not make a secret of it." Hitler then made a specific reference to the Jews—his rhetoric against them increasing in the wake of the failure of the Évian conference and just one month before the atrocities of *Kristallnacht*. "Further, we know that the international Jewish fiend looms threateningly behind the scenes on stage and it does so today just as it did yesterday."

What Hitler was doing, of course, was using his old tactic of exaggerating potential threats to Germany. He had seen the lack of desire in the German population for another war and so he now sought to overstate the possible danger from others as a reason why Germany should prepare for conflict. He would then, over the next months, couple this rhetoric with feeding the sense of indignation felt in some quarters in Germany that all of the "wrongs" of Versailles had still not been put right—specifically the return of German territory lost to the Poles at the end of the First World War. In pursuit of this policy he was helped by the enormous trust that many Germans now placed in him. "People at that time really were enthusiastic," says Professor Norbert Frei, "and now they had the experience of a couple of very good years under Nazism—if you are not a Jew or not a political opponent of the Nazis then you had a rather good experience. And people loved Hitler, most of the Germans loved Hitler at that stage, not because he intended to go to war but just because he achieved all these things without going to war . . . The Germans at that time were even talking about Hitler as 'General Bloodless,' a military person who was able to achieve all these things without spilling blood."[50]

Amongst the Nazi faithful, like Bruno Hähnel, the events of the autumn of 1938 had only served to reinforce their belief in Hitler's judgement. "People followed all these events with great interest, of course," he says, "but in the meantime we had adopted an attitude whereby one said that the Führer would manage. The Führer would do the right thing. And people were also proud of the fact that European political leaders came to Munich. Again we saw this as an advantage and our conviction that Adolf Hitler had achieved significance in the world was strengthened."[51]

Hitler knew that this attitude of trust—that he would "do the right thing"—was based on faith in his charismatic leadership. But much of that confidence flowed from his perceived ability to increase Germany's influence and power whilst avoiding war. So he now faced the difficult task of shifting public perception more towards the acceptance of military conflict, whilst keeping faith in his charisma intact. In a speech to top German journalists in Munich on 10 November 1938 he outlined—remarkably frankly and openly—both the problem he faced and the possible solution. He admitted that, "For decades the circumstances have forced me to talk almost exclusively of peace." And that the trouble was that this might have led Germans to believe that the "present regime" was determined to "keep the peace at all costs"—something that he confessed would be an "incorrect assessment" of the aims of Nazism. So the challenge both for the regime and for these journalists was now to create an attitude amongst the general population that "there are things that, if they cannot be enforced by peaceful means, must be enforced by means of violence." And the feeling had to be created amongst ordinary Germans that "if things cannot be settled amicably, force will have to be used, but in any case things cannot go on like this." To achieve this end "it was necessary to shine light on certain foreign policy events in such a way that the inner voice of the German people naturally cried out for the application of force."[52]

Hitler said he took pride in "slowly grinding down the nerves" of his opponents—specifically the authorities in Czechoslovakia. He had been able to do this, the implication was clear, because he possessed a strong inner core of belief in himself. And it thus followed that to Hitler the question of the "self-confidence" of the German people was crucial given what was to come. The "whole German people," he said, "must learn to believe in final victory so fanatically that even if we were occasionally defeated, the nation would regard it from an overall point of view and say, this is a temporary phase: victory will be ours in the end!" Hitler then announced how he believed this goal could be accomplished. The key was consistently to state that "the Leadership is always right!" And whilst Hitler accepted that the leaders of Germany "must be allowed to make mistakes" it was important to realise that "all of us can only survive if we do not let the world see our mistakes . . . " Once a decision had been made, Hitler demanded that "the whole nation closes ranks behind that decision. There must be a united front and then whatever is not quite right about the decision will be compensated for by the determination with which the nation stands behind it . . . "

Hitler made this revealing speech in Munich on the day after the atrocities of *Kristallnacht*—and so it is significant that he chose not to mention the attacks. Indeed, as far as the historical record shows, he never discussed them either publicly or privately. As with the Jewish boycott in 1933, Hitler intuitively realised that his authority might be damaged if those non-Jewish Germans who objected to seeing their Jewish neighbours beaten up, imprisoned in concentration camps and even murdered were able to link his name to the atrocities. Yet none of these events would have happened unless he had desired them.

But despite Hitler's attempt to act as if the atrocities of 9–10 November 1938 had not happened, *Kristallnacht* still marked a decisive moment both in the history of the Third Reich and in the perception of Hitler as a leader—in Germany and elsewhere. Less than a week after *Kristallnacht*, on 16 November 1938, Ludwig Beck remarked in a private conversation that he now felt Hitler was a "psychopath through and through" and that "I have warned and warned [the German generals]—and at last I stood alone."[53]

In London, *Kristallnacht* dramatically altered the views of Lord Halifax, the British Foreign Secretary. Having previously gone along with Chamberlain's actions at Munich and his announcement that the agreement represented "peace for our time,"[54] Halifax now told a meeting of the Foreign Policy Committee that recent events demonstrated that "crazy persons" had managed to "secure control" of Germany. He felt that "the immediate objective [of the British government] should be the correction of the false impression that we were decadent, spineless and could with impunity be kicked about."⁵⁵

Halifax, who later admitted privately that he was "rather anti-Semitic,"⁵⁶ was appalled at the Nazis' actions against the Jews. He felt a line had been crossed. Neville Chamberlain, however, did not. Whilst no doubt deploring the violence of *Kristallnacht,* he did not see these events as especially relevant to Britain's security or German foreign policy intentions. He had invested a great deal of his own personal authority in trusting Hitler and was not about to admit he had been wrong—at least, not yet.⁵⁷

How close Hitler was to laying bare before the German people the true measure of his ambitions is clear from the speech he gave in the Reichstag on 30 January 1939. Lasting more than two hours, the speech is infamous for the "prophecy" Hitler made about the Jews, one that echoed the views expressed in the SS magazine, *Das Schwarze Korps,* in the months before.⁵⁸ "Should international financial Jewry succeed," said Hitler, "both within and beyond Europe, in plunging mankind into yet another world war, then the result will not be a Bolshevisation of the earth and the victory of Jewry, but the annihilation of the Jewish race in Europe."⁵⁹

The speech is also noteworthy for Hitler's statement about his second obsession—*Lebensraum.* He said that Germany faced a simple choice in the face of gross over-population: either carry on exporting German manufacturing goods in order to generate money to buy food imports, or gain more territory, and he made it obvious that he favoured the latter. Just how that *Lebensraum* would be gained was not spelt out—though since Hitler also said that Germany had peaceful relations with nations to the west, south and north, by omitting "the east" from the list he pointed the way his ambitions lay.

It was a remarkable performance by Hitler, given at some risk to his charismatic leadership and his popularity. For though he dotted his speech with references to his desire for peace, the threat of war hung over his whole performance. Still, the subtext of the speech was faithful to the tactics he had suggested to German journalists on the morning after *Kristallnacht*—Hitler was indeed saying that "if things cannot be settled amicably, force will have to be used, but in any case things cannot go on like this." And Hitler was still riding high on a wave of trust from millions of Germans in the wake of the peaceful resolution at Munich. Allied to this emotional faith in their Führer's judgement was still the recurring emphasis on that old familiar justification for action—the "righting of the wrongs" of Versailles. This allowed Germans, like Luftwaffe officer Karl Boehm-Tettelbach, to still maintain that Hitler "had something good in mind."[60] Why was it, Boehm-Tettelbach asked, that the Allies from the First World War—Britain, France and America—"after so many years still consider the Treaty of Versailles as valid? That's impossible!"[61]

Another reason, sometimes overlooked, why Hitler was able to press on towards war with his charismatic leadership intact, was that his own past behaviour helped create the very dangers he now claimed motivated his current actions—much as how distaste for mental patients had been created by the sordid conditions in which they now existed as a result of the Nazis' cuts in funding for mental hospitals.[62] For example, Hitler said he wanted Germany to rearm massively because other nations were a threat, yet the scale of Germany's rearmament caused these other nations to want to rearm themselves. He said the American press was sympathetic to Jews and yet he created that sympathy by the way German Jews were treated.

By alienating the Western powers, by stoking up a potential financial meltdown in Germany by pursuing a programme of massive rearmament, by creating an atmosphere in which war could only be stopped by Germany losing prestige—something Hitler could not contemplate—Hitler made war all but inevitable. By the time he gave his speech in the Reichstag on 30 January 1939, Hitler had gained more than almost anyone had ever thought possible—he had created a Greater Germany from Carinthia in the south to Flensburg in the north. From Aachen in the west to Königsberg and Vienna in the east. But it was not enough.

There were now few obstacles inside Germany to Hitler's desire for conflict. By January 1939 any opposition within the German army had been all but swept away. On 18 December 1938, for example, Brauchitsch wrote in instructions on how German officers should be trained that "Adolf Hitler, the resourceful Führer, who transformed the profound teaching of 'front-line comradeship' [*Frontkämpfertum*] into the ideology of National Socialism, has built and secured the new Greater German Reich for us . . . There is tremendous change in all areas. A new German man has grown up in the Third Reich, full of ideals . . . Across all classes a new unique national community [*Volksgemeinschaft*] has been created to which we all belong—the people, the Wehrmacht and the party. Staunch is our loyalty, firm our trust, to the man who created all this, who caused this miracle by his faith and will."[63]

Yet only four months before, in September 1938, General Alfred Jodl of the Wehrmacht High Command had written in his diary, "It is deeply sad that the Führer has the whole people behind him, but not the leading generals of the army. In my opinion, only through action can they make up for what they have sinned by lack of obedience. It's the same problem as in 1914. There is only one disobedience in the army, that of the generals—and ultimately this results from their arrogance. They cannot believe and obey any more, because they do not recognise the genius of the Führer, in whom some of them surely still see the corporal of the world war, but not the greatest statesman since Bismarck."[64]

From a refusal "to recognise the Führer's genius" to "staunch" loyalty for a leader who has created a "miracle" is quite a journey in four months. And it was only made possible by the Munich agreement, combined with the power of Hitler's charismatic leadership. Hitler had said he was certain that all would turn out well—and everything had turned out better than his generals could have hoped. All that was left now, many of these senior army figures must have felt, was to do what millions of other Germans were already doing—and to have "faith" in the Führer's judgement.

Hitler was moving closer to war. He showed every sign of feeling aggrieved—despite having received the Sudetenland—that Czechoslovakia still existed in any form. Via Joachim Ribbentrop, Hitler put pressure on the Slovaks to declare their independence from the rest of the Czech state—and the Slovak parliament duly did on 14 March 1939. What was left of Czechoslovakia—chiefly Bohemia and Moravia—was now immensely vulnerable to Nazi aggression. Given the Slovak secession, the assurances given by Britain and France about the integrity of Czechoslovakia at the Munich conference were now all but meaningless. The Czechoslovakia they had agreed to champion no longer existed.

The new Czech government under President Hácha had tried not to offend Hitler since the Munich conference and the loss of the Sudetenland, but there was nothing—short of their own destruction—that they could do that would make him happy. On 14 March, President Hácha and his Foreign Minister, František Chvalkovský, arrived in Berlin to plead with Hitler not to order a German invasion of the remaining Czech lands. Hitler received them in the vast new Reich Chancellery designed by Albert Speer, opened two months before. Hitler had wanted this building to intimidate foreign statesmen. Visitors had to walk over slippery marble along a reception hall twice as long as the Hall of Mirrors in Versailles to reach Hitler's office. Once admitted into his presence they would notice an inlay on his desk that, as Speer recalls, showed "a sword half drawn from its sheath." "Good, good," Hitler had said when he saw the design, "when the diplomats sitting in front of me at this desk see that, they'll learn to shiver and shake."[65]

When Hitler finally deigned to meet Hácha at one o'clock in the morning—having finished watching a comedy film—he told him that in five hours' time German troops would invade the remainder of the Czech lands. Hácha collapsed and had to be revived by Theodor Morell, Hitler's doctor. At four o'clock in the morning, in order to avoid bloodshed, he agreed to hand over the remainder of Czechoslovakia into German hands.

Czechs like Anna Krautwurmowa were terrified. They remembered how Czech citizens had fled from the Sudetenland in the face of German aggression: "The Czechs who were returning from the borderlands told us how they were attacked and beaten with rifle butts. People had to flee, flee with their small children. That's how it was, they were heartless. They were truly heartless, merciless, and they swore at our people for no reason."[66]

These remaining Czech lands had no German-speaking majority within them. This was not about regaining Germans or German territory lost at the end of the First World War. This was imperialist aggression. "Why should they have the right [to invade]?" asks Anna Krautwurmowa. "This was the Czech Republic. Czechoslovakia. Why should they have any rights over another country?" In the days after the Germans moved into Prague and took the Czechs under their "protection" this was a question that many others were asking—including those in powerful positions, like Sir Alexander Cadogan of the British Foreign Office. "I'm afraid we have reached the cross roads," he wrote in his diary on 20 March 1939. "I always said that, as long as Hitler could pretend he was incorporating Germans in the Reich, we could pretend that he had a case. If he proceeded to gobble up other nationalities, that would be the time to call 'Halt!'"[67]

By the end of March, Britain had guaranteed to protect three countries against any future German aggression—Greece, Romania and Poland. This was a setback for Hitler, because he was still clinging to the hope that France and Britain could somehow be persuaded to give Germany a free hand in eastern Europe. His ambition was—as it had always been—to gain land in the west of the Soviet Union. To that end he had been testing Polish reaction to some form of deal with Germany—one that would turn Poland into a country dominated by the Nazis but without the need for a German invasion, rather like the arrangement just reached with Slovakia. He had already shown "goodwill" to the Poles, Hitler thought, by allowing them to gain territory from Czechoslovakia around Teschen at the time of the Sudetenland crisis. But now, armed with the British guarantee, the Poles were not going to let the Nazis bully them.

Hitler's foreign policy "vision" had remained the same—war with the "blood stained criminals" of the Soviet Union—but the realities of European geography had defeated him. There were too many troublesome countries between Germany and the Soviet Union to make his dream easy to achieve. War with Poland seemed inevitable, and—most likely—war with Britain and France as well. Ironically, in an effort to protect his army from a long-term war on two fronts, Hitler concluded a non-aggression pact with the Soviet Union, signed by Ribbentrop in Moscow in the early hours of 24 August 1939.

In many respects, for Hitler, this was all something of a mess. He was about to fight the wrong opponent—Britain—having made a pact with the wrong country, the Soviet Union. And it demonstrates in stark terms one of the great failures of his leadership. He had clarity of vision—which all charismatic leaders need—and he had the ability to react to short-term problems—which all politicians need—but he did not have the skill to link the two parts together in a coherent whole. Five years before, in a speech at the Nuremberg rally recorded in *Triumph of the Will*, Hitler had called for the Nazi party to be "unchangeable in its doctrine" but "supple and adaptable in its tactics." But Hitler had been too "supple and adaptable in his tactics" to gain the goals that his "unchangeable" doctrine demanded.

In any case, almost certainly Hitler's idea of an alliance with Britain had been misconceived from the first. One of the weaknesses of Hitler as a leader was that he constructed his "vision" of the way he felt Germany's future ought to be without adequate intelligence about the views of his potential adversaries. "His illusions and wish-dreams were a direct outgrowth of his unrealistic mode of working and thinking,"[68] wrote Albert Speer. "Hitler actually knew nothing about his enemies and even refused information that was available to him. Instead, he trusted his inspirations." And as far as Britain's intentions went, Hitler's "inspirations" were plain wrong. As Professor Anita Prażmowska says, the British made a straightforward "strategic evaluation" in spring 1939 and came to the conclusion that "the balance of power in Europe" was "tipping dangerously against British interests."[69] This, rather than any grand ideological or humanitarian concern, was what led them to contemplate war. Indeed, it's hard to see how any British government would have permitted Germany to create a gigantic empire in central and eastern Europe.

Hitler had been furious when he heard that Chamberlain had issued guarantees to Poland after the German occupation of the Czech lands in March 1939, angry that Chamberlain had not continued to act true to his behaviour at the time of Munich and simply acceded to German demands. Hitler doesn't seem to have realised the extent to which the behaviour of others changed in response to his own. Chamberlain had trusted Hitler, and Hitler had broken his word so he would not be trusted again. Hitler's own self-obsession, his focus on his own "will," blinded him to the fact that the people he dealt with were capable of radically changing their views about him.

Nevertheless, Hitler now had control over the only institution that could have stopped him from leading Germany to war—the army. It was a dominance which fully revealed itself at a conference at the Berghof on 22 August 1939. Hitler told his generals that "fundamentally all depends on me, on my existence . . . There will probably never again in the future be a man with more authority than I have."[70] Hitler ordered his military commanders in the forthcoming war to "harden" their "hearts" against the enemy.

However, even within the Nazi elite there were some—most notably Hermann Göring—who were now fighting an internal battle between their "faith" in the charismatic leadership of Adolf Hitler and their anxiety about the practical consequences of war. Göring was a more complex character than the bluff, bullying caricature that is often presented, and his views about the road Hitler was travelling were complex. It wasn't that Göring was against Nazi aggression—quite the contrary. He had encouraged Hitler to progress with the *Anschluss* and had taken some delight in describing to President Hácha just what his bombers would do if let loose on Prague. What Göring worried about—as did Hitler's Generals—was a wide-ranging conflict that involved Britain, France and potentially America and the Soviet Union as well. Göring was happily married to the actress Emmy Sonnemann and was father to a daughter, Edda, who was just over a year old. They lived in epic splendour at his vast estate at Carinhall in the Schorfheide forest and at his grand house in Berlin. Life for Göring was good. Why would he want to help start a war that might risk all this? Göring had demonstrated this anxiety when he famously quarrelled with Joachim Ribbentrop at the time of Munich, saying to the bellicose Foreign Minister that he, Göring, understood about war, and that whilst if war came he would be in the first aircraft into battle, he would insist Ribbentrop was in the seat next to him.[71]

On the other hand, Göring—as we have already seen many times in this history—was an absolute believer in the charisma of Adolf Hitler. In his latest obsequious remarks in public, spoken in the Reichstag after Hitler's speech on 30 January 1939, Göring had promised to "blindly" follow Hitler, a man he said who had "restored to us a life worth living, a life splendid and magnificent."[72]

But despite this promise to "blindly" follow Hitler, Göring still wanted to avoid war. Hence the appearance on the scene, in early July 1939, of an enthusiastic amateur diplomat called Birger Dahlerus. Göring had known Dahlerus, a forty-nine-year-old Swedish businessman, for years. Now Dahlerus, appalled at the prospect of war and with influential friends in Britain, approached Göring and offered to try and work for peace between the German and British governments. Göring leapt at the opportunity to use Dahlerus and met with seven senior British businessmen at a house in the north of Germany on 7 August. Several more meetings followed, with the calm, measured Swede eventually discussing German intentions—having been briefed by Göring—with Neville Chamberlain, Lord Halifax and Sir Alexander Cadogan at the end of August in London.

It was a mission that was doomed from the start. The British would not countenance forcing the Poles to give up any territory to the Germans—given the German occupation of the Czech lands another Munich was inconceivable—and Hitler was set not only on taking Danzig and the Polish corridor but on gaining *Lebensraum* in the east as well.

Göring knew all this. He had even heard Hitler state baldly "There will be a war"[73] at a military conference back in May. So why was Göring wasting so much time on Dahlerus? One possibility was that he felt excluded by the presence of Ribbentrop at Hitler's side, and saw this escapade as a way of worming his way back into the centre of events. But from the account Dahlerus gives of that summer it seems more likely that Göring was actually trying to do what he could to avert a war with the British. That's also the impression conveyed by the bizarre scene Sir Alexander Cadogan described on 30 August,[74] with Dahlerus in the British Foreign Office on the phone to Göring, quizzing him about whether a compromise was possible between Germany and Britain—which, of course, it never was.

Göring owed his power, fame and riches to his position in the Nazi state—a position only made possible by his belief in the charismatic leadership of Adolf Hitler. Now Göring was experiencing one of the downsides of that belief—for if you follow a leader out of blind faith then you have few options if you subsequently fear the journey will take you to a place you do not want to be.

Göring arranged a meeting between Dahlerus and Hitler in the Reich Chancellery in the early hours of 27 August, at which Dahlerus hand-delivered a letter from Lord Halifax expressing the British desire for peace. That Göring thought this anodyne note could change anything showed both how desperate he was to avoid war with the British, and how anxious he was to please Hitler by demonstrating his influence with powerful figures in the British government.

Dahlerus was taken on the same grand route through the new Reich Chancellery to Hitler's office that Hácha had followed a few months before. When Hitler met Dahlerus he stared intently at him and then launched into a monologue about German history. Dahlerus noticed how Hitler managed to work himself up into a state of excitement—seemingly without outside stimuli. "He had a seductive way of putting his own viewpoint in the most favourable light," wrote Dahlerus, "but he suffered from lamentable incapacity to see or respect the other party's point of view."[75] Hitler boasted about the power of the German armed forces, and when he mentioned the strength of the Luftwaffe, Göring—who had been sitting quietly thus far—"giggled contentedly."

By now Dahlerus had formed the view that Hitler's "mental equilibrium was patently unstable" and so, when he could get a word in, he spoke softly in an attempt to calm the German leader. But when Dahlerus mentioned that Britain and France were also powerful military nations the reaction was instantaneous. Hitler "suddenly got up and becoming very much excited and nervous, walked up and down saying, as though to himself, that Germany was irresistible and could defeat her adversaries by means of a rapid war. Suddenly he stopped in the middle of the room and stood there staring. His voice was blurred and his behaviour that of a completely abnormal person. He spoke in staccato phrases, and it was clear that his thoughts were concentrated on the tasks that awaited him in case of war. 'If there should be war,' he said, *'dann werde ich U Boote bauen, U Boote bauen, U Boote, U Boote, U Boote.'* ['I will build U boats, build U boats, U boats, U boats, U boats.'] His voice became more indistinct and finally one could not follow him at all. Then he pulled himself together, raised his voice as though addressing a large audience and shrieked, *'Ich werde Flugzeuge bauen, Flugzeuge bauen, Flugzeuge, Flugzeuge, und ich werde meine Feinde vernichten.'* ['I will build planes, build planes, planes, planes, and I will destroy my enemies.'] He seemed more like a phantom from a story book than a real person."[76]

The meeting ended with Dahlerus trying to discover just what Hitler wanted from the Poles. But, like many others before him, he found it impossible to get Hitler to articulate detailed terms. Dahlerus left, appalled both by Hitler's behaviour and by the way Göring abased himself before his Führer.

Whilst as a piece of political history this remarkable encounter is not hard to explain—Hitler must have felt that he should exploit even the slightest chance that Britain could be persuaded to stay out of any conflict over Poland, though he knew how unlikely such an outcome was—as an insight into Hitler the charismatic leader it is a good deal more intriguing. Dahlerus, never having met Hitler before, did not find Hitler "charismatic": indeed, he wrote that he "had not seen a trace of the extraordinary fascination which he was popularly supposed to exercise upon everyone."[77] In fact, Dahlerus thought Hitler was not of sound mind.

Hitler, of course, lost his temper on a regular basis and had never had the ability to conduct normal negotiations over a long period, politely and in detail. Equally, he had before used his ability to self-generate his anger as a tactic in diplomatic discussions—most notably when the Austrian Chancellor Kurt Schuschnigg visited the Berghof on 12 February

1938. Hitler ranted and raved at Schuschnigg in the morning and then switched in an instant into a convivial host when he sat down to lunch with the Austrian delegation. Dr. Otto Pirkham, an Austrian diplomat present that day, noticed that Schuschnigg was "very depressed"[78] at lunch after being lambasted by Hitler—almost in a state of shock.

But Hitler did not appear to be using his ranting as a conscious negotiating ploy with Dahlerus. In this instance Dahlerus appears to have encountered an important aspect of the real Hitler. We have already seen how a central part of Hitler's personality was his limitless capacity to hate, and here that was allied to an emotionality that was given such free rein as to appear out of control. The ability to feel events emotionally and to demonstrate that emotion to others was a crucial part of his charismatic appeal, and before Hitler's audience felt emotion, he had to feel it first.

But, increasingly, Hitler's displays of raw emotion were resulting in other European statesmen and diplomats thinking that he was—as Dahlerus did—"patently unstable." By this time Nevile Henderson, the British ambassador to Berlin, for example, thought Hitler was "quite mad" and had "crossed the borderline of insanity."[79] Yet, still, Hitler was the unchallenged leader of Germany. Indeed, Göring had witnessed Hitler's tirade in front of Dahlerus with equanimity.

The reasons why Göring—along with countless other Germans—carried on backing Hitler during this decisive period offer insights into the way they experienced his leadership. In the first place, Göring had witnessed Hitler's passionate harangues for years. And whilst foreigners might think Hitler "mad," Göring and the rest of the Nazi elite were not predisposed to notice when the line between passion and dangerous instability was crossed. Manfred Schröder, for instance, was a young German diplomat and Nazi party member who witnessed Hitler's behaviour at first hand in the Reich Chancellery immediately after President Hácha had been forced to agree to give up the Czech lands. Hitler was "talking the whole time"[80] and "dictating to two secretaries" at once. At the time Schröder took this hyperactive behaviour as the sign of a "genius at work" but "when I look back today and I have the clear picture of him standing up and then sitting down again I think he was behaving like an absolute maniac." From charismatic "genius" to "absolute maniac"—this was the same person's judgement about Hitler, altered only by time and experience.

Another familiar belief that many who supported Hitler could fall back on in times of anxiety was the notion that Hitler was unduly influenced by wild and radical advisers. Just as Goebbels had decided at the Bamberg conference back in 1926 that Hitler was criticising Gregor Strasser's plans because he had fallen into the clutches of the unsavoury Nazi leaders in Bavaria, so a number of people now blamed Ribbentrop, the war-mongering Foreign Secretary, for Germany's rush to war. The question in the German Foreign Office, according to Manfred von Schröder, was now, "How can we get rid of Ribbentrop and get a direct contact with Hitler?" Paradoxically, this view that Hitler was somehow being led astray could co-exist with the overwhelming feeling that Hitler—deep down—knew what was best for Germany. Once again, this belief relied both upon the vast and seemingly unshakeable certainty that Hitler constantly demonstrated in his own judgement, and the fact that his recent adventures in foreign policy had all come right for Germany in the end. "Any doubts I might have had were quelled by the self-assurance Hitler showed," wrote Albert Speer. "In those days he seemed to me like a hero of ancient myth who unhesitatingly, in full consciousness of his strength, could enter and masterfully meet the test of the wildest undertakings."[81]

Nevile Henderson also suspected that the key to Adolf Hitler's success might be to do with his boundless self-confidence, backed up by his intuitive sense of what to do next. Henderson, like Dahlerus, never found Hitler charismatic and puzzled throughout his time in Berlin "wherein the greatness of Hitler lay, by what means he had succeeded as the undisputed Leader of a great people, and what was—to me—the hidden source of his influence over his followers and of their complete subservience to him."[82] One answer, Henderson discovered, was the Führer's followers' confidence in his intuition. "I constantly asked those in closest touch with Hitler in what his chief quality consisted. I was told almost unanimously, in his *Fingerspitzengefuehl* [tip of the finger feeling]."[83]

Closely allied to this faith in Hitler was a sense that the Führer was somehow "destined" to lead Germany to wherever he chose. "This man—Hitler—is Germany's fate for good or evil," said Werner von Fritsch, after he'd been forced to resign as head of the German army. And Fritsch was in little doubt where Hitler was taking Germany, warning that he would now "drag us all" into "the abyss."[84]

However, in the summer of 1939, many Germans still believed that

Hitler could prevent the war against Poland becoming a wider conflict. "We had had many examples of the Western powers leaving Hitler alone, including Munich, including the occupation of Prague,"[85] says Ulrich de Maizière, then a young army officer. And when news came of the Nazi-Soviet non-aggression pact on 24 August 1939 it seemed as if Hitler had, once again, achieved a foreign policy triumph from nowhere. Now, whatever else happened, it appeared the Germans would not face the same two-front war, trapped between Britain and France in the West and Russia in the East, as they had twenty-five years before.

The Wehrmacht invaded Poland on 1 September 1939 and two days later Britain and France declared war on Germany. All that Ulrich de Maizière could now envisage was that, "Predicting with certainty [what would now happen] was by no means obvious."[86]

PART THREE

RISK AND REWARD

12

THE GREAT GAMBLE

Despite decades of historical research, a number of myths about Hitler and Nazism still persist in the popular consciousness. One of the most pervasive is that the German victory over the French in 1940 was made possible because of the superiority of German equipment—crucially, that the Wehrmacht had more tanks to enable them to pioneer Blitzkrieg tactics. But this is not the case. In fact, the Germans had *fewer* tanks than the Allies on the Western Front, and a study of the decisive period from the start of the war through to the defeat of the French—from September 1939 to the summer of 1940—reveals a much more complex matrix of reasons for Hitler's success, one in which his charisma played a vital role. Hitler's vision, his certainty, his oratory, his ability to release the limitless ambitions of his followers and create an atmosphere of intense excitement at the possibility of making history—all of this played a part in ensuring German victory.

Above all, this is the period of the great gamble. And here, too, we confront another popular myth—that the greatest risk Hitler ever took was thought at the time to be his decision to invade the Soviet Union. But, in reality, his decision to attack the French was considered much more risky—so much so that the German offensive on the Western Front in the spring of 1940 was looked on as one of the greatest military gambles in history. According to conventional wisdom at the time, the German attack ought not to have succeeded.[1] Moreover, during this period Hitler not only had to persuade his generals to do his bidding and attack west, but also decide on the nature of the war against Poland and the form that the Nazi occupation would take.

However, there is nothing mysterious about the military destruction of Poland, which the Germans accomplished within weeks. Warsaw may have fallen only on 28 September, but the fate of Poland had been clear eleven days before when the Red Army, acting in consultation with the Germans, marched into eastern Poland to seize their share of Polish territory. Trapped between Hitler and Stalin—who were acting as Allies in the dismemberment of Poland under the secret protocol of the Nazi-Soviet non-aggression pact—the Poles never had a chance.

But if the military action was straightforward, Nazi policy within occupied Poland was anything but. A senior German military officer like General Johannes Blaskowitz could still maintain during interrogation in 1947 that he had felt at the time that, "A war to wipe out the political and economic loss resulting from the creation of the Polish Corridor and to lessen the threat to separated East Prussia surrounded by Poland and Lithuania was regarded as a sacred duty though a sad necessity."[2] In effect, he claimed that he was fighting a war to "right the wrongs of Versailles."

A war for these ends also had the wholehearted support of ethnic Germans who had been left trapped at the end of the First World War when territory that had been German for generations had been handed over to Poland. "Well, the Treaty of Versailles to us, who were living there, was a difficult and hard experience, because it meant that we were cut off from the Reich," says Charles Bleeker Kohlsaat, a member of a prominent ethnic German family in western Poland. He hoped that Hitler would create a new Germany and include all ethnic Germans within it. "When there were broadcasts of the Führer's speeches, Hitler's speeches, we were glued to the radio and listened with interest to what he was saying. Listening to the Führer's speeches, we believed that it was a miracle that Hitler was performing, and we thought that he would bring the Reich to a new greatness and we were full of enthusiasm about this man's achievements . . . And everybody was fascinated, as long as you did not look behind the scenes—and the average person did not look behind the scenes—you thought, gosh, this man is really achieving something, that is a proper German."[3]

Thus for Germans like Blaskowitz, Kohlsaat and millions of others, this was not an "ideological" war but part of Hitler's promise to restore German territory and honour after the humiliation of Versailles. In so far as they were influenced by Hitler's charisma, their support was based to a large extent on this shared goal. But it soon became clear that they were mistaken. This was not a conventional war to reclaim lost territory at all. As Professor Mary Fulbrook, who has made a special study of this period, puts it, "If you look at the invasion of Poland in September 1939 you see in the very first week of the war the first mass atrocities against civilians, against Jewish women and children and old people . . . If you take just the first week of the war and you look at Eastern Upper Silesia you get burnings of synagogues with people inside the synagogue dying in the flames. You get atrocities with the killing of men, women, children and old people in all the houses surrounding the synagogue in Będzin [on 8 September 1939]; this is a massive atrocity . . . we're talking about several hundred civilians being burnt alive or shot while they were trying to escape, or jumping into the river to put the flames out and being shot if they popped their heads out of the water for air."[4] Though these attacks were smaller in scale than the mass murders that would accompany the German invasion of the Soviet Union in the summer of 1941, they were, as Fulbrook says, "nevertheless an outrage which is not normal warfare and is not like the kinds of things that we saw with atrocities in the First World War, where there were atrocities but there was some kind of legitimation in military terms for them, in a way that there wasn't here. This was racial."

German soldiers like Wilhelm Moses, who was a member of a Wehrmacht transport unit, were shocked at what they saw. He witnessed the SS Germania hanging seven or eight Poles in a public square whilst a brass band played. This, plus the other horrors he saw, led him to be "ashamed about everything . . . And I no longer felt German . . . I had already got to the point where I said, 'If a bullet were to hit me, I would no longer have to be ashamed to say that I'm German, later, once the war is over.'"[5]

The following year, 1940, Charles Bleeker Kohlsaat also experienced an event that made him realise the true nature of the Nazi occupation of

Poland: "We were sitting on the balcony on a Sunday having breakfast. Suddenly a cart drove into the courtyard . . . When I looked down I saw the horses and recognised the farmer . . . So my mother said, 'Go and see what he wants.' So I ran to the courtyard and walked over to the vehicle, where the farmer's Polish farmhand was sitting, whom I also knew, at least by sight. And next to him sat a man whom I did not know. He was still a young man, and I took a look at him while he was talking to himself. It was as if he was in shock and he was babbling to himself.

"When I got nearer to the cart and took a closer look at the man, I noticed that his feet were tied. And the man was saying to himself, 'Me good worker, can drive with horses.' So I said to the farmhand, 'Who is this?' He said, 'That's a Jew.'

"So I ran back to the house and told them all about it. I felt very important, because that was the first living Jew I had ever seen. Afterwards my mother said, 'Go downstairs to see the housekeeper and tell her to make him something to eat.'

"So I went downstairs to see the housekeeper, and she said, 'Well, all I have left is a very meagre meal indeed.' And I was handed a blue pot with a carrying handle, which contained milk soup, a slightly sour-tasting soup with potatoes in it.

"When I was leaving the kitchen, I had to tell them the story downstairs of course. That took a moment and I had to wait for the food to heat through, so when I was leaving the house by the side entrance, I heard voices coming from the front steps. As I turned around, I saw my grandmother standing at the top of the stairs and two policemen at the bottom of the flight of steps, and they said, 'Where is the Jew?'

"To which my grandmother said, 'My grandson has just gone to bring him something to eat.' Then one of them got out his truncheon, held the truncheon and said, 'He can have a taste of this first; [after we take him away] he will get more, but until then this will have to do.' To which my grandmother, putting her hands on her hips, said, 'Tell me, are you not ashamed of yourself at all?' But he only shrugged and said, 'But it's only a Jew.' They then took the Jew away. He was probably hanged there that very same day, I don't know."

The Bleeker Kohlsaats tried to come to terms with the terrible events they witnessed in Poland—all perpetrated under the leadership of a man they had thought was a "proper German"—by attempting to convince themselves that all of those Poles who suffered at the hands of the occupying forces must have been guilty of some offence or other. The man they had longed to save them, to come to their rescue, could surely not be ordering the murder of innocent people, could he? As Kohlsaat says, "People would say, 'Good heavens, the great and glorious Adolf Hitler must be entirely unaware of what his people get up to here, otherwise he would never let this happen.' We were deeply ashamed about the behaviour of several [German] people whom we observed on the street; the way they displayed the attitude of the master race, the way they showed off their uniform, the whole notion that the Poles were inferior people, all that made us deeply ashamed and it depressed us too. We laughed at them [the Poles], but we did not treat them badly, we just mocked them in secret. Said things like, 'Look, just look at those nitwits!' But that was no reason to treat them badly, we wouldn't have done that, that was not the done thing, that was not right, and everything was geared towards etiquette, wasn't it? A German doesn't do things like that, right? But then the Germans came and they did do it!"

Even before the September invasion the Nazis had made plans to target specific Polish groups. In July 1939 the decision had been taken to form five (later expanded to six) special task groups—*Einsatzgruppen*—who would operate behind the front line and destroy the Polish governing class.[6] Reinhard Heydrich told senior members of the security police on 7 September that the leadership strata of Poland had to be "rendered harmless."[7] As for the two million Polish Jews, they were particularly vulnerable, with thousands killed in the first months of the war and the rest subject to imprisonment in ghettos. The first large ghetto—containing 230,000 Jews—was sealed in Łódź at the end of April 1940. All this was sanctioned by Adolf Hitler, who according to Goebbels, found the Poles "more animals than human beings" and thought that "the filth of the Poles is unimaginable." Hitler's "judgement" on the Poles, said Goebbels, was "annihilatory."[8]

Nor was it the case that the atrocities in Poland were solely committed by members of the Nazi party apparatus—the SS or the *Einsatzgruppen*. Elements of the German army also committed crimes. "The achievements and successes of the Polish campaign must not let it be overlooked, that some of our officers lack a firm inner attitude," wrote Brauchitsch in a decree to all German officers in October 1939. "An alarming number of cases such as wrongful confiscation, unlawful seizure, personal enrichment, embezzlement and theft, abuse or harassment of subordinates, partly in excitement, partly in senseless drunkenness, disobedience with severe consequences for the subordinate troops, rape of a married woman, etc, paint the picture of mercenary manners that cannot be condemned too strongly."[9]

But that has to be set against a background in which a number of German officers—like General Johannes Blaskowitz—were appalled at the systematic atrocities committed by Nazi functionaries. Like Beck before him, Blaskowitz had never succumbed to the charisma of Adolf Hitler. But he was part of that substantial group of army officers who had been affected by the consequences of Versailles—in particular Blaskowitz detested the Polish "corridor" which separated Eastern Prussia, his own birthplace, from the rest of Germany.

Blaskowitz was the son of a Protestant pastor, and he himself was a devout Christian. He was also cultured and extremely self-possessed. Hitler disliked him, believing before the war that he was a timid general. Nonetheless, Blaskowitz had led the German 8th Army with distinction at the battle of Bzura, west of Warsaw, the largest engagement of the Polish war. More than 150,000 Polish soldiers surrendered to the Germans, caught in a vast encirclement. But despite this success Hitler was still not impressed by Blaskowitz when he met him in Poland on 13 September. Hitler remarked later that Blaskowitz did not seem to have "understood his mission." By this cryptic remark Hitler almost certainly meant that Blaskowitz was resolutely "old school"—certainly not a commander for the future. "I'm looking for hard men," Hitler told his adjutant that same day. "I need fanatical National Socialists."[10] Knowing that Hitler wanted Blaskowitz removed—and believing the charges against him to be unfair—General Halder, Chief of the Army General Staff, supported a study of Blaskowitz which demonstrated how well he had conducted himself during the invasion.[11] Hitler remained unimpressed, but Blaskowitz remained in Poland.

A conflict between some of the old school officers and the "hard men" of National Socialism over the treatment of the Poles was always likely. An early sign was when General Halder recorded in his diary on 19 September 1939 that Reinhard Heydrich of the SS had said that "housecleaning" would now take place in Poland of the "Jews, intelligentsia, clergy, nobility."

However, Halder wrote that the "Army insists that 'housecleaning' be deferred until army has withdrawn and the country has been turned over to civil administration. Early December."[12] ("Housecleaning," of course, was one of many different euphemisms the Nazis were subsequently to use during the war to describe their atrocities. And, as we have seen, this "housecleaning" certainly wasn't "deferred" until December. In fact, one estimate is that 50,000 Poles had been executed by the Germans by the end of 1939.)[13]

Halder was informed by General Eduard Wagner, after a meeting with Hitler, that Poland was to become a land of "cheap slaves"[14] and that the army must confine itself to "military matters." The aim was to create "total disorganisation" within Poland. Halder called this a "devilish plan" in his diary. Significantly, the day before Halder wrote this entry, 17 October 1939, Hitler had ordered that the SS and other non-army security units should be considered as outside of the jurisdiction of the army. If the army leadership now saw the SS doing something they disliked in Poland they no longer had any legal way of pursuing the perpetrators.

Nazi-occupied western Poland—not forgetting that eastern Poland was in the hands of the Soviets, who were pursuing their own "devilish plan" of ethnic re-organisation—was to be divided into two. One section, "the General Government" centred on Krakow and, under the control of Nazi stalwart Hans Frank, was to be a kind of dumping ground holding those excluded from life in the Reich, whilst the other was to be incorporated into Germany. This German portion was further divided into several new districts or *Gaue*. The two biggest were Danzig/Western Prussia ruled by Albert Forster and the Warthegau, under Arthur Greiser. These men, both *Gauleiters*, or district leaders, plus their respective higher SS comanders, were charged with racially re-ordering Poland in the most brutal way imaginable. General Johannes Blaskowitz, the army commander in Poland, was all but sidelined.

This didn't stop Hans Frank taking an intense dislike to Blaskowitz and his leadership of the army in Poland. When Goebbels visited Frank on 2 November 1939 the Nazi governor complained that the German army in Poland were not "racially aware"[15] and were hindering him in his work. The dislike was mutual. Helmuth Stieff, a German staff officer, was appalled at the effects of Frank's rule of the General Government when he visited Warsaw in November 1939. "The bulk of the millions of popu-

lation of the city eke out a miserable existence somewhere and somehow,"
he wrote to his wife, "one cannot tell what they live on. It is an unspeak-
able tragedy that is unfolding there. One has also no idea how [long]
this will go on . . . It is a city and a population which is doomed . . . it is
depressing if you are in a beautiful hotel room eating roast goose and at
the same time see how women, who used to have important roles perhaps
only three months ago, sell themselves for a loaf of bread to our soldiers
in order to live their miserable life a little longer . . . The extermination
of entire generations of women and children is possible only by subhu-
mans that no longer deserve the name German. I am ashamed of being a
German."[16]

At the end of his letter, Steiff mentioned that he had met with General Blaskowitz who had "poured his heart out to me and told me about
his concerns and worries." But it seems unlikely at this stage that Blaskowitz blamed Hitler directly for the crimes he knew were being committed in Poland. Blaskowitz seems to have been on a similar trajectory of
discovery as General Beck had been before him. At least initially, it was
much easier for both Beck and Blaskowitz—much less a matter of searing
self-reproach—to act as if the blame for these atrocities lay at the door of
the SS or other Nazi party fanatics rather than the German head of state.
Even if, in their hearts, they might have thought otherwise.

During the autumn of 1939 Blaskowitz gathered evidence of the crimes
the SS were committing in Poland and then, finally, on 16 November he
submitted a report to the Head of the German Army, Brauchitsch. The
document then passed to Hitler's military adjutant, Major Gerhard Engel,
who showed it to Hitler. No copies remain of Blaskowitz's report, but we
do know Hitler's reaction to it, because Engel recorded his response. "He
takes the note calmly at first, but then starts off again with serious allegations against the 'childish attitudes' in the leadership of the army. You do
not lead a war with Salvation Army methods. Also, a long-held aversion
became confirmed. He had never trusted General Blaskowitz. He had also
been against his appointment to the command of an army and deems it
right to remove Blaskowitz, because unsuitable, from this post."[17]

Yet Blaskowitz was not relieved of his command. Halder and
Brauchitsch simply ignored Hitler's views. Blaskowitz was able to stay in
his job in Poland in the face of strident criticism from the man who was
not only head of state, but head of the German armed forces as well. Just

as before the war, Hitler felt unable to exercise the kind of control over army appointments that Stalin did.

Blaskowitz's report turned up at one of the toughest moments in Hitler's relationship with his generals. Difficulties had been growing since a meeting he had held with his senior military commanders just under three months before, on 27 September 1939. It was at least as dramatic an encounter as the one in November 1937 at which Hitler had declared that war was all but inevitable. Because now Hitler announced that he wanted "immediate plans"[18] to be drawn up for an attack against France. This was devastating news to the army commanders. Just a few weeks before they had been hoping that Britain and France would stay out of the war completely, and they still feared an attack from the West. Germany was especially vulnerable at this moment, given that the bulk of German forces were still in eastern Europe. And now, instead of calling for a period of retrenchment and then hopefully coming to some kind of peaceful accommodation with Britain and France, Hitler was telling them that they should prepare for an invasion of France as soon as possible.

It's difficult to grasp today how wild Hitler's idea must have sounded to these generals. Because we all know the eventual result—a dramatic German victory in the spring of 1940—there is a tendency to read history backwards and to think that somehow an invasion of France would have seemed a sensible option for the Germans at the time. It didn't. The British and French not only possessed more tanks than the Germans, their tanks were better. The French had the Char B tank with a 75mm cannon and 60mm of armour, far superior to any fighting vehicle the Germans used at the time. In addition, as Professor Adam Tooze says, a careful study of the German armaments programme around this time reveals that Hitler's thinking was still resolutely old-fashioned. "If we look in closer focus at the first months of the war, the extraordinary thing is that the programmes that Hitler prioritises in the initial months of the war are not an increased speed of build-up for the tank arm but, in fact, a huge ammunitions programme which is designed to avoid the munitions crisis which had crippled the German offensive in the autumn of 1914. So he's an infantryman of the First World War, and well remembers the crisis of German ammunition supply which had allegedly bogged down the German army in the first phase of the First World War. And that's the Führer challenge of December 1939, not to increase production of tanks but to triple the production of ammunition in the next six months. So the kind of war that Hitler even at that point seems to envision is a slogging match to the Channel."[19]

It was thus scarcely credible to the German general staff—almost all of whom had bitter personal experience of the last "slogging match to the Channel"—that Hitler could contemplate a swift invasion of France. Senior army officers agreed amongst themselves that it simply wasn't possible—one estimate of the earliest such an offensive could be contemplated was 1942.[20]

In this assessment they shared the opinion of their enemies. The French, in particular, were supremely confident of victory over the Germans, with some even thinking that the Nazi regime would soon fall apart without the need for outside intervention. One contemporary report from the military intelligence experts of the *Deuxième Bureau* (France's external military intelligence agency) said that, "According to intelligence from good sources, the Hitler regime will continue to hold power until the spring of 1940—then be replaced by Communism."[21]

The crisis deepened when Hitler, infuriated by the lack of enthusiasm shown by his generals for an attack on France, harangued them once again on 10 October. Just as he had at the infamous November 1937 meeting, he read from a lengthy prepared manuscript. Once again he was demonstrating an extraordinary style of leadership; he had decided entirely on his own what was best for Germany and the job of his generals was merely one of implementation. There had been no prior consultation with his military experts before he arrived at his decision, no logistical analysis to see if his goal was even possible.

At one level this leadership technique was effective. It served to demonstrate that Hitler believed he was a "unique genius," a charismatic leader who did not need the input of others. It also knocked the confidence of anyone who opposed him—they were continually forced to react to Hitler's views rather than participating in the policy decision beforehand. However, it was also high risk. At this stage of the war, Hitler relied to a large extent on the power of his own persuasive techniques to control his military high command. And so when he couldn't persuade his audience that he was right, he encountered difficulties that other, less charismatic, dictators never had to confront.

Having failed to convince his generals that an attack on France was sensible, Hitler now faced growing opposition. An insight into General Halder's state of mind is provided by his diary entry for 14 October 1939. After a meeting with Brauchitsch he wrote: "Three possibilities: attack, wait, change."[22] By "change," Halder and Brauchitsch meant a change in leadership—the sidelining, if not the complete removal, of Adolf Hitler. There was a recent precedent for this kind of action. During the First World War two senior German commanders—Ludendorff and Hindenburg—had taken control of all strategic military decisions, leaving Kaiser Wilhelm II on the periphery of power. And it had been another general—Wilhelm Groener—who had delivered the news to the Kaiser in November 1918 that he should abdicate. But Halder and Brauchitsch also recognised that none of the options they had in front of them were ideal—especially if they opted for "change," since "it is essentially negative and tends to render us vulnerable."[23]

Halder and Brauchitsch did not think that an invasion of France was out of the question on moral or legal grounds. They simply thought that the German army was not up to the task in the immediate future. They thus objected not to fighting a war of aggression in the west—merely to losing it. And they were not alone in thinking this. On 3 November Halder wrote, "None of the Higher Hq [i.e., Headquarters] thinks that the offensive ordered by OKW [i.e., the supreme command of the armed forces who worked directly with Hitler] has any prospect of success."[24] Brauchitsch and Halder now, however reluctantly, contemplated a coup against Hitler.

Meanwhile, many of the old familiar faces from the aborted coup attempt the previous year—included Ludwig Beck—also plotted to stop Hitler taking Germany into a disastrous war against the French. One idea was for units loyal to the conspirators to march on Hitler's headquarters and arrest him after the attack in the west had been launched. Hitler would be removed and Beck would become the new head of the German state.[25]

When Brauchitsch saw Hitler on 5 November he attempted to persuade him that the army was not ready for an attack on France, and said that the invasion of Poland had revealed a number of problems with discipline. He even compared the attitude of the Wehrmacht in 1939 with that of the German army towards the end of the First World War. Hitler—predictably—lost his temper. He threatened to travel immediately to the front and find out what was going on himself. Even more worrying for Brauchitsch was Hitler's assertion that the army lacked the will to go into battle as he wished. Hitler talked about the "spirit of Zossen"[26] (the army wartime headquarters was close to the village of Zossen, south of Berlin) and said he would obliterate this defeatism. Devastated by Hitler's attack, Brauchitsch said after the meeting that he would take no active part in any coup. Halder, worried that Hitler suspected senior officers were plotting against him, also gave up the idea of leading a plot against the Führer.

It was a revealing moment. Brauchitsch had heard nothing during the 5 November meeting with Hitler to make him less anxious about the proposed Western offensive. In fact, the situation for Halder and Brauchitsch grew worse later that same day, since the order to invade France was issued by Hitler shortly after the meeting—with the attack due to start on 12 November. Yet now, even with the knowledge that Hitler had named the day for the launch of this massive campaign they felt the Germans would lose, they failed to act.

Their fundamental misjudgement had been to think that any action against Hitler would be analogous with the sidelining and eventual ejection of the Kaiser twenty-one years before. Unlike the Kaiser, Hitler was still considered a trusted leader by millions of Germans. Although the Germans were at war with the British and French, and there was uncertainty and concern about how this war would end, the Führer had also orchestrated the swift defeat of the Poles and the re-incorporation into the Reich of Danzig and the Polish corridor, as well as all the territory lost to Poland at Versailles. As a result, some—like Walter Mauth, then sixteen years old—thought, "When the war with Poland was over within three weeks . . . we thought we were unbeatable."[27]

Further evidence of just how popular Hitler was with the general German population was on show that November as a result of events in Munich. Three days after his ill-tempered meeting with Brauchitsch, Hitler arrived in Munich for the sixteenth anniversary of the Beer Hall Putsch. He gave a speech at the Bürgerbräukeller and then hurried back to Munich station to take the train to Berlin. Around ten minutes after he left the Bürgerbräukeller a bomb, concealed in a pillar, exploded. Over several months, Georg Elser, a carpenter, had managed to work secretly during the night at the beer cellar and had concealed the bomb just behind the rostrum where Hitler was to speak. Elser, a former supporter of the German Communist party who was angry about the war, had decided that the only way to improve Germany's situation was to kill Hitler and other Nazi leaders.

Elser was a lone assassin who had acted without help from others. Hitler was lucky to survive, and he put his escape down to the actions of his own personal providence once again. But what's significant is the public reaction to news of the attempt to murder Hitler. One report compiled by the SD, the intelligence branch of the SS, revealed that, "The attempted assassination in Munich has strengthened the notion of togetherness within the German population greatly," and that, "love for the Führer has grown even more . . . "[28] Another report, from December 1939, said that, "Ever since the outbreak of the war and especially after the attempted assassination in Munich, many shop-owners have taken to putting up images of the Führer in their window-displays. In some cases this tribute to the Führer is still carried out in a most distasteful way. A window of a shop for spirits in Kiel for example is reported to display the Führer's image amidst numerous bottles of spirits with the slogan, 'We will never surrender!' "[29]

At one level this enthusiastic support for Hitler is not surprising. For more than six years Goebbels' propaganda had been pumping out the message that Hitler was a quasi-mystical figure whose presence was essential for Germany's future success and security. That, plus the succession of foreign policy triumphs before the outbreak of war, all cast a long shadow. It was also possible for many people to still revere Hitler yet to be anxious about the war and the effects of economic measures—like the recent War Economy Decree—which materially affected their earnings.

What is less obvious is why the various small groups of plotters didn't fully grasp from the start that—unlike the Kaiser—Hitler still had access to this immense reservoir of trust and reverence. Charismatic leadership is strengthened and reinforced by success, and Hitler had not yet failed. This was the lesson that General Wilhelm Ritter von Leeb learnt when he tried to rally support for a coup against Hitler in the wake of the crushing of Brauchitsch at the 5 November meeting. The date Hitler had fixed for the invasion, 12 November, had been postponed because of new intelligence about the weather and concerns over Allied troop movements—in fact, it was to be rescheduled and then postponed many times more before the eventual start date of 10 May 1940.

However, at the end of 1939, conflict with France still seemed imminent. Von Leeb called the planned attack in the west "mad."[30] He was also outraged at the atrocities in Poland. He protested to Halder that the German "police" actions in Poland were "unworthy of a civilised nation."[31] Von Leeb tried to enlist the help of fellow generals, Bock and Rundstedt, in preparing a coup—but neither was interested. And ultimately it was one of Leeb's own officers, corps commander General Geyr von Schweppenburg,[32] who remarked that it was possible that the ordinary soldiers and junior officers would simply refuse to move against Hitler. This was a judgement confirmed, after the war, by another senior German officer in the west, Walther Nehring, who said that it would have been "futile" to order his men to turn against the regime because "amongst the majority of the young soldiers, Hitler's prestige was already entrenched too deeply."[33]

On 23 November, Hitler spoke to about two hundred senior military leaders at the Reich Chancellery, the latest in a series of attempts to enthuse his generals about the forthcoming conflict in the west. It was an open contest between Hitler's vision on the one hand and the people he knew were necessary to implement this vision on the other. And Hitler knew this was a battle he had to win.

Once again, all of Hitler's familiar techniques of persuasion were evident. Crucial was the sense that he, as an individual, was the only person who really mattered. "The fate of the Reich depends only on me,"[34] he said, portraying himself as the charismatic warlord sent to save Germany. And, as before, he announced he had come before his generals, "to tell" them of his decisions.

His speech contained a history lesson—designed to demonstrate how he had previously been proved right by events, even though others had doubted him—and smatterings of his own brutal philosophy: "In fighting I see the fate of all creatures. Nobody can avoid fighting if he does not want to go under." He said his mission was clear—to obtain *Lebensraum* for a people who desperately needed it.

It was this kind of talk that led Hugh Trevor-Roper in his essay "The Mind of Adolf Hitler" to conclude that for Hitler "the purpose of human life" was "merely that Germans should be the masters of the world" and that "to him it was simply a question of more cakes for Germans and less for non-Germans."[35] But that is to underestimate Hitler's appeal to his generals. He offered not just a practical goal—that Germans must conquer more territory—but a philosophical justification: that life is a permanent struggle and we are all animals who must fight or die. It was a call to release the beast that lurked inside every human being. The speech is replete with the word "annihilate"—Hitler said he sought "to annihilate everyone who is opposed to me . . . I want to annihilate the enemy." Long before he announced what is generally considered his "war of annihilation" against the Soviet Union, Hitler is seen here wanting to practise "annihilation" in the west. Moreover, his speech was also a call to seek sanctuary in the certainty of absolutes. "I have to choose between victory or annihilation," he said. "I choose victory." As we have seen, this posing of "either/or" choices was one of Hitler's common tactics, as was his threat to kill himself if events went against him: "I shall never survive the defeat of my people."

Hitler obviously felt this lengthy speech had not been enough to motivate Brauchitsch and Halder, and so called them to his office after the conference in order to restate his unhappiness with the attitude of the army leadership, referring once more to the "spirit of Zossen."[36] Brauchitsch "offered to resign"[37] but Hitler told him to stay and do his "duty."

Meanwhile, Halder and his colleagues had been reluctantly planning the invasion in the West—even though they believed they had no chance of success. They were right to be so negative. If the Germans had invaded following the plans as they existed at the start of November, the result would have been either immediate defeat or the kind of stalemate that bled Germany dry on the Western Front during the First World War. Gradually, however, the plans began to change. More resources started to be devoted to von Rundstedt's Army Group A, the force which had always been charged with protecting the southern flank of Bock's Army Group B as it moved to subdue Holland and attack Belgium. Nonetheless, by the time of Hitler's conference on 23 November, "Case Yellow" (*"Fall Gelb"*), as the attack plan was called, was still a mishmash with neither army group designated as the priority force.

General Erich von Manstein now argued that the only way to have a chance of defeating the Allies in France—as opposed to creating a period of impasse—was to make Army Group A the dominant offensive force. He proposed that Bock's Army Group B invade Belgium in an attempt to convince the Allies that they were the main German attacking force, whilst the armoured units of group A further south would travel through the forest of the Ardennes, cross the river Meuse and make a dash for the Channel coast where the river Somme meets the sea. Huge numbers of British and French soldiers would then be trapped between the two pincers of group A and group B. However, as Professor Adam Tooze says, "This is an operation of unprecedented logistical risk and gives the opponents of Germany—Britain, France, Belgium and Holland—the chance, if they're sufficiently well organised, to mount a devastating counterattack on Germany and on the pincer moving across northern France. And for this reason the Germans fully understand that if this plan fails they've lost the war . . . The gamble bears the possibility of total victory . . . but also a risk of catastrophic defeat, which they're fully conscious of."[38]

Despite—or most likely because of—the immenseness of the risk, this became the plan that Hitler favoured, after Manstein had lobbied him personally about it. The idea of armoured units operating at speed had been developed by General Guderian in his book *Achtung Panzer!* published two years before, and Halder had seen in Poland how important it was for armoured units to lead the attack. So there were various hands on the development of the final draft of Plan Yellow—and happenstance played a part too when the Allies found a copy of the original, conventional plan of attack after a German plane crashed in Belgium in January 1940. As a result the Germans felt it prudent to change the nature of the forthcoming offensive.

Nonetheless, the fundamental reason why this revolutionary approach to the invasion of France was adopted was the will of Adolf Hitler. Hitler always set a vision—in this case "invade the West"—and then sought ideas of how this could be implemented in detail from others. But what he had also done was to demonstrate time and again his attraction to the all-or-nothing gamble. The occupation of the Rhineland, the *Anschluss,* the Munich crisis—all involved risking the fate of Germany. Hitler saw his ability to take risks as another sign of the greatness of his leadership and had contempt for those who chose the safe options in life. "The men of Munich," he said in August 1939, "will not take the risk."[39] It was precisely Hitler's near addiction to risk that so disturbed traditional officers like Ludwig Beck. However, there were others who felt that this very quality meant that Hitler would be open to new ideas.

Another feature of Hitler's leadership that underpinned all these discussions about the invasion of France would come much more obviously to the fore after the Germans' triumphant victory. Hitler offered Germans not only excitement and the chance to make history, but linked this with the idea that one should act now, today, this moment. Hitler often referred to the fact that he only had one brief life in order to accomplish his aims—and he feared he would not reach old age. He was in a hurry, and he conveyed that sense of urgency to everyone around him. And this was exacerbated by his lack of belief in an afterlife. The sub-text of many of his speeches around this period is clear—you have one life, you will die and be extinguished forever whether you spend your time taking huge and exciting risks with the intention of changing the world, or working quietly in an office. You decide. A boring life or a thrilling one—both lead to an eternity of nothingness. It was obvious which road Hitler wished to travel. As he said at the end of his 23 November speech to his generals, "I have decided to live my life so that I can stand unashamed when I have to die."

Moreover, the plan appealed to Hitler's desire to surprise his enemy. "The factor of surprise is half the battle,"[40] said Hitler later. "That's why one cannot go on repeating an operation indefinitely, simply because it has been successful." And Hitler had recognised as early as October 1939, long before he heard of the Manstein plan, that his opponents in the West were particularly vulnerable to the unexpected. "The Führer emphasises that we must not fall back into the tactics of linear battles of the [First] World War," wrote General von Bock in his diary on 25 October, "that we had to force the enemy through fast, sharp attacks and swift advances of motorised and tank units to operate and act quickly, [something] which was not in the nature of both the systematic French and the ponderous Englishman."[41]

It was this insight that was to prove vital in the battle to come. Subsequent wargaming of the Manstein plan at the German army headquarters at Zossen confirmed that the whole offensive turned on one single question: how soon would the Allies recognise that the main thrust of attack was not through Belgium but the Ardennes? If the Germans were not across the River Meuse in eastern France in four days then the British and French would have time to realise what was happening and divert substantial forces to stop them. It was already clear in the planning stage that the city of Sedan, which straddled the Meuse, would be crucial. Take

Sedan and be across the Meuse swiftly and there was no insuperable natural obstacle facing Army Group A all the way to the French coast at the bay of the Somme. (Here, in the context of the decision of the German leadership to embrace this radical version of Plan Yellow, history also played a part. The German armed forces existed in the shadow of the First World War and Manstein's plan was a chance to avenge that loss—not just to defeat the French but to humiliate them.)

Ultimately, Hitler hoped, it did not matter if the Allies possessed more tanks than the Germans—as long as those tanks remained in the wrong place. This, of course, was the aspect of the gamble that was to pay off spectacularly. The Allies were brimming with over-confidence about the fight to come and this over-confidence was to prove their undoing. So arrogant was General Maurice Gamelin, the commander of the French armed forces, that he had told his senior officers back in September 1939 that if the Germans attacked in the spring of 1940 then he was certain of victory.[42]

Equally confident of victory was Adolf Hitler. Indeed, one of the many remarkable aspects of the planning for the attack on France was that the one constant throughout all of the variations of tactics and strategy was Hitler's certainty that all would come well. General Halder recorded in his diary on 17 March that Hitler was "manifestly confident of success"[43]—this against a background of deep anxiety from many individual German commanders. On 14 February Halder wrote that Generals Guderian and von Wietersheim "plainly show lack of confidence"[44] in the operation, and on 25 February he headed his entry on a meeting with Fedor von Bock, who was to command Army Group B in the attack, with the single word, "Worries."[45]

Before Plan Yellow went ahead Hitler sprang another surprise on the Allies—the Germans invaded Denmark and Norway. Hitler knew it was essential for the health of the German war machine to protect iron ore supplies from neutral Sweden, most of which reached Germany via the Norwegian port of Narvik. There had long been rumours about a possible Allied attack in Scandinavia and, as it transpired, the German action, starting on 9 April, coincided almost exactly with an attempt by the British to mine Norwegian waters.

On land the Germans triumphed in Denmark within hours and made swift gains in Norway, but at sea the *Kriegsmarine* lost more than a dozen warships. Nonetheless, despite this success for the Royal Navy, Allied soldiers failed to defeat the Germans in Norway and the subsequent controversy about the failure of the Norwegian campaign led to the resignation of Chamberlain and the appointment of Winston Churchill as British Prime Minister on 10 May 1940—coincidentally the same day that the German invasion of France and the Low Countries began.

The Wehrmacht attacked the Allies with 112 divisions, less than 10 per cent of them armoured, and to begin with both the British and French thought that the Germans were behaving exactly as expected. The early movement of Bock's Army Group B into neutral Belgium confirmed to General Gamelin that his assessment that the main thrust of attack would be in the north was correct. One French officer who saw him that day remembers Gamelin walking about humming with a contended expression on his face.[46] It seemed logical, to the French and British, that the Germans would attack both into Belgium and Holland in order to gain air bases from which to attack Great Britain.

Allied forces advanced, as planned, into Belgium in order to engage the enemy. By 14 May, at the battles of Hannut and Breda, the French had more than held their own against the Germans. However, there were already signs that action could be expected elsewhere. By 12 May, reports of the massive advance of German Army Group A through the Ardennes forest had reached the Allies, though this was initially dismissed as a flanking manoeuvre to support the main area of conflict in Belgium. But soon it was obvious that the Germans were threatening Sedan and intended to cross the River Meuse. On 13 May, Gamelin learnt that some German units had already crossed the Meuse to the north of Sedan, via the weir at Houx. That same day the Luftwaffe launched an intense and concentrated bombardment in Sedan. And by 14 May the Germans had succeeded in crossing the Meuse at several places along the river. It was devastating news for the French. One officer witnessed the commander of the north-eastern front, General Alphonse-Joseph Georges, break down in tears as he said "there have been some failures"[47] at Sedan. The next day, the Prime Minister of France, Paul Reynaud, rang Winston Churchill at 7:30 in the morning. Churchill picked up the phone by his bedside to hear Reynaud say "evidently under stress" the words, "We have been defeated . . . We are beaten; we have lost the battle."[48]

It was an extraordinary moment in military history. Almost, as Paul-

Émile Caton put it in the title of his book about the Battle for France, *Une Guerre Perdue en 4 Jours*—"A War Lost in 4 Days."[49] And it is scarcely possible to exaggerate the effect of this swift triumph over the Allies on the collective German psyche. Erwin Rommel, who had petitioned Hitler to be allowed command of a panzer division in the attack, remarked that what had happened was "hardly conceivable." Tanks from his 7th Panzer division, a spearhead unit of Army Group A, "had broken through and were driving deep into enemy territory. It was not just a beautiful dream. It was reality."[50]

This "beautiful dream" had been made possible not only by Hitler's insistence on the adoption of the risky Manstein plan and a catalogue of failures by the Allies, but by the use of an innovative method of command—one previously developed by the Prussian Army and which now meshed perfectly with the way Hitler operated his own leadership. The Prussian Army, as Professor Robert Citino says, developed a "certain kind of military culture" that arose out of "Prussia's geography, traditions, and position within Europe and relative lack of resources. So this was a state that almost always tried to fight so-called 'short and lively' wars, a term in fact coined by Frederick the Great in the eighteenth century. 'Short and lively' wars which were translated into relatively rapid victories over the enemy's main force within the first six or eight weeks of the fighting . . . I think this was always what set Germany apart from its neighbours, it was a state that was crammed into a relatively uncomfortable spot in Central Europe with a relatively low base of resources and certainly a smaller population than the coalition of enemies that Germany could potentially be fighting."[51]

This necessity to fight "short and lively" wars in turn meant that commanders on the battlefield could never rely on tried and tested defensive tactics. As Citino says, "Frederick the Great back in the eighteenth century laid out Prussian tactical doctrine in a pithy sense: the Prussian army always attacks. He had a standing order for his cavalry forces that they must always get their charge in first and not wait to be charged by the enemy. That notion of a kind of bulldog level of aggression coupled with a rapidity of manoeuvre had been a German tradition for a good long time."

In parallel with this "bulldog" approach to war, the German army developed a concept of *Auftragstaktik* or mission command. More so than

any of their opponents, the German army practised delegation. Battlefield commanders were given objectives to fulfil but thereafter permitted a level of independent decision-making that was unheard of in the
British or French armies. Rommel's own actions during the invasion of
France perfectly exemplify the German method of making war. Units of
Rommel's 7th Panzer were amongst the first to cross the River Meuse at
Houx on 12 May—much to the astonishment of the Allies, since around
the hamlet of Houx the Meuse runs through a deep gorge which makes
this ideal defensive territory. Soldiers of the French Ninth Army had dug
in on the opposite bank ready to fight. But a series of decisions Rommel and his men made on the spot—from setting fire to several houses
to create a smokescreen, to organising a rope and pulley system over the
river—helped make the crossing of the Meuse a possibility. Above all,
Rommel was following the Prussian doctrine of acting swiftly and with
surprise. The French commanders had anticipated that they would have
several days to prepare their defences, having blown up all the bridges
over the Meuse. Thanks to Rommel's speed of movement they had only
hours.

Rommel, though an exceptional general, was in reality doing no more
than was expected of all German battlefield commanders—even down to
NCOs. As General Manstein wrote after the war, "The German method
is really rooted in the German character, which—contrary to all the non-
sense talked about 'blind obedience'—has a strong streak of individuality
and, possibly as part of its Germanic heritage, finds certain pleasure in
taking risks."[52]

Whilst on a number of occasions we have seen how German generals were initially appalled at the extent of the risks Hitler was prepared
to run on issues of grand strategy—as shown by both the Hossbach
meeting in 1937 and his decision to invade France—paradoxically, at
the operational level, the German army valued the ability of the individual commander to take calculated risks in battle on his own initiative.
Indeed, *Auftragstaktik*—in the sense of "mission command"—had also
been a core principle of Hitler's own leadership in the domestic field. "I
never had a conference with Schacht [German minister of economics in
the 1930s]," said Hitler, "to discover what means were at our disposal. I
restricted myself to saying simply, 'This is what I require, and this is what
I must have.'"[53] A core part of Hitler's charismatic leadership was thus

his desire for his subordinates to choose the way they wanted to fulfil his grand vision—the essence of the military doctrine of *Auftragstaktik*.

All this was in stark contrast, in May 1940, to the way some of the solders in the Allied armies were led. Edward Oates, for example, was serving with the British Royal Engineers in France and he experienced at first hand the lack of *Auftragstaktik* during the retreat: "I can remember some Belgians, they'd got brass helmets and there was quite a few of them, and they said, you know, 'We want an officer. If we can have an officer we'll fight, but we don't know what to do' . . . I was [also] a bit surprised, I suppose, that the French army gave up so easily, but I hadn't even thought about it. We were just ordinary soldiers and we did what we were told. We hadn't got any strategy or thoughts about where you fought battles or anything, we were just there."[54]

But whilst at the grand strategic level Hitler was keen to take risks and embrace the concept of surprise, there were signs that if events did not transpire exactly as he had expected on the battlefield he could be both timid and indecisive. Goebbels, as we have already noted, was one of a number of Nazi leaders who had identified this characteristic in Hitler before the war.[55] Now his generals witnessed the same qualities. During the Norwegian operation, for example, General Walter Warlimont felt Hitler had shown "truly terrifying weakness of character"[56] after events did not go to plan, and now on 17 May when Hitler announced that Army Group A was vulnerable to flank attack, Halder recorded, "The Führer is terribly nervous. Frightened by his own success, he is afraid to take any chance and so would rather pull the reins on us."[57] The next morning Hitler raged and screamed at Halder and ordered the advance west stopped, only to change his mind at six in the evening. "So the right thing is being done after all," wrote Halder, "but in an atmosphere of bad feeling . . . "[58]

At first sight these two qualities in Hitler—risk-taking and indecision allied with apparent timidity—seem at odds with each other. That was certainly how Halder saw it. On 6 June 1940, towards the end of the campaign in France, he wrote that Hitler thought the plans of the High Command were too "hazardous" and that he wanted to play "absolutely safe." Halder had problems reconciling this attitude with his previous experience of Hitler as the all or nothing gambler: " . . . there just isn't a spark of the spirit that would dare put high stakes on a single throw."[59]

But Halder was wrong. These two aspects of Hitler's leadership were not polar opposites but both consequences of the way Hitler's decision-making process worked. As we have seen, Hitler decided on policy in a way that would be anathema to many of those in power today. Instead of consulting with interested parties, reviewing options and then arriving at a considered decision, Hitler shut himself alone in his room and waited for inspiration. "The spirit of decision does not mean acting at all costs," he said. "The spirit of decision consists simply in not hesitating when an inner conviction commands you to act."[60] Once his "inner conviction" had told him what to do, Hitler then used all of his powers of persuasion to convince those around him that this was the correct and logical way forward. But one of the many problems with this way of deciding what to do was that it was ill suited to structured day-to-day meetings where countless small decisions had to be taken. How could Hitler wait for his "inner conviction" to reveal itself on issues like the exact movements of one particular division of the German army? The solution, of course, would have been for Hitler to let Halder and the others at Army High Command headquarters make these decisions themselves whilst working towards the overall vision that he had set by virtue of this "inner conviction." But he couldn't do this. And the reason is not hard to find—his lack of trust in their decision-making capability. Had not the handful of people now trying to run this campaign at the highest level, chiefly Halder and Brauchitsch, been the ones who had been so against the invasion of France in the first place?

It's ironic, against that background, that the greatest popular example of Hitler's micro-management and timidity during this campaign—the decision to halt German forces in front of Dunkirk on 24 May—was not Hitler's decision at all. As Professor Sir Ian Kershaw says, Hitler "was actually agreeing to the suggestion put forward by the commander of the German forces in the West, General—rapidly to become Field Marshal—von Rundstedt, who then wanted to preserve the tanks for what they saw as their greater need, which was to destroy the French troops by moving south against them. And Göring had promised Hitler that the British troops would be bombed to bits from the air anyway. So for 24 hours Hitler went along with that decision, realised subsequently it was a mistake and then backtracked from it, but by then it was too late and the British were on their way to getting away from Dunkirk. But it was actually

Hitler at that stage still going along with the advice of his generals, not overriding it as he came to do increasingly as the war went on."[61]

As a result of the German delay in moving on Dunkirk, more than 800 civilian vessels—fishing boats, pleasure steamers, tugs—arrived to help the Royal Navy ferry the troops across the Channel to England. In all, more than 330,000 Allied soldiers were rescued. The British government had initially thought only about 40,000 could be saved. But, still, the situation looked bleak for the Allies. Not only had France fallen to the Germans within six weeks, with the armistice signed on 22 June, but the British had been forced to retreat with little more than the clothes they stood up in. "All their vehicles have been left on the beach," says military historian Professor Geoffrey Wawro. "Most of their field artillery, anti-tank guns, ammunition, fuel stocks, all have been left to the Germans. So it's going to take an awful long time to build them up, and in fact you're going to see old, antiquated vehicles running around in the Western Desert because the good stuff was all left behind at Dunkirk."[62]

In June 1940 Hitler was enjoying the high point of his entire career. The French, Norwegians, Danish, Belgians and Dutch were all under German rule—and this tremendous conquest had been achieved in a matter of weeks. More than 1.2 million prisoners of war had been captured and the Germans had suffered a loss of fewer than 50,000 casualties.[63] Keitel, as a result of all this success, would now call Hitler *Grösster Feldherr aller Zeiten*—"the greatest military leader of all time." Hitler now only faced one problem—the British. Their refusal to do what he wanted would test his charismatic leadership as never before.

13

CHARISMA AND OVERCONFIDENCE

On 6 July 1940 Hitler drove back into Berlin, after overseeing the capitulation of France, to scenes of joy bordering on hysteria. Hundreds of thousands of Berliners crammed the streets to cheer him. Schoolboys climbed lampposts to see their Führer. Flowers were strewn under his car. A forest of waving swastika flags lined the route. All of this elation, all of this ecstasy was focused on this one, slight, individual. If Hitler had not thought before that he was an infallible figure sent by Providence to gain greatness for Germany, then surely he must have believed it at this moment.

We can get an insight into Hitler's mentality in the wake of the fall of France by the views he expressed a few weeks before, when he went on an early-morning tour of Paris. After visiting the most important tourist sites—including the Pantheon, the Opéra and Napoleon's tomb—Hitler told Albert Speer that he had "often considered whether we would not have to destroy Paris" because the city was beautiful and was thus a rival to Berlin. But he had now decided not to annihilate the French capital because one day the greatness of Berlin would make Paris "only . . . a shadow" by comparison. Speer thought these words demonstrated that Hitler "contained a multitude of selves, from a person deeply aware of

his responsibilities all the way to a ruthless and mankind-hating nihilist."¹
But a better view might be that this incident showed Hitler wallowing in
the immensity of his individual power. He—and he alone—could now
decide if one of the most glorious cities on earth would continue to exist.

Hitler's self-confidence, his self-belief was simply overweening. So
much so that he felt able to announce at a meeting with his military
commanders in late July 1940 that since Britain's position was "hopeless"
then "the war is won by us."² It's a moment that perfectly encapsulates
the advantages and disadvantages of charismatic leadership. Because the
very qualities that had allowed Hitler to play such a pivotal role in the victory over France would now turn out to be the very qualities that would
help ensure Germany's slide into defeat. Hitler, over the next months,
would demonstrate just where overconfidence born of charismatic leadership can lead.

The central problem the Germans now faced was that Britain did not
accept that the war was lost. In a speech to the Reichstag on 9 July Hitler
made an "an appeal to reason" to England (by which he meant Britain)
claiming that he saw "no compelling reason"³ for the war to continue. But
it was an "appeal" that the British were destined to reject. During a series
of meetings of the War Cabinet held several weeks before, at the lowest
point of British fortunes when it was thought that many fewer soldiers
would escape from France than eventually did, Churchill had debated
with his colleagues what Britain's stance should be and then orchestrated
a decision to fight on against Germany. Churchill's persuasive logic had
been that under any peace treaty signed immediately in the wake of the
defeat of France, Hitler would demand the effective disarmament of Britain and as a result the country would be "completely at his mercy." Consequently, said Churchill, "we should get no worse terms if we went on
fighting, even if we were beaten, than were open to us now."⁴

Hitler now had discussions⁵ with Grand Admiral Raeder about the
possibility of a seaborne invasion on the south coast of England, but the
evidence is that both men doubted that such an action was practicable.
And they were right to have such doubts. As Professor Adam Tooze says,
"They [the Germans] hadn't started thinking about a war with Britain,
let alone an invasion, until May 1938. The naval armaments programme
doesn't get into gear until January 1939. For the preceding five years Britain had been outspending Germany on the navy so the already enormous

gap between the German navy and the British navy in 1933 had not been shrinking but growing larger every year. So when they then also go on to lose the vast majority of their modern naval forces in the Norwegian debacle which, from a German naval point of view, is a catastrophe, they essentially do not have a surface navy with which to protect an invasion in the summer of 1940."[6]

Against this background, Hitler's "War Directive No. 16" which called for the preparation of "Operation Sea Lion" (*Unternehmen Seelöwe*)—the invasion of Britain—is a work of almost ludicrous optimism. It stated that before the attack could take place the Royal Air Force needed to be so damaged that it posed no appreciable threat to the invasion, and that the Straits of Dover had to be "sealed" by mines to prevent the Royal Navy attacking the Germans as they crossed the Channel. But, as Andrew Roberts says, "even in the event that the RAF was neutralised . . . I don't think the Germans were going to be able to invade successfully in 1940. I think that the actual plans needed to get an army across the Channel were just not in place. There weren't enough of those flat-bottom boats, they weren't particularly seaworthy and if the Royal Navy had got amongst them there would have been a massacre."[7] None of which, of course, is to denigrate the sacrifice made by "the Few" during the Battle of Britain that summer and early autumn, but only to acknowledge that both Hitler and Grand Admiral Raeder always understood that an invasion of Britain in 1940 was a scarcely credible option. Indeed, on 22 July 1940 Hitler explicitly told Brauchitsch that he thought the crossing of the Channel was a "very hazardous" undertaking and should be undertaken only if there was "no other way" of dealing with Britain.[8]

This all led to a moment of immense paradox. In July 1940, on the one hand, Hitler was at the peak of his appeal to the German people as a charismatic warlord. As Walter Mauth, then seventeen years old, says, "Everywhere the war lasted three or four weeks and everything went like clockwork. German soldiers were obviously unstoppable. And given this situation we all were—to be honest—enthusiastic, even those who had previously had a different attitude towards the entire regime. All of a sudden, considering everything worked so well and nobody had been able to stop us, we were suddenly all nationalists. Wherever German soldiers were nobody else could get a foothold. It was really like that."[9]

But, on the other hand, the charismatic warlord who had led Germany to these military achievements could not end the war with Britain as he wished. Britain—as Hitler saw it—whose puny, ineffective army had collapsed and then run away from the beaches of Dunkirk.

Why wouldn't the British now admit defeat? The evidence points to Hitler's genuine bewilderment at Britain's intransigence. As Halder recorded on 13 July, Hitler remained "greatly puzzled"[10] by Britain's "persistent unwillingness" to make peace. Hitler might have been received with rapture by Berliners on 6 July, he might have led Germany to the "greatest and most glorious victory of all time" but he could not make Britain leave the conflict. This, notwithstanding the fact that Lord Halifax, in a radio broadcast on 22 July, made Britain's reasons for the rejection of Hitler's "appeal for peace" clear. "He [i.e., Hitler] says he has no desire to destroy the British Empire, but there was in his speech no suggestion that peace must be based on justice, no word of recognition that the other nations of Europe had any right to self-determination, the principle which he has so often invoked for Germans. His only appeal was to the base instinct of fear, and his only arguments were threats . . . Nor has any one any doubt that if Hitler were to succeed it would be the end, for many besides ourselves, of all those things which, as we say, make life worth living. We realise that the struggle may cost us everything, but just because the things we are defending are worth any sacrifice, it is a noble privilege to be the defenders of things so precious."[11]

Hitler was to spend the rest of the war wondering why the British did not make peace at this moment. He could not grasp that there were those in Britain who genuinely believed that "the things we are defending are worth any sacrifice." His attitude is all the more surprising since he himself so embraced the "all or nothing" approach the British were adopting. It is as if he ascribed to himself the motives of principle and honour and expected others to behave with base pragmatism.

Hitler's actions in the summer of 1940 also illustrate a gigantic weakness in the way his leadership operated in practical terms. By relying on his "inner conviction," Hitler made little attempt to understand the developing views of his enemies. He did not grasp that British resistance had its roots in the destruction of the belief that the German leader could be trusted to keep his word. This was the basis on which Churchill could say, in March 1940, when still First Lord of the Admiralty, "There are thoughtless, dilettante or purblind worldlings who sometimes ask us,

'What is it that Britain and France are fighting for?' To this I make the answer, 'If we left off fighting, you would soon find out.' "[12]

There were also worrying signs for Hitler that Britain would be supported by America in the forthcoming struggle. "It is not an ordinary war," said President Franklin Roosevelt, speaking on 19 July 1940 at the Democratic National Convention. "It is a revolution imposed by force of arms which threatens all men everywhere. It is a revolution which proposes not to set men free but to reduce them to slavery, to reduce them to slavery in the interests of a dictatorship which has already shown the nature and the extent of the advantage which it hopes to obtain. That is the fact which dominates our world and which dominates the lives of all of us, each and every one of us. In the face of the danger which confronts our time, no individual retains or can hope to retain the right of personal choice which free men enjoy in times of peace."

The contrast is thus striking between the immense faith that many Germans now placed in Hitler's ability to lead them to victory, and his complete inability to convince the British, and their friends the Americans, that Germany had already won the war. As a result, the pressure on Hitler was enormous. He and he alone would have to decide the way out of this new situation. The German High Command, basking in the success of the historic victory over France—Hitler had recently rewarded eight generals for their role in the campaign by raising them to the rank of Field Marshal—now needed to be told what to do next.

One option was to invade Britain. But not only was such an action considered risky in the extreme, but Hitler was unsure whether it was wise to destroy the British Empire, which he saw as a useful counterweight to American or Asian dominance of the seas, or to occupy Britain which—like Germany—was a relatively overpopulated nation which could not feed itself without importing food. Another option was to engage British forces in the Mediterranean by capturing Gibraltar and the Suez canal, at the same time as U-boat attacks in the Atlantic on convoys from America were increased in an attempt to starve the British to the negotiating table. And then there was the final option, at first sight the most bizarre of all: break the non-aggression pact and turn on Stalin. "Hitler had this notion," says Professor Sir Ian Kershaw, "which sounds really odd today, but the idea that he put forward: we defeat London via Moscow, knock out the Soviet Union in a quick *blitzkrieg* war, take about four or five months, by the end of the year we'll destroy the Soviet Union, Britain will then be bereft of its only potential ally in Europe and the Americans will now keep back to their own hemisphere. So by another route we will have won the war."[13]

It was this option that, of course, the Germans finally adopted when they marched into the Soviet Union in the largest invasion in history on Sunday, 22 June 1941. And it is this decision that is still often seen as the most powerful example of Hitler's charismatic rule. How else, the popular argument goes, could Hitler have convinced his generals to do something as crazy as declare war on Stalin? After all, as Field Marshal Montgomery famously said, "Rule One" of warfare is "don't march on Moscow."[14] General Halder also fuelled this idea when he said after the war that he had held a meeting with Brauchitsch in July 1940 and said that Hitler was a "fool"[15] for wanting a conflict against the Soviet Union. But this does not properly represent the thinking at the time. Whatever private misgivings Halder may or may not have possessed in 1940, far from protesting about the invasion of the Soviet Union, as he had pro-tested about the invasion of France the year before, he had begun consid-ering on his own initiative the merits of just such an adventure only days after the end of the campaign in France.[16] Nor did the Germans necessar-ily believe that it was a "rule" of warfare not to march on Moscow. For Montgomery's grasp of history was sketchy. Whilst it was true that Napo-leon's campaign had ended in disaster, there had been previous successful invasions of Russia. Tokhtamysh, for example, a descendant of Hitler's hero Genghis Khan, had entered Moscow in 1382 and presided over the death of more than twenty thousand Muscovites. And Hitler's generals knew that there was an example in their own lifetimes that could serve as a model for how a war against the Soviet Union could be managed. The treaty of Brest–Litovsk between the Germans and the nascent Soviet state in March 1918 gave Germany huge tracts of land in the east including Belorussia, the Ukraine and the Baltic States. The Germans had lost this territory in the wider settlements at the end of the First World War, but the memory of this successful land grab into Soviet territory remained. As German historian Golo Mann put it, "Brest–Litovsk has been called the forgotten peace, but the Germans have not forgotten it. They know that they defeated Russia and sometimes they look upon this proudly as the real, if unrewarded, achievement of the war."[17]

Hitler's decision to consider an invasion of the Soviet Union made all the more sense to his military commanders when compared with the various other options open to them. Hitler discussed all this with them at a meeting on 31 July 1940 at the Berghof.[18] The first half of the conference was taken up with a lengthy and gloomy report from Grand Admiral Raeder about the prospects of an invasion of Great Britain. Raeder dared, in front of Hitler, to propose postponing any invasion until the following year—this even before the results of a concerted Luftwaffe attack on the British were known. Hitler, normally made furious by lack of enthusiasm from his military leaders, then voiced his own "scepticism" about the feasibility of an invasion. He went on to say that if a decision was taken not to mount an invasion of Britain then "our action must be directed to eliminate all factors that let England hope for a change in the situation." And this, in turn, meant that Russia—Hitler persistently called the Soviet Union "Russia" although Russia was only one of more than a dozen Soviet republics—must be "smashed." Planning for an offensive against the Soviet Union now proceeded in parallel with half-hearted attempts to pull together a coherent plan to invade Britain, stopping only when "Operation Sea Lion" was finally postponed in September 1940.

The idea of an invasion of the Soviet Union made practical sense to many of those who worked for Hitler. Not least because there was evidence from the poor performance of the Red Army during their invasion of Finland the previous winter that Soviet forces were anything but first rate, weakened as they were by the purges of the 1930s. As we have seen, Hitler never attempted a similar widespread removal of army officers who were not outright supporters of the Nazis. Indeed, according to Goebbels, Hitler thought Stalin was "probably sick in the brain"[19] for killing or otherwise dismissing some of the Red Army's most experienced officers on the merest suspicion of political unreliability.

All this meant that German officers like Peter von der Groeben felt not only that they could approach any conflict with the Soviet Union with some confidence, but the fundamental reasoning behind the attack was sound. "From my perspective, it [the German invasion of the Soviet Union] was in some way—above all from a military point of view—almost inevitable. What was the situation? France had been defeated. The attempt to wrestle England to the ground with the famous Operation Sea Lion had failed, because it had not been possible to gain air supremacy—on the contrary, losses against the English Air Force had been incurred. It was clear that in the foreseeable future, within two years, America would enter the war on the side of our opponents. It is known that Roosevelt was determined to wage this war from the outset. And so the question arose of what could be done to be able to stand up to them, to this threat. And on the other side there was the extremely unstable Russia, which made increasingly big demands . . . hence the—in my view—absolute necessity arose to remove the Russian threat before America could go into action . . . People thought, and the military leaders were among them, that it would be relatively easy to eliminate the Russian army with one short, forceful blow. Based on the information I knew about, which we had about the Russian army, I also believed that it would not be much of a problem."[20]

Invading the Soviet Union would also, of course, allow Hitler the opportunity to pursue the basic aim of *Lebensraum* he had outlined in *Mein Kampf* sixteen years before. Gone would be the ties of the pragmatic non-aggression pact with Stalin. At last Hitler could lead the Germans against the "headquarters," as he saw it, of the "Judaeo–Bolshevist world conspiracy."[21] And, not surprisingly, those SS men like Walter Traphöner who had always believed this Nazi propaganda, welcomed the idea of conflict with the Soviet Union. "We wanted to prevent Bolshevism from ruling the world, you see . . . And we were committed to preventing them from flooding still further into Europe."[22]

But even though, as far as Hitler and his comrades were concerned, there were both practical and ideological reasons why it now made sense to consider an attack on the Soviet Union, there was an obvious flaw in their logic. Hitler said on 31 July that "Russia is the factor on which Britain is relying the most"—but this assertion was simply not true. Key figures in the British government had always been suspicious of the Soviet Union and most certainly were not relying on Stalin. Chamberlain, Lord Halifax and Churchill had all expressed dislike for the Communists. As recently as 31 March 1940, Churchill had stated publicly that he felt the Soviets had just demonstrated in Finland the "ravages" which Communism—"that deadly mental and moral disease"—makes "upon the fibre of any nation."[23] Moreover, Stalin's strategy had up to now been to keep out of the war in order to let the Germans and the Western Allies bleed each other dry. And whilst it was true that there were growing strains in the Nazis' relationship with Stalin—not least over the Soviet occupation of the Baltic States in the summer of 1940—there were still no signs that Stalin wanted war with Germany.

It was not Russia that Britain relied upon to carry on fighting the war, but America. On 20 May 1940, one of the grimmest days during the Battle for France, Churchill had written to President Roosevelt saying, "If this country was left by the United States to its fate, no one would have the right to blame those then responsible if they made the best terms they could for the surviving inhabitants."[24] Churchill, as Professor David Reynolds reminds us, "always had the United States in his frame of reference. He was half American and he had long argued that Britain should form an alliance with the United States and draw America into European affairs, so that was something that mattered to him in a way it didn't instinctively to Halifax or to Chamberlain. Having said that, given the way the war changes so dramatically in the summer of 1940, any British leader would have had to start looking to America in a new way because it was the only source of significant support."[25]

The Americans, long before they entered the war in December 1941 after the Japanese attack on Pearl Harbor, were offering military support to the British. Most famously, in December 1940 after his re-election as President, Roosevelt committed the United States to Lend-Lease and thus to provide equipment to the British and not expect immediate payment in return. But even before that date the Americans were supporting the British war effort. Indeed, in July 1940 Churchill knew that the Americans planned to provide the British with more than 10,000 aircraft within a year and a half.[26] That, plus the 15,000 planes the British were making themselves in the same period, meant that the British were expanding the RAF faster than the Germans were growing the Luftwaffe.

The only practical way the flow of goods from America could be stopped, of course, was by sinking merchant ships as they crossed the Atlantic. And here too the Germans faced problems. The U-boat programme had been neglected for years as the emphasis of the German navy building programme had shifted to a long-term plan to create a giant surface battle fleet. By the start of the war the German navy had less than three dozen U-boats able to challenge the Allied merchant convoys in the north Atlantic. And only twenty additional U-boats had been constructed by the time of the fall of France in June 1940.[27]

In discussions with his generals, Hitler attempted to deal with the threat from America by logic which—even for him—was tortured. He argued that if Russia was defeated then this would allow the Japanese to more easily focus on their own territorial expansion in Asia and the Pacific, thus causing conflict between the Americans and the Japanese. The Americans, by implication, would then be occupied protecting their interests on the other side of the world. In addition, Hitler asserted, even if the Americans wanted to fight in Europe, it would take several years for them to be battle ready, by which time the Nazis would be in control of mainland Europe and, benefiting from the raw materials drawn from their new eastern empire, impregnable to attack.[28]

It was a strategy built on hope. Hitler hoped the Americans would be unable to support the British war effort if, as he hoped, the Japanese forced a conflict with them in the Pacific. Simultaneously, he hoped the British would make a compromise peace once the Soviets were defeated. Hope piled on hope piled on hope. Even Hitler could not conceal the fact that he could not actually make any of this happen. He could not order the German army across the Atlantic to defeat the Americans, he could not, it appeared, even order them across the English Channel to defeat the British. Moreover, as a central European by birth and inclination, Hitler had never shown any sign of embracing naval conquest. He believed Germany should expand on mainland Europe.

Yet despite all of this, no one seriously questioned Hitler's analysis in the summer of 1940. The charismatic aura around him had intensified— now anyone approaching him did so with the knowledge of his recent success. Hitler had said Germany could defeat France and those that had doubted him had been proven wrong. Now he claimed Britain and America could be defeated by attacking the Soviet Union. And according to confidential SD reports monitoring public opinion towards the end of 1940, many in the general population—as yet ignorant of Hitler's exact plans for the future—were happy to put their faith in his judgement. "When the Führer speaks, all doubts fall away . . ."[29] was one remark from a citizen of Schwerin in northern Germany, judged "typical" by the SD. Another report, from the summer of 1940 said that Hitler's speech on his return from France "was perceived with emotion [*Ergriffenheit*] and enthusiasm everywhere" with one person capturing the prevailing mood with the words, "The Führer's speech seemed like a cleansing thunderstorm."[30]

Adolf Hitler, seated far right, as an ordinary soldier in the 16th Bavarian Reserve Regiment, known as the "List" Regiment after the name of its colonel. A number of Hitler's comrades thought him a bit odd.

Hitler in the early 1920s as an embryonic politician in Munich. Note the deliberate attempt to appear "respectable" with newly-trimmed moustache and bourgeois clothing.

Hermann Göring, who joined the Nazi party in 1922 and was wounded during the Beer Hall Putsch the following year. He was one of the most strident believers in the "charisma" of Adolf Hitler.

Ernst Röhm in the uniform of a German officer. Hugely influential during the early days of the Nazi party, Röhm would later command the Nazi stormtroopers and then be murdered on Hitler's orders in 1934.

Dietrich Eckart, a dissolute writer and vicious anti-Semite who was one of the first to recognise the political potential of Adolf Hitler. Eckart died in 1923 but remained one of the few people that Hitler spoke of with reverence.

Joseph Goebbels, who held a PhD in German literature, was instrumental in creating the "Hitler myth"—the idea that Hitler was infallible. Working across print, radio and film, Goebbels became the most powerful propagandist the world has ever seen.

General Erich Ludendorff (left) and Adolf Hitler (right) at the time of their trial in 1924 for involvement in the Beer Hall Putsch. Ludendorff, a hero of the First World War, was initially helpful to Hitler, but was soon discarded once Hitler decided that he, and he alone, was the leader Germany needed.

Nazi stormtroopers and other far-right paramilitary units arrive in
Munich to take part in the Beer Hall Putsch in November 1923.
The putsch was an incompetent attempt to start a revolution,
but Hitler later turned this failure into a heroic myth.

Hitler outside Landsberg prison in Bavaria in December 1924 on
his release after serving just nine months of a five-year sentence for his
part in the Beer Hall Putsch. He emerged from prison, having written
Mein Kampf, convinced that he was Germany's saviour.

Hitler with an adoring group of young supporters. Hitler always targeted the young in particular, believing that this strategy would help ensure the future of the Nazi movement for a thousand years.

„Nimmer wird das Reich zerstöret — wenn ihr einig seid und treu"

1

Nationalsozialisten

A propaganda poster from 1933 showing President Hindenburg and Adolf Hitler. It reads: "The Reich will never be destroyed when you stay united and loyal" and was thus a deliberate attempt to link Hitler with the more "respectable" Hindenburg.

Hitler at the 1934 Nazi rally in Nuremberg—the rally featured in the
film *Triumph of the Will*. These rallies, with their elaborate staging,
played a vital part in the creation of a "charismatic" aura around Hitler.

A number of correspondents noticed how the crowds—and women in
particular—were almost ecstatic in the presence of Hitler at parades and rallies.

A gigantic crowd of Austrians gathered in the Heldenplatz in the centre of Vienna to hear Hitler speak on 15 March 1938, and to celebrate the union of Austria with Nazi Germany.

Ludwig Beck, Chief of Staff of the German Army in the 1930s. He never found Hitler "charismatic" but felt that he still offered the best chance of a German rebirth. Beck realised too late that Hitler would lead Germany into a war that it would lose.

Hitler as Chancellor of
Germany and Führer
of the German people
in the 1930s. Here he
demonstrates his famous
"stare." He would hold
the eyes of the person
looking at him much
longer than was normal.

Once the Nazis gained power, German Jews were hugely at risk. Here Nazi stormtroopers humiliate a Jewish man and non-Jewish woman who were in a relationship.

German shops damaged during *Kristallnacht*—the "night of the broken glass"—on 9–10 November 1938. Nazi stormtroopers ran almost beserk through Germany, smashing Jewish property, burning synagogues and attacking Jews.

In the wake of the *Anschluss*—the union between Germany and Austria in 1938—there was an outpouring of anti-Semitic action. Below, Austrian Jews are forced to scrub the streets.

Neville Chamberlain, the British Prime Minister, visits Germany during the Sudetenland crisis. He was unable to comprehend that Hitler, the leader of a cultured European state, might actually *want* to provoke a European war.

Hitler watches as victorious German troops pass by in celebration of the subjugation of Poland. The Nazis, assisted by the Soviets who attacked Poland from the East, had taken little more than a month to defeat the Polish army.

Hermann Göring, Commander-in-Chief of
the German air force, Walter von Brauchitsch,
head of the army, and Adolf Hitler (from left
to right) in the spring of 1941. These three
men would play crucial roles in the invasion
of the Soviet Union just a few weeks later.

Hitler in Munich after the initial
attempt to defeat the Red Army in
1941 had failed. But many still had
faith in him as a charismatic leader.

A military conference attended by the Italian leader, Benito Mussolini (far left) in
April 1942. Next to Mussolini is Alfred Jodl, Chief of the Operations staff of the
German Armed Forces High Command (OKW), then Hitler, then Field Marshal
Wilhelm Keitel, Head of OKW, then Ugo Cavallero, Chief of the Italian Supreme
Command and finally Eckhard Christian, a Luftwaffe staff officer.

Hubert Lanzinger's portrait of Hitler, as a knight in shining armour holding a Nazi standard, reflects a desire to see Hitler as a heroic figure from German myth.

Hitler plots his next move in the summer of 1942 as German troops advance east into the Russian heartland. Heinrich Himmler, on the left of the photograph, has just organised a massive increase in the killing capacity of Nazi death camps.

A member of a German *Einsatzgruppen* shoots a Soviet civilian—most likely a Jew—after the German invasion of the Soviet Union. These killing squads operated behind the front line, and by the autumn of 1941 were murdering Jewish women and children as well as men.

German soldiers are marched out of Stalingrad as prisoners of war after the German defeat in February 1943. Nearly 100,000 Germans were captured by the Red Army at the battle of Stalingrad—and the vast majority would die in Soviet captivity.

Hitler with his dog Blondi. Hitler had been fond of dogs for many years—he had been distraught when a fox terrier he had adopted in the First World War went missing. Blondi died in the Führerbunker in April 1945 when Hitler ordered a sample of poison to be tried on the dog before he took it himself.

A pensive Hitler during a flight in 1943. With the Soviets fighting back on the Eastern Front and American forces already in Britain preparing for an Allied invasion of France, prospects for the Nazis were bleak.

Hitler talks to decorated Luftwaffe officers at the Berghof in 1944. These young men will have been taught about the "infallibility" of their "charismatic" Führer since 1933.

Hitler's theatrical gestures were an important part of his speech-making.
What mattered most to Hitler was the emotion he generated in his speeches
as he attempted to make a connection with his audience.

Claus von Stauffenberg, the
German officer who planted a
bomb at the Wolf's Lair in East
Prussia in an attempt to kill Hitler
on 20 July 1944.

The damage Stauffenberg's bomb did to the
conference room at the Wolf's Lair. Hitler said
that he survived the attack because "Providence"
wished him to continue his "life's mission."

In the end, Hitler brought little but destruction to the world. Not just to Berlin—here with the ruins of the Reichstag in the distance—but to much of Europe. Hitler's legacy included the most monumental crime of all history—the Holocaust.

Such an attitude was also made possible by the sense of superiority that had been drummed into the Germans, a feeling confirmed by the victory over France. "We had been taught that only the Germans were valuable human beings," one student at the time later remembered. "There was a little booklet called 'German inventors, German poets, German musicians,' nothing else existed. And we devoured it, and we were absolutely convinced that we were the greatest. And we would listen to the news flashes and we were incredibly proud and moved and frequently many people would shed tears of pride. You have to imagine it—I cannot understand it today—but it was just like that . . . even my sceptical father said 'we,' now he suddenly said 'we,' whereas before, when he was telling us stories from the war and so on, he would use 'I,' but now it was suddenly 'we.' 'We' are splendid fellows!"[31]

Hitler's decision to turn on the Soviets tapped into a mix of memory, practicality and romance—a potent combination that Hitler knew how to manipulate. Ever since the Teutonic Knights had gained land in the Baltic states in the thirteenth century, tales of chivalry and conquest had been told about the German conquest of the "East." More recently, the Germans who had fought in the army on Soviet territory in the First World War, and in the *Freikorps* in the Baltic states in the war's immediate aftermath, had formed their own opinion of this vast space to set against the myths of old. "Deepest Russia, without a glimmer of Central European *Kultur* [culture], Asia, steppe, swamps, claustrophobic underworld," recalled one German soldier, "and a godforsaken wasteland of slime."[32] Another saw the Germans as a civilising force in this wild landscape, as "pioneers of *Kultur*" and "thus, whether aware or not, the German soldier becomes a teacher in the enemy land."[33] Moreover, current German military planners knew that they relied on imports from the Soviet Union—particularly of oil and grain—to be able to carry on fighting the war. What if Stalin threatened to stop supplying this vital material? Why not, instead, fight to gain permanent and secure access to these raw materials once and for all?

The arrival of the Soviet Foreign Minister, Vyacheslav Molotov, in Berlin on 12 November 1940 served only to make that option all the more attractive for Hitler. Molotov had been invited to discuss the relationship between the Soviet Union and Germany, fifteen months after the signing of the non-aggression pact. The Soviet Foreign Minister's style of leader-

ship was the opposite of Hitler's. He was so adept at sitting through inter-
minable meetings that he had earned the nickname "stone arse." He dealt
in practical, everyday concerns and was suspicious of ambitious flights of
fancy. The antithesis of charisma himself, Molotov was the last person to
be swayed by Hitler's grand visions. And so it proved during their meetings in the Reich Chancellery on 12 and 13 November.

Hitler began by emphasising in his opening remarks to Molotov that
he wanted to talk in "bold outline" about the relationship between the
Soviet Union and Germany. Hitler thus sought to avoid "petty momentary considerations." He then raised the "problem of America" implying
that American aid for Britain was actually part of a cynical ploy to "further
their own rearmament and to reinforce their military power by acquiring
bases."[34] But it wouldn't be until "1970 or 1980" that America would be
in a position to "seriously endanger" other nations. In the meantime,
Hitler suggested that perhaps the Soviet Union could participate in the
Tripartite Pact, the recently signed agreement between Germany, Italy
and Japan.

But Molotov demonstrated that "petty momentary considerations"
were precisely what interested him. He brushed away Hitler's desire to
talk in broad terms and tried to focus the conversation on immediate
practical issues like Germany's intentions towards Finland. Hitler, having dealt swiftly with this question ("Finland remained in the sphere of
influence of Russia"), conjured up a future world "after the conquest of
England" when "the British Empire would be apportioned as a gigantic worldwide estate in bankruptcy of 40 million square kilometres. In
this bankrupt estate there would be for Russia access to the ice-free and
really open ocean." But Molotov could not have been less interested in
the future dismemberment of the assets of a country that had yet to be
beaten—and indeed might not ever be beaten. At a later meeting on the
same trip to Berlin he explicitly said to Ribbentrop that he was aware that
the German plans for the future were based on the "assumption" that the
war against Britain "had already actually been won."

Molotov's rejection—almost scorn—of Hitler's charisma was predictable not only given his own personality but also Stalin's contempt for
this style of leadership. Stalin had beaten at least two "charismatic" rivals
in the race to succeed Lenin—Zinoviev and Trotsky—and had achieved
his success by cunning and the exercise of raw power. Hitler thrived on

rhetoric—it was the basis of his appeal—while Stalin had a totally different view of leadership. "One should distrust words," he said. "Deeds are more important than words."[35] Not surprisingly, the talks with Molotov were unsuccessful, and on 18 December 1940, shortly after they ended, Hitler issued the formal directive for Operation Barbarossa (*Unternehmen Barbarossa*)—the invasion of the Soviet Union.

Meantime, events in Poland continued to demonstrate how the interrelationship between Hitler and his followers could create immense dynamism and destructiveness. Just as before the war, Hitler's lack of definition of precise aims was a key factor in his leadership of his ideological supporters. In the words of Professor Norbert Frei, "The key to it was to be vague . . . you don't get a consistent picture even if you are at the top of the hierarchy."[36] As Joseph Goebbels said on 5 April 1940 during a confidential briefing for the German press, "Today, when someone asks you how we conceive of the new Europe, we must say, we do not know. Certainly we have an idea. But if we dress it in words it will immediately create enemies and increase the resistance . . . Today we say '*Lebensraum*.' Everyone can imagine what they want. We will know what we want when the time is right."[37]

Amongst the new rulers of Poland this form of leadership was a recipe for the most astonishing level of violence and chaos. For example, Arthur Greiser, ruler of the newly created area called the Warthegau in Poland, and Arthur Forster, Nazis boss of Danzig/West Prussia, both exercised enormous individual power without reference to any other authority. Both were "Gauleiters," or district leaders (the Reich was divided into "Gau" or "districts," each with its own "Gauleiter"). These men—and they were all men—were appointed directly by Hitler and reported directly to him. Many had been with him from the beginning of the Nazi movement. Albert Forster, for instance, had become a Nazi stormtrooper in 1923 when he was twenty-one years old. Forster and Greiser had both been told by Hitler that "they had ten years to tell him that Germanisation of their provinces was complete and he would ask no questions about their methods."[38] As a result, since both felt free to complete their tasks however they liked, they each approached the job differently. Greiser, a close associate of Himmler, utilised approved Nazi methods in determining who was "German" in his area of Poland and who was not. Forster, equally brutal but rather more laissez-faire in his methods, thought it would be quicker to work out which villages appeared Germanic and then "Germanise" the inhabitants en masse. In both cases the consequences for those not considered "German" could be catastrophic—deportation to the General Government, starvation and death was the fate that awaited many of them.

The situation in Poland was rendered even more chaotic by the arrival of several hundred thousand ethnic Germans who, by agreement with Stalin, were able to emigrate to the "Reich" from areas like the Baltic States within the newly-expanded Soviet Union. It came as a shock to many of them to discover that the "Reich" in which they were now told to make their home was not within the pre-war boundaries of Germany but in the newly incorporated territories that until recently had been part of Poland. Some of the new immigrants were simply given flats and businesses expropriated from Poles who had been deported or Jews who were now imprisoned in ghettos. However, the majority of ethnic Germans did not find new homes but languished in reception camps waiting for the Nazi authorities to sort matters out.

Presiding over all of this human torment was Heinrich Himmler. He, in common with other Nazi rulers in Poland like Forster and Greiser, had been given enormous latitude by Hitler to use whatever methods he thought were necessary to reorganise Poland on racial grounds. And Himmler knew very well that Hitler would support the adoption of violent and radical measures to get the job done. Himmler, just thirty-nine years old in the summer of 1940, was still a veteran of the Nazi movement. He had taken part in the Beer Hall Putsch in 1923 and then turned against his old patron, Ernst Röhm, at the Night of the Long Knives in 1934.

Moreover, Himmler was also a passionate believer in the prime importance of "race" in human history. "We need to be clear about one thing," he told a gathering of Nazi gauleiters in February 1940, "we are firmly convinced, I believe it, just as I believe in a God, I believe that our blood, the Nordic blood, is actually the best blood on this earth . . . In a thousand centuries this Nordic blood will still be the best. There is no other. We are superior to everything and everyone. Once we are liberated from inhibitions and restraints, there is no one who can surpass us in quality and strength."[39]

In pursuit of "the best blood" Himmler had been appointed as "Reich Commissar for the Strengthening of German Nationhood" by Hitler back in October 1939, and in this capacity he had been attempting one of the largest ethnic reorganisations of human beings in history. Or, as Goebbels put it, writing in his diary in January 1940, "Himmler is presently shifting populations. Not always successfully."[40]

A necessary precondition for the latitude which Himmler exercised over the violent actions in the East was, not surprisingly, Hitler's confidence that Himmler was both intensely loyal to him and subscribed to his "charismatic genius." Back in January 1923, even before he had experienced personal dealings with Hitler, Himmler wrote: "He is in truth a great man and above all a true and pure one."[41] But notwithstanding Hitler's confidence in Himmler's loyalty, the SS leader still had to push his desired changes through against other competing Nazi power interests in Poland. When, for example, Himmler objected to the lax manner in which Albert Forster implemented racial selection in Danzig/West Prussia he found he could do little to enforce his will, since Forster, as a gauleiter, had direct access to Hitler. Himmler also had problems with Göring who had pursued objections from Hans Frank, the Nazi ruler of the General Government, after Frank had complained to Göring, in his capacity as Head of the Four Year Plan, about the effect of mass deportations to his area of Poland made in pursuit of Himmler's racial reorganisation.

But Himmler was an expert at manoeuvring his way through this maze of conflicting job titles and ambitions. He knew that Hitler disliked reading memoranda and most often wanted his subordinates to anticipate his needs by listening for verbal cues. That, after all, had been how Himmler had understood what was required of both him as an individual, and the SS as a whole, at the time of the attack on Röhm and the SA leadership. But Himmler also realised that very occasionally it was beneficial to put proposals in writing before Hitler. This, he knew, should only be done when there was an express need for a clear decision from the Führer and when the moment for the approach was propitious. In May 1940 he felt both of these conditions were met when he wrote a long memorandum for Hitler called "Some Thoughts on the Treatment of the Alien Population in the East." There was an obvious need for guidance from Hitler about how racial policy in Poland should be implemented, and the memo was timed to reach Hitler at a moment when the Germans were making progress in the Battle for France.

Himmler was not going to Hitler with problems that he wanted solved. Instead, he was offering a way of developing what he knew was

Hitler's vision for the east. He proposed that the "non-German" population of the "eastern territories" should be kept as ignorant slaves and only
be taught the following: "Simple arithmetic to no more than 500, writing
of the name, a doctrine that there is a divine commandment to obey the
Germans, to be honest, hardworking and virtuous. Reading, I think, is
not necessary."[42] Meantime, the land was to be scoured for children of
"our blood" who would be snatched and taken to be reared in Germany.

It was exactly the kind of radical and racist plan that was calculated to
appeal to Hitler—and it did. He said to Himmler that he considered the
memo *"gut und richtig"* ("good and correct"). "This is the way decisions
are made," says Professor Christopher Browning. "Hitler does not draw
up an elaborate plan, sign it and pass it down the line. What you get is an
encouragement to Himmler to fight it out with the others and the ability
now to invoke Hitler's approval if they don't give way. And Hitler can
still back out later, of course. You see, he's reserving his options, but he's
encouraging Himmler, who has anticipated that this is really the sort of
long-range thing that Hitler would like."[43]

This system of a "vision from above," which was then left to subordinates to define and put into effect, created a tendency for those subordinates to promise far more than they could ever deliver. Unlike the
generals who had, for example, raised sober objections to Hitler's plan to
invade France, dedicated believers in Hitler's charisma like Himmler and
Göring sought to please their boss by offering assurances that the near
impossible—sometimes the actual impossible—could be achieved. By the
summer of 1940 Göring had already demonstrated this propensity many
times; in the economic field by setting unrealistic targets in the Four Year
Plan, and in the military arena by assuring Hitler that the Luftwaffe could
destroy the Allied troops gathered on the beaches of Dunkirk. Himmler
had also shown that he could not deliver his ambitious plans for racial
reorganisation. Not only had the massive shifting of Poles within Poland
caused administrative and economic chaos, but several hundred thousand
ethnic Germans who had arrived in the new Reich full of hope for the
future were now forced to live in transit camps because there was nowhere
else for them to go. Yet in his 15 May memo Himmler ignored all these
problems and, instead, argued for a further expansion of the racial reorganisation of the east. Himmler, like Göring, knew that above all else
Hitler was attracted to plans that exuded both optimism and radicalism.

A further consequence of this aspect of Hitler's charismatic leadership was the way his immediate subordinates came to mimic their Führer's tendency to ignore practical problems that stood in the way of an ultimate goal. Himmler demonstrated this quality countless times, but most obviously during his first visit to Auschwitz concentration camp in the spring of 1941. Auschwitz, at this period in its development, was a concentration camp designed to strike terror into the Polish population of Upper Silesia. When the camp opened in June 1940 the first inmates were Polish political prisoners. Though many did die there as a result of appalling mistreatment, it was not yet a place of systematic extermination. Himmler decided to visit the camp because he knew that the giant chemical conglomerate I G Farben was interested in opening a new factory nearby. He hoped that Auschwitz could provide some of the workers for this proposed synthetic rubber, or *"Buna,"* complex.

On 1 March 1941 Himmler met the commandant of Auschwitz, Rudolf Höss, together with other local Nazis including the Gauleiter of Upper Silesia, Fritz Bracht. Himmler announced that the camp would now be expanded three-fold and dismissed a series of objections to his plans—like the problem of drainage—with the words, "Gentlemen, the camp will be expanded. My reasons for it are far more important than your objections."[44] It was a line that could just as easily have come from Hitler, and one that is—on any reflection—nonsensical, since the practical objections to Himmler's plans remained, no matter how much he wanted them pushed through. Later that day Rudolf Höss tried once more to convince Himmler of the seriousness of the problems he faced in trying to expand the capacity of the camp from 10,000 inmates to 30,000 inmates. "I want to hear no more about difficulties!" said Himmler in response. "For an SS officer there are no difficulties! When they come up, it's his job to get rid of them. How you do that is your business, not mine!"

Whilst this is—it must be said—a truly bizarre system of administration, there were underlying reasons why—for longer than one might have supposed—it continued to operate. Hitler had emphasised for years that goals could be achieved primarily by willpower and by faith—and he claimed to have demonstrated that reality himself via achievements like the Nazi seizure of power and the victory over France. More significant, though, was that the people who would suffer from a failure to achieve these ambitious goals were often those the Nazis either didn't care about or actually wished to see suffer. In the case of the Poles, the thousands who died on the trains sent to the General Government, or who starved to death after they arrived and found nothing to eat and nowhere to stay, could be dismissed by the Nazis as an unimportant part of the "leaderless labouring class."

This tendency to set ludicrous goals and then dismiss the consequent suffering when they were not fulfilled was most apparent in the context of Nazi policy towards the Jews. The Nazis had a large number of Polish Jews under their control by the end of September 1939—nearly two million—and Hitler's initial "vision" for them followed naturally on from the pre-war policy goals of persecution and expulsion. Several thousand Polish Jews were shot by special task forces—*Einsatzgruppen*—but many more were ordered into ghettos prior to their deportation. And the potential for individual commanders to use their own discretion in their work was built into the plan at an early stage. Reinhard Heydrich, in a list of instructions for *Einsatzgruppen* leaders, wrote, "It is obvious that the forthcoming tasks cannot be determined from here in all their details. The following instructions and guidelines only serve the purpose of urging the leaders of the *Einsatzgruppen* to reflect for themselves on practical considerations."[45]

On 29 September Hitler said that he wanted the Jews moved to the south-east corner of the new Nazi empire, between the Bug and Vistula rivers,[46] a remote area near the border with the Soviet-occupied zone of Poland, where they would be forced into work camps. Adolf Eichmann, a thirty-three-year-old SS captain (*Hauptsturmführer*) who had been instrumental in organising the deportation of Jews from Austria after the *Anschluss*, heard about this idea and immediately tried to implement it. There is no evidence that Eichmann was ordered to do so. Rather he decided on his own initiative to see if he could organise the deportations that he believed his superiors desired. On October 6, Eichmann met with the chief of the Gestapo, Heinrich Müller, who was in favour of some trial deportations to see if the system worked. Over the next few days Eichmann exceeded this brief and started to plan the deportation of Jews from as far afield as Vienna. Incredibly, given the short timescale involved, the first train containing nearly a thousand Jews left for south-east Poland from what is now Ostrava in the Czech Republic on 18 October, just three weeks after Hitler had made his wishes clear.[47] On 20 October, a train left Vienna with around the same number of Jews.

In seeking to deport Jews from Vienna, Eichmann was also trying to solve a "problem" that the Nazis had created for themselves in the wake of the *Anschluss* and the vast Aryanisation programme that they had imposed before the war. By shutting down or appropriating Jewish businesses, the Nazis had made it impossible for many Jews to earn a living. If the Jews were not then able to emigrate, they would then become a "burden" on the Nazi state. Even before the war, one Nazi planner, Walter Rafelsberger,[48] had proposed that the Jews who remained should be forced into camps where they would be made to work on construction projects. Now, in wartime conditions, ideas similar to Rafelsberger's must have seemed attainable.

However, not surprisingly, Eichmann's plan collapsed into chaos, creating appalling suffering once the Jews arrived at the town of Nisko in the Lublin region of Poland. There was no accommodation for them—they were ordered to build their own huts—and many of them were taken towards the border with Soviet-occupied Poland and told to go away and never come back. In November 1939 further transports of Jews were banned and the scheme abandoned, though some Jews continued to languish in the makeshift camp in Nisko until spring 1940.

It had been Himmler who had ordered Eichmann's initiative to be cancelled—not because of the suffering of the Jews who had been caught up in this venture, but because his current priority was organising the transportation of the incoming ethnic Germans from Soviet territory, and Eichmann's Nisko project was diverting resources. Himmler also had his own plans for deporting the Polish Jews down into the General Government. It was the huge administrative problems caused by this improvised scheme that had led to complaints being made to Göring and Himmler's subsequent memo to Hitler in May 1940.

However, short-lived as the Nisko scheme was, it is nonetheless revealing of the nature of the Nazi system of leadership—particularly as it related to the Jewish question. Hitler was scarcely involved, yet his own imprimatur was crucial. Such was the nature of his leadership that a mere indication that he favoured a particular course of action—regardless of the practical difficulties of implementation—was enough to provoke one of his underlings to act, even one as junior as Adolf Eichmann. Indeed, as subsequent developments in the Nazis' anti-Semitic policy demonstrated, so strong was the sense emanating from Hitler that wild dreams could be considered practical possibilities, that the Führer did not have to initiate all of the visions himself—others, knowing the kind of world he wanted, could do the work for him. Hitler had created an atmosphere in which, as Himmler said in his speech in February 1940, the Nazis could be "liberated from inhibitions and restraints."

By the summer of 1940, not only had Eichmann's Nisko plan proved impossible to implement, but so had Himmler's idea of shipping the Polish Jews to the General Government. Meanwhile, Polish Jews had been confined in ghettos in the larger cities like Warsaw, Łódź and Krakow where many were already dying of disease and malnutrition. Estera Frankiel, for instance, who with her family had been imprisoned in the Łódź ghetto in the spring of 1940, says that conditions were so bad that "one only thought about how one could survive this [single] day."[49] Ghettos, which had originally been intended only as a temporary measure before the Jews could be deported, were now acting as long-term prisons. The suffering was immense. One Pole who saw conditions in the Warsaw ghetto in 1941 wrote in his diary, "The majority are nightmare figures, ghosts of former human beings, miserable destitutes, pathetic remains of humanity . . . On the streets children are crying in vain, children who are dying of hunger. They howl, beg, sing, moan, shiver with cold, without underwear, without clothing, without shoes, in rags, sacks, flannel which are bound in strips round the emaciated skeletons, children swollen with hunger, disfigured, half conscious, already completely grown-up at the age of five, gloomy and weary of life."[50]

Senior Nazis like Heinrich Himmler and Hans Frank were not only indifferent to this suffering, they actually wanted something like it to occur. "Give the Jews short shrift. A joy to finally tackle the Jewish race physically. The more that die the better,"[51] Hans Frank had said in November 1939 in the context of the doomed plan to send the Jews east of the river Vistula.

It was in an attempt to pursue the original idea of the expulsion of the Jews that an official in the German Foreign Office, Franz Rademacher, proposed in the summer of 1940 the strange and radical solution of sending the Jews to the French colony of Madagascar, an island off the south-eastern coast of Africa. The idea of expelling the Jews to some-where far away from Europe was not new. Paul de Lagarde, a nineteenth-century German anti-Semite,[52] had first proposed sending the Jews to Madagascar—not, of course, for their welfare, since he favoured their destruction in one way or another.[53] (Lagarde also espoused many other ideas long before the Nazis adopted them—like hatred of liberalism and a desire for Germany to gain additional territory.) More recently, Himmler had also mentioned in his May 1940 memo that he hoped "to see the term 'Jews' completely eliminated through the possibility of large-scale migra-tion of all Jews to Africa or some other colony."

But it was Rademacher who now brought the Madagascar idea to the fore. Rademacher was not just a career diplomat, but also a commit-ted Nazi, and had recently been appointed head of the Jewish section (*Judenreferat*) within the German Foreign Office. He believed that the defeat of France—together with, as he supposed, the imminent capitu-lation of Britain and thus the end of hostilities in Europe—opened up a whole new vista of possible options. One was that "western Jews" be "removed from Europe, to Madagascar, for example."[54] Rademacher's memo suggesting this option was written to his boss, Under Secretary Martin Luther and dated 3 June 1940. But just three weeks later Reinhard Heydrich, aware of Rademacher's attempt to involve the Foreign Office in what he considered was his business, told Ribbentrop, German For-eign Secretary, that he wanted to be part of these discussions. As a result, six weeks later, Eichmann delivered a lengthy proposal for sending four million Jews to Madagascar where they would live—and in due course die—supervised by the SS.

That Hitler endorsed such proposals is certain. He told Mussolini that summer about the Madagascar plan and Goebbels recorded in his diary on 17 August after meeting Hitler, "We want later to transport the Jews to Madagascar."[55] The news even reached the Jews imprisoned in the Łódź ghetto. "Then there was talk about Madagascar," says Estera Fren-kiel, who by the summer of 1940 was working as a secretary within the ghetto administration. "I myself heard about this at the time, how Rich-ter from the Gestapo said to Rumkowski [the Jewish head of the Ghetto], 'We shall move all of you to Madagascar and there, you will be King of the Jews or the President . . . ' "[56] In fact, the Jews would almost certainly have suffered a catastrophic fate if they had been sent to Madagascar—the pre-war assessment made by the Polish Lepecki commission reported that fewer than 10,000 families could be accommodated on Madagascar,[57] while the Nazis planned on sending four million Jews there.

The Madagascar plan lasted little longer than Eichmann's Nisko debacle. It had always been dependent on Britain making peace—the Jews could never be transported to Africa unless the shipping lanes were secure. But its brief history is nonetheless significant since it demonstrates the extent to which the ideological believers around Hitler were prepared to think in extreme terms about the possible fate of the Jews.

The planning for the forthcoming war against the Soviet Union was developed alongside these increasingly radical ideas about the treatment of Jews in particular and the Polish population in general. These elements all worked together to produce a remarkable outpouring of murderous—indeed genocidal—proposals. Pioneering research by German scholars over the last twenty years has demonstrated how the "state-secretaries" (officials akin to Permanent Under Secretaries in the British governmental model) in the Nazi system theorised in wild and expansive terms about the potential removal and starvation of millions of people. They were motivated, in part, by the belief that there were simply too many people in this part of the world already. Werner Conze, later a professor at the Reich University in Posen, wrote just before the war that, "In large areas of eastern Central Europe, rural overpopulation is one of the most serious social and political problems of the present day."[58] Influenced by the theories of social scientists like Paul Mombert, these Nazi planners thought that a so-called "optimum population" could be calculated for any particular territory. As a consequence they argued that there was a massive surplus population in the areas the Nazis already occupied in the east and those they sought to occupy as a result of the invasion of the Soviet Union. They were also aware, of course, of a previous dramatic reduction in the population of one region the Nazis sought to occupy. Between 1932 and 1933 Stalin had presided over a famine in Ukraine that had resulted in a death toll of at least six million.[59] Scholars still debate whether Stalin wanted this number of Ukranians to die in the drive towards Soviet modernisation, but what is certain is that by the outbreak of the Second World War the Nazis had a clear example before them of how the population of Eastern Europe could be drastically reduced by famine in a short period of time.

For these Nazi planners the war was most certainly a liberation. As Dr. Dietrich Troschke, a young economist who worked in the General Government, wrote in his diary in April 1940, "Those who are on service in the east find themselves in a unique situation. Every individual is confronted with extraordinary opportunities. Nobody could ever have imagined a posting that offers so much more in the way of challenges, responsibility and scope for initiative than anything else they have done in their entire lives."[60]

As Professor Christopher Browning puts it, Nazi planners felt "a certain intoxication in making history . . . People get high on the notion that they are going beyond what anybody else has done before, that they're going to make history in an exhilarating way that has no precedent. What you get is this strange mixture of people with great technocratic abilities and expertise in planning that also have these utopian visions, and these utopian visions are very intoxicating. And it's that combination of utopian intoxication and technocratic expertise that the Nazis blend in ways that produce this extraordinary destructiveness or, in this case, plans for extraordinary destructiveness."[61]

As we have seen, for Hitler the war was "ideological" from the moment German troops entered Poland in September 1939, but the consequences of this ideological thinking were now about to be seen with more intensity and on a greater scale in the war against the Soviet Union. Hitler made this desire explicit in an infamous speech he gave to senior German officers on 10 March 1941, when he stated that the forthcoming war against the Soviet Union was a "war of annihilation."[62] Specifically he called for the "annihilation of the Bolshevist commissars and of the Communist intelligentsia."

One junior German army officer, who knew of the decision to kill Soviet political officers (the "commissars") before the invasion of the Soviet Union and accepted it, later recalled his thinking at the time: "The difference [between fighting the Soviets and fighting on the Western Front] was that the Russian people or the Red Army soldier was considered an inferior person and that it was a mass action, that is, there were masses of Russian soldiers. And this strength, this quantitative superiority of people had to be changed . . . They [the Nazi leaders] said there is no time left, we have to fight, we have to press on and it doesn't matter whether a few more Russian people die on the way. It is an inferior group of people . . . these were inferior people who in fact gave us the moral right to destroy them, to exterminate them in part, so they would no longer be a danger for us . . . The Bolshevik was always portrayed with a bloody knife between his teeth, as someone who only ever destroys, shoots people, and batters them to death and tortures and deports to the camps in Siberia . . . These were Bolsheviks who were capable of any atrocity and violence, they must never play any leading role in the world."[63]

It was against this background of Hitler's desire to fight a "war of annihilation" against an "inferior group of people" that a group of state secretaries, army officers and other officials met on 2 May 1941. The view they formed at the meeting was expressed in the first two points of their concluding memorandum: "1. The war can only continue to be waged if the entire Wehrmacht is fed from Russia during the third year of the war. 2. As a result, x million people will doubtless starve, if that which is necessary for us is extracted from the land."[64] By the "third year of the war" these officials meant the period from September 1941 to August 1942. And the figure of "x" million was later revealed to be "30 million."[65]

This extraordinary "starvation plan" document—one that, in the context of the subsequent understandable focus on the horrors of the Holocaust, has not received the attention it should—did not appear by chance at this meeting, but was rather the result of a chain of causation that led to Hitler. The only senior government figure attending the meeting, Alfred Rosenberg, had a discussion planned with Hitler later that day to discuss "the questions of the East in more detail,"[66] and no doubt wanted to be able to make concrete proposals that would appeal to his Führer. Then there was the structural consequence of Hitler not wanting his senior ministers to meet together to discuss policy—the last Cabinet meeting had been held in 1938—which meant that meetings at the level *below* Cabinet ministers, the level of the state secretaries, became crucial.[67] (It was no accident that one of the most infamous meetings of the entire war—the discussion at the Wannsee conference in January 1942 about the fate of the Jews—was also conducted, like the 2 May "starvation" meeting, at this state secretary level.) There was also the important way Hitler's leadership, both in content and form, influenced the men who on 2 May proposed starving millions of people to death. Not only had Hitler already announced that this was to be a war of "annihilation," but he had demonstrated countless times before how he wished his followers to pursue "radical" solutions.

As a result, there is every reason to suppose that the men around the conference table on 2 May 1941 believed that they were serving the interests both of their leader and of their country by planning for 30 million people to starve to death. In particular, they remembered how the Allies had blockaded Germany in the First World War in an attempt to starve the country into submission. As a consequence, says Professor Adam Tooze, "what you see in the rhetoric of 1940–42 is this sort of inverting move where they say 'somebody's going to starve, but it isn't going to be us this time.'" And unlike the decisions about the Holocaust which were most often communicated in euphemistic terms (people to be killed, for instance, were said to be subject to *Sonderbehandlung,* or "special treatment"), the Hunger Plan was "explicitly documented in instructions issued to the German occupying forces. So commanders of German garrisons in the rear areas have explicit instructions which say should you feel minded to distribute food to starving Russians, remind yourself and your subordinates that what is at stake here is nothing less than the survival of the Reich and the continuation of the war into its second, third, fourth year."[68]

This kind of logic, of course, is an application of Hitler's own way of looking at the world in "either/or" terms—"either we annihilate the enemy or we are annihilated instead." This simple, emotion-based way of reducing complex questions to absolute alternatives had been a key component of Hitler's charismatic leadership from his earliest beer hall speeches. It was no surprise, therefore, that just days before the invasion of the Soviet Union Hitler spoke in similar terms to Joseph Goebbels: "The Führer says that we must gain the victory no matter whether we do right or wrong. We have so much to answer for anyhow that we must gain the victory because otherwise our whole people . . . will be wiped out."[69]

The starvation plan, like a whole host of Nazi plans before it, ultimately proved unworkable on the scale envisaged—German forces lacked the resources to imprison millions of people in every Soviet city and leave them to starve to death. But there were a number of places where the underlying thinking behind the plan was put into effect. The German army, for instance, laid siege to Leningrad (today's St. Petersburg) between September 1941 and January 1944 with the result that over 600,000 civilians died—many from lack of food. And the desire not to "waste" valuable food on the enemy was one of the key reasons for the death of more than three million Soviet prisoners of war in German captivity. There were also individual cities, like Kharkov in the east of Ukraine, where the German authorities did try and impose a starvation policy. Kharkov was the most populous Soviet city the German army occupied during the war. It was clear from the moment they arrived in October 1941 until they were finally expelled by the Red Army in August 1943[70] that seizing food from the locals was very much on their minds. "One soldier rushed into our room," says Inna Gavrilchenko, then a fifteen-year-old Ukrainian schoolgirl, "and started searching. He rushed behind the bookcases and started searching there and throwing out some things, throwing out books . . . Then he found some sugar, we had some sugar."[71]

Having stolen supplies from the inhabitants of Kharkov, the Germans sealed the city as best they could to stop the locals leaving, and then only offered food to the few Soviet people who helped them run the city. The rest—around 100,000 citizens—were left to starve to death. Inna Gavrilchenko watched as her own father died of hunger—and she came to know the signs of starvation well. "First of all, when you are starving, your body lacks proteins. And your body starts swelling. But it doesn't swell all over the body. It begins with your hands, or your feet. So, if you look at an arm, it looks like a stick with a boxer's glove on. And you can't clench your fist, make a fist, because your fingers wouldn't bend. They are so swollen. And the same with your legs—your legs are like sticks—your feet are swollen. Then the belly is swollen and there's a very special swelling on your face. It is just parts of the face that get swollen. And it disfigures faces. And one more thing, in the final stages of starvation, your lips get somehow stretched, and it's what they call a hungry grin. You don't know whether a person is grinning or crying. But the teeth are bare. Then, diarrhoea, the so called hungry diarrhoea. And then comes a bitter taste in the mouth. And some rash. On your tongue and then the mouth—a red rash."[72]

Some Germans relished the destruction of the people of Kharkov. When, for example, Anatoly Reva, then a small boy, approached a group of German soldiers and begged for some food, he was handed a bag full of human excrement. "They didn't have any kind of human feelings," he says. "They didn't feel sorry for the children."[73] But other Germans did show some compassion, as Inna Gavrilchenko recalls: "I was going along the street and it was already rather late in the afternoon—it was past three, I think, and it was growing dark. And I knew that after four I could be shot [for being out on the street], but I couldn't walk any faster and I had a long way to go home. And I saw a small German soldier, I remember that he was very small, and I stopped him and asked him what time it was. And I remember that it was past three, well past three. And he asked me, 'Where are you going?' I said, 'Home.' And he said, 'Is it far from here?' I said, 'Rather.' And he said, 'Oh right, I'll walk you there.' And he walked me up, nearly up to my place and then he looked at me and I remember he had something—a bag or something—and he looked at me. I stood silent for a minute and then he produced a piece of sausage. And gave it to me. I was quite at a loss, and he ran away . . . so the Germans were different. Germans were different and you can't possibly say that those who were SS were all bad, and those who were not SS were good. You can't say so. They were different."[74]

These contrasting experiences at the hands of the German occupiers of Kharkov illustrate a broader issue—for it was one thing to meet in a warm office in Berlin and demand that 30 million people be left to starve in the Soviet Union, and quite another to witness personally the suffering of dying women and children. Many German soldiers were able to accept the reasons why these people had to die in this way, but some were not. The starvation plan took no account of the feelings of the people who were supposed to implement it. And, demonstrably, not every German was heartless. This was an issue that Hitler failed to recognise. At the core of his speeches and his orders—indeed, at the core of his nature—was a lack of compassion. A belief that individuals did not matter but a *"Volk"*—a "people"—did. He assumed that he could persuade millions of Germans to pursue his policies with the same brutality that he possessed. Often he succeeded—but sometimes he didn't.

The forthcoming war with the Soviet Union also offered the Nazis other possible "solutions" to their self-created Jewish "problem." Hitler met Hans Frank, ruler of the General Government, on 17 March 1941 and told him that far from being the dumping ground of the Reich, his goal was to make the General Government "free" of Jews, "with the aim of this area becoming a purely German land over the course of 15 to 20 years."[75] Other related documents around this period make it clear that the Jews were to be sent into conquered Soviet territory once the war against

Stalin—which Hitler thought would only last a few weeks—was won.[76] The Nisko plan had failed, the Madagascar plan had failed, but now the prospect of controlling the wastelands of the Soviet Union offered a way for the Nazis to remove the Jews from the Reich.

Such a deportation would—like the other wartime plans that preceded it—almost certainly have had genocidal consequences. Not only had the Nazis already planned for 30 million Soviet citizens to die of hunger in the territory into which they intended to send the Jews, but Hitler told General Jodl on 3 March 1941, in the context of the forthcoming invasion, that "The Jewish–Bolshevik intelligentsia, hitherto the oppressor of the people, must be eliminated."[77] Moreover, special *Einsatzgruppen* units under the direction of Reinhard Heydrich were formed to operate immediately behind the advancing German troops, tasked with fomenting pogroms against the Soviet Jews and shooting "Jews in the service of the party or the state."[78] At this planning stage, the majority of the army leadership accepted not just the existence of the *Einsatzgruppen,* but all of the various practical consequences of this "war of annihilation"—from the decision to kill Soviet political officers and the immediate shooting of partisan fighters, to the imposition of mass reprisals against whole communities in case of civilian resistance.

Hitler was about to get the war he had always desired: a fight to the death against what he believed was the most dangerous regime in the world. That he wanted to conquer territory in the west of the Soviet Union is not surprising—he had stated as much in *Mein Kampf* in 1924. What is more surprising is that he had reached a point in the spring of 1941 that he was able to bring so many people with him on this bloody journey. As we have seen, there were a whole host of reasons why he was able to achieve this end—from the practical to the ideological. But the one overarching reason why so many millions of Germans accepted this new war in the East was their faith in the judgement of Adolf Hitler—a faith based on a combination of his past successes and his charismatic leadership. Yet even during the planning stage this new conflict looked risky in the extreme. It was obvious early in 1941, for example, from the work of General Georg Thomas,[79] that the German Army scarcely had enough fuel for two months' warfare in the Soviet Union, and only if they reached the oil of the Caucasus—more than two thousand miles from Berlin—could the army obtain the necessary fuel needed in the future.

Yet even if the Germans managed to get to the Caucasus swiftly enough, which was doubtful, there remained the problem of transporting that oil back to where it was needed within the German empire.

In a proclamation to the German people on 22 June 1941, Hitler claimed that he had been forced to order an attack on the Soviet Union because the Western Allies had secretly been plotting Germany's destruction with Stalin and the Soviet leadership: "It has become necessary to oppose this conspiracy of the Jewish–Anglo-Saxon warmongers and likewise the Jewish ruling powers in the Bolshevik control station at Moscow."[80] But it was a shallow pretence—an obvious part of what Churchill called "his usual formalities of perfidy."[81] The truth was that Hitler had initiated what he himself called the "greatest struggle in the history of the world"[82] because he wanted it to happen. And this one decision would do more than anything else to hasten the defeat of Germany and the destruction of his charismatic leadership.

14

FALSE HOPE AND THE
MURDER OF MILLIONS

As the first soldiers of the Wehrmacht crossed into Soviet territory in the early hours of Sunday, 22 June 1941, they initiated not only the largest and bloodiest invasion in history, but the greatest test yet in Hitler's leadership—one that would ultimately reveal the brittleness of his charismatic rule.

The consensus amongst the Germans—and not only the Germans—was that the Soviet Union would be swiftly defeated. As Professor Sir Ian Kershaw says, "At the time Hitler thought five months would do it, Goebbels thought four months, some of the generals thought less than that. This was a collective German lunacy, if you want to see it in that sense. But the American intelligence forces thought that this would be [over in] between three and six weeks, they reckoned that the Red Army was in no position to withstand the Wehrmacht. And British intelligence also thought this was a foregone conclusion and the Germans would win in the Soviet Union."[1]

With hindsight, knowing as we do the immense industrial and human resources which the Soviet Union was able to mobilise for this war, it seems almost incomprehensible that there was such a widespread view—amongst the Allies as well as the Germans—that Stalin's regime would crumble. But this confidence in a swift German victory was based on what appeared to be rational calculation. As we have seen, it was widely thought that Stalin had gravely weakened the Red Army by the purges of the 1930s and that this had contributed to the poor Soviet showing during the recent Finnish war. This was then seen against the seemingly miraculous German victory in little more than six weeks against France. But underlying each of these apparently rational views were elements of prejudice. A number of senior figures in the West despised the regime in the Soviet Union and were prepared to think the worst of it. Conveniently forgotten by many in the Alliance by the time of the "Big Three" conferences at Tehran and Yalta, was the lacklustre rhetoric President Roosevelt had initially used in support of Stalin in June 1941. One American senator—Bennett Clark of Missouri—had even said, "It's a case of dog eat dog. Stalin is as bloody-handed as Hitler. I don't think we should help either one."[2] Whilst a senior British general wrote in his diary on 29 June 1941, "I avoid the expression 'Allies,' for the Russians are a dirty lot of murdering thieves themselves, and double crossers of the deepest dye."[3]

As for the reasons behind the German victory in France, this was ascribed by the Allies to the brilliance of the Wehrmacht—this "terrible military machine" as Churchill described the German army in his speech on 22 June 1941—rather than to the incompetence of the British and French. Churchill in that same speech talked of the "mechanised armies" that Hitler had launched on the Soviet Union, but as we have seen the truth was that the British and French armies were more mechanised than the Germans at the time of the invasion of France. It was understandable, of course, that the Allied leadership preferred to focus on the strength of their enemy rather than their own previous ineptness, but the consequence was to exaggerate the material strength of the German army.

In the first days of the war, as the Germans pushed through into the Soviet Union in three great thrusts—from Army Groups North, Centre and South—it seemed as if the prophecy of an easy victory over the Red Army had been correct. Peter von der Groeben, then a young major, recalls that "We thought that it would all be over by Christmas."[4] Carlheinz Behnke, with the SS-Panzer Division Wiking, "assumed" together with his comrades that victory "would all happen quite quickly, as had been the case throughout France, that we would definitely manage the stretch up to the Caucasus so as to then fight against Turkey and Syria. That's what we believed at the time ... And we were longing to be deployed, and on 22 June we said, now we'll get our chance, and now we'll be able to prove ourselves too, now in the East we'll be able to carry on what our comrades started earlier, at the beginning of the war. So a Blitzkrieg, that's what we expected. At the time we were 17, 18 years old, young, and we entered this war in a rather carefree way ... we now had the chance to prove ourselves as soldiers and we wanted to demonstrate that we were every bit as capable as our predecessors ... Well, we thought that we'd have things under control by the onset of winter, which gave us four to five months. That was the general feeling. And the initial successes proved us right. And right at the beginning, once the border fortifications had been broken through, we took hundreds of thousands of Russians prisoner, and then it was clear that, as far as we were concerned, it was a question of weeks or months until this huge empire would crumble and we would have achieved our goal."[5]

Within a week the Germans were poised to take Minsk, capital of Belorussia. Guderian's 2nd Panzer Group appeared to be recreating the success of France—in fact, exceeding it, since within just five days they had travelled nearly two hundred miles into the Soviet Union. Back home in Germany this all seemed to be confirmation that victory would be easy and swift. "In the weekly newsreels we would see glorious pictures of the German army with all the soldiers singing and waving and cheering," remembers Maria Mauth, then a student, "and that was infectious, of course, it must have been a doddle! We thought about it in these terms and believed it for a long time too. Whatever the Führer said was true. And I am convinced that 90 per cent of people believed it. I did too for a long time. I also believed, gosh, he has achieved so much already! And that was it. He had achieved so much."[6]

General Franz Halder, in his diary on 3 July 1941, was equally as enthusiastic, writing, "It is thus probably no overstatement to say that the Russian campaign has been won in the space of two weeks."[7] But even in an entry suffused with hubris as much as this one, Halder felt compelled to add that it was still important to deny "the enemy possession of his production centres and so prevent his raising a new army with the aid of his gigantic industrial potential and his inexhaustible manpower resources."

The Germans knew that they had not only to achieve victory over the Soviet Union, but victory in a hurry. They needed to snatch the industrial resources of the Soviet state in order to support their own effort against their increasingly well-armed opponents in the West. On 26 June 1941, just over a week before Halder's vainglorious boast that the "Russian campaign has been won," Field Marshal Erhard Milch, a close associate of Göring's and "Air Inspector General," revealed at a meeting with other senior military commanders that, "The combined production [of aircraft engines] in England and the U.S.A. surpassed the overall production of Germany and Italy as early as 1 May 1941, and would, at the current state of German production, be twice as much as German production in late 1942."[8] And Milch gave this pessimistic assessment, remember, before America had formally entered the war.

By the summer of 1941 Hitler and his generals were beginning to realise that their over-confidence in the wake of the victory over France had made them blind to the difficulties they would encounter in their struggle against the Red Army. On 11 August, Halder wrote, "The whole situation makes it increasingly plain that we have underestimated the Russian colossus . . . The time factor favours them, as they are near their own resources, while we are moving farther and farther away from ours."[9] The supply problem grew so bad that by the end of August the Germans had suffered more than 400,000 casualties and yet had little more than half that number immediately available to fill their shoes.[10]

The situation was exacerbated by a dispute that had rumbled on between Hitler and his generals since almost the first moment of the decision to move on the Soviet Union. The controversy focused on the extent to which the advance on Moscow was a priority for the Wehrmacht. Halder and many of his colleagues thought it ought to be an absolute priority, whilst Hitler favoured the destruction of Leningrad and the advance towards the Crimea and then the Caucasus over any attack on the Soviet capital. In the middle of August Halder submitted a memorandum forcefully calling for Army Group Centre to push on to Moscow. But General Alfred Jodl, chief of the operations staff at OKW (officers of the supreme command of the armed forces), felt it was important to have continued faith in Hitler's judgement. When on 20 August 1941 one of Halder's officers argued that he should support the advance on Moscow, Jodl replied, "We must not try to compel him [i.e., Hitler] to do something which goes against his inner convictions. His intuition has generally been right."[11] (Reliance on a leader's "inner convictions" and "intuition" is, of course, axiomatic of a reliance on charismatic leadership.)

Hitler's verdict on the dispute, in a directive on 21 August, was to reaffirm that the capture of Moscow before winter should not be the "principal" object of the campaign, but rather the focus should be on the occupation of the Crimea and the advance towards the oil fields of the Caucasus. Halder was furious, writing that Hitler was to "blame"[12] for the way the campaign was going and that the high command of the army was being treated in an "absolutely outrageous" way. But Halder was behaving disingenuously. He had been prepared to share credit back in early July when he thought the campaign had been "won" in a matter of a few weeks, yet now took none of the responsibility for "underestimating" his opponent. Hitler was an obvious and easy target for blame when events did not go as expected—but the responsibility for failure was not his alone.

Heinz Guderian, commander of 2nd Panzer Group—also known as Panzergroup Guderian—was also angry at Hitler's decision not to push on to Moscow but to turn south instead. He saw Hitler on 23 August and forcefully put his case for carrying on the attack to the Soviet capital. He used every argument he could think of to persuade Hitler. But it was useless. Having allowed Guderian to speak at length, Hitler then simply explained to him why he was wrong. Economic considerations were paramount and conquering the Ukraine was more important than attacking Moscow. "I here saw for the first time a spectacle with which I was later to become very familiar," wrote Guderian after the war. "All those present nodded in agreement with every sentence that Hitler uttered, while I was left alone with my point of view . . . In view of the OKW's unanimous opposition to my remarks, I avoided all further argument on that occasion . . . "[13] Neither Brauchitsch nor Halder—the senior figures in the OKH, the Army high command—were present at the meeting, and Guderian's sense of isolation was total. Hitler had created the structure of the OKW in the wake of the Blomberg/Fritsch crisis three years before, and this system, plus his own charismatic dominance of the staff of the OKW, made his position at the time all but impregnable. Leading figures in the OKW, like Jodl, had become little more than cheerleaders.

But the strain of the war was still getting to Hitler. When Goebbels visited Hitler's headquarters in East Prussia that August he thought the Führer "looks a little worn out and sick. This is probably due to his dysentery, and probably also to the fact that the last few weeks have worn him out so harshly. This is not surprising. Today the responsibility for a whole continent rests on his shoulders."[14]

However, despite the difficulties of the war against the Soviet Union, Hitler's love of conflict and bloodshed had not been quashed. During his after-dinner monologues that autumn he called for a war "every 15 or 20 years"[15] and demanded the "sacrifice" (i.e., death) of 10 per cent of Germans in battle. The death of so many Germans on the Eastern Front meant nothing to him. Pressure merely stirred his desire for greater carnage and greater vengeance. His fundamental nihilism was on show once again a few weeks later when he said, "The earth continues to go round, whether it's the man who kills the tiger or the tiger who eats the man. The stronger asserts his will, it's the law of nature. The world doesn't change; its laws are eternal."[16] It was an attitude—a way of seeing the world free of all moral or ethical responsibility to other nations or people—which was, as we have seen, at the core of the reason why so many of his followers could feel "intoxicated" by the possibilities the war offered. What few people who embraced Hitler's vision seem to have thought through—at least until events started to go against them—was the full logic of this philosophy: if you don't win then you "deserve" to be exterminated yourself. However, Hitler was one of the small number of Nazis who had fully accepted this reasoning from the beginning. He had even built a life or death commitment into the party programme of the Nazis as far back as February 1920, ending the document with the words, "The leaders of the Party promise to work ruthlessly—if necessary at the cost of their own lives—to implement this programme."[17] Now, by calling for a war of "annihilation" against the Soviet Union, Hitler understood that by his own logic this also meant a similar fate for Germany if the war was lost. Indeed, he privately said as much in January 1942, calling for the German people to "disappear" unless they were prepared to give their "body and soul in order to survive."[18]

Hitler hid none of his potentially apocalyptic beliefs from those around him. But as long as success seemed assured it was not necessary for them to dwell on the consequences of failure. And after the anxieties of August 1941 it did seem as if all might come right for the Germans in the autumn, when Guderian—despite his belief that strategically this action was a mistake—led his 2nd Panzer Group south from Army Group Centre to join forces with units from Rundstedt's Army Group South. The result, by the end of September, was the largest encirclement action in history as 650,000 Red Army soldiers were trapped during the Battle for Kiev. It seemed to be another triumph for Hitler's judgement.

Hitler watched the newsreels of the destruction of so many Soviet soldiers and said he was "thrilled"[19] by the sight. All this carnage reminded him of the First World War. That conflict, he said, had been responsible for the death of his "idealism" about war. Trench warfare, he reiterated, had taught him that life is a "cruel struggle" and had no other purpose than "the preservation of the species." He proceeded to apply that lesson to the war in the east by ordering that Leningrad should vanish from the surface of the earth. The German Army was told not to accept the surrender of the inhabitants of the encircled city, since feeding and housing these people was not considered a German responsibility.[20]

Hitler then returned briefly to Berlin to give a speech at the Sportpalast on 3 October 1941. Here he once again repeated his fantasy of how Germany had been forced into a war against the Soviet Union because of a secret conspiracy by Stalin to attack the Reich. But he reassured the German people that "everything" since 22 June "has gone according to plan."[21] Even more than that, he announced that "this opponent has already broken down and will never rise again." Six days later, on 9 October, in the light of news that five Soviet armies had been encircled in the twin battle of Vyazma/Bryansk, the Reich press chief, Otto Dietrich, announced that "the campaign in the east has been decided."[22] Over the next few days the German press followed suit: the *Münchener Zeitung*'s (Munich News) headline was "Soviets Defeated!"; the *Hannoverscher Kurier*'s (Hanover Courier): "Europe is saved: Freed from Stalin by the Führer's military genius"; and the *Völkischer Beobachter* boasted "Success of the Eastern Campaign assured!"[23]

But the success of the Eastern Campaign was most certainly not assured, and Hitler had risked a great deal by making the speech he did at the Sportpalast. "Pure charisma," Max Weber wrote, "does not know any 'legitimacy' other than that flowing from personal strength, that is, one which is constantly being proved"[24]—and it was potentially damaging for Hitler to assert that a victory had taken place when in fact it had not. Moreover, Hitler spoke those words knowing that the war in the east could well continue into the following year—as Halder makes explicit in his diary on 13 September 1941.[25]

Hitler now agreed that the German army could at last advance directly on Moscow in *Unternehmen Taifun* (Operation Typhoon) and the Wehrmacht managed to launch almost two million men against the Red Army in front of the Soviet capital in a last attempt to deliver a decisive blow before winter came. As German Army Group Centre pushed forward that October, Hitler himself became intoxicated by the vision of what could now be achieved in the Soviet Union. His after-dinner monologues delivered that month to his followers at his headquarters in East Prussia show Hitler at his most authentic: in his determination to destroy the lives of millions of Soviet citizens ("there's only one duty: to Germanise this country by the immigration of Germans, and to look upon the natives as Redskins"[26]); his desire to lay waste to cities ("I have no feelings about the idea of wiping out Kiev, Moscow or St. Petersburg"[27]); the intensity of his hatred of the Jews ("let nobody tell me that all the same we can't park them in the marshy parts of Russia!"[28]). But Hitler did not confine his rants only to the war in the east, he also discoursed on Christianity ("taken to its logical extreme, Christianity would mean the systematic cultivation of human failure"[29]); on the construction of bathroom appliances ("what's the point of having a hundred different models for wash-basins?"[30]); on his love of bearing grudges and seeking vengeance ("I have numerous accounts to settle, about which I cannot think today. But that doesn't mean I forgot them"[31]). It all reveals Hitler, as Hugh Trevor-Roper wrote, as the "coarsest, cruelest, least magnanimous conqueror the world has ever known."[32] But it also demonstrates once again core elements of his charismatic leadership—his certainty, his liberation from conventional morals, and his excitement and exhilaration at the vastness of the possibilities ahead. And despite his almost daily interference with the details of the military campaign—something that infuriated Halder—Hitler still claimed in October 1941 that his best subordinates took 95 per cent of his decisions for him,[33] intuitively knowing what he would like.

As Hitler spoke these words, there was growing panic in Moscow. Stalin even contemplated fleeing the city but eventually decided to stay and impose a state of siege on the capital. But the success of the German army was not sustainable. Not only were their supply lines overstretched but soon new Red Army units would arrive, released from bases in Siberia because of intelligence reaching Stalin that Japan, Hitler's ally, had no plans to attack the Soviet Union from the Far East.

By the start of December 1941 German soldiers were just twelve miles from the Kremlin. But this was as close to the centre of Moscow as they would ever get, as on 5 December 1941 the Soviets launched a counter-attack with around seventy divisions—more than a million Red Army troops—committed to the fight. The Germans, already weakened by lack of supplies—particularly lack of proper clothing and cold-weather pro-tection for their weapons and vehicles—struggled to contain the Soviet offensive.

It was perhaps the single most decisive moment in the history of the war. For Professor Adam Tooze this is "an absolutely crucial turning point . . . It's the first battle defeat suffered by the German army in quite a long time, since the end of the First World War"[34]; for Sir Ian Kershaw it's the "first major setback" for the Germans, one which means that "war is going to be prolonged indefinitely"[35]; and for Professor Richard Evans, it's "the first time the Germans are actually stopped in their tracks and they don't know what to do."[36] As a result the German leadership were placed in a position where they feel "completely clueless."

Ulrich de Maizière, then a Wehrmacht officer serving on the Eastern Front, describes it as a devastating time: "You have to imagine what goes on in the mind of a young general staff officer of 29 years of age, who is convinced in August [1941] that it will be all over in September, who thinks it will take longer in October and in December realises it will last at least three more years."[37] And, for de Maizière, the events of December 1941 also demonstrated the appalling lack of preparation that had been made by the German leadership for a winter war. "In one night we lost five hundred men in the division, they froze to death . . . " Those same harsh winter conditions also showed the resilience of the Soviets, who were "very capable of bearing hardship, very modest in terms of their own requirements. They were very courageous, but not very imaginative. They were uncommonly hardy and had a capacity to bear suffering. They could survive two or three winter nights out in the open with a few sunflower seeds in their pockets or a few grains of corn. They got their fluid intake from the snow. I myself have witnessed that a young woman gave birth one night to a child on a woollen blanket and heap of straw in a wooden hut and then went to work in the stable the following day . . . One saw the primitive accommodation, the primitive villages, the way they lived, and one did have the feeling that this is a people that cannot compare with central and western European countries in terms of their level of development."

But now these "not very imaginative" people living in "primitive" circumstances were fighting back successfully against the Germans. Soldiers Nazi propaganda described as "subhuman" appeared to be defeating the supermen of the "master race." More than that, German newspapers—sanctioned by the state—had only a few weeks before declared that the Soviets were "defeated" and Hitler had said unequivocally that the Red Army would "never rise again." The unreasoned, almost hysterical optimism in these statements had also been reflected in the orders given to Heinz Guderian on 13 November, just three weeks before the launch of the offensive against the Soviet capital. He had been told to take his Panzers more than two hundred miles east of Moscow to cut off the city from reinforcements. It was an impossible request that reflected none of the reality on the ground—as achievable as an order to invade the moon. The fantasy nature of life in Hitler's bunker in Berlin in the last days of the war has often been remarked upon. The fantasy nature of life in the Führer's headquarters in East Prussia in the autumn and early winter of 1941 has received less attention, but is at least as revealing.

Hitler was now in denial. When he was told, just before the Soviet offensive in December, that the Wehrmacht could not be supplied with adequate amounts of steel, he simply refused to accept that "no raw materials are available" because "he has now conquered all of Europe."[38] And on 29 November 1941, when informed by his own Armaments Minister, Fritz Todt, that "the war can no longer be won militarily," and that the only way of stopping the conflict was by some form of political solution, Hitler replied that he could see no way of ending the war in such a way.[39]

Many of the central components of Hitler's charismatic appeal—his certainty, his force of will, his refusal to admit defeat, his faith in his own destiny—were beginning to be perceived as dangerous weaknesses by some of those who had put their trust in him. An idea of the inner tension a number of his most senior military figures were enduring, as they attempted to reconcile the reality they were learning from those beneath them with the intransigence of their leader, can be seen from the catalogue of illness and dismissal that winter. Field Marshal Brauchitsch had a heart attack on 9 November 1941.[40] The anxiety and stress of the eastern campaign had—both Hitler and Halder agreed—contributed to the breakdown in his health. Hitler removed Brauchitsch from command on 19 December 1941. The day before, Hitler had granted Field Marshal von Bock's request to be replaced as commander of Army Group Centre. Bock had been outraged by the decision not to push forward earlier on Moscow; however, he wrote that his request to be relieved was motivated by a stomach illness from which he had not recovered.

The stress of the fight on the Eastern Front was breaking the spirit of those tasked with meeting impossible logistical demands. On 17 November 1941, General Ernst Udet committed suicide. As the Luftwaffe's Head of Equipment he had endured the added pressure of working for Hermann Göring, a man who consistently made unattainable promises to Hitler. During the Battle of Britain, Udet had personally experienced how Göring's pattern of wild promise, followed inevitably by crashing disappointment, could affect him. Having assured Hitler that the RAF would be defeated, Göring dealt with the failure of the Luftwaffe to deliver the desired result by placing large amounts of the blame on Udet.

Hitler now had a series of important personnel decisions to take, and the most important was who should replace Brauchitsch as head of the army. Hitler needed someone on whom he could utterly rely. Someone, he must have felt, given this list of sick and feeble military commanders, who was tough enough to deal with the stress of this war of annihilation. And by this point the only man who measured up to all this, in Hitler's view, was Adolf Hitler. He appointed himself the head of the German army and added this title to his growing list—which now included Supreme Commander in Chief of all German armed forces, Chancellor, Führer of the German people, and head of state.

Hitler's strength as a charismatic leader had always been to set the overarching vision and leave the details to his subordinates. But now the days of staying in his room until noon, and then taking a long lunch and a walk in the mountains until tea, were over. His reaction to adversity was to pile more work on himself. In the process he sent out the clear message to his military subordinates that he knew better than they did—not just in vision, but in detail.

This new reality was demonstrated during one of his first meetings as head of the army. On 20 December 1941, Hitler met General Guderian for an epic five-hour conference. Guderian travelled to Hitler's headquarters in the belief that "our Supreme Command would listen to sensible propositions when they were laid before it by a general who knew the front."⁴¹ He believed that his unit should mount a tactical retreat in the face of the Soviet offensive—in fact, as Hitler learnt at this meeting, they were already retreating. Hitler vehemently disagreed, insisting that they stay where they were. He suggested they blast holes in the frozen earth to create shelters. Guderian dismissed the idea, and argued that huge numbers of his soldiers would die if they did not pull back. Hitler's response was revealing. "Do you think Frederick the Great's grenadiers were anxious to die?" he asked. And like Frederick the Great, Hitler argued, "I, too, am entitled to ask any German soldier to lay down his life." Guderian replied that every soldier knew that in war time he risked his life, but that "the intentions I have heard expressed will lead to losses that are utterly disproportionate to the results that will be achieved."

Searching for an explanation for Guderian's behaviour, Hitler seems to have found the answer in the tank commander's desire to protect his men. "You have been too deeply impressed by the suffering of the soldiers," he said. "You feel too much pity for them. You should stand back more. Believe me, things appear clearer when examined at longer range."⁴²

Guderian, having failed to convince Hitler of the wisdom of tactical retreat, left East Prussia for the front. Less than a week later he was sacked. And he was not the only general to lose his job. Around three dozen generals would be removed in the wake of the December crisis. Then, on 17 January, Field Marshal Walther von Reichenau, who had been one of the first senior officers to support Hitler in the early 1930s, collapsed and died of a stroke.

Hitler would have seen all this as evidence of Darwinian selection; if his generals were not tough enough then so be it. He would replace them with other, tougher men. Indeed, the necessity for "toughness" was a theme of the order he sent to Army Group Centre on 20 December. "The fanatical will to defend the land on which the troops are standing must be injected into them with every possible means, even the toughest."⁴³

Whether or not Hitler's decision to order the army to stand its ground that winter made good tactical sense is still open to debate. Whilst the outright crisis did ease by spring, this was in part the result of inept decisions taken by Stalin, and because German officers did move their troops back some miles to more defendable positions when they thought it necessary. What is clear, however, is that this marks the moment when Hitler demonstrated that he could not be trusted to keep his promises to the German people. The enemy had not been destroyed as he had promised back in October.

The situation in December was made still worse for Hitler by the entry of America into the war as a result of the Japanese attack on Pearl Harbor on 7 December. Four days later, Hitler—and thus Germany—declared war on America. In doing so, Hitler would have felt he was doing little more than formalising a state of conflict that had existed unofficially for months. American ships were already protecting British convoys in the Atlantic and Roosevelt had made obvious his commitment to helping Churchill.[44] In any case, Hitler felt, the Americans would now be involved in a war in the Pacific and it would be some time before their troops could also be fighting in Europe. Hitler's focus thus remained on the war in the East.

But not exclusively. Because Hitler had also been making important decisions in two areas of secret Nazi policy—the adult euthanasia scheme and the persecution of the Jews. How he dealt with both of these issues during this vital period tells us a great deal not just about the cold cruelty at the heart of the Nazi state, but also how Hitler carefully managed his charismatic reputation in the face of potentially unpopular decisions.

By early summer 1941 the euthanasia action against the severely disabled had been in operation for nearly two years. Since German doctors would not participate in the scheme without some form of official backing Hitler had been forced, back in October 1939, to sign a note authorising Phillip Bouhler of the Party Chancellery and his own doctor, Karl Brandt, to conduct "mercy" killings. Hitler saw the war as ideal cover to pursue the policy; significantly he deliberately backdated the note he wrote in October 1939 to 1 September and the invasion of Poland. But despite the existence of this document he wanted to keep his own name out of this business as much as possible. Hitler subsequently refused, for example, to allow formal legislation to be passed which would associate him directly with the killings.[45]

By 1941 several killing centres had been established within Germany to murder selected disabled people—adults as well as children. The killing procedure that evolved at places like Sonnenstein mental hospital near Dresden had obvious similarities with the technique used subsequently to murder Jews in the extermination camps—the patients were told to undress because they were to take a "shower" and were then gassed once the "shower" room had been sealed. Those involved in the crime did their best to keep the process secret—patients were often moved between a number of asylums before finally arriving at a killing centre—but since in many cases the victims had families who still cared about their welfare, and since the killings were conducted inside Germany, it proved hard not to let news about the action slip out. There were a number of occasions where it was obvious what had happened once the notice of the fictitious cause of death was posted to the relatives. In one case, for example, the cause of death was reported as appendicitis, but the patient's appendix had actually been taken out years before.[46]

Cardinal August Count von Galen, Bishop of Münster, famously protested publicly about the euthanasia campaign on 3 August 1941. From the pulpit he declaimed that it was obvious that incurable patients were being killed, and he railed against the whole idea of "worthless life." He also pointed out that once the idea of killing people like the mentally ill had been accepted then others could soon be at risk—like soldiers who returned severely injured from the front line. He also made reference to the British bombing raids on Germany—allowing for the possible inference that this was some kind of divine retribution on Germany.

In the wake of Galen's actions, and after the publication and distribution of thousands of copies of his eloquent outrage, it looked like the Nazis faced a growing movement of public protest. Nazi authorities had already seen discontent develop in Catholic areas of Germany when, starting earlier in 1941, they had introduced a variety of restrictive measures—like the removal of nuns from teaching. The protests later crystallised around the decision to ban crucifixes in schools. This resulted in petitions and even street demonstrations. Significantly, many of the protestors claimed that they were completely behind Hitler, but that his underlings must be acting against his wishes whilst he was away fighting the war. "You wear brown shirts on the outside," wrote one protestor, talking about the local Nazi party officials, "but on the inside you are Bolsheviks and Jews, otherwise you could not act behind the Führer's back. Our Führer does not order such things. Every day he cares for his soldiers in the field and not

for taking the crucifixes out of school . . ."⁴⁷ Another letter from Maria
Aigner, who lived in a village north of Munich, read, "As a mother of
eight, our Führer awarded me with the *Mutterkreuz* (mother's cross) in
gold. It is incomprehensible to me that my youngest, whom last Monday
I led to school for the first time, should not see a crucifix there, after his
seven siblings have grown up in the shadow of the crucifix hitherto. Of
my five sons, two already fulfil their duty as soldiers and the crucifix in
school has certainly not harmed them, but it was to them an example of
the highest commitment. I often contemplate and cannot solve the mystery, how such a measure is possible at all, since our Führer stands by his
soldiers in the East and fights against Bolshevism."⁴⁸

We've already seen the positive benefit that Hitler gained from the
belief amongst many ordinary Germans that the everyday problems they
faced at the hands of Nazi officials were not the work directly of their
Führer, and that "if only he knew" what was happening then all would be
put right. But here we see a more problematic side of that arrangement
as far as Hitler was concerned, and one explanation of why he tried to
distance himself from policies that might prove unpopular—even though
he desired their implementation. If Hitler had openly supported measures like the removal of crucifixes from schools or the euthanasia killings then he knew that many of his supporters—in particular, millions of
Christians—would be disillusioned.

So, despite the complete loathing Hitler expressed for Christianity
in private, senior Nazis ensured that the ban on crucifixes in schools was
lifted. Moreover, not only did Hitler not throw Bishop Galen into a concentration camp for so openly challenging the euthanasia policy, but on
24 August 1941 he stopped the transportation of the disabled to the killing
centres. Over ninety thousand people had been murdered so far during
the euthanasia action. But the killings did not completely stop. The programme of murdering selected sick prisoners from concentration camps
under a procedure named 14f 13 continued, and individual asylums still
carried on killing a number of patients on site. All this, however, was
much easier for the Nazis to keep secret than the widespread transportation of patients to the killing centres had been.

What this all demonstrated was the latent power of the Church to
mobilise popular protest. Hitler recognised this and spoke privately that
autumn of wanting Christianity to die a "slow" death, whilst understand-

ing the obvious dangers of provoking discontent. "The main thing," he said, "is to be clever in this matter and not to look for a struggle where it can be avoided."[49]

But whilst he avoided directly challenging the Church during 1941, Hitler did increase measures against the Jews. Not only was Hitler's hatred of Jews almost visceral in a way his dislike of Christians was not, but the Jews could not mobilise protest against their treatment in the way that millions of Christians could. They had few friends inside the Reich with the courage to stand up for them. Whilst Bishop Galen protested about the euthanasia scheme, for instance, he made no mention of the persecution of the Jews.

Moreover, unlike the euthanasia action where Hitler had never spoken publicly about his desire to see the disabled killed, he had explicitly spoken in the Reichstag on 30 January 1939 about the fate he desired for the Jews in the event of war, saying infamously that if the "International Jewish financiers" caused a world war then the "annihilation of the Jewish race in Europe" would follow.

But Hitler had not, by the start of 1941, pursued such a policy. Jews had been mistreated, persecuted and imprisoned in ghettos in Poland. Many thousands had died, but there had been no systematic plan in place to annihilate them. One reason was because Hitler wanted, as we have seen, to make peace with Britain and in the process prevent America from interfering—as he saw it—in European affairs. A policy of mass murder of the Jews would have been an obstacle in the way of such a goal. But the prospect of the war against the Soviet Union offered new possibilities. As Professor Omar Bartov says, "the war in the Soviet Union provides the perfect cover for genocide on that scale, and I mean cover in all ways. Cover vis-à-vis the international community, cover vis-à-vis your own population, even cover vis-à-vis the people who are doing it, because then you're involved in such a brutal war in which so many millions of people die, that killing another group doesn't seem very different. And I have to say that if you look at genocide in the twentieth century more generally you will find that it almost always happens either at a time of war or is at least described as war, as happening within a war, and a war for existence, not just any war."[50]

A meeting between Hermann Göring and Reinhard Heydrich on 26 March 1941 demonstrated the accuracy of this judgement. Here the plan to deport the Jews to the barren reaches of the Soviet Union was discussed and endorsed. That Hitler approved of such an idea is certain, since he personally told Hans Frank on 25 March that the General Government was, over time, to become "free of Jews."[51] These Jews, it was clear, would be sent further east to languish and eventually die.

In parallel with this policy of expulsion to a wilderness within what was shortly expected to be the new Nazi sphere of influence, went a more immediate plan to kill selected Jews behind the lines as the German Army advanced into the Soviet Union. Reinhard Heydrich's 2 July 1941 directive to the *Einsatzgruppen* demonstrates that he wanted these killings to be seen in the context of the overall war of annihilation against the Soviet Union that Hitler had declared. The action was described as an attempt to eliminate communist and "Jewish" influence and control, and as such was easier for many senior German army commanders to accept than an outright policy of mass extermination. The memory of the attempted Communist revolution in Germany after the First World War, and the perception that Jewish figures had instigated it, was still raw. For Carl-heinz Behnke of the Waffen SS—someone who had joined the Hitler Youth at the age of eleven in 1933 and volunteered for an SS Panzer Division in 1940—the link between Judaism and Communism was obvious. "The Jews were simply regarded as the leadership class or as those who were firmly in control over there in the Soviet Union." Moreover, he felt, "they were attempting to somehow gain control over the German nation . . . that was after all the aim of Bolshevism, to spread westwards to the Atlantic and to then spread Bolshevism throughout Europe. And I don't think that aim can be dismissed."[52]

The "solution" that Hitler then encouraged to deal with the Jewish "leadership class" in the Soviet Union might subsequently be seen as too radical or too risky by many Germans, but large numbers still accepted that some kind of action should be taken against the Jews in the Soviet Union and their unease only related to the degree of radicalism involved. The Nazi regime, after all, had been stoking hatred and fear of the Bolsheviks amongst the German population for years before the unexpected non-aggression pact of August 1939 with Stalin. However, Hitler also knew that there was bound not only to be foreign opposition to the idea of shooting Soviet Jews in cold blood, but that these killings would be something only the most extreme anti-Semite would be likely to endorse.

So just as he had with the Jewish boycott of April 1933 and in the aftermath of *Kristallnacht* in 1938, Hitler kept his own name and prestige apart from these potentially damaging actions.

Once the conflict had begun Himmler ordered several more SS units to reinforce the work of the *Einsatzgruppen* in the Soviet Union and the killing extended over the summer and early autumn of 1941 to include the murder of Jewish women and children. This all occurred after Hitler had met Himmler on 15 July at his headquarters in East Prussia. An idea of what was on Hitler's mind at the time can be gleaned from a speech he gave to select Nazi leaders the next day. He declared that he wanted to create a "garden of Eden" in the east for Germans, and this should be achieved by "shooting everyone who even looks [at us] askance."[53] Hitler was also talking during the summer and autumn of 1941 of leaving the populations of cities like Leningrad to starve to death, so the increasing intensity of the action against the Jews of the Soviet Union can be seen as part of a wider aim of destroying millions of lives in the east.

By now there was also another plan for the radical ethnic re-ordering of the Nazi empire in the east under active consideration. On 15 July 1941, less than a month after the invasion had been launched, Himmler received a draft of *Generalplan Ost* (General Plan East), a wide-ranging vision for the settlement of the eastern territories that imagined the disappearance of large numbers of the indigenous population. Professor Konrad Meyer-Hetling, an academic expert in rural and town planning—as well as an SS colonel—played a crucial part in the construction of the document. As the plan subsequently proceeded through various drafts it became clear that the number of people to be removed would almost certainly have been higher than 40 million.[54] It was never specified explicitly where these people were to be removed to, or if and how they were to be murdered. Most likely, they too were to be shipped to the wilds of the occupied far eastern Soviet Union and simply left to die. Since the Germans did not conquer the Soviet Union as they had planned, the *Generalplan Ost* was never implemented in full, but it does show the context in which the fate of the Jews was considered in the summer and autumn of 1941. It is also another example of how highly intelligent people like Meyer-Hetling felt liberated by the regime to dream up fantastical quasi-utopian plans that would result in unimaginable suffering for millions of people. (After the war, and a short period of imprisonment, Meyer-

Hetling resumed his academic career as a Professor at Hanover Technical University.)

The shooting of Jews in the Soviet Union also provided the background against which decisions about the fate of Jews in Poland, Germany and other Nazi-occupied territories were about to be taken. The original idea had been to deport these Jews into the Soviet Union once the war was over. But now several leading Nazis, like Joseph Goebbels, Gauleiter of Berlin as well as Propaganda Minister, and Karl Kaufmann, the Gauleiter of Hamburg, asked Hitler to consider bringing forward that plan and deport German Jews almost immediately. Everyone involved in this process knew that a move of this significance could only be taken with Hitler's approval. In response, Hitler told Goebbels in August 1941 that his "prophecy" made in the Reichstag in January 1939 to destroy the Jews if they "provoked" another world war was coming true. "In the East the Jews have had to settle their account; in Germany they have partly settled and will have to pay even more in future."[55]

In September 1941, Hitler agreed to deport the German Jews, and just a few weeks later the Jews of Hamburg were sent east. One non-Jewish German who watched a column of Jews trail by on the way to Hamburg railway station recalls that around a fifth of people welcomed their departure, saying "Thank goodness these useless eaters are vanishing"[56] but most just looked on in silence.

The Jews from Hamburg were not sent directly into the occupied Soviet Union but were transported to the already overcrowded Łódź ghetto in Poland. Their arrival created a crisis that by December 1941 led to a plan to murder selected Jews from the ghetto in gas vans based at an extermination centre at Chelmno, 120 miles north of Łódź. But most of the 60,000 Jews deported from the "Old Reich" between October 1941 and February 1942 were sent directly into the area of the Soviet Union in which the *Einsatzgruppen* operated. Some were shot immediately on arrival, whilst others were housed in ghettos—and Soviet Jews were murdered to make space for them.

The fact that the Jews were "sent away" from the Reich undoubtedly helped ordinary Germans not to think about their possible fate. From September 1941 German Jews had been forced to wear a yellow star to mark them out, and this caused even some supporters of the regime to feel "sorry"[57] for their Jewish neighbours. But once these same Jewish neighbours were transported to the east then many people simply banished them from their minds.

Hitler seems to have been acting that autumn and winter out of his visceral feelings of hatred for the Jews rather than any carefully thought through strategy. As we've seen, whilst he'd decided in September 1941 that German Jews should be deported east, there was no detailed plan in place about exactly where they should go—Himmler had to improvise a solution. All that was certain was that the future for these Jews was extremely bleak.

By the end of 1941 several different techniques of murder were in development or operation: gas vans—in which victims were forced into the back of a sealed van and then carbon monoxide gas from the exhaust was used to kill them—were at work, particularly at Chelmno; the *Einsatzgruppen* continued mass shooting behind the lines in the Soviet Union; the building of the first fixed extermination camp started at Belzec in south-east Poland—Belzec was to use the exhaust from powerful diesel engines to kill, to begin with, "unproductive" Jews from nearby ghettos; and at Auschwitz main camp in Upper Silesia the deputy commandant was experimenting with the use of a powerful insecticide called Zyklon B to kill Soviet prisoners of war and the sick. Within a few months this technique would also be used to kill Jews from the surrounding area.

No written order from Hitler to kill the Jews that autumn has ever been found. Instead, his rhetoric continued to set the broad and murderous goals whilst the system did the rest. That December, in the wake of both the Red Army's counter-offensive and the Japanese attack on Pearl Harbor, Hitler's vision for the fate of the Jews grew still more apocalyptic. In his speech to the Reichstag on 11 December, Hitler claimed the "sheer, satanic malice" of the Jews was behind Roosevelt's decision to embark on a "foreign policy diversion"—by which he meant military support for Britain. Hitler, just as he had in his speeches in the early 1920s, thus claimed that the Jews were behind the policies of both the Communist Soviet Union and the capitalist United States.

The next day, 12 December, Hitler spoke to Reich leaders and, as recorded by Goebbels, said that since the Jews had brought about a world war then "they would experience their own extermination."[58] Four days later on 16 December, Hans Frank, who had just heard Hitler speak, said at a meeting in Krakow that "we must exterminate the Jews wherever we find them." In Berlin, said Frank, he had been told to "liquidate" the Jews.[59] A month later, on 20 January 1942, the infamous Wannsee conference took place just outside Berlin. Here Reinhard Heydrich discussed various issues related to the fate of the Jews, including the definition of just who should be considered a "Jew" in the context of the deportations.

It is tempting to see all this as a relatively straightforward chain of causation. Hitler announces a decision to exterminate the Jews on 12 December 1941 and then the various bodies charged with implementing this decision move into operation. But this would be wrong. Hitler's comments on 12 December did not amount to an announcement of an all-encompassing Europe-wide extermination programme, and contrary to popular belief the question of murdering all the Jews by gassing them was *not* raised at the Wannsee conference. Whilst there was discussion of a plan to kill the Jews in the General Government more quickly (these Jews were the ones Hans Frank had referred to in his "liquidate them yourselves" speech of 16 December) Heydrich wanted other Jews who were fit enough to be sent to the east to build giant roads. Here large numbers were still expected to die, but this was not the master plan for the Holocaust as we know it. It wouldn't be until spring 1942, two months after Wannsee, that the first foreign Jews—from Slovakia—arrived at Auschwitz–Birkenau. Many of them were subsequently murdered, though not immediately on arrival, in improvised gas chambers converted from peasant cottages. The death camps of Sobibor and Belzec also started killing around the same time—but the majority of people killed here were Polish Jews, indeed, Jews from the General Government. It was not until early summer that foreign Jews began arriving.

Only by the summer of 1942 was it clear that the "Final Solution" meant absolute "extermination" of all the Jews under Nazi control and that this policy was to be put into practice here and now, not at some point "after" the war had been won. By August, Jews from Western Europe were no longer sent to ghettos in Poland but direct to extermination camps—only one of which, Auschwitz, had the capacity to "select" any appreciable number of Jews from arriving transports and put them to work, before the rest were murdered. Belzec, Sobibor and Treblinka were all solely death camps, where arriving Jews had a more than 99 per cent chance of being murdered by gassing within a few hours of arrival. The practical and emotional reality of that bare statistic is recalled by Toivi

Blatt, a Polish Jew sent to Sobibor in 1943. He was one of the tiny number of Jews selected by the Nazis to work in the camp and thus temporarily able to postpone their own deaths. He remembers the arrival of "a Dutch transport of about 3,000 Jews" into Sobibor, " . . . we helped them with their heavy luggage and later we were told to divide women and children one side, men the other side . . . I was with another few young men standing, yelling. I asked them to leave their luggage—women were told to leave their handbags, just throw them on the side. At that point I noticed their eyes—in the women's eyes some kind of anxiety, they were afraid. Because what do you have in a handbag—the most important stuff. One woman didn't want to leave it and the German hit her with a whip . . . They didn't know they will die in a few minutes. Once their hair was cut, they were told to go further up from the barracks just a few minutes to the gas chamber. And I'm sure that this trap was so perfect, I'm sure when they were in the gas chambers and gas came out of the shower heads instead of water, probably they were thinking that it was some kind of malfunction. I remember once [another] transport from Holland, it came in the middle of the night. Three thousand people arrived and when they were already taken out of the gas chambers to be burnt I remember thinking it was a beautiful night, the stars—and 3,000 people died. Nothing happened. The stars are in the same place."[60]

Toivi Blatt defied the statistics and survived Sobibor because he managed to escape in a mass breakout in October 1943. The killings he bears witness to were to become—rightly so—symbolic of the rule of Adolf Hitler. But the decision-making process which led to the gas chambers of Sobibor and the other death camps was neither simple nor straightforward. There was not one moment of absolute decision, but rather a series of points of escalation: at the time of the invasion of the Soviet Union; the autumn 1941 deportation of the Jews; the December meetings between key Nazi leaders in the wake of Pearl Harbor; the move during 1942 to extend the killing to Jews across the whole Nazi empire.

It is almost as if the Nazis were finding out—step by step—just how radical they could be in their treatment of the Jews. No one else in history had travelled this road before. No one had ever tried to comb Europe in order to exterminate an entire people—men, women and children. As Professor David Ceserani says, "what makes the 'Final Solution,' as it becomes, so extraordinary, is that finding it impossible to simply remove the Jews and dump them and then ignore them whatever happens to them, the decision is made to remove them to places where they will be killed for sure and that great efforts will be made to murder them. Not all of them all at once necessarily, because some will be preserved for labour, but they would ultimately all be killed. They wouldn't just die on an island off the coast of Africa, in Siberia, on a reservation, of typhus, starvation, whatever. They would be killed. That is radical. It is unprecedented."[61]

Hitler was responsible for all this not just because he wanted it to happen. He was responsible because his charismatic leadership played a vital part in legitimising the whole murderous scheme to his subordinates. Throughout the speeches, diary entries and other documents of the time one finds reference to the ultimate legitimising source—the Führer. At times of anxiety, at moments when doubt crept into the strongest resolve, always there was the comfort that this was all done "in accordance with the wishes of the Führer."[62] As Goebbels wrote in his diary in March 1942 in the context of the "barbaric" penalty to be "exacted" on the Jews, "The Führer is the untiring pioneer and spokesman for a radical solution that is demanded by the very nature of things and which is inevitable."[63]

Once Hitler's followers embraced his vision and were reassured that he would support them in the quest to kill Jews, this released a rush of initiatives from below. Hitler thus created a much more dynamic system of destruction than one which called on him to authorise every detail. What was happening here was more than just the application to the "Final Solution" of the German army's concept of *Auftragstaktik*[64]—"mission command." The German army permitted *Auftragstaktik* only within a strict hierarchy of command, whereas in the context of the killing of the Jews there was competition between various agencies in the Nazi state to solve the "Jewish question." Indeed, the Wannsee conference was convened by Reinhard Heydrich partly in an attempt to put an end to this conflict and assert SS control. Nor were those involved in key roles of the killing process merely coming up with different ideas to implement a clearly defined vision—as would be the case with the application of *Auftragstaktik*. The evolution of the "Final Solution" was a genuine two-way process, with substantive initiatives from below subsequently approved or discouraged by decisions at the highest level. It was a system that even permitted a relatively low-level functionary like *Sturmbannführer* (Major) Rolf-Heinz

Höppner of the SS to suggest to his boss Adolf Eichmann in July 1941 that "the most humane" solution to a forthcoming food shortage in the Łódź ghetto might be to "finish off those of the Jews who are not fit for work by some quick-working device."[65]

Nazis like Höppner felt able to use their initiative and come up with their own "solutions" to their self-created Jewish "problem." This, plus their own anti-Semitic beliefs, led to one of the most significant consequences of Hitler's charismatic leadership—the internalisation of responsibility. Far from many of these individuals subsequently claiming that they had merely "acted under orders" when they had participated in the extermination process, they thought what they had done was "right" at the time. Adolf Eichmann, for instance, said to his colleagues in 1945 that the knowledge that he had played a part in the death of millions of Jews "gave him such extraordinary satisfaction that he would leap into his grave laughing."[66] Even much further down the chain of command, Hans Friedrich, a soldier with the 1st SS Infantry Brigade who personally shot Jews in the autumn of 1941, felt able to say more than sixty years later that he had "no" feelings for the Jews he killed because his "hatred towards the Jews is too great."[67]

Behind all of this was the figure of Adolf Hitler—authorising, supporting, and endorsing the killing process. During 1942, Hitler showed he was prepared to compromise and act pragmatically in relation to forced workers from the east—in April, after representations from Albert Speer, Hitler agreed that their conditions could be made less onerous[68]—but not in relation to the Jews. They were all destined to be murdered—regardless of any other wartime consideration. Indeed, it is not going too far to assert that by this time Hitler saw one *point* of the war, that the Jews should die.

PART FOUR

BLOOD AND DEATH

15

LAST CHANCE

December 1941 marked a fundamental turning point in the war: from that moment onwards defeat seemed by far the most likely outcome for the Nazis. The failure of the German Blitzkrieg to secure victory in the Soviet Union; the entry of America into the war; the huge logistical difficulties the Nazis faced in trying to rule an empire in the east whilst simultaneously murdering millions of the inhabitants—all were compelling reasons why this was the beginning of the end.

Albert Schneider, then in a German unit in front of Moscow, was one of the soldiers who thought at the time that "the war had already been lost—that was actually the end of it all . . . even though at the time the retreat had not even begun." And he didn't just feel this because of the military setbacks the Germans had suffered, but because of the behaviour of German forces in these occupied lands. "People [i.e., Soviet citizens] were systematically robbed of everything . . . everybody who lived in this village [nearby] was robbed, the cellars were searched to see if there were potatoes [in them] and so on, without any consideration, as to whether the people might starve to death themselves . . . I am of the opinion that if the people had been decently treated, we might even have won the war."[1]

Typically, Hitler, with the help of Goebbels, blamed other people for the failure to defeat the Soviets, chiefly his generals. Hitler described Brauchitsch, for instance, in March 1942 as a "vain, cowardly wretch who could not even appraise the situation, much less master it." Goebbels, who recorded Hitler's views in his diary, then wrote, apparently without irony, "By his [i.e., Brauchitsch's] constant interference and consistent disobedience he completely spoiled the entire plan for the eastern campaign as it was designed with crystal clarity by the Führer."[2]

Hitler was also helped by the inept way that Stalin was now acting as supreme commander of the Soviet forces. On 5 January 1942 Stalin called for a series of near simultaneous offensives along the entire front. It was a ridiculously ambitious idea and he pushed it through despite objections from his military experts. The failure of the Red Army to exploit the gains of December 1941 outside Moscow was epitomised by the disastrous Kharkov offensive in May 1942, when several Soviet armies were encircled and more than 200,000 Red Army soldiers taken prisoner.

But, nonetheless, the fundamental difficulties the Germans faced still remained. In particular, Britain's position had been immeasurably strengthened by America's entry into the war. "No American will think it wrong of me," wrote Churchill when he heard of the Japanese attack on Pearl Harbor, "if I proclaim that to have the United States at our side was to me the greatest joy. I do not pretend to have measured accurately the martial might of Japan, but at this very moment to know the United States was in the war, up to the neck and in to the death. So we had won after all!"[3]

Churchill was right. Hitler had been unable to cross the Channel in 1940 to invade Britain, and invading America was out of the question. So how *could* Germany win? Hitler still clung to the view that if the Soviet Union could be defeated then somehow the Western Allies could be contained. And in a remarkable example of the faith that still remained in his charismatic leadership, many of those who served in the German army continued to believe in him. Carlheinz Behnke of the Waffen SS, for example, was certain that all would come well: "At the time we were unconditionally prepared to pledge ourselves to the Führer . . . There was still fascination, you see, when we saw him in Berlin [in the autumn of 1942]. That was the only time that I saw him close up during the war, the speech to the officer cadets at the Sportpalast. And at the time we were still impressed, he was wearing a field grey uniform, the Iron Cross first class was the only decoration. Even in retrospect, I have to say, when I hear his speech again, I'm fascinated, not that I would want [that time] back again, but that's what it was like then. And it's difficult to convey it to the children, the grandchildren, if you weren't part of it yourself at the time."[4]

A key part of his continued support for Hitler during 1942 was his belief that his leader's goals were not just correct but inspiring. "He developed a vision which was inconceivable. It was a utopian view. We were fascinated . . . The fact that *Lebensraum* was being moved towards the East in a common Great Europe. At the time I thought that was right. Without giving a thought to all the things associated with it, killing people and so on and so forth . . . And nowadays we sometimes say in jest, we can be glad that we lost the war, because otherwise I would be a regional commander, a gauleiter, somewhere and be performing my duties somewhere far away from home . . . I think we simply felt superior somehow, you see. Superior to the Slavonic peoples. It seems naïve today when you think about it. This huge empire!"[5]

Joachim Stempel, then an officer with the 14th Panzer Division, was also full of confidence in 1942. "I can only say that we were all inspired by the belief and the conviction that we would succeed in whatever we did." He and his comrades thought "there is nothing that we cannot achieve, albeit with difficulty, with a lack of equipment, and there was always the belief and the conviction that the leadership would take care of everything."[6]

In 1942 Wilhelm Roes desperately wanted to serve with the Waffen SS. He had been inspired by a recruiting poster of a blonde SS man with "this sort of look coming from his eyes." But because he wanted to join before he was eighteen he needed the approval of his father. "I told him [that approval was needed], and he beamed, that his oldest son was going to become a real soldier, in the Waffen SS! Of course he signed it . . . 1 June 1942 I turned 17, and on 8 June I was called up."

Roes joined the SS Leibstandarte—a unit his father proudly told him was "the most elite unit of the Waffen SS." He still remembers the "honour code" of the SS: "We were not allowed to lock our lockers because people do not steal in the Leibstandarte." Roes also received ideological instruction that built on an education that had already been spent—since he was seven years old—under the control of the Nazis. 'What else did we have as propaganda? We had political courses . . . the story of Adolf Hitler's life. I could recite that to you today, the development of the Nazi Party, of the SS. At that time we were told the Second World War which we were now fighting wouldn't be possible without the First World War. Adolf Hitler had been a soldier in the First World War himself, and his party cannot tolerate that such large territories are being taken away, and the colonies, that we have to get it back to the way it was before. That was our motivation. We were fed with that, and we swallowed it. I was very proud, extremely proud."7

When on leave, Roes flaunted his membership of the Leibstandarte. "When we came to a place, to a pub or some place, in our uniform—with Adolf Hitler written there [on the sleeve], our uniforms were fabulous—I could see a girl and say I'm going to go out with her. We come from the Liebstandarte—ooh! We were in Italy, I will never forget that, we came to a hairdresser's, in Milan, a twenties place, everything in chrome—we'd never seen anything like it. We walked in there, every seat was occupied. The Italian hairdressers screamed something, everybody got up, and we all got their seats. We weren't normal soldiers, we were the vision of something very special. Of course that impressed us."

As for the mission of the SS to conquer an eastern empire, and in the process confront an "inferior" people, Roes says he "simply believed what the propaganda said. So if the propaganda said this is a Russian subhuman, we're more valuable, we have to beat them, defeat them, to get the land we need in order to live [then we believed it]. And at the age of seventeen I had no ideas of whether we had too much land or not enough land. I couldn't understand this 'subhuman.' That was said and I believed it, not just me but everybody almost. The few who didn't [believe it] didn't dare say anything. It's a generation problem. You will not be able to understand the mentality of people [at the time]. We were seventeen, we were used to obeying. We were used to believing what we were told. At the beginning it had been right what we were told. That's what it was, that Hitler's a superman."

Yet there were already signs that a growing number of German soldiers—and their relatives—were beginning to doubt Hitler's superhuman qualities. One indication of this trend was the wording of death notices in the German press—specifically, how often relatives mentioned that their sons had died "for the Führer" rather than "for Germany." In the *Fränkischer Kurier*[8] (Frankish Courier), for instance, a newspaper from the south of Germany, Hitler had been mentioned in more than 40 per cent of the death notices in the summer of 1940, but this dropped to just 12 per cent in the second half of 1942. In addition, starting in the spring of 1942, records show there was an increase in the volume of people brought before the court in Munich charged with making derogatory remarks about the Nazis.[9]

This same shift in the attitude of the general German population can also be seen in the reaction to Hitler's speech to the Reichstag on 26 April 1942—the last time the Reichstag would meet. Hitler's attempt to put a gloss on events in this speech would have cheered only diehard Nazis. He blamed the unexpected bad weather for the problems on the Eastern Front—weather, he said, which "even in these areas occurs only once every hundred years"[10]—and the Allies for starting the war. Crucially, what Hitler *didn't* say was exactly how the war would be won. In fact, there was a worrying hint, for the German population, of nihilism within the speech. "We Germans have everything to win in this struggle of 'to be or not to be' because losing the war would anyway be our end."[11] What's more, the ostensible reason Hitler had said he wanted to address the Reichstag—in order to get parliament to vote to confirm his total authority over the legal system—seemed irrelevant. Hadn't Hitler already got total authority over the state?

Meeting with Hitler straight after his speech, Goebbels felt that "He was very happy to have got it all off his chest."[12] But just two days later Goebbels wrote, "The conclusion arrived at [in the Foreign Press] is that the Führer's speech represents, as it were, the cry of a drowning man." A negative response was even to be found amongst German listeners. A secret report Goebbels received said that the German people registered "some scepticism about the military situation. Above all, since the Führer spoke of a second winter campaign in the east, people believe that he, too, is not convinced that the war against the Soviet Union can be finished this summer."[13] The consequence was that the speech had "spread a feeling of insecurity."

This sense that Hitler's charismatic appeal was waning was further intensified by the visit of Mussolini on 29 April, just three days after Hitler's speech. The atmosphere of the encounter was memorably captured by

the diaries of the Italian Foreign Minister—and Mussolini's son-in-law—
the resolutely cynical Count Galeazzo Ciano. "There is much cordiality,"
he wrote on their arrival at Salzburg, "which puts me on my guard. The
courtesy of the Germans is always in inverse ratio to their good fortune."[14]
The next day, describing the Italian delegation's meeting with the Führer,
he says, "Hitler talks, talks, talks. Mussolini suffers—he, who is in the
habit of talking himself, and who, instead, practically has to keep quiet.
On the second day, after lunch, when everything has been said, Hitler
talked uninterruptedly for an hour and 40 minutes . . . Those, however,
who dreaded the ordeal less than we did were the Germans. Poor people.
They have to take it every day, and I am certain there isn't a gesture, a
word, or a pause which they don't know by heart. General Jodl, after an
epic struggle, finally went to sleep on the sofa."[15]

Hitler, of course, had always behaved in this way—even, as we have
seen, boring on at length to his flatmate in Vienna before the First World
War. What was new was the sense that the charismatic link between him
and his audience that had first appeared in the beer halls of Munich just
over twenty years ago was deteriorating. And the reasons for this aren't
as simple as one might think. It isn't necessarily the case that charismatic
authority is weakened by a leader's lack of success—Hitler and the Nazis
were dramatically unsuccessful at the time of the Beer Hall Putsch, for
example, but the perception of Hitler's charisma amongst his supporters
actually increased after his trial for treason. It's rather that the problem for
a charismatic leader comes when a pattern of failure develops—especially
once a perception grows that the promises of the leader cannot be trusted.

In Hitler's case, the difficulties he faced in April 1942 can be traced
back to his speech the previous October, when he all but promised that
the war against the Soviet Union was won. By now the German population knew that their leader had been spectacularly wrong. Not only that,
but he was beginning to seem at the mercy of events rather than their
master. How, for example, Germany could defeat America was a topic
that Hitler shied away from—and people noticed. It was certainly spotted
by Ciano, who wrote on 30 April 1942, "In my opinion, the thought of
what the Americans can and will do disturbs them all, and the Germans
shut their eyes in order not to see. But this does not keep the more intelligent and the more honest from thinking about what America can do,
and they feel shivers running down their spines."[16]

However, the testimony of former soldiers like Wilhelm Roes and Carlheinz Behnke, as well as the reaction of many other Germans at the time, does demonstrate that there was still significant support for Hitler as a charismatic leader in 1942. It all remained a question of faith, and different people would have their faith questioned at different times. For the absolute believers, it was possible—as events became bleaker—for their faith to remain undiminished. After all, as Göring said back in September 1936, "through the genius of the Führer things which were apparently impossible have very quickly become reality."[17]

But the tendency for this faith in Hitler to create a sense of unreality about the war was immense. And that sense of unreality spread to Hitler himself who would believe only what he wanted to believe about the strength of the Red Army. This led General Halder to write in despair, "This chronic tendency to underrate enemy capabilities is gradually assuming grotesque proportions and develops into a positive danger. The situation is getting more and more intolerable. There is no room for any serious work."[18]

But as spring turned to summer in 1942 it seemed that, superficially at least, things were going better for Hitler after the setbacks of the winter. In the Far East the Japanese were engaging the Americans, even if they had just lost crucial aircraft carriers at the Battle of Midway in June 1942; in the Western Desert, Erwin Rommel was fast making himself a German hero, most especially when the Afrika Korps seized Tobruk on 20 June and took 30,000 Allied prisoners; in the Arctic sea, in early July, German submarines and planes laid waste to the Allied convoy PQ 17 and destroyed 24 of 39 ships en route with supplies to the Soviet Union—a disaster for the Allies which led to the temporary suspension of all Arctic convoys; and on the steppes of southern Russia the German army's new offensive, *Fall Blau* (Operation Blue), was making swift progress southeast towards Stalingrad and the Russian oil fields of the Caucasus. Indeed, Hitler was so confident that in late July he ordered the forces of Operation Blue to be split. Army Group A would move south towards the oil fields and Army Group B would continue east towards Stalingrad. It demonstrated over-confidence on a massive scale—though over-confidence born of a desperation to finish the war in the East quickly—and carried within it the seeds of the calamity that would befall the German 6th Army in Stalingrad in six months' time.

A similar, almost bizarre level of over-confidence was also being demonstrated by one of Hitler's longest-serving followers, Hermann Göring. By now Göring had so appropriated to himself Hitler's refusal to listen to practical objections that he felt able, in August 1942, to harangue a gathering of senior Nazis—including Reich Commissioners—as if he was a brutal headmaster talking to children who needed a good thrashing. "God knows," he said, "you are not sent out there [to countries occupied by the Nazis] to work for the welfare of the people in your charge, but to get the utmost out of them, so that the German people can live. That is what I expect of your exertions. This everlasting concern about foreign peoples must cease now, once and for all. I have here before me reports on what you are expected to deliver. It is nothing at all when I consider your territories. It makes no difference to me in this connection if you say that your people will starve. Let them do so, as long as no German collapses from hunger."[19] Göring then demanded a huge increase in food deliveries to the German homeland—seemingly upping the quotas as if on a whim. "Last year France delivered 550,000 tons of grain," said Göring, "and now I demand 1.2 million tons. Two weeks from now a plan will be submitted how it can be handled. There will be no more discussion about it."

However, an appeal to the "will" of the individual only stood a chance of working when there was a possibility of success. It was no use demanding raw materials when there were simply none to give. But this straightforward reality did not prevent Göring, Himmler or indeed Hitler from demanding the impossible. On 11 August 1942, just five days after Göring's meeting, Hitler met Paul Pleiger, a talented industrialist who was now responsible for ensuring that sufficient coal was available for Germany's wartime needs. Pleiger explained to Hitler that coal output was declining—he needed experienced miners to be allocated to him, but was only promised malnourished labour from the east. Hitler listened to him and then replied that if there was a shortage of coal then the output of steel could not be increased, and if the output of steel could not be increased then the war would be lost. How could Pleiger answer such a statement? He simply replied that he would do all that was "humanly possible" to meet the targets that Hitler desired.[20]

Whilst Hitler's behaviour at the meeting with Pleiger was illustrative of the immense dangers of charismatic leadership, it at least demonstrated that he was still trying to act as a charismatic leader. But other decisions around the same time show that Hitler must also have had inner doubts as to whether he really was still that kind of leader at all. On 9 September 1942 Hitler removed Field Marshal List from command of Army Group A. Increasingly desperate for swift success, Hitler believed that List had been dragging his feet. This action in itself was not surprising—Hitler had removed other military commanders before. It was Hitler's choice of replacement that was so significant—because Hitler chose himself.

This was Hitler's strangest appointment yet. Even leaving aside the new ludicrous chain of command that meant Hitler now reported to himself many times over,[21] it was impossible for him to exercise effective command over soldiers more than a thousand miles away. This decision, coupled with the removal that same month of General Halder as army chief of staff—whose last diary entry states "my nerves are worn out"[22]—and his replacement with Kurt Zeitzler, an officer known for his sycophancy, demonstrated a growing air of desperation at the Führer's headquarters.

Hitler certainly had good reason by now to doubt the practical ability of the German army to win this war. By the autumn of 1942 the supply situation for the army was so bad that General Fromm, head of the Army Armament Supply, wrote in a report that Hitler should find an immediate political solution and end the war.[23] This was the background against which Hitler started to become fixated on one city on the Eastern Front—Stalingrad. Units of the 6th Army, part of Army Group B, reached the river Volga in August 1942 and by the start of September the Germans were fighting in the city. "[Hitler] was not achieving what he wanted from the Caucasus," says Antony Beevor, who has made a particular study of this battle, "and so the 6th Army was ordered to capture Stalingrad, and this was where his obsession with the city that bore Stalin's name became a trap. It was the bait, and it's always a great disaster in war when a commander becomes obsessed with a particular objective and he loses sight of the wider picture."[24]

Stalingrad marked the turning point in perceptions of Hitler's charismatic leadership. For soldiers of the 6th Army, like Joachim Stempel, this was the moment when their faith was destroyed. As a young officer with 14th Panzer Division he had advanced across the Russian steppes that summer full of optimism. When he reached Stalingrad, a city that lay in a narrow strip along the western bank of the Volga, the wide river that divided European Russia from Asia, he and his comrades thought "it would be simply a matter of time before we were able to push the enemy back to the eastern shore."[25] They had been buoyed by the success of the Germans at the Battle of Kharkov four months before, and the relative ease with which they had begun their advance in Operation Blue.

But once within Stalingrad they faced determined and fierce resistance from the Soviet troops. "There were snipers firing from everywhere," says Stempel, "from any hole, from any corner, from any chimney of a burned-down house, from any pile of earth . . . [there were] a lot of [Soviet] women in uniform, who proved to be excellent snipers and who made our life there a living hell." Another problem for the soldiers of the 6th Army, many of whom had ridden across the steppes in tanks, was the alien nature of hand-to-hand combat amidst the wreckage of houses and factories. "We were totally unfamiliar with that and we had not been trained for it either . . . you had to make your way to the front, ducking, crouching, kneeling, [and] shots rang out from all sides—from the front, from behind, from above, from below. And all around you was the noise of the artillery salvoes hitting what was left of the factory buildings . . . Seeing your opponent is an indescribable feeling, when you are suddenly facing one another. [You think] 'he wants to kill me, I have to kill him.' I can't describe that feeling. There is no hesitating or consideration of humane feelings . . . We were repeatedly told, 'Another 100 metres, then you've done it! [i.e., reached the Volga].' But how can it be done if you just don't have the strength? And it was terrible too for our people bringing supplies, when, under cover of darkness, they finally brought the food to the front in thermal containers, even though it had got completely cold by then, and then they were suddenly killed by the Russians from behind. And we were waiting for the food which never arrived because they had been caught, taken prisoner or even shot by Russian scouts or reconnaissance patrols, behind our backs." As each day went by, Stempel saw that "each attack resulted in such a high number of losses that it was easy to calculate how long it would be before there was no one left."

The difficulties of the 6th Army in Stalingrad were compounded by the promise made by Adolf Hitler in a speech on 30 September 1942. "You can rest assured," he said, "no human being can remove us from this place."[26] It was an even more explicit statement than the one he had given the year before about victory in the Soviet campaign. Now—in unequivocal terms—Hitler had said that the German army would never retreat from Stalingrad. Carlheinz Behnke, then a junior officer in the Waffen SS, heard Hitler give his speech and say "We will take Stalingrad!" And he and his comrades "didn't doubt it at all. Not at all."[27]

We can never know for certain what was the motivation for Hitler's promise about Stalingrad. Perhaps his decision was influenced by the fact that the city bore Stalin's name. More likely it was that Hitler realised that he needed to rebuild confidence in his promises after the debacle of the previous year, and here was a promise to the German people that he genuinely thought he could deliver. In addition, as Antony Beevor says, Hitler "somehow believed that if the German soldier holds firm he will always be right. It was this whole notion, 'the triumph of the will,' and the idea that somehow moral decision and decisiveness would overcome everything."[28]

But as autumn turned to winter it became clear that the German 6th Army could not remove soldiers of the Soviet 62nd Army completely from the city. Under the command of Vasily Chuikov—a man so tough that he used to beat up his own officers if they displeased him—Red Army soldiers clung to the western bank of the river Volga or lived deep in the rubble of shattered buildings. "Our principle was, we'll put claws in the throat of the enemy and hold them very close," says Anatoly Mereshko, then a young Soviet officer at Stalingrad, "that way you can stay alive. These were Chuikov's tactics."[29]

As the Soviet 62nd Army held out in Stalingrad, an offensive was being prepared to relieve them by two of Stalin's most brilliant generals— Zhukov and Vasilevskii. The plan—codenamed Operation Uranus—was for a vast encirclement operation. Red Army soldiers would not, to begin with, attack Stalingrad itself but press against the flanks of the enemy, up to a hundred miles away to the far west of the city, and confront the weaker Romanian units that protected German supply lines. The operation, launched on 19 November 1942, was a spectacular success—just four days later the Red Army had succeeded in completely cutting off the Germans in Stalingrad.

The success of Operation Uranus laid bare a series of flaws in Hitler's leadership. More than anything, it showed the consequences of his immense arrogance: he had grossly underestimated the Soviets' capacity to resist. Specifically, he had dismissed their ability to learn intelligently from the tactics of the German army. Because Soviet forces had

behaved in a particular way in the past—for example by walking into a
trap set by the Germans at the Battle of Kharkov, back in the spring—he
thought they would behave in a similar way in the future. But from the
highest level of the Soviet government—Joseph Stalin—to the lowest
ordinary soldier, the Soviet military machine had changed. In recent
months Stalin had become less dictatorial as far as his senior generals
were concerned—he had, for instance, allowed Zhukov and Vasilevskii
to initiate and then develop Operation Uranus unhindered—whilst
improvements had also been made in the training and coordination of
individual units. Most importantly, the Soviets had developed techniques
of *maskirovka*—deception—to conceal their military build-up from the
Germans.

Hitler's underestimation of the capacity of the enemy had spread to
his commanders. On 23 October 1941, just a few weeks before the launch
of Operation Uranus, the new chief of the General Staff, Kurt Zeitzler,
had declared that the Soviets were 'in no position to mount a major offensive with any far-reaching objective.'[30] Yet Hitler, even in the face of the
surprising Soviet success in encircling the 6th Army, still continued to
underrate his opponents. *Unternehmen Wintersturm* (Operation Winter
Storm), Manstein's attempt to relieve the stricken 6th Army, was never
adequately resourced and the rescue attempt was called off after less than
a week. As for Göring's boast that the Luftwaffe could adequately supply
the 6th Army from the air—that turned out to be mere wishful thinking.
As a consequence of the German failure to relieve the 6th Army, conditions inside the encirclement grew increasingly grim. "After Christmas,
things deteriorated rapidly in terms of morale, and, not only in terms
of morale, there was also the question of [lack of] food, supplies,"[31] says
Gerhard Hindenlang, a German battalion commander at Stalingrad.

But still, many of the soldiers of the 6th Army hoped for rescue. They
would listen and think they heard the advancing tanks of their German
liberators. As one officer trapped inside Stalingrad put it, "I believed that
the Führer would not give us up; that he wouldn't sacrifice the 6th Army;
that he would get the 6th Army out of there."[32]

They were wrong. Their Führer had given them up. All that was left
for Hitler was to attempt to engineer a Wagnerian ending to the saga by
promoting the commander of the 6th Army, Friedrich Paulus, to Field
Marshal on 30 January 1943, just before Stalingrad fell. Since no German

Field Marshal had ever allowed himself to be captured by the enemy it was a clear sign that Hitler wanted Paulus to kill himself. But Paulus decided not to take his own life and was captured by the Red Army. Hitler's reaction was a mix of fury and disbelief. "It hurts me so much,"[33] Hitler said when he heard the news, "because the heroism of so many soldiers is destroyed by a single, spineless weakling . . . "

The transcript of Hitler's words that day reveals a growing side to his leadership—one that would be on display to the world just over two years later—the desire to embrace death in defeat. "What does that mean, 'life'?" asked Hitler. " . . . the individual has to die. What remains alive beyond the individual is the people. But how can one fear this moment—through which one [can free] oneself from misery . . . "[34] Instead of entering into "national immortality"[35] Paulus had "preferred" to go to Moscow, where "rats will eat" him in the Lubyanka prison. Moreover, Paulus had set a dangerous precedent—now other officers in the future might not fight to the death. Hitler was certain how the end ought to come: " . . . you gather yourselves together, build an all-round defence, and shoot yourself with the last cartridge. If you imagine that a woman, after being insulted a few times, has so much pride that she goes out, locks herself in, and shoots herself dead immediately—then I have no respect for a soldier [who prefers] going into captivity."[36]

Ever since he had joined the German Workers' Party twenty-three years before, Hitler had shown himself to be a gambler, prepared to take huge risks on enterprises that could so plainly go either way. He had also said that he had assumed the Battle of Stalingrad would end "heroically"—and by "heroically" he meant, if necessary, in a last suicidal stand. In this respect, Paulus and many of the other commanders of the 6th Army had let him down. He would shortly try and ensure that millions of other Germans did not.

THE DEATH OF CHARISMA

The shame of Stalingrad caused a widespread deterioration in belief in Hitler's charisma. What's extraordinary, therefore, is that Hitler held out as leader of Germany for two years more. One explanation sometimes given for this phenomenon is that the Nazi regime began to rely more on terror and threat to stay in power—elements of coercion that had always existed but which now became more prevalent. But that's only part of the story. Hitler's charismatic appeal did not entirely disappear and its legacy cast a long and destructive shadow.

Hitler sought to limit the damage to his prestige caused by events in Stalingrad in a number of ways. The most obvious was that he simply did not appear in public during this time of defeat. It was Goebbels who was given the hapless task of reading out a lengthy proclamation from Hitler on 30 January 1943, the tenth anniversary of his appointment as chancellor. And it was left to Göring, speaking that same day on the radio, to articulate why the German people should still have faith in Hitler. The reason he gave was straightforward; "Providence" had sent Hitler to Germany and allowed this "simple fighter" from the First World War to attain greatness. So how could one believe that what was happening now was all "senseless"?[1] It was an obvious attempt to appeal for "faith" in Hitler's charisma to be continued, if not redoubled. It was, in essence, the same simple admonition the 6th Army had received from Hitler's headquarters just a few days before their surrender—which was to always remember that the "Führer knows best."[2]

There were obvious difficulties in following this advice. For Hitler had unquestionably broken his promise made the previous September that "no one" would ever get the Wehrmacht out of Stalingrad. And, as other events in the first half of 1943 demonstrated, simply exhorting the German armed forces to fight on, in the face of the obvious advantages the Allies now possessed, scarcely deserved to be called a strategy at all. Take, for example, what was now happening in the Battle of the Atlantic. In May 1943 the German navy was forced to withdraw all U-boats from the North Atlantic—an outright admission of German defeat. Jürgen Oesten, one of the most successful U-boat captains of the war, explains why, from his perspective, this decision had to be taken: "If a U-boat got hold of a convoy then, of course, it gave the relevant signal and then the other U-boats were in position to adjust their course accordingly, so that they got hold of the convoys as well . . . and this system was working reasonably well as long as the escort vessels were not in a position to detect the boats at night . . . [But] from the second half of 1942 onwards the [British] escort vessels were able to find the direction of the [U-boat] wireless signal, so that if a submarine in the vicinity of the convoy gave a signal, the destroyers could be in a position to come directly to the U-boat. The second thing was that radar development was far quicker on the British side than in Germany, and the escort vessels were equipped with radar, so from then onwards the escort vessels were in a position, as well, to detect the boats by means of radar at night [and] they were in the position to find the direction of the U-boat as soon as the U-boat gave a wireless signal. In these two respects the Allies were superior and therefore we had to stop the war in the Atlantic, early in the months of 1943. We stopped all submarine war in the North Atlantic because the boats were no longer safe enough."[3]

In addition to Allied advances in radar technology, the code breakers at Bletchley Park in England had broken the German naval Enigma code, and this, plus better air defence of Atlantic convoys, meant the lifeline across the sea between America and Britain could not be broken. It symbolised one key reason the Nazis were losing the war—they did not have the time or resources to innovate. After any initial success the Germans might have, the initiative rapidly passed to their better-equipped and more numerous opponents. For all of the bluster of the new Armaments Minister, Albert Speer, and for all of the hints of German "wonder weapons" to come, the consequences of this reality in 1943 were inescapable—Germany could not win this war. The German navy had no answer to Allied technological advances in the Atlantic, and the German army had no answer to the increasing strategic awareness and power of the Red Army on the Eastern Front.

As for the German air force, the inability of the Luftwaffe to protect German cities and towns from attack was on show for all to see. Extensive bombing of the industrial Ruhr region began in March 1943 and the fire storms in Hamburg, as a result of bombing raids in late July, killed more people—40,000—than lost their lives in London in the entire course of the Blitz. In the bomber war, just as with the Battle of the Atlantic, it was this same combination of greater Allied innovation and resources that was now making the Germans suffer.

Just before the Hamburg firestorm, on 25 July, the Italians had demonstrated how they were prepared to deal with their own charismatic leader, Benito Mussolini, who had so inspired Adolf Hitler and the Nazis back in the early 1920s. Seeing which way the war was going, the Grand Fascist Council voted to remove him from power and Mussolini was arrested as he left an audience with the king. Shortly afterwards the Italians broke off their alliance with Germany and tried to exit the war. "Not very honourable, certainly, whenever you betray a friend, an ally, but it happens, it happens," says Mario Mondello, an Italian diplomat at the time and a member of the Italian National Fascist Party. "We are more realistic, sometimes, than the Germans are. Of course, being realistic we are not faithful to the present chief and so on. I don't say it is a noble thing, but it is our character."[4]

However, it was much more than any perceived variation in "character" between Germans and Italians that enabled Hitler to stay on in power nearly two years longer than Mussolini. An important difference between the two countries was structural. Mussolini had not dismantled, as Hitler had, all of the various institutions that could hold him to account. The Italian king was head of state—not Mussolini—and it was still possible for members of a Fascist Council to meet and declare their lack of confidence in Mussolini via a vote. None of that could happen in Nazi Germany. Hitler had always been more alert to any possible challenge to his authority—becoming head of state himself in 1934 and letting the Cabinet wither and die as a political forum before the outbreak of war.

Meanwhile, Hitler continued to rely on personal appeals to motivate his generals. Some months after Mussolini had been deposed, Peter von der Groeben, then chief of operations for German Army Group Centre, attended a meeting with other senior commanders at Hitler's headquarters at the Wolf's Lair in East Prussia. Von der Groeben watched as Hitler and the generals "discussed for two hours whether the one and only tank division we had, had been deployed correctly . . . So one was standing in the background and getting more and more desperate . . . And at the end of every meeting he [i.e., Hitler] would always personally turn to the field marshal in charge and say, 'But you're not going to abandon me,' and he took both his hands and shook them . . . He had an immense ability to manipulate and influence people."[5] The aristocratic von der Groeben also reveals that Hitler's conduct during these encounters was most certainly not that of a madman. "I can only judge all this from these meetings which I attended, but he was always above reproach in all respects. I never experienced any kind of abusive behaviour or anything of the kind."

Johann-Adolf Graf von Kielmansegg, an officer on the German General Staff, witnessed the motivating effect Hitler continued to possess. He and his friends called it "the Wehrmacht high command bug" and whenever a new officer arrived they would ask themselves, "How long will it be before he catches it?" Kielmansegg believed that one could only become infected with this "bug" when in close contact with Hitler. "The only time when I was under the spell, so to speak, was when Hitler gave me a very personal order for Marshal Antonescu, the Romanian leader at the time. There were only three of us. The head of the general staff on the left, Hitler in the middle and me on the right. And I stood there. And the head of the general staff said [to Hitler], 'You want to give Count Johann-Adolf Kielmansegg a personal order.' I was his emissary you might say. So Hitler turned around and looked at me. And at that moment I had the strong feeling, 'This man knows exactly what you are thinking.' That's the feeling I had."[6]

Nicolaus von Below, Hitler's Luftwaffe adjutant, recalls that Hitler "never betrayed a sign of weakness nor indicated that he saw any situation as hopeless . . . It fascinated me to see how he contrived to put a positive value on setbacks and even succeeded in convincing those who worked closely with him."[7] In part, Hitler achieved this effect by using the same methods he had for years—staring longer into someone's eyes than normal, a sense of stillness in the moment, an absolute lack of doubt, and a direct and personal appeal for loyalty. But by now every officer who stood in front of Hitler also knew that they were in the presence of a man who had over the last three years led Germany to great victories—and these successes had not been forgotten, even now, in the face of recent defeats. Maybe, just maybe, the Führer did still know "best."

Senior officers like Karl Dönitz, who were also committed followers of Hitler, were particularly susceptible to this aspect of his appeal. Jürgen Oesten, for example, remembers accompanying Dönitz to a wartime meeting with Hitler. Before he entered the room to meet the Führer, Dönitz had told Oesten how he was going to express his doubts about the ability of the Navy to achieve what Hitler wanted. Dönitz then went into the room to see Hitler. But when he emerged, Dönitz was transformed. He was now full of confidence about the way ahead, and says Oesten, "floating on a sea of emotion."[8]

"I experienced examples of it," confirms Ulrich de Maizière, who as an officer of the General Staff was present at meetings with Hitler towards the end of the war, "of men who came to tell him it could not go on any longer—and even said that to him. And then he talked for an hour and then they went and said, 'I want to give it another try' . . . Well, he had an enormously strong will, you know, and he had powers of persuasion that could gloss over any rational arguments . . . if he ordered the attack on the Caucasus and the logistics expert told him that there wasn't enough fuel then he would say, 'then just seize the petrol. I don't care, it will be done.'"[9]

Just as before, Hitler's powers of persuasion only worked on those who were predisposed to succumb to them. For example, Günther von Below, a colonel who was captured at Stalingrad, was not susceptible. "For me, Hitler was never a superior or some overwhelming leadership personality. I never had that feeling. He never made much of an impression on me. You may think now that this is my attitude 50 years after the event, but I know for certain that I never felt like that about him. He never fascinated me."[10] But the reason why von Below did not succumb to Hitler's personal appeal is not hard to find—he was never that bowled over by anyone he ever met. "I have always been very matter of fact myself, for my entire life," he admits. "And my wife once said, 'You are always so damned matter of fact.'"

For those who were inclined to be carried away on a "sea of emotion" after meeting Hitler, the consequences were comforting—but often short term. For though there were obvious reasons why Hitler's charisma still had an effect—after all, who in the German High Command *wanted* to believe that the war was lost?—one needed to possess considerable powers of self-deception to pretend that Hitler's promises of a brighter future could still be met. In June 1944, for example, General Kurt Zeitzler, who had long been looked on as a man who shared Hitler's optimism, simply could not take the pressure any more. He had a nervous breakdown and walked away from his job as Chief of Staff of the German army.

But Hitler's undoubted ability to persuade many of those he met to "give it another try" has to be set against other powerful reasons to continue the fight that had little to do with any charismatic powers he might still have possessed. First was the knowledge of the crimes that had been committed since the war began, particularly since the invasion of the Soviet Union. This could be a powerful motivating factor, as Heinrich Himmler well knew. So much so that he deliberately spelled out just what the SS had been up to when he spoke in Posen on 6 October 1943 to a gathering of senior Nazis. He told them explicitly that the extermination of the Jews was taking place and that by the end of the year the "Jewish question" would be "solved." Moreover, he said, it had been necessary to kill Jewish women and children as well as men to prevent a race of "avengers" growing up and seeking retribution in the future. Significantly, as he neared the end of his speech, Himmler told his audience, "You now know about it."[11]

Sharing knowledge of the mass murder of millions of people across the Nazi elite was an effective way of creating a communal sense of responsibility to fight to the bitter end. Just how potent this was can be gauged by the difficulties Albert Speer's presence at this 6 October meeting caused him in later life. After all, how could he portray himself as a "good Nazi," someone who had sought to mitigate Hitler's call for the destruction of German infrastructure in the last days of the war, when in the autumn of 1943 he had been told all about the extermination of the

Jews? Not surprisingly, Speer fiercely—if unconvincingly—persisted to his last breath that he had left the meeting early and never heard Himmler's words at Posen.

Knowledge of the atrocities committed in the east was not, of course, confined to the Nazi elite. Peter von der Groeben, for instance, learnt exactly what had been taking place when he was coordinating a tactical retreat as a commander with Army Group Centre. An SS officer approached him and said, "I hear you want to evacuate the territory over there." Von der Groeben said that was correct, only to hear the SS man reply, "No, that is not possible." And when von der Groeben asked why, he was told because "that's where the mass graves are." The SS man then pulled a series of photographs from his pocket, showing what looked like "turnip pits," but which were in fact where the SS had buried their victims. "Under no circumstances must this fall into the hands of the Russians," said the SS officer. "Well, my dear chap," said von der Groeben, "you see to it that this will be removed."

"That was the first time," says von der Groeben, "that I heard about what those people had been up to . . . There was no reason for me to give him a sermon there and then, you know. I was in no position to do so. Yes, I was horrified, horrified—as far as I can remember. Let us assume that I was really deeply horrified and shaken by it, which I don't remember. What should I have done? What could I have done?

"So could I have gone to my field marshal and reported what I had just found out? I don't remember what I actually told him. Or else I could go home and say 'well, I won't go along with this any more.' But that was entirely out of the question. What would you have done? You tell me."[12]

Von der Groeben also reveals another reason why, despite learning about these mass killings, he felt he should carry on serving Hitler as best he could: "Those [Germans] fighting in Russia, they still had the idea that under all circumstances they had to prevent the Russians from getting into Germany—also into East Prussia, where I came from. And for that reason, of course, in spite of all fundamental doubts and rejections, one did try for as long as possible to do one's best and to prevent it by military means." Anxieties such as these were all set against the background of increased coercion and use of terror by Nazi authorities; and in that context it was no accident that Heinrich Himmler was appointed Minister of the Interior in August 1943.

But no amount of threat, guilt, or fear, could alter the fact that Germany was losing the war. The failure of *Unternehmen Zitadelle* (Operation Citadel), the German summer offensive around Kursk in 1943, marked the end of any pretence that the Wehrmacht could mount a successful major counter-attack on the Eastern Front. But still officers close to Hitler, like Nicolaus von Below, retained faith in their Führer. "For some time I had not believed in victory," said von Below, "but neither did I foresee defeat. At the end of 1943 I was convinced that Hitler could still find a political and military solution. In this paradoxical belief I was not alone."[13]

Nonetheless, in early 1944, Fritz Darges, Hitler's SS Adjutant, describes the mood at the Führer's headquarters as "subdued." "We were worried every time another general staff officer arrived. What bad news would he bring us this time?" But it remained obvious to Darges and his comrades that their Führer would fight to the very end regardless of any possible consideration. "Hitler used to say, 'I don't give up at five minutes before midnight. I give up at five minutes after midnight.' And who would have asked him to give up anyway? '*Mein Führer,* do you think it's still possible to win the war?' Can you tell me who would have dared to ask him that?"[14] Darges expresses the reason why he felt it was impossible to give up by way of a metaphor—one cannot "get off a moving train." Others compared their predicament to sailors trapped on a boat in a storm.

However, there were also German officers who had formed a very different view—who had decided that not only was the war lost, but that the only way to avoid further suffering was to kill Hitler. The core conspirators were a group of army officers of noble birth. One of the leaders, for example, Henning von Tresckow, a major general and chief of operations for Army Group Centre, came from an aristocratic family in East Germany. Like Ludwig Beck, he had initially seen Hitler as a useful political leader who would strengthen the German army and attempt to "right the wrongs" of Versailles. And despite playing a part in the dramatic German victory over France in 1940, he was politically sophisticated enough to recognise that if the British ever gained the Americans as allies then Germany would inevitably be defeated.[15]

Once in a senior position, Tresckow appointed other officers sympathetic to his views to positions around him. This led directly to a plan to shoot Hitler on his visit to Army Group Centre on 13 March 1943. It was called off only because of lack of support at the last minute from Field

Marshal Kluge—the overall commander of Army Group Centre who had previously expressed support for the conspiracy. "Again and again he [Kluge] brought up various arguments," wrote Fabian von Schlabrendorff, another of the conspirators, "claiming that neither the world nor the German people nor the German soldier would understand such an act at this time."[16]

Still determined to kill Hitler, Tresckow then wrapped up a bomb, pretending it was two bottles of Cointreau,[17] and gave it to Heinz Brandt, a lieutenant colonel who was travelling on Hitler's plane. Tresckow hoped the bomb would explode in mid-air, killing everyone on the flight. The advantage of this approach, according to von Schlabrendorff, was that "the stigma of an assassination would be avoided, and Hitler's death could be attributed—officially, at least—to an accidental plane crash."[18] But the bomb failed to go off.

The following week, Rudolf Christoph von Gersdorff—a baron— made another attempt on Hitler's life. Gersdorff, a close confidant of Tresckow's at Army Group Centre, planned to blow up Hitler when he attended an exhibition of captured Red Army weapons in Berlin on 21 March 1943. Under his uniform Gersdorff concealed two bombs, and then accompanied Hitler round the exhibition. But Hitler stayed for a shorter time than expected and Gersdorff—who had set delayed-action time fuses to the bombs—had to rush to the toilet and dismantle them.

For army officers admitted into Hitler's presence, there existed an easier way to kill him than turning oneself into a human bomb. Simply take out a pistol and pull the trigger. "Many people say, 'Were you checked for weapons?'" says Peter von der Groeben. "'No.' 'So why didn't anybody shoot him?' I could have done it, any time. I had my briefcase with me, and of course I could have carried a pistol in there. And I was two steps away from him, I only had to draw and fire . . . I will tell you exactly why [I didn't do it]. In the first place I was afraid, it would have been the end of me, and, secondly, as a colonel, I didn't really feel it was my mission to interfere with fate in this way."[19]

For some conspirators, like Georg von Boeselager, another aristocratic German officer who wanted to see Hitler dead, it just wasn't emotionally possible to shoot Hitler, face to face. He revealed[20] that, despite his proven courage in battle, he did not feel "equal to the job." "Even a hunter is gripped with feverish anticipation when the long awaited object of his hunt finally appears within his sights," wrote Fabian von Schlabrendorff, who was sympathetic to Boeselager's inability to shoot Hitler. "How much greater then is the turmoil in one's heart and mind when, after overcoming a multitude of obstacles, and with the knowledge that the odds are unfavourable, one pulls out a gun at the risk of one's life, fully aware that success or failure of the deed will decide the fate of millions!"[21] To get round this problem Boeselager proposed leading a group of soldiers against Hitler's armed bodyguard and then killing Hitler in the subsequent fire-fight—an impractical solution that was never adopted.

If Hitler had visited Army Group Centre for a second time, then the conspirators would have tried to kill him by opening fire on him simultaneously in what they called a "collective assassination" attempt. This method of killing Hitler was designed to "help ease the burden felt by any person with a conscience."[22] But Hitler never returned after the March 1943 trip.

A year later, in March 1944, one conspirator finally emerged who was prepared to try and shoot Hitler face to face. Rittmeister Eberhard von Breitenbuch, an aide to Field Marshal Busch, was set to pull his pistol from his pocket and kill the Führer at a military conference at the Berghof. But, by happenstance, junior officers were not admitted into Hitler's presence that day.[23]

Four months afterwards, the most famous assassination attempt on Hitler—the 20 July 1944 plot—was carried out by a man who decided not to shoot the Führer, but once again to try and blow him up. Claus Schenk Graf von Stauffenberg—who was so blue-blooded that he had been born in a castle—placed a bomb in a briefcase under the conference table during one of Hitler's midday military meetings at the Wolf's Lair. Stauffenberg then left to fly to Berlin in order to coordinate the resistance effort there. The bomb exploded at 12:50, but Hitler, as is well known, survived this assassination attempt with only minor injuries.

At about five o'clock that same evening Ludwig Beck appeared at the office of the German Army High Command on the Bendlerstrasse in Berlin. He had been part of the plot against Hitler—off and on—for years now and had been chosen by the conspirators as the new head of state because, as Hans Gisevius, a diplomat who had helped plan the attempted coup, wrote, "General Ludwig Beck, in truth, stood above all the parties . . . Beck was the only general with an unimpaired reputation, the only general who had voluntarily resigned."[24]

The problem now was that neither Beck nor the other conspirators could be certain that Hitler was dead. Keitel, speaking from the Wolf's Lair, had told other officers at the Bendlerstrasse that Hitler had suffered only slight injuries in the assassination attempt. But was he telling the truth? There also remained the question of the allegiance of the other soldiers in Berlin. Beck asked General Friedrich Olbricht, a fellow conspirator, about the loyalty of the guards he had posted outside the building. Beck specifically wanted to know if these men were prepared to die for Olbricht. It was a question that cut to the heart of the coup attempt. That there were still those around Hitler who were prepared to die for him was axiomatic. The SS Leibstandarte Adolf Hitler—the Life Guards of Adolf Hitler—had, like all of the SS formations, as its very motto, *Meine Ehre heisst Treue* ("My honour is called loyalty"). But would Olbricht's soldiers die for him if forces loyal to Hitler attacked? Olbricht could only reply, "I don't know."[25]

Hitler's continuing ability to generate immediate personal loyalty was demonstrated in dramatic terms that same night, when a dithering Major Otto-Ernst Remer of the Grossdeutschland regiment was handed the phone by Joseph Goebbels and heard Hitler at the other end of the line. "Do you recognise me, Major Remer," asked Hitler, "do you recognise my voice?"[26] Remer replied that he did, and Hitler then ordered him to help put down the coup. Remer immediately obeyed.

After the war, Remer said that he felt "the whole conspiracy was organised in a dilettante fashion . . . Any putsch such as Stauffenberg's had to succeed in killing Hitler because it was to him that the oath [of loyalty] was sworn. This could not be achieved by cowardly placing a bomb in a corner—he should have had the courage to use a pistol and shoot Hitler. This is what a real man would have done and I would have respected him."[27] This is an unfair judgement on Stauffenberg—he was a man of considerable bravery who had not felt able to kill himself in the attempt on Hitler because he believed he was needed later in Berlin to help organise the coup. As for Remer he was undoubtably a deeply unpleasant character—after the war he was a Holocaust denier—but here his other substantive point is correct. Hitler's death was essential for the coup to succeed. Indeed, the failure of the 20 July 1944 plot demonstrated in stark terms how central Adolf Hitler, as one single individual, was to the Nazi state. The question potential supporters of the plot had raised after the bomb went off had been simply this, "did Hitler still live?" Field Marshal Kluge, Commander-in-Chief West, for example, had vacillated in his support for the coup attempt before, but only came firmly to the view that he could not commit to the enterprise after it appeared that Hitler had survived. So even as late as July 1944, after the near collapse of German Army Group Centre in the wake of the Soviet offensive that had begun the previous month, Hitler's physical presence on this earth was enough to break the conspiracy. The Italians had not had to kill Mussolini to remove him from power. But only death would destroy Hitler's hold over Germany.

By half-past nine in the evening on 20 July, less than five hours after Beck had said he was head of state, there was a fire fight at the Bendlerstrasse as soldiers loyal to Hitler attempted to retake the building. They succeeded with relative ease and Beck was captured. He then asked if he could take the opportunity to kill himself. Friedrich Fromm, commander in chief of the German Home Army, agreed. (Fromm was implicated in the planning stages of the plot, though he had refused earlier in the evening to take part.) Beck held a pistol to his own head and pulled the trigger, but the bullet only grazed him and much to his surprise Beck found he was still alive. Fromm then ordered Stauffenberg and a number of the other key conspirators taken out of the building and shot. Beck was then given a second opportunity to kill himself. Once again he pulled the trigger, and this time the bullet rendered him unconscious—but still not dead. Beck was only finally killed by a third shot, this from a German soldier loyal to Adolf Hitler.

After the war the conspirators were treated as heroes, as Germans attempted to deal with this troubled history. But at the time they were reviled—and not just by Hitler and other loyalists. "The soldiers at the front," says Ulrich de Maizière, "the mass of frontline officers, initially had no sympathy for the assassination attempt at all because they had the feeling that the supreme commander was being murdered behind their backs. They did not know what the motive was . . . they only knew that the Führer of the Reich was meant to be murdered. For me it was a different thing because I knew the perpetrators and knew their motives. And so I regretted that the attempt had not been a success, but I could not say anything like this."[28]

Reports compiled in the aftermath of the bomb attack by the SD, the intelligence division of the SS, confirm de Maizière's judgement that the majority of soldiers were appalled by this attempt on Hitler's life—and not just soldiers but members of the general population as well.[29] Hitler was still seen by many as a selfless individual who was doing his best to prevent Germany's defeat. Yes, there had been setbacks, but with the Red Army drawing near, and an Allied commitment expressed the previous year to only accept "unconditional surrender" from the Germans, many felt, to use Darges' words, that this was no time to "to get off a moving train."

Hitler now appointed General Heinz Guderian as Chief of Staff of the German Army to succeed the departed Zeitzler. Hitler had sacked Guderian back in December 1941, but now this previously lucky commander—who had helped conquer France and led a spectacular drive towards Moscow in the early days of the invasion of the Soviet Union—was back in favour. Hitler made plain to Guderian at their meeting on 21 July 1944 that he would never tolerate his new Chief of Staff saying he wanted to resign—Zeitzler had offered his resignation five times before he had eventually walked out, and Hitler now insisted on someone who would stick to the job.

Guderian initially found Hitler's manner in the wake of the attempt on his life, "astonishingly calm"[30] but it soon became clear that "the deep distrust he already felt for mankind in general, and for General Staff officers and generals in particular, now became profound hatred . . . It had already been difficult enough dealing with him; it now became a torture that grew steadily worse from month to month. He frequently lost all self-control and his language grew increasingly violent."[31]

Guderian not only took on the job as Chief of Staff, but he served on the notorious "Court of Honour" which expelled officers from the army on suspicion of knowledge of the bomb plot, and then left them to be tried—and invariably executed—by the "People's Courts." This, and other actions of collaboration with the Nazi regime, have led military historians like Professor Robert Citino to form a profoundly negative opinion on Guderian's character. "He had been given a vast estate in occupied Poland—that obviously meant the Polish inhabitants had been evicted from it—and this was a man thoroughly wedded to the regime, still receiving large bribes from the Third Reich up to the very last moments of the war. And so I would say he's a relatively unsavoury character and his unsavouriness only came out by the diligent work of large numbers of historians in the decades following the Second World War. As a field commander, if I were asked to take an objective—City B—and here are your forces, and who would you like to carry out the manoeuvres, I might still call Heinz Guderian—wherever he is in the hereafter—and see if we could work out some terms. As an arbiter of what is right and wrong and the notion that there still can be morality even in wartime, he'd be the last person I'd call."[32]

But mere self-interest doesn't fully explain Guderian's motives in serving Hitler as Chief of Staff of the German army. Nor does the effect of any lingering "charisma" Hitler may still have possessed offer an explanation—as we have seen, Guderian was immune to this aspect of Hitler's leadership and had lost his job back in December 1941 in large part because he was prepared to argue with the Führer. The chief reason Guderian carried on supporting Hitler to the extent he did was surely because, as he puts it in his memoirs, "the Eastern Front was tottering on the edge of an abyss from which it was necessary to save millions of German soldiers and civilians. I should have regarded myself as a shabby coward if I had refused to attempt to save the eastern armies and my homeland, eastern Germany."[33]

Not that, as Professor Citino says, one should take at face value everything Guderian says in his memoirs. His protestations about his extreme distaste at having to serve on the "Court of Honour" and persecute his colleagues ring false. Much more sincere is his anger directed at the perpetrators of the bomb plot. Guderian felt it was doomed to fail even if Hitler had died. This was because, above all else, Guderian was focused on the looming problem of the Soviet advance—and here he has a point, since the conspirators had no more idea how to extricate Germany from the war against Stalin and prevent the Soviets taking revenge for their suffering than Hitler did.

By now, it was this fear of what the Red Army might do that dominated the minds of many Germans. "Children," the popular soldiers' saying went, "enjoy the war—the peace will be dreadful!"[34] And just three months after the failed bomb plot Germans gained an insight into how the new occupiers of their country might behave when Soviet troops moved on to German soil in East Prussia. On 20 October 1944, the Red

Army captured the small town of Nemmersdorf and committed a series of atrocities. The exact scale of the crimes committed at Nemmersdorf has been debated ever since,[35] but the fact that the Red Army murdered civilians and raped women is not in doubt. Colonel-General Reinhardt, for example, visited the area on 25 October and wrote to his wife the next day, "The Bolsheviks had ravaged like wild beasts, including [the] murder of children, not to mention acts of violence against women and girls, whom they had also murdered."[36]

For Hitler—and for millions of other Germans—what happened at Nemmersdorf symbolised the reason to keep on fighting. "They're animals from the steppes of Asia," Hitler said when he learnt about Nemmersdorf, "and the war I am waging against them is a war for the dignity of European mankind."[37] There is no record that Hitler felt any irony in this suggestion, given that the war of "annihilation" he had instigated against the Soviet Union had already cost the lives of many millions; and one of the main reasons for the atrocities committed against German civilians was the desire of Red Army soldiers for vengeance.

Nonetheless, the suffering of the Germans at the hands of the Soviets—even if it can in part be understood—cannot be excused. Anna Seddig was just one of hundreds of thousands of German women fleeing west who was abused. She was carrying her one-year-old son Siegfried with her. "Nothing to eat. Siegfried was thirsty and although I was pregnant again I still breastfed him. I also let snow melt in my mouth so that he could drink it. We had the snow after all." One night, seeking shelter for herself and her baby, she encountered a group of Red Army soldiers. "The Russians came and shone their torches on me. And one said 'Now, woman, you will get a place to stay.' And the place to stay was an air-raid shelter. There was a table in it. And in that night one Russian after another raped me there on the table. It's like being dead. Your whole body is gripped by cramp. You feel repulsion. Repulsion, I can't express it any other way. It was all against our will. They considered us fair game. I can't tell how many men there were—ten, fifteen. It just went on and on. There were so many, one after the other. One of them, I remember, also wanted me, but then he said, 'How many comrades have already been here? Put your clothes on.'"[38]

The broader picture was bleaker than ever for the Germans. The scale of the resources the Allies could now produce dwarfed anything the Germans could manage. In the year 1944, for instance, the Germans made fewer than 35,000 fighters and bombers—whilst together, Britain, America and the Soviet Union produced nearly 130,000.[39] And despite the desperate dreams of "wonder weapons" in development or of a split occurring between the Western Allies and Stalin, Germany's fate by the end of 1944 was obvious. Starved of raw materials—the Soviet capture of Romanian oil wells in April 1944 had been a devastating blow—the German war machine could last for only a few months more. But the cost, in human terms, of carrying on the war would be tremendous. Just under two million Germans had died during 1944, and those numbers would increase proportionately in 1945 with more than 400,000 killed in January alone.[40]

Hitler still tried to project certainty that all would eventually come well, and this was an important factor in maintaining the will to fight amongst the leaders of the Nazi movement. In the presence of a select group of Nazi believers, his optimism could still be infectious. In early December, just before the launch of the doomed German offensive in the Ardennes, Hitler so enthused Joseph Goebbels about the wonderful future ahead that the Propaganda Minister had trouble sleeping.[41]

However, even Hitler, whose ability never to demonstrate self-pity born of "neediness" had been a core part of his charismatic appeal, was now finding it hard to conceal his own belief that Germany would lose the war. After the failure of the German attack in the Ardennes, Nicolaus von Below heard Hitler confess that he believed the end was near, and he could only promise that he would never "capitulate" but "would take a world down with us."[42]

Increasingly, there was a sense of defeatism amongst sections of the German population, and the Gestapo was charged with the task of shooting "looters, deserters and other rabble."[43] It also seemed that the belief that "the Führer knows best" was collapsing amongst those who had fought for the regime. In March 1945, only one in five German prisoners of war held in the West had faith in Hitler—at the start of the year three times as many had expressed confidence in their Führer.[44]

Ulrich de Maizière, then a lieutenant colonel, offers a vivid portrait of the fast declining leader of the Third Reich: "By that time Hitler was already a sick man, with a severe shaking paralysis in his right arm, a shuffling gait, blue glasses, poor eyesight, so that everything had to be put before him in large letters. But he had lost none of his demonic charisma. In this final phase I perhaps had to make night-time presentations 10 to 15 times as 1A [i.e., Chief of Operations] in the Operations Department and I had the following two experiences. On the one hand he was a man, I am now talking of the human effect that he exuded, a man of indescribable, demonic effect on other people, whom only very, very few people were able to resist. And those who were constantly in his environment were totally subject to him. I know only very few people who succeeded in resisting the personal charisma of this man, no matter how ugly he was to look at. The second thing, however, which was much more dangerous, was that he was a man with a mental illness, to the extent that he had a hypertrophic self-identification with the German people, that he lived in such self-identification with the German people. He was subjectively convinced, and I heard this from his own mouth, that the German nation would not survive his end and the end of National Socialism. It would be destined to collapse. That was sick."[45]

That Hitler did not want to see Germany handed over to the victors intact is certainly true. He told Albert Speer in March 1945, "If the war is lost, the people will be lost also. It is not necessary to worry about what the German people will need for elemental survival. On the contrary, it is best for us to destroy even these things. For the nation has proved to be the weaker, and the future belongs solely to the stronger eastern nation. In any case only those who are inferior will remain after this struggle, for the good have already been killed."[46]

It was a view that ought not to have surprised Speer or any member of the Nazi elite or, indeed, anyone who had ever read *Mein Kampf.* The logic was inescapable in Hitler's mind. Life was a permanent struggle and the "weaker" *deserve* to die. It was a vision of strength, power and conquest that had been attractive when the Nazis were the ones winning—but which now had wholly nihilistic consequences in defeat. Speer professed to have been horrified at Hitler's desire to leave Germany in ruins, but it was wholly predictable. Hitler was simply being consistent with the world view he had first expressed in print in 1924.

It's a moment that symbolises the calamitous consequences of believing in Hitler's charismatic leadership. Hitler had always talked of never allowing a "repeat" of 1918 when the German army had surrendered whilst still on foreign soil. But the way in which the First World War had ended now seemed to be a model of compassion compared with the finale Hitler contemplated.

There were Germans—particularly those who directly faced the Red Army—who subscribed to Hitler's view that they should die rather than survive defeat. Rudolf Escherich was one of them. He was a member of a Luftwaffe squadron near the river Oder in the East of Germany. "We were all young, enthusiastic pilots, and were burning to do something to fight for the salvation of our Fatherland—even if it was practically hopeless."[47] He and twelve of his colleagues agreed to participate in a kamikaze-style operation called "Special Mission Freedom." Before taking part they all signed a letter saying, "We sacrifice ourselves voluntarily for our Führer, our homeland and for Germany." The plan was to crash their planes, loaded down with 500kg bombs, into the bridges over the river Oder. But the mission was a failure—Escherich lost his way in thick fog and then the operation was abandoned once the Red Army swiftly crossed the river.

What remains intriguing is the motivation of these pilots. Escherich says he would "certainly not" have flown such a suicide mission against the Western Allies. "In the West, they were civilised, they treated their prisoners of war in a half humane fashion and you could expect them to treat the defeated German population more or less decently. But the Russians were not like this." When reminded of the appalling atrocities the Germans had committed on Soviet territory, and how this must have been part of the motivation for the Soviets behaving as they did, Escherich says, "In such a situation, you don't ask yourself these questions. We were now confronted by the Russians overwhelming us, our whole population. And then you don't ask yourself about what had gone on before and whether we had once done injustice to them."

But, as Rudolf Escherich might have predicted, on the Western Front there were many Germans who were not prepared to "sacrifice" themselves "for our Führer, our homeland and for Germany." In March 1945, the month before Escherich's attempted suicide mission, Hitler expressed his outrage at the numbers of German soldiers who were allowing themselves to be captured in the West. "In some places," said Hitler, "no resistance at all—immediate and easy surrender to the Americans. It's a disgrace."[48] True to his ultra-Darwinian beliefs, Hitler blamed the existence of the Geneva convention for the willingness of Germans to surrender, arguing that if he made it "clear to everyone" that he treated "enemy prisoners ruthlessly, without consideration for reprisals" then Germans would be less willing to be captured as a consequence.

Meanwhile the Allied bombing campaign had intensified still further—most famously with the attack on Dresden on 13 February 1945. "The air war is still the great tale of woe in the present situation," wrote Goebbels in his diary on 2 March 1945. "The Anglo–Americans have again made very heavy raids on western and south-eastern Germany with damage wholly impossible to set out in detail. The situation becomes daily more intolerable and we have no means of defending ourselves against this catastrophe."[49]

Goebbels wrote these words exactly two weeks before the Allies launched a devastating attack on the medieval German city of Würzburg in Franconia. On 16 March 1945, 226 RAF Lancaster bombers dropped almost 1,000 tons of bombs—mostly incendiaries designed to create a firestorm—on Würzburg. More than 80 per cent of the city's centre was destroyed—proportionately greater destruction than at Dresden. "The whole town was on fire," says Christl Dehm, who experienced the attack, "and time-delay bombs were exploding everywhere. And everywhere fear, and the screams of the wounded, and people burning alive who couldn't save themselves. Dreadful images."[50]

But terrible as the effects of the bombing were, it's worth remembering one of the conclusions of the United States Strategic Bombing Survey, conducted after the war: "The mental reaction of the German people to air attack is significant. Under ruthless Nazi control they showed surprising resistance to the terror and hardships of repeated air attack, to the destruction of their homes and belongings, and to the conditions under which they were reduced to live. Their morale, their belief in ultimate victory or satisfactory compromise, and their confidence in their leaders declined, but they continued to work efficiently as long as the physical means of production remained."[51]

The conclusion of the Americans was that this "resistance" demonstrated that "the power of a police state over its people cannot be underestimated." No doubt fear of reprisals by the regime was a factor in ensuring the bombing campaign did not lead to open civil disobedience. But the feeling of hopelessness and lack of alternative options in the face of the Soviet advance also played a part.

Even his gauleiters—some of his most dedicated followers—were no longer all in thrall to Hitler by the time of their last meeting on 24 February. Nicolaus von Below, who witnessed the encounter, said that Hitler "attempted to convince his listeners that he alone could correctly judge the situation. But the powers of suggestion he had employed in the past to mesmerise this circle were gone."[52] Still, unnoticed by von Below, amongst one or two of these core believers there lingered the remnants of belief. After his speech Hitler sat down to eat with the gauleiters and launched into a monologue. Listening to him, Gauleiter Rudolf Jordan, of Magdeburg-Anhalt, felt the depressed mood "evaporate." It was the "old Hitler" on show.[53]

However, as the Soviets closed on Berlin, the number of those who continued to have faith in Adolf Hitler declined still further. Even many of those closest to him did not share his belief that it was necessary to extinguish one's own life as the flame of the Third Reich died. Heinrich Himmler—"loyal Heinrich" as Hitler called him—had certainly imagined a world beyond Allied victory. This man who had helped implement the extermination of the Jews now sought to save some of them. On 5 February 1945 a train left for Switzerland containing 1,200 Jews from Theresienstadt concentration camp in Czechoslovakia. Himmler had agreed a deal with the American Union of Orthodox Rabbis to exchange Jews for cash—and a different train was planned to leave every two weeks.[54] Hitler was furious when he heard the news and ordered Himmler not to proceed with any more such ventures. But this didn't stop Himmler personally meeting Norbert Masur, an emissary of the World Jewish Congress, on 21 April and discussing handing over 1,000 women from Ravensbrück concentration camp. The meeting took place at the home of Himmler's masseur, Felix Kersten, and according to Kersten, Himmler told him just before the encounter, "I want to bury the hatchet between us and the Jews. If I had my own way, many things would have been done differently."[55]

The day before—Hitler's fifty-sixth birthday—Himmler, along with a number of other leading figures in the Third Reich, including Hermann Göring, had taken their leave of Hitler at the Führerbunker in Berlin. For years they and the other prominent Nazis had been rivals, divided amongst each other as they sought to please their Führer. Now they were united only in their desire to escape from him. It was a rare case, as Professor Sir Ian Kershaw memorably remarked, "of the sinking ship leaving the rat."[56]

On 23 April, Himmler met the Swedish diplomat, Count Folke Bernadotte. Himmler, believing Hitler would shortly commit suicide—if he had not already done so—authorised Bernadotte to tell the Western Allies that Germany would unconditionally surrender to them, though not to the Red Army. When the news was broadcast on BBC Radio, Hitler could scarcely believe the "betrayal." "Of course, Hitler was outraged in the extreme," says Bernd Freiherr Freytag von Loringhoven, one of the last German officers still in the bunker. "Militarily there was no hope left. And now this move had been made by the man he probably had trusted most. This man had deserted him and had approached the Allies. As a result, the following night Hitler took the logical step and dictated his personal and political will and within two days he was dead."[57]

Of all of the Nazi elite who had previously expressed belief in Hitler's charisma, only the propaganda minister, Joseph Goebbels—along with his wife and six children—chose to die in the bunker with him. Goebbels' wife, Magda, was one of the few who probably still retained their faith in Hitler to the very end, but it is doubtful if her husband now believed in Hitler's charismatic leadership quite so much. Most likely, Goebbels had worked through all of the various possibilities for his future and saw death alongside Hitler as the most sensible. If Goebbels had been captured by the Allies—and how could someone as physically distinctive hope to hide from discovery—he knew he faced almost certain execution. But if he stayed with Hitler then he believed he could become a hero himself. He had said as much just a few days before, on 17 April, at a meeting with his staff at the propaganda ministry, when he explained that the reason they should not try to flee from Berlin was because in a "hundred years time" a film would be made about this epic period that would mean they would then be "brought back to life." As a result, "Everybody now has a chance to choose the part which he will play in the film a hundred years hence. I can assure you that it will be a fine and elevating picture. And for the sake of this prospect it is worth standing fast."[58]

While Goebbels tried to create his own "film" ending to his life, Hitler was, according to his secretary Traudl Junge, now "leading his shadowy life" wandering "restlessly around the rooms"[59] of the bunker under the garden of the Reich Chancellery. "The atmosphere in the bunker was absolutely macabre," confirms Bernd Freiherr Freytag von Loringhoven. "The people there no longer had anything to do. They were hanging around in the corridors, waiting for news. The enemy was close at hand. So the main topic in the bunker was 'How do I kill myself?' "[60]

Just before midnight on 28 April, Hitler dictated a political testament—one that is remarkably consistent with his earliest expression of belief, the letter he wrote in September 1919 at the behest of Karl Mayr. Both documents exude hatred of the Jews. In his political testament Hitler blames the Jews for the outbreak of the Second World War and ends with the words, "Above all I charge the leaders of the nation and those under them to scrupulous observance of the laws of race and to merciless opposition to the universal poisoner of all peoples, international Jewry."[61] Neither document contains an iota of humanity, and they both reveal a mind fixed in certain belief. Even as he died Hitler did not blame himself for any of the calamities he had brought upon the world. Instead, he claimed that "In these three decades I have been actuated solely by love and loyalty to my people in all my thoughts, acts, and life."

Hitler had not changed—all the elements that had enabled him to become a charismatic leader still existed within him until his last breath. What had changed was other people's perception of him. Since charisma is only created in an interaction between an individual and a receptive audience, repeated failure and broken promises had badly damaged Hitler's charismatic appeal not only amongst the broad German population, but amongst many of his core supporters.

Adolf Hitler committed suicide just after 3:30 in the afternoon of 30 April 1945. He shot himself in the head as he bit on a capsule of poison that had previously been supplied to him by Himmler. So distrustful of "loyal Heinrich" had Hitler been at the end of his life that he insisted that a sample of the poison first be tried on his dog, Blondi, to ensure that Himmler had not planned to deceive him and allow the Allies to capture him alive.[62]

ACKNOWLEDGEMENTS

There are many people I need to thank. Janice Hadlow, Controller of BBC2, and Martin Davidson, BBC History commissioner, were both enthusiastic about this idea and I am grateful for their support.

Professor Sir Ian Kershaw was historical consultant to the TV series and also read a draft of this book and offered his thoughts and criticisms. I have written elsewhere of the debt I owe him—he has been a friend and colleague for almost twenty years now—but I need to reiterate my gratitude to him here. It has been my colossal good fortune to be able to work closely with one of the most brilliant historical scholars of the last hundred years. But, I hasten to add, the views and judgements expressed in this book are entirely my own.

Another old friend and colleague, Detlef Siebert, who also worked with me for many years on various television series on Nazism, read through this book and offered his criticisms. He is as generous as he is intelligent.

I also benefited from the long discussions I had with a whole galaxy of the world's best historians for my educational website WW2History.com. Also, of course, I thank the BBC, and in particular my last boss, Keith Scholey, for permission to use transcript material from my previous TV series on Nazism.

Working with me on the television series, Ann Cattini was a beacon of stability as Production Executive. In Germany, Dr. Frank Stucke was an excellent Associate Producer, and I also benefited very much from the archival research work of two talented young German academics, Fabian Wendler and Julia Pietsch. Martin Patmore, who has filmed almost everything I have made for the last twenty years, did his usual fine job as cameraman, as did the film editors, Alan Lygo, Jamie Hay and Simon Holland. Monika Rubel and her team at 24 Frames films in Munich were a tremendous help with the drama sections of the series, and impressively endured my foibles as a drama director. John Kennedy and his son Christopher deserve special mention as Graphic Designers—their work on the TV series was quite exceptional.

At Ebury Press, my editor Albert DePetrillo, and my publisher, Jake Lingwood, were good friends to this project over several years. My American publisher, Dan Frank of Pantheon books, made a number of insightful comments, whilst my literary agent, Andrew Nurnberg, remains as important in my working life as ever. My wife, Helena, used her considerable business skills to manage our independent production company, and offered me constant support with this book as well. My children, Oliver, Camilla and Benedict, were more supportive than I deserve. They have lived with my obsession with this subject all their lives—and that's a long time. My eldest son, Oliver, has just graduated from Cambridge and my daughter, Camilla, has a place at Oxford to read History (though not this period of history . . .).

I have dedicated this book to my parents, who both died at the age of forty-nine. Now that I reach my mid-fifties the idea that they died so young, in the circumstances they did, seems more obscene to me than ever.

NOTES

EPIGRAPHS
1. Entry for 18 January 1942, evening, *Hitler's Table Talk, 1941–1944*, introduced and with a new preface by Hugh Trevor-Roper, Phoenix Press, 2002, p221.
2. Konrad Heiden, introduction to *Mein Kampf* by Adolf Hitler, Houghton Mifflin, 1971, pxxi.

INTRODUCTION
1. Hitler confessed this to Leni Riefenstahl quoted in: *A Memoir* by Leni Riefenstahl, Picador, 1992, p178.
2. Konrad Heiden, *The Fuehrer*, Robinson Publishing, 1999, first published 1944, p35. Heiden expresses the contradiction in Hitler, thus: "As a human figure, lamentable; as a political mind, one of the most tremendous phenomena of all world history."
3. Hitler's words, 18 January 1942, in *Hitler's Table Talk*, p221.
4. See Max Weber, *Essays in Sociology*, Routledge, 1998, p245.
5. Weber, *Essays*. In particular pp245–264.
6. Laurence Rees, *Their Darkest Hour*, Ebury Press, 2007, ppviii–x.

CHAPTER ONE
1. August Kubizek, *The Young Hitler I Knew*, Greenhill Books, 2006, pp157–9.
2. ibid., pp126–7.
3. Hitler, *Mein Kampf*, pp154–5.
4. Quoted in English in Konrad Heiden, *The Fuehrer*, pp70–72. Quoted in German in Eberhard Jäckel, *Hitler: Sämtliche Aufzeichnungen 1905–1924*, Stuttgart, 1980, pp64–69. Reproduction in the Bundesarchiv (BArch) NS 26/4.

298 Notes to Pages 12–18

5. Quoted in Robert G. L. Waite, *Vanguard of Nazism, the Free Corps Movement in Postwar Germany 1918 to 1923,* Harvard University Press, 1952, p22.

6. *Mein Kampf,* p165.

7. See Thomas Weber, *Hitler's First War,* Oxford University Press, 2010.

8. Quoted ibid., p215. Weber also makes the point that regimental dispatch runners were more likely to get recommended for awards than front line soldiers—but that, of course, does not mean that Hitler was not bravely doing a dangerous job.

9. Balthasar Brandmayer, *Meldegänger Hitler 1914–1918,* Munich/Kolbermoor 1933, pp71–2.

10. See, for example, the interrogation of Max Amman at Nuremberg, 5 November 1947 NARA RG238-M1019–2, and Balthasar Brandmayer, *Meldegänger Hitler,* pp72 and 105.

11. BArch, N 28/6 Ludwig Beck to Frau Wilhelm Beck, 28 November 1918, quoted in Klaus-Jürgen Müller, *General Ludwig Beck,* Boppard am Rhein, 1980, pp323–328.

12. Laurence Rees, *The Nazis: A Warning from History,* BBC Books, 2005, p15.

13. Previously unpublished testimony.

14. Interestingly, Hitler was treated in the "psychiatric" department of Pasewalk for "psychosomatic" blindness. See Weber, p221.

15. Hitler, *Mein Kampf,* p202.

16. Anton Joachimsthaler has written extensively on this subject in *Korrektur einer Biographie: Adolf Hitler 1908–1920,* Munich 1989, see pp201–213. The original documents are in the Bavarian State Archive, Batl. Anordnung des Demob.Batl, vom 3.4.1919. 2 Inf. Regt., Bund 19 Bayrisches Hauptstaatsarchiv (BayHStA), Abt. IV. Joachimsthaler also remarks that Hitler's regiment renamed their barracks after the Socialist revolutionary Karl Liebknecht, p209.

17. Joachimsthaler, p213.

18. See the views of Anton Joachimsthaler expressed in *The Making of Adolf Hitler,* produced by Tilman Remme, executive producer Laurence Rees, BBC 2, 2002.

19. See Ian Kershaw, *Hitler: Hubris,* Allen Lane, 2002, p119.

20. Weber, *Hitler's First War,* p252.

21. Karl Mayr (writing as "Anon"), "I Was Hitler's Boss," *Current History,* Vol. 1, No. 3 (November 1941), 193.

22. BayHStA, Abt. II Gruppen Kdo. 4 Bd. 50/6, quoted in Ernst Deuerlein, *Hitler's Eintritt in die Politik und die Reichswehr,* Vierteljahreshefte für Zeitgeschichte (VfZ), Vol. 7, No. 2 (1959), pp191–2.

23. Previously unpublished testimony.
24. Quoted in Deuerlein, *Hitler's Eintritt*, p200. Original is in the Bavarian State Archive. *Auszüge aus den Berichten der zum Aufklärungskommando Beyschlag befohlenen Soldaten*, Bay HStA. Ab II Gruppen Kdo 4 Bd 50/5. Handschriftlich.
25. BayHStA, RWGrKdo 4/314. Quoted in Eberhard Jäckel, *Hitler: Sämtliche Aufzeichnungen 1905–1924*, Stuttgart, 1980, pp88–90.
26. ibid.

CHAPTER TWO

1. Kurt Lüdecke, *I Knew Hitler*, Jarrolds, 1938, pp22–25.
2. Kubizek, *Young Hitler*, p33.
3. ibid., p157.
4. Previously unpublished testimony.
5. Previously unpublished testimony.
6. Hitler speech of 12 April 1922 in N. H. Baynes (Editor), *Speeches of Adolf Hitler: Early speeches, 1922–1924, and Other Selections*, Howard Fertig, 2006, p5.
7. Hitler speech of 28 July 1922, ibid., p29. Also quoted by Eberhard Jaeckel, Jäckel, *Hitler: Sämtliche Aufzeichnungen 1905–1924*. First published in *Völkischer Beobachter*,16 August 1922.
8. First published in *Völkischer Beobachter*, 22 April 1922.
9. Interview with author for WW2History.com.
10. Hitler speech of 12 April 1922, Baynes, p6.
11. Baynes, pp15–16.
12. Previously unpublished testimony.
13. Previously unpublished testimony.
14. Hans Frank, *Im Angesicht des Galgens*, Munich/Grafelfing, 1953, pp39–42.
15. Roger Manvell and Heinrich Fraenkel, *Göring*, Greenhill Books, 2005, pp36–37.
16. *Trial of the German War Criminals: Proceedings of the International Military Tribunal* (British edition), IX, pp64–65.
17. Hitler did not "hypnotise" his audience—in the sense of convincing them to act against their will. But the pioneering work of the Hungarian scholar, Sándor Ferenczi, on the nature of hypnotism and suggestion does offer an insight into some of the psychological reasons which might have been behind Hitler's effectiveness as a speaker in these early post–First World War years. Crucially, Ferenczi pointed out that "Everything speaks much more in favour of the view that in hypnotism and suggestion the chief work

is performed not by the hypnotist and suggestor, but by the person himself." Ferenczi went as far as to state that you can't be hypnotised—or be the subject of "suggestion"—unless you consent. Moreover, Ferenczi believed that it was immensely helpful for any person who wishes to practise suggestion, to possess "an imposing appearance . . . a penetrating glance, and a stern expression of countenance . . . It is [also] generally recognised that a self-confident manner, the reputation of previous successes . . . help in the successful effect of suggestion." In addition, for Ferenczi the "suggestor" was a kind of "father figure." He thought that "a preliminary condition of every successful suggestion is that the hypnotist shall figure as a 'grown up' to the hypnotised subject. The former must be able to arouse in the latter the same feelings of love or fear, the same conviction of infallibility, as those with which his parents inspired him as a child." (See Sándor Ferenczi, *First Contributions to Psycho-Analysis* [first published in Hungarian, 1909], translation by Ernest Jones M.D., The Hogarth Press and the Institute of Psychoanalysis, 1952, pp59–71.) One must not take all this too far in the case of Hitler, since he most certainly did not "hypnotise" his supporters in the manner of a stage hypnotist. Those who followed him did so willingly and out of their own choice. Equally, Ferenczi writes with a certainty which would on occasion benefit from nuance and qualification—as in his statement that "In our innermost soul we are still children, and we remain so throughout life." But it is striking, nonetheless, how much this early Hitler conforms to Ferenczi's view of the successful "suggestor." Even at this age—he was just thirty-three in 1922—Hitler was positioning himself as a "father figure," calling on the youth of Germany to follow him and offering "fatherly" advice and admonition. And as for Ferenczi's view that the successful suggestor must create a "conviction of infallibility," well, a "conviction of infallibility" was exactly what Hitler tried to project from his first political speech onwards.

18. Kubizek, *Young Hitler*, p182.
19. Hitler speech of 12 April 1922, Baynes, p12.
20. See also the work of the "crowd theorists," pioneered by Emile Durkheim. E. Durkheim, *The Elementary Forms of Religious Life*, Simon and Schuster, 1995.
21. Konrad Heiden, *The Fuehrer*, Robinson Publishing, 1999, pp91–2.
22. Otto Strasser, *Hitler and I*, Jonathan Cape, 1940, pp76–77.
23. Sir Nevile Henderson, *Failure of a Mission*, Hodder and Stoughton, 1940, p179.
24. Previously unpublished testimony.

25. Rees, *The Nazis: A Warning from History*, pp32–33.

26. Weber, *Hitler's First War*, p257.

27. Ernst H. Posse, *Die politischen Kampfbünde Deutschlands*, Berlin, 1931, pp46–7 quoted in Robert G. L. Waite, *Vanguard of Nazism, the Free Corps Movement in Postwar Germany 1918–1923*, Harvard University Press, 1952, p266.

28. Not quoted in Waite but in the original, Ernst H. Posse, *Die politischen Kampfbünde Deutschlands*, Berlin, 1931, p46.

29. Previously unpublished testimony.

30. Heinrich Hoffmann, *Hitler Was My Friend*, London, 1955, p46.

31. Karl Mayr (writing as "Anon"), "I Was Hitler's Boss," *Current History*, Vol. 1, No. 3, (November 1941).

32. ibid.

33. Kubizek, *Young Hitler*, p42.

34. Charles de Gaulle, *The Edge of the Sword*, Greenwood Press, 1960, p58.

35. ibid., p65–6.

CHAPTER THREE

1. Weber, *Essays in Sociology*, p262.

2. Rees, *Nazis: A Warning from History*, p26.

3. Friedrich Nietzsche, *The Birth of Tragedy and the Genealogy of Morals*, translated by Francis Golffing, Doubleday Anchor Books, 1956, p186.

4. Peter Viereck, "Stefan George's Cosmic Circle," *Decision*, October 1941, p49.

5. Previously unpublished testimony.

6. Previously unpublished testimony.

7. Kubizek, *Young Hitler*, p185.

8. ibid., p83.

9. Previously unpublished testimony.

10. Ludwig Gengler, *Kampfflieger Rudolf Berthold*, Germany, 1934, quoted p178.

11. Joachim C. Fest, *Hitler*, Harcourt Brace Jovanovich, 1974, p132.

12. ibid., p133.

13. Quoted by Margarate Plewnia, *Auf dem Weg zu Hitler*, Bremen, 1970, p67. She in turn quotes Albert Zoller, *Hitler privat—Erlebnisbericht seiner Geheimsekretärin*, Droste, Düsseldorf, 1949, p118.

14. ibid., p55.

15. *IMT testimony* of Julius Streicher, Friday, 26 April 1946.

16. Waite, *Vanguard of Nazism*, p267.

17. Otto Strasser, *Hitler and I*, p86.

18. Bruce Campbell, *The SA Generals and The Rise of Nazism*, University Press of Kentucky, 1998, pp18–20.
19. Werner Maser, *Der Sturm auf die Republik*, Frankfurt, Athenäum-Verlag, 1965, p356.
20. *Völkischer Beobachter*, 6 December 1922.
21. Rees, *The Nazis: A Warning from History*, p25.
22. Previously unpublished testimony.
23. See, for example, Strasser, *Hitler and I*, p57.
24. Albrecht Tyrell, *Führer befiehl . . . Selbstzeugnisse aus der "Kampfzeit" der NSDAP, Dokumentation und Analyse*, Düsseldorf, 1969, pp281–3. Tyrell quotes extracts from *Der Hitler Prozess vor dem Volksgericht in München, Zweiter Teil*, München, 1924, Hitler's closing words, pp85–91. English translation in J. Noakes and G. Pridham, *Nazism 1919–1945, Vol. 1*, Exeter University Press, 1983, p35.
25. Previously unpublished testimony.
26. Neithardt had been the judge in January 1922 at the trial of Hitler and other Nazis accused of a brawl at the Löwenbräu beer cellar in Munich the previous September and had petitioned his own superiors to be lenient to Hitler. See Rees, *The Nazis: A Warning from History*, p28.
27. *The Times*, 2 April 1924.

CHAPTER FOUR

1. Weber, *Essays*, p250.
2. Hitler, *Mein Kampf*, p288.
3. ibid., p306.
4. See p102.
5. Ernest Becker, *The Denial of Death*, Free Press Paperbacks, 1997, p282.
6. ibid., p27.
7. Hitler, *Mein Kampf*, p290.
8. ibid., p305.
9. ibid., p679.
10. ibid., p654.
11. ibid., p661.
12. Previously unpublished testimony.
13. Laurence Rees, *Their Darkest Hour*, Ebury Press, 2007, p206.
14. Previously unpublished testimony.
15. Dennis Mack Smith, *Mussolini: A Biography*, Vintage Books, New York, 1983, p172.
16. See Professor Browning's views, pp23–24.

17. Konrad Heiden, introduction to *Mein Kampf* by Adolf Hitler, pxx.
18. Hitler, *Mein Kampf*, p581.
19. Ian Kershaw, *Hitler: Hubris*, pp242–243.
20. Lüdecke, *I Knew Hitler*, pp217–8.
21. Goebbels' diary, entry for 15 February 1926. Unless otherwise footnoted, all entries from the Goebbels diaries are taken from: Elke Fröhlich (ed.), *Die Tagebücher von Joseph Goebbels. Teil I: Aufzeichnungen 1923–1941; Teil II: Diktate 1941–1945*, Munich 1993–2005.
22. ibid., entry for 13 April 1926.
23. ibid., entry for 19 April 1926.
24. In particular Otto Strasser—see *Hitler and I*, p100.
25. Uriel Tal, *Political Faith of Nazism prior to the Holocaust*, Tel Aviv University, 1978, p30.
26. John Whittam, "Mussolini and The Cult of the Leader," *New Perspective*, Vol. 3, No. 3, March 1998.
27. In English in Ian Kershaw, *The Hitler Myth*, Oxford University Press, 1987, p27. Also quoted in Albrecht Tyrell, *Führer befiehl . . . Dokumentation und Analyse*, Düsseldorf, 1969, p173.
28. Becker, *Denial of Death*, p193.
29. Joseph Goebbels, *Der Angriff* (Berlin, 30 April 1928). Quoted by Joseph Goebbels, *Der Angriff. Aufsätze aus der Kampfzeit*, Munich, 1935, pp71–73.
30. Walter Frank, *Franz Ritter von Epp: Der Weg eines deutschen Soldaten*, Hamburg, 1934, pp141–2.
31. Adam Tooze, *The Wages of Destruction*, Penguin, 2007, p13.
32. Previously unpublished testimony.

CHAPTER FIVE

1. Hitler 1932 election speech at Eberswald. Archive featured in episode 1, *The Nazis: A Warning from History*, BBC2, 1997.
2. Richard Bessel, "The Potempa Murder," *Central European History*, 10, 1977, pp241–54.
3. Previously unpublished testimony.
4. Previously unpublished testimony.
5. Albert Speer, *Inside the Third Reich*, Phoenix, 1995, p46.
6. ibid., p46.
7. ibid., p66.
8 ibid., p44.
9. Previously unpublished testimony.
10. Previously unpublished testimony.

11. Previously unpublished testimony.
12. Tal, *Political Faith of Nazism prior to the Holocaust*, p28.
13. Thomas Ferguson and Peter Temin, "Made in Germany: The German Currency Crisis of July 1931," *Research in Economic History*, Vol. 21 (2003), pp1–53.
14. Previously unpublished testimony.
15. Weber, *Hitler's First War*, p272.
16. Previously unpublished testimony.
17. Weber, p283.
18. Nathaniel Shaler, *The Individual: A Study of Life and Death*, D. Appleton and Company, New York, 1902, p199.
19. Ernst Hanfstaengl, *15 Jahre mit Hitler, Zwischen Weissem und Braunem Haus*, 1980, pp232–6, and Heinrich Hoffman, *Hitler Was My Friend*, London, 1955, pp151–2. See also Walter C. Langer, *A Psychological Profile of Adolph Hitler. His Life and Legend*, Office of Strategic Services Washington, D.C. Online at: www.nizkor.org. For the detail of Hitler's alleged sexual perversion, see Robert Waite, *The Psychopathic God: Adolf Hitler*, Basic Books, 1977. But it is all essentially hearsay evidence and unpersuasive. More recently an attempt has been made to claim Hitler was homosexual—see Lothar Machtan, *The Hidden Hitler*, Basic Books, 2001—but this is also unconvincing. Ian Kershaw's review of Machtan's book in *Die Welt* 13.10.2001 http://www .welt.de/print-welt/article481144/Der_ungerade_Weg.html raises questions about the theory.
20. Riefenstahl, *A Memoir*, p180.
21. Goebbels' diary, entry for 26 June 1930, p183f.
22. Previously unpublished testimony.
23. Previously unpublished testimony.
24. Previously unpublished testimony.
25. Otto Meissner, *Aufzeichnung über die Besprechung des Herrn Reichspräsidenten mit Adolf Hitler am 13. August 1932 nachmittags 4.15*. Quoted by: Walther Hubatsch, *Hindenburg und der Staat. Aus den Papieren des Generalfeldmarschalls und Reichspräsidenten von 1878 bis 1934*, Göttingen, 1955, p338. In English in Noakes and Pridham, Vol. 1, p104.

CHAPTER SIX

1. Goebbels' diary, entry for 13 August 1932.
2. Tal, *Political Faith of Nazism Prior to the Holocaust*, p7.
3. Franz von Papen, *Memoirs*, London, 1952, pp162–3. In German in Franz von Papen, *Der Wahrheit eine Gasse*, Munich, 1952, p195.
4. Von Papen, *Memoirs*, p279.

5. Testimony of Göring from Day 80, Nuremberg Tribunal, 13 March 1946.
6. Von Papen, *Memoirs*, p162.
7. Oldest source for this famous remark is Konrad Heiden, *Adolf Hitler. Das Zeitalter der Verantwortungslosigkeit. Eine Biographie*, Zürich, 1936, p278.
8. Hinrich Lohse, *Der Fall Strasser*, held in *Forschungsstelle für die Geschichte des Nationalsozialismus* in Hamburg. In English in Noakes and Pridham, Vol. 1, p111.
9. Peter D. Stachura, *Gregor Strasser and the Rise of Nazism*, George Allen & Unwin, 1983, p104.
10. Otto Strasser, *History in My Time*, Jonathan Cape, 1941, p240.
11. Stachura, *Gregor Strasser and the Rise of Nazism*, p116.
12. Hinrich Lohse, *Der Fall Strasser*. In English in Noakes and Pridham, Vol. 1, p113.
13. Strasser, *History in My Time*, p236. Also, see von Papen, *Memoirs* for a reproduction of the gift, facing p279.
14. See notes made on 2 December 1933 by Lutz Graf von Schwerin von Krosigk, Reichs Finance Minister, quoted in Wolfram Pyta, *Vorbereitungen für den militärischen Ausnahmezustand unter Papen/Schleicher*, Militärgeschichtliche Mitteilungen, 51, 1992, pp385–428.
15. Previously unpublished testimony.
16. Previously unpublished testimony.
17. Rees, *The Nazis: A Warning from History*, p43.
18. Von Papen, *Memoirs*, p251.
19. Previously unpublished testimony.

CHAPTER SEVEN

1. Manvell, *Göring*, p95.
2. ibid., p97.
3. Previously unpublished testimony.
4. Previously unpublished testimony.
5. Walther Hofer, *Der Nationalsozialismus: Dokumente 1933–1945*, Frankfurt am Main, 1957, p55. Hitler speech 10 March 1933. First published in Reichsgesetzblatt RGBl 1933, Teil I, Nr. 17, p83.
6. *Völkischer Beobachter*, 13 March 1933.
7. Previously unpublished testimony.
8. Previously unpublished testimony.
9. *Völkischer Beobachter*, 24 March 1933.
10. Alan Bullock, *Hitler: A Study in Tyranny*, London, 1967, pp128–9.
11. Max Domarus, *Hitler: Speeches and Proclamations 1932–1945 Volume One:*

1932 to 1934, Bolchazy-Carducci Publishers, 1990, Hitler statement 23 March 1933, p273.

12. ibid., pp292–3.
13. Previously unpublished testimony.
14. *Völkischer Beobachter,* 29 March 1933.
15. *Daily Telegraph* interview with Adolf Hitler, published *Völkischer Beobachter,* 28 July 1934. Quoted in English in Domarus, *Vol. 1,* 1990, p317.
16. Joseph Goebbels, *My Part in Germany's Fight,* London, 1938, p248.
17. Previously unpublished testimony.
18. Klaus Hildebrand, *The Foreign Policy of the Third Reich,* Batsford, London, 1973, pp31–32.
19. Interview with author for WW2History.com.
20. Quoted in Hans-Adolf Jacobsen and Werner Jochmann (editors), *Ausgewaehlte Dokumente zur Geschichte des Nationalsozialismus 1933–1945,* Band II. Bielefeld, 1961. First published in *NSDAP: Nationalsozialistische Monatshefte,* 4 June, 1933.
21. Previously unpublished testimony.
22. Previously unpublished testimony.
23. From the account by Field-Marshal von Weichs quoted in Robert J. O'Neill, *The German Army and the Nazi Party 1933–1939,* Corgi Books, 1968, p67.
24. ibid.
25. Kurt Gossweiler, *Die Röhm-Affäre. Hintergründe—Zusammenhänge—Auswirkungen,* Köln, 1983, p68.
26 Quoted in Hans-Adolf Jacobsen and Werner Jochmann (eds.), *Dokumente zur Geschichte des Nationalsozialismus 1933–1945,* Band II, Bielefeld, 1961.
27. Tooze, *Wages of Destruction,* p67.
28. Kershaw, *Hubris,* p511.
29. Rudolf Diels, *Lucifer ante Portas,* Stuttgart, 1950, pp379–82. Also in Kershaw, *Hubris,* p505.
30. From an account by Kempka, "Hitler's Chauffeur," quoted in Noakes and Pridham, Vol. 1, pp178–179.
31. *Deutsche Allgemeine Zeitung* (DAZ), No. 302, 2 July 1934.
32. *Völkischer Beobachter,* 3 July 1934.
33. Previously unpublished testimony.
34. *Völkischer Beobachter,* 1 July 1934.
35. Previously unpublished testimony.
36. Previously unpublished testimony.
37. Previously unpublished testimony.

38. See, for example, the views of Professor Norbert Frei about the "modernity" and "barbarism" of the Nazis, expressed in his interview with the author at: WW2History.com.

39. Rudolf Semmler, *Goebbels, The Man Next to Hitler*, London, 1947, see diary entry for 12 December 1941.

40. Previously unpublished testimony.

41. Hermann Göring, *Aufbau einer Nation*, Berlin, 1934, pp51–2. (Also quoted, though in a slightly different translation, in Arthur Schweitzer, *The Age of Charisma*, Nelson Hall, Chicago, 1984, p83.)

42. David Welch, *Propaganda and the German Cinema 1933–1945*, Oxford University Press, 1983, p147.

43. Riefenstahl, *Memoirs*, p101.

44. William L. Shirer, *Berlin Diary 1934–41*, John Hopkins, 2002, p21.

45. George Orwell, *The Collected Essays, Journalism and Letters of George Orwell*, Volume 2, Eds. Sonia Orwell and Ian Angus, Harcourt Brace Jovanovich, 1968.

46. ibid.

47. Hitler Speech of 8 November 1935, p727, Domarus, *Vol. II*.

48. Max Domarus, *Hitler—Reden und Proklamationen 1932–1945—kommentiert von einem deutschen Zeitgenossen*, Band I, Würzburg, 1962, p641.

49. Shirer, *Berlin Diary*, pp17–18.

50. See p23.

51. W. Breucker (Ludendorff's adjutant), *Die Tragik Ludendorffs*, Oldenburg, 1953, p107; also in English in J.C.R. Wright, *Above Parties: The Political Attitudes of the German Protestant Church Leadership 1918–1933*, Oxford, 1974, p78.

52. Speer, *Inside The Third Reich*, p150.

53. Hans-Jochen Gamm. *Der braune Kult* (Hamburg, 1962) 213–4, quoted in English in Robert G. L. Waite, *The Psychopathic God: Adolf Hitler*, Basic Books, New York, 1977, p29.

54. Previously unpublished testimony.

55. Domarus, *Vol. II*, p790.

56. Hitler speech 23 November 1937, quoted in Arthur Schweitzer, *The Age of Charisma*, Nelson Hall, Chicago, 1984, p75.

57. Richard Steigmann-Gall, *The Holy Reich—Nazi Conceptions of Christianity*, Cambridge University Press, 2003, p2.

58. Goebbels' diary, entry for 8 April 1941.

59. Entry for 13 December 1941, *Hitler's Table Talk*, pp142–145.

60. Laurence Rees, *Selling Politics*, BBC Books, 1992, p50.

61. Wilfred von Oven, interview in *Goebbels: Master of Propaganda*, written and produced by Laurence Rees, BBC 2, 1992.
62. *Völkischer Beobachter*, 1 February 1934.
63. Rees, *Selling Politics*, p21.
64. *Die zukünftige Arbeit und Gestaltung des deutschen Rundfunks*. Ansprache Goebbels an die Intendanten und Direktoren der Rundfunkgesellschaften, Berlin, Haus des Rundfunks, 25.3.1933, in Helmut Heiber (ed.), Goebbels Reden. Band 1: 1932–1939. Düsseldorf, 1971, p94.
65. Welch, *Propaganda and the German Cinema*, p158.
66. ibid., p170.
67. Rees, *Selling Politics*, p51.
68. Weber, *Essays*, p248.
69. Goebbels' diary, entry for 5 July 1941.
70. Weber, *Essays*, p248.
71. Tooze, *Wages of Destruction*, pp37–166.
72. Interview with author for WW2History.com.
73. Rees, *Their Darkest Hour*, p196.

CHAPTER EIGHT

1. Hitler, *Mein Kampf*, pp118–119.
2. J.R.C. Wright, *Above Parties—the Political Attitudes of the German Protestant Church Leadership 1918–1933*, OUP, 1974, p54.
3. Previously unpublished testimony.
4. Wolfgang Ruge, Wolfgang Schumann (eds.), *Dokumente zur Deutschen Geschichte*, Berlin, 1977, p116.
5. Previously unpublished testimony.
6. Domarus, *Vol. II*, p938.
7. Jonathan Glover, *Humanity—a Moral History of the Twentieth Century*, Pimlico, 2000, pp361–2.
8. Previously unpublished testimony.
9. Previously unpublished testimony.
10. *Aufzeichnung ohne Unterschrift* (August 1936), in *Akten zur Deutschen Auswärtigen Politik 1918–1945*. Göttingen, 1977. Serie C: 1933–1936. "Das Dritte Reich: Die Ersten Jahre," Band V, 2, 26. Mai bis 31. Oktober 1936. Dokumentnummer 490, pp793–801.
11. Rees, *Selling Politics*, p81.
12. International Military Tribunal (IMT) *Der Prozess gegen die Hauptkriegsverbrecher vor dem Internationalen Militärgerichtshof Nürnberg*, 1. November 1945—1. Oktober 1946, Band XXXVI, Nürnberg, 1948, p489ff.

13. ibid.

14. Henderson, *Failure of a Mission*, p159.

15. Göring's announcement on arrival at the ministry of economics, as heard by Wilhelm Ter-Nedden (recorded in interview with him filmed by the author).

16. Tooze, *Wages of Destruction*, p198.

17. Previously unpublished testimony.

18. BArch N 28/4. Quoted in Klaus-Jürgen Müller, *General Ludwig Beck*, Boppard am Rhein, 1980, pp497–8.

19. Previously unpublished testimony.

20. Nicholas Reynolds, *Treason Was No Crime: Ludwig Beck, Chief of the German General Staff*, William Kimber, 1976, pp73–74.

21. BArch N 81/2 and OKW 898.

CHAPTER NINE

1. BArch NS 10/550.

2. Henderson, *Failure of a Mission*, p282.

3. Previously unpublished testimony.

4. Previously unpublished testimony.

5. O'Neill, *German Army*, pp190–191.

6. Friedrich Hossbach, *Zwischen Wehrmacht und Hitler 1934–1938*, Göttingen, 1965, p191.

7. O'Neill, *German Army*, p201.

8. Karl-Heinz Janssen, *Der Sturz der Generäle: Hitler und die Blomberg-Fritsch-Krise 1938*, Munich, 1994, p55.

9. Simon Sebag Montefiore, *Stalin: The Court of the Red Tsar*, Phoenix, 2007, pp221–222.

10. Robert Service, *Stalin—A Biography*, Macmillan, 2004, p348.

11. BArch N 28/4.Quoted in German in Müller, *General Ludwig Beck*, pp498–501. It is not clear whether Beck intended this paper to aid his own thinking or be given to colleagues.

12. Reynolds, *Treason Was No Crime*, p128.

13. Harold C. Deutsch, *The Conspiracy Against Hitler in the Twilight War*, University of Minnesota, 1968, p34.

14. Reynolds, *Treason Was No Crime*, p138.

15. Previously unpublished testimony.

16. Walter Görlitz, *Generalfeldmarschall Keitel, Verbrecher oder Offizier? Erinnerungen, Briefe, Dokumente des Chefs OKW*, Göttingen, 1961, p179.

17. Previously unpublished testimony.

18. Previously unpublished testimony.
19. Previously unpublished testimony.
20. Previously unpublished testimony.
21. Interview *The Nazis: A Warning from History*, episode 3, "The Wrong War," BBC2, 1997.
22. Domarus, *Vol. II*, p1050.
23. ibid., p1057.
24. Von Papen, *Memoirs*, p438.
25. Rees, *Nazis: A Warning from History*, p100.
26. Reynolds, *Treason Was No Crime*, p144.

CHAPTER TEN

1. Albert Speer, *Inside the Third Reich*, p100.
2. Remark by Albert Speer, according to his brother Hermann, quoted in Michael Thad Allen, *The Business of Genocide—the SS, Slave Labor, and the Concentration Camps*, University of North Carolina Press, 2002, p59.
3. M. J. Drake, I. W. Mills and D. Cranston, "The Chequered History of Vasectomy," *British Journal of Urology*, pp475–81, September 1999.
4. Previously unpublished testimony.
5. Interview with author for WW2History.com.
6. See Ernst Klee, *"Euthanasie" im NS-Staat: Die "Vernichtung lebensunwerten Lebens,"* Frankfurt/M., S. Fischer, 1983, p86.
7. Hitler, *Mein Kampf*, p688.
8. Robert Jay Lifton in his classic study, *The Nazi Doctors*, Basic Books, 2000, confirms that "the great majority" of the doctors he interviewed "approved of the sterilization laws at the time," p29.
9. *Völkischer Beobachter*, 2 August 1929.
10. Karl Binding, Alfred Hoche, *Die Freigabe der Vernichtung lebensunwerten Lebens. Ihr Maß und ihre Form*, Leipzig, 1920, p56f.
11. Previously unpublished testimony.
12. See, for example, Rudolf Ramm, *Aerztliche Rechts—und Standeskunde: Der Arzt als Gesundheitserzieher*, Berlin: W deGruyter, 1943, pp79–80.
13. Welch, *Propaganda*, p123.
14. See E. Klee (ed.), *Dokumente zur "Euthansie,"* Frankfurt, 1985, p63.
15. Previously unpublished testimony.
16. Karl Brandt, Hitler's own doctor, overheard the remark and recalled it in evidence at the Nuremberg Doctors trial in 1947—see *USMT Nuremberg, Case I (Medical Case). Transcript of Proceedings*, p2482.
17. *Völkischer Beobachter*, 2 August 1929.

18. Ian Kershaw, *Hitler 1889–1936: Hubris*, pp527–591.
19. *Rede Hitlers vor Kreisleitern auf der Ordensburg Vogelsang am 29. April 1937*, in Hildegard von Kotze and Helmut Krausnick (eds.), *Es spricht der Führer. 7 exemplarische Hitler-Reden*, Gütersloh, 1966, pp123–177.
20. Quote from Reinhard Spitzy, Rees, *Nazis: A Warning from History*, p94.
21. ibid., pp100–101.
22. Ronnie S. Landau, *The Nazi Holocaust*, London, I. B.Tauris, 2006, pp137–140. Reported *New York Times*, 27 March 1938, p25.
23. *Manchester Guardian*, 23 May 1936.
24. Golda Meir, *My Life*, Weidenfeld and Nicolson, 1975, p127.
25. *Völkischer Beobachter*, 13 July 1938.
26. Hitler speech, 12 September 1938, Domarus, *Vol. 2*, p1153.
27. Interview for WW2History.com.
28. Previously unpublished testimony.
29. Previously unpublished testimony.
30. *Dieses Pack ist schlimmer!* (This bunch is worse!), *Das Schwarze Korps, Zeitung der Schutzstaffeln der NSDAP*, Organ der Reichsführung SS, Berlin, 17 November 1938, No. 46, Vol. 4, front page.
31. *Damit wir uns recht verstehen* (Let us be quite honest) *Das Schwarze Korps, Zeitung der Schutzstaffeln der NSDAP*, Organ der Reichsführung SS, Berlin, 1 December 1938, No. 48, Vol. 4, p2.
32. *Juden, was nun?* (Jews, what now?), *Das Schwarze Korps. Zeitung der Schutzstaffeln der NSDAP*, Organ der Reichsführung SS, Berlin, 24 November 1938, No. 47, Vol. 4, front page.

CHAPTER ELEVEN

1. William L. Shirer, *Berlin Diary 1934–1939*, The John Hopkins University Press, 2002, entry for 31 August 1939, p191.
2. BArch RW 19/41, p56, Wehrwirtschaftsinspektion [War Economy Inspection] VII (Munich), Wirtschaftsbericht [economic report] August 1938, 9. 9. 1938.
3. BArch RW 19/41, p35, Wehrwirtschaftsinspektion [War Economy Inspection] VII (Munich), Wirtschaftsbericht [economic report], October 1938, 18. 11. 1938.
4. Leonidas E. Hill, *Die Weizsäcker Papiere 1933–1950*, Frankfurt a. M./Berlin/Wien, 1974, p142.
5. Douglass, Frederick, speech at Canandaigua, New York, August 3, 1857. Full text in John W. Blassingame (ed.), *The Frederick Douglass Papers*, Vol. 3: 1855–63. Yale University Press, 1979, p204.

6. Previously unpublished testimony.
7. F. Wiedemann, *Der Mann der Feldherr werden wollte,* Kettwig, 1964, pp127–8.
8. ibid.
9. Klaus-Jürgen Müller, *General Ludwig Beck, Studien und Dokumente zur politisch-militärischen Vorstellungswelt und Tätigkeit des Generalstabschefs des deutschen Heeres 1933–1938,* Boppard am Rhein, 1980, pp502–512.
10. Müller, *General Ludwig Beck,* pp521ff. Original in BArch (Freiburg), N 28/3.
11. Reynolds, *Treason Was No Crime,* pp119–120.
12. Notes for a presentation by the chief of staff, army, 19 July 1938, with additional suggestions of 16 July 1938, quoted by Müller, *General Ludwig Beck. Studien und Dokumente zur politisch-militärischen Vorstellungswelt und Tätigkeit des Generalstabschefs des deutschen Heeres 1933–1938,* Boppard am Rhein 1980, pp554–556. Original in: BArch N 28/4.
13. Previously unpublished testimony.
14. Quoted by Müller, *General Ludwig Beck,* pp521–528. Original in: BArch N 28/3.
15. Speech 6 November 1933, quoted in William L. Shirer, *The Rise and Fall of the Third Reich,* Crest, 1962, p343.
16. Edgar Röhricht, *Pflicht und Gewissen. Erinnerungen eines deutschen Generals 1932 bis 1944,* Stuttgart, 1965, pp119ff.
17. Quoted in Müller, *General Ludwig Beck,* pp542–550.
18. Quoted by Müller, *General Ludwig Beck,* pp554–556. Original in: BArch N 28/4.
19. Interview with the author for WW2History.com.
20. BArch N 19/6, Nachlass von Weichs, Erinnerungen, Bd. 2: Weimar und Nürnberg—Anschluß Österreichs, Besetzung Sudetenland und Böhmen-Mähren—1. Teil, 1937–1939 (estate von Weichs, memoirs, Vol. 2: Weimar and Nuremberg—Anschluss of Austria, occupation of Sudetenland and Böhmen-Mähren—part 1 [handwritten], 1937–1939).
21. Sir Ian Kershaw, *Hitler 1936–1945: Nemesis,* Penguin, 2001, p103.
22. Fritz Redl, "Group Emotion and Leadership," *Psychiatry,* 1942, Vol. V, pp573–596.
23. Sir Frank Roberts testimony in episode 3 of BBC TV, *The Nazis: A Warning from History,* 1997.
24. Hitler speech, 12 September 1938, Domarus, *Vol. II,* p1153.
25. Meeting on 30 August, 1938, Cabinet Office Papers (National Archive, Kew), CAB 23/94.
26. David Reynolds, *Summits: Six Meetings that Shaped the Twentieth Century,* Allen Lane, 2007, p37.

27. Chamberlain's letter to his sister Ida, 19 September 1938. See Reynolds, *Summits*, p55.
28. John Julius Norwich (editor), *The Duff Cooper Diaries*, Phoenix, 2006, entry for 17 September 1938, p260.
29. Ivone Kirkpatrick, *The Inner Circle*, Macmillan, 1959, pp94–97.
30. Lloyd George, writing in the *Daily Express*, 17 September 1936.
31. *The Duff Cooper Diaries*, entry for 17 September 1938, p260.
32. David Dilks (ed.), *The Diaries of Sir Alexander Cadogan* (1938–1945), Cassel, 1971. Entry for Saturday, 24 September 1938, p103.
33. Reynolds, *Summits*, p60.
34. As said to Birger Dahlerus, August 1939. Birger Dahlerus, *The Last Attempt*, Hutchinson, 1947, p73.
35. Reynolds, *Summits*, p107.
36. ibid., p111.
37. Previously unpublished testimony.
38. Interview with author for WW2History.com.
39. Goebbels' diary, entry for 29 September 1938.
40. Quoted in Weizsäcker's diary on 9 September 1938, Leonidas E. Hill, *Die Weizsäcker Papiere 1933–1950*, Frankfurt am M./Berlin/Wien 1974, p145.
41. For example, Gerd Überschär, *Generaloberst Franz Halder*, Göttingen, 1991; Ian Kershaw, *Nemesis*; Reynolds, *Summits*.
42. Ben Pimlott (ed.), *The Second World War Diaries of Hugh Dalton 1940–1945*, Jonathan Cape, 1986, entry for 23 February 1945, p836.
43. Laurence Rees, *World War Two. Behind Closed Doors: Stalin, the Nazis and the West*, BBC Books, 2008, pp345–411.
44. Besprechung bei Generalfeldmarschall Göring am 14.10.38, 10:00, im Reichsluftfahrtministerium, Dokument 1301-PS, in *Der Prozess gegen die Hauptkriegsverbrecher vor dem Internationalen Militärgerichtshof Nürnberg*, 1. November 1945–1. Oktober 1946, Band XXVII, Nürnberg, 1948, pp160–164.
45. Interview with author for WW2History.com.
46. Tooze, *Wages*, p294.
47. Kershaw, *Nemesis*, p161.
48. Besprechung bei Generalfeldmarschall Göring am 14.10.38, 10:00, im Reichsluftfahrtministerium, Dokument 1301-PS, in *Der Prozess gegen die Hauptkriegsverbrecher vor dem Internationalen Militärgerichtshof Nürnberg*, 1. November 1945–1. Oktober 1946, Band XXVII, Nürnberg, 1948, pp160–164.
49. Domarus, *Vol. II*, p1223.
50. Interview with author for WW2History.com.
51. Previously unpublished testimony.

52. "Rede Hitlers vor der deutsche Presse (10 November 1938)," *Vierteljahrshefte für Zeitgeschichte*, Vol. 6 (1958), No. 2, pp175–191.

53. Visit to Beck on 16 November 1938. Transcript of Holtzmann's affidavit dated 19 April 1946; attachment to a letter from Robert Holtzman to Ricarda Huch, 8 June 1946, Institut für Zeitgeschichte (IfZ) Munich, ZS/A-26a/1, pp13f.

54. Words spoken by Chamberlain outside 10 Downing Street on 30 September 1938.

55. CAB 27/624 32nd, 14 November 1938.

56. Peake Papers, 19 February 1957, quoted in Andrew Roberts, *The Holy Fox, The Life of Lord Halifax,* Phoenix, 1997, p128.

57. ibid., p128.

58. See pp143–144.

59. Domarus, *Vol. III*, p1449.

60. Rees, *The Nazis: A Warning from History,* p109.

61. Previously unpublished testimony.

62. See pp135–136.

63. Secret decree of the Supreme Commander of the Army, General von Brauchitsch, on the education of the officer corps, 18 December 1938. Quoted by: Klaus-Jürgen Müller, *Armee und Drittes Reich 1933–1939. Darstellung und Dokumentation*, unter Mitarbeit von Ernst Willi Hansen, Paderborn, 1987, pp180–182. And: *Offiziere im Bild von Dokumenten aus drei Jahrhunderten*, Militärgeschichtliches Forschungsamt, Stuttgart, 1964. The Original is in: Militärgeschichtliches Forschungsamt (MGFA), H 7/30, Sammelheft zu Oberkommando des Heeres Nr. 300/40g PA (2) Ia vom 25.10.1940.

64. Jodl diary entry for 13 September 1938. "Aus den Tagebüchern des Chefs der Abteilung Landesverteidigung, dann Wehrmachtsführungsamt im OKW, Oberst d. G. Jodl," quoted in Jacobsen and Jochmann (eds.), *Ausgewählte Dokumente zur Geschichte des Nationalsozialismus 1933–1945.* Jodl's diary is also reproduced in *Der Prozess gegen die Hauptkriegsverbrecher vor dem Internationalen Militärgerichtshof Nürnberg,* 1. November 1940–1. Oktober 1946, Volume XXVIII, Nürnberg, 1948, Dokument 1780-PS, pp345–393. The original is in: BArch N 69 (estate Jodl).

65. Speer, *Inside the Third Reich,* p172.

66. Testimony in episode 3 of BBC TV, *The Nazis: A Warning from History.*

67. Cadogan diary, entry for 20 March 1938, p161.

68. Speer, *Inside the Third Reich*, p239.

69. Interview with author for WW2History.com.

70. Führer address to the commanders-in-chief on 22 August 1939, *Akten*

zur deutschen auswärtigen Politik 1918–1945 (ADAP), aus dem Archiv des Deutschen Auswärtigen Amts, Serie D, 1937–1945, Band VII, Göttingen u. a., 1953, pp167–170, pp171–172.

71. Kershaw, *Nemesis,* p120.

72. Domarus, *Vol. III*, p1459.

73. Meeting of 23 May 1939, in *Akten zur deutschen auswärtigen Politik 1918–1945* (ADAP), aus dem Archiv des Deutschen Auswärtigen Amts, Serie D, 1937–1945, Band VI, Göttingen u. a., 1956, pp477–483. This document is also part of the evidence in the Nuremberg trial, document 79-L, cf.: *Der Prozess gegen die Hauptkriegsverbrecher vor dem Internationalen Militärgerichtshof Nürnberg,* 1. November 1945–1. Oktober 1946, Volume XXXVII, Nürnberg, 1946.

74. Cadogan diary, entry for 30 August 1939, p205.

75. Dahlerus, *The Last Attempt*, p60.

76. ibid., p62.

77. ibid., p70.

78. Previously unpublished testimony.

79. Kershaw, *Nemesis*, p92.

80. Rees, *Their Darkest Hour*, p210.

81. Speer, *Inside the Third Reich*, p235.

82. Henderson, *Failure of a Mission*, p39.

83. ibid., p73.

84. 20 December 1938, *Diary of Ulrich von Hassell.* Ulrich von Hassell, *Die Hassell-Tagebücher. Aufzeichnungen vom Andern Deutschland.* Nach der Handschrift revidierte und erweiterte Ausgabe unter Mitarbeit von Klaus Peter Reiß, ed. Friedrich Freiherr Hiller von Gaertringen, Siedler Verlag, Berlin, 1988, pp67–72.

85. Previously unpublished testimony.

86. Previously unpublished testimony.

CHAPTER TWELVE

1. Indeed, even now if the battles are played out on computer simulations, the Allies always win. See Ernest R. May, *Strange Victory, Hitler's conquest of France*, I. B.Tauris, 2000, p6.

2. Memorandum Brief of the Prosecution, Crimes against Peace: Counts one and four; Planning, Preparing, Initiating and Waging Wars of Aggression and Invasions, the Common Plan or Conspiracy, 26 August 1948, Records of the United States Nuremberg War Crimes Trials Interrogations, 1946–1949. 898, Roll 58, 30.

3. Previously unpublished testimony.
4. Interview with author for WW2History.com.
5. Rees, *The Nazis: A Warning from History*, p114.
6. Martin Kitchen, *The Third Reich, Charisma and Community*, Longman, 2008, p306.
7. ibid., p307.
8. Kershaw, *Nemesis*, p245.
9. Decree of the ObdH [Commander-in-Chief of the Army], Colonel General von Brauchitsch, to the officers of the army, Berlin 25.10.1939, BArch N 104/3. Quoted in: Helmuth Groscurth, *Tagebücher eines Abwehroffiziers 1938–1940. Mit weiteren Dokumenten zur Militäropposition gegen Hitler*, hrsg. von Helmut Krausnick und Harold C. Deutsch unter Mitarbeit von Hildegard von Kotze, Deutsche Verlags-Anstalt, Stuttgart, 1970, p386.
10. Richard Hargreaves, *Blitzkrieg Unleashed*, Stackpole Books (U.S.A.), 2010, p158.
11. Richard Giziowski, *The Enigma of General Blaskowitz*, Hippocrene Books, New York, and Leo Cooper Books, London, 1997, p143.
12. Charles Burdick and Hans-Adolf Jacobson (editors), *The Halder War Diary 1939–1942*, Greenhill Books, 1988, entry for 19 September 1939, p57.
13. Bogdan Musial, *Deutsche Zivilverwaltung und Judenverfolgung im Generalgouvernement*, Wiesbaden, 1999, p106; this figure also quoted in Christopher Browning, *The Origins of the Final Solution*, Heinemann, 2004, p35.
14. *Halder War Diary*, entry for 18 October 1939, p73.
15. Goebbels' diary, entry for 2 November 1939, quoted in Giziowski, *Enigma*, p162.
16. Letter of 21 November 1939, Ausgewählte Briefe von Generalmajor Helmuth Stieff (hingerichtet am 8 August 1944), in: *Vierteljahreshefte für Zeitgeschichte (VfZ)*, Vol. 2, 1954, No. 3, pp291–305. Sections of the letter (but not all these extracts, which are taken from the German original) also in English in Giziowski, *Enigma*, p164.
17. *Heeresadjutant bei Hitler 1938–1943. Aufzeichnungen des Majors Engel*, hrsg. und kommentiert von Hildegard von Kotze, Stuttgart, 1974, p67f. A copy of the diary is in the Institut für Zeitgeschichte (IfZ) Munich, ED 53.
18. *Halder War Diary*, entry for 27 September 1939.
19. Interview with author for WW2History.com.
20. *Kriegstagebuch des Oberkommandos der Wehrmacht* (Wehrmachtführungsstab), Band I: 1 August 1940–31 Dezember 1941, geführt von Helmuth Greiner, Bernard & Graefe Verlag für Wehrwesen, Frankfurt am Main, 1965, p950.

21. May, *Strange Victory*, p287.
22. *Halder War Diary*, entry for 14 October 1939, p72.
23. ibid.
24. ibid., entry for 3 November 1939, p76.
25. Institut für Zeitgeschichte (IfZ) Munich, ZS 603 (von Dohnanyi), *Protokoll der Besprechung mit Frau von Dohnanyi am 1.12.52*, p14f.
26. Kershaw, *Hubris*, pp269–270.
27. Previously unpublished testimony.
28. Bericht zur innenpolitischen Lage (Nr. 15) 13. November 1939, in: *Meldungen aus dem Reich 1938–1945. Die geheimen Lageberichte des Sicherheitsdienstes der SS*. Hrsg. u. eingel. von Heinz Boberach. Band 3, Herrsching, 1984, pp449–456.
29. Meldungen aus dem Reich (Nr. 28) 13. Dezember 1939, in: *Meldungen aus dem Reich 1938–1945. Die geheimen Lageberichte des Sicherheitsdienstes der SS*. Hrsg. u. eingel. von Heinz Boberach. Band 3, Herrsching, 1984, pp563–573.
30. Georg Mayer (ed.), Generalfeldmarschall Wilhelm Ritter von Leeb, entry for 9 October 1939, *Tagebuchaufzeichnungen und Lagebeurteilungen aus zwei Weltkriegen*, Deutsche Verlags-Anstalt, Stuttgart, 1976, pp187–188.
31. Letter of Wilhelm Ritter von Leeb to Franz Halder on 19 December 1939, typewritten draft; in the original there is a handwritten annotation "send via courier on 20 December 1939. Becker, Major." From *Tagebuchaufzeichnungen und Lagebeurteilungen aus zwei Weltkriegen*, Stuttgart, 1976, pp473–474. A carbon copy of the typewritten draft is in von Leeb's estate in the Bavarian main state archive, BayHStA, Abt. IV Kriegsarchiv, Nachlass Wilhelm Ritter von Leeb.
32. Helmuth Groscurth, *Tagebücher eines Abwehroffiziers 1938–1940*. Mit weiteren Dokumenten zur Militäropposition gegen Hitler, hrsg. von Helmut Krausnick und Harold C. Deutsch unter Mitarbeit von Hildegard von Kotze, Stuttgart, 1970, p222.
33. Letter written by Walther Nehring, a general of the armoured corps, to Geyr von Schweppenburg on 26 October 1967 about whether his [Nehring's] armoured regiment would have acted against Hitler. Document in Institut für Zeitgeschichte (IfZ) Munich, ED 91/16.
34. Hitler's 23 November 1939 speech, Domarus, *Vol. III*, p1887.
35. Hugh Trevor-Roper, *The Mind of Adolf Hitler*, in *Hitler's Table Talk*, Phoenix Press, 2002, pxxxvii.
36. *Halder War Diary*, entry for 23 November, p80.
37. From Brauchitsch's testimony at Nuremberg, IMT *Vol. XX*, p628.
38. Interview with author for WW2History.com.

39. *Halder War Diary*, entry for 14 August 1939, p20.

40. *Hitler's Table Talk*, 17 September 1941, p32.

41. Klaus Gerbet (ed.), *Generalfeldmarschall Fedor von Bock. Zwischen Pflicht und Verweigerung. Das Kriegstagebuch*, Herbig Verlag, München/Berlin, 1995, p67f.

42. General Édouard Réquin witnessed this remark by Gamelin, quoted in Claude Paillat, *Désastre, Les Dossiers secrets de la France contemporaine*, Vol. 4, Part 2, Laffont, 1985, p185.

43. *Halder War Diary*, entry for 17 March 1940, p106.

44. ibid., p99.

45. ibid., p103.

46. General Andrew Beaufre, *Le Drame de 1940*, translated in English as *The Fall of France*, Cassell, 1965, p180.

47. May, *Strange Victory*, p413.

48. Winston Churchill, *Their Finest Hour, The Second World War, Vol. II*, Penguin Books, 2005, p38.

49. Paul-Émile Caton, *Une Guerre perdue en 4 Jours*, L'Amitié par le Livre, 1969.

50. Originally published in B. H. Liddell-Hart (ed.), *The Rommel Papers*, New York: Harcourt, Brace and Co., 1953 [www.eyewitnesstohistory.com, "Blitzkrieg, 1940"].

51. Interview with the author for WW2History.com.

52. Erich von Manstein, *Lost Victories*, Presidio Press, 1982, p383. (This memoir should be read with extreme care—it seems to have been written largely to absolve Manstein of deserved guilt for his actions in the East, and subsequent scholarly research reveals it to be unreliable on the Eastern campaign in general and Manstein's own actions in particular.)

53. *Hitler's Table Talk*, 16 August 1942, p635.

54. Interview with Edward Oates in the testimony section of WW2History.com.

55. See p64.

56. Kershaw, *Nemesis*, p289, Walter Warlimont, *Inside Hitler's Headquarters*, London, Weidenfeld and Nicolson, 1964, pp76, 79–80.

57. ibid., 17 May 1940, p149.

58. ibid., 18 May 1940, pp150–151.

59. *Halder War Diary*, entry for 6 June 1940, p182.

60. *Hitler's Table Talk*, 17 September 1941, p31.

61. Interview with author for WW2History.com.

62. Interview with author for WW2History.com.

63. Tooze, *Wages*, p370.

CHAPTER THIRTEEN

1. Hitler visit to Paris, 23 June 1940, described in: Speer, *Inside the Third Reich*, pp248–9.
2. *Halder War Diary*, entry for 22 July 1940, p230.
3. Hitler speech, 19 July 1940, Domarus, *Vol. III*, p2062.
4. War Cabinet minutes of 27 May 1940, Public Record Office Cab 65/13 and Cab 66/7.
5. Meeting held on 11 July 1940 at the Berghof.
6. Interview with author for WW2History.com.
7. Interview with author for WW2History.com.
8. *Halder War Diary*, entry for 22 July 1940, p230.
9. Previously unpublished testimony.
10. *Halder War Diary*, entry for 13 July 1940, p227.
11. Lord Halifax, BBC Radio broadcast, 22 July 1940.
12. Winston Churchill, BBC Radio broadcast, 31 March 1940.
13. Interview with author for WW2History.com.
14. Alun Chalfont, *Montgomery of Alamein*, Weidenfeld and Nicolson, 1976, p318.
15. Halder, *Spruchkammeraussage*, 20 September 1948, Institut für Zeitgeschichte (IfZ) Munich, ZS 240/6, p446.
16. *Halder War Diary*, entry for 3 July 1940 in discussion with Hans von Greiffenberg, p220.
17. Vejas Gabriel Liulevicius, *War Land on the Eastern Front: Culture, National Identity and German Occupation in World War I*, University of Cambridge Press, 2004, p249.
18. *Halder War Diary*, entry for 31 July 1940, pp241–246.
19. Goebbels' diary, entry for 10 July 1937.
20. Previously unpublished testimony.
21. Hitler speech to Nuremberg Party rally, 13 September 1937.
22. Previously unpublished testimony.
23. Winston Churchill, BBC Radio broadcast, 31 March 1940.
24. Warren F. Kimball, *Churchill and Roosevelt: The Complete Correspondence*: Vol. I, William Collins, 1984, WSC to FDR. 20 May 1940, C-11x, p40.
25. Interview with author for WW2History.com.
26. Tooze, *Wages*, p405.
27. ibid., p399.
28. *Halder War Diary*, entry for 31 July 1940, pp241–246.
29. Ian Kershaw, *The Hitler Myth*, p157, from Meldungen aus dem Reich (Nr. 141), 14 November 1940, in Heinz Boberach (ed.), *Meldungen aus dem Reich*

1938–1945. Die geheimen Lageberichte des Sicherheitsdienstes der SS, Vol. 5, Herrsching, 1984, pp1762–1774.

30. Meldungen aus dem Reich (Nr. 107) 22 Juli 1940, in Heinz Boberach (ed.), *Meldungen aus dem Reich 1938–1945*, pp1402–1412.

31. Previously unpublished testimony from Maria Mauth.

32. Liulevicius, *War Land*, p278.

33. ibid.

34. BArch RM 41/40.

35. Stalin meeting, 9 August 1944, with Polish delegation, held in the Kremlin, Moscow. *Documents of Polish-Soviet Relations 1939–1945*, Vol. 2, 1943–1945, General Sikorski Historical Institute, p334, doc 189.

36. Interview with author for WW2History.com

37. Secret statement of Dr. Goebbels to invited representatives of the German press, 5 April 1940, in Hans-Adolf Jacobsen, *Der zweite Weltkrieg. Grundzüge der Politik und Strategie in Dokumenten*, Fischer Bücherei, Frankfurt am Main/Hamburg, 1965, pp180–181.

38. Rees, *The Nazis: A Warning from History*, p112.

39. Heinrich Himmler: Speech to gauleiters and other party representatives, 29 February 1940, quoted in Bradley F. Smith and Agnes F. Petersen (eds.), *Heinrich Himmler. Geheimreden 1933 bis 1945 und andere Ansprachen*, Frankfurt/M., Berlin, Wien, Propyläen Verlag, 1974, pp115–144.

40. Goebbels' diary, entry for 24 January 1940.

41. Peter Longerich, *Heinrich Himmler, Biographie*, Munich, 2010, pp86, 797.

42. Heinrich Himmler, *"Some Thoughts on the Treatment of the Alien Population in the East,"* 15 May 1940, in Wolfgang Michalka (ed.), *Das Dritte Reich. Dokumente zur Innen und Außenpolitik, Vol. 2: Weltmachtsanspruch und nationaler Zusammenbruch 1939–1945*, München, 1985, pp163–166.

43. Interview with author, quoted in Rees, *The Nazis: A Warning from History*, p133.

44. Rudolf Höss, *Commandant of Auschwitz*, London, Phoenix Press, 2000, p390 and Höss interrogation by Jan Sehn, Krakow, 7–8 November 1946, Instytut Pamieci Narodowej, Warsaw NTN 103.

45. Express letter of the Chief of the Reich Main Security Office, R. Heydrich, to the commanders of the security police's task forces regarding the consecutive steps and methods of the "Final Solution to the Jewish Question," 21 September 1939. The letter is a Nuremberg document (Doc. 3363-PS) and reproduced in *Der Prozess gegen die Hauptkriegsverbrecher vor dem Internationalen Militärgerichtshof Nürnberg*, 1 November 1945–1. Oktober 1946, Band XXXII, Nürnberg, 1948.

46. Noakes and Pridham, *Vol. III,* p1053.
47. Christopher Browning, *The Origins of the Final Solution*, London, William Heinemann, 2004, pp36–43.
48. Götz Aly and Susanne Heim, *Architects of Annihilation*, London, Weidenfeld and Nicolson, 2002, p21.
49. Previously unpublished testimony.
50. Diary of Stanislav Rozycki, in Landau, *The Nazi Holocaust,* p158.
51. Excerpts from the speech of General-Governor Hans Frank at a meeting of the district leaders and city commissioners of the district of Radom concerning the plan to concentrate the Polish and Jewish population in the General Government, 25 November 1939. *Faschismus-Getto-Massenmord. Dokumentation über Ausrottung und Widerstand der Juden in Polen während des zweiten Weltkrieges,* hrsg. vom Jüdischen Historischen Institut Warschau, ausgewählt, bearbeitet und eingeleitet von Tatiana Berenstein u.a., Rütten & Löning, Berlin, 1960, p46. The original is in: Archive of the Jewish Historical Institute in Warsaw (Zydowski Instytut Historyczny), Varia I, Nr. 33.
52. Fritz Stern, *The Politics of Cultural Despair*, University of California, 1974, pxix.
53. For a full discussion of the ideas of Paul de Lagarde, see Stern, *Politics of Cultural Despair*, Chapter 1, pp3–83.
54. Kershaw, *Nemesis*, p321.
55. Goebbels' diary, entry for 17 August 1940.
56. Previously unpublished testimony.
57. Browning, *Origins of the Final Solution*, p82.
58. Aly and Heim, *Architects of Annihilation*, p58.
59. Service, *Stalin*, p312.
60. Aly and Heim, *Architects*, p118.
61. Interview with author for WW2History.com.
62. *Halder War Diary*, entry for 30 March 1941, p346.
63. Previously unpublished testimony from Bernhard Bechler, ADC (junior officer) to General Eugen Müller (General for "Special Duties") autumn 1940 to spring 1942.
64. Alex J. Kay, "Germany's Staatssekretäre, Mass Starvation and the Meeting of 2 May 1941," *Journal of Contemporary History,* Vol. 41 (4), p685. Also see the work of Christian Gerlach, *Kalkulierte Morde: Die deutsche Wirtschafts- und Vernichtungspolitik in Weissrussland 1941 bis 1944*, Hamburg, 2000.
65. Kay, *JCH,* p689.
66. *Rosenberg diary*, 1 and 6 May 1941, published in Frankfurter Rundschau no 140, 22.6.1971, quoted in Kay, *JCH,* p692.

67. A point made by Mark Roseman, *The Villa, the Lake, the Meeting, Wannsee and the Final Solution,* Allen Lane, 2002, p57 and also by Kay, *JCH,* p688.

68. Interview with author for WW2History.com.

69. Goebbels' diary, entry for 16 June 1941.

70. The Red Army briefly recaptured the city in February 1943, only for the Germans to recapture it in March.

71. Previously unpublished testimony.

72. Previously unpublished testimony.

73. Laurence Rees, *War of the Century,* BBC Books, 1999, p99.

74. Previously unpublished testimony.

75. Frank's official diary, 25 March 1941 [Krakow, Cabinet meeting and discussion]. Werner Präg and Wolfgang Jacobmeyer (eds.), *Das Diensttagebuch des deutschen Generalgouverneurs in Polen 1939–1945,* Stuttgart, Deutsche Verlags-Anstalt, 1975, pp335–338.

76. Peter Longerich, *The Unwritten Order,* Stroud, Tempus, 2001, pp57–62.

77. ibid., p63.

78. Instruction dated 12 July 1941, quoted in H. Buchheim, M. Broszat, H. Krausnick, H-A. Jacobsen, *Anatomy of the SS State,* London, Collins, 1968, p62.

79. Barry A. Leach, *German Strategy Against Russia 1939–1941,* Oxford University Press, 1973, pp140–145.

80. Hitler proclamation, 22 June 1941, Domarus, *Vol. IV,* p2451.

81. Churchill speech, 22 June 1941.

82. Hitler proclamation to soldiers of the Eastern Front, 3 October 1941, Domarus, *Vol. IV,* p2491.

CHAPTER FOURTEEN

1. Interview with author for WW2History.com.

2. Quoted in *New York Times,* 24 June 1941, p7.

3. Words of Lt. General Henry Powell, deputy to General Sir Alan Brooke, Chief of the Imperial Defence Staff, quoted in Joan Beaumont, *Comrades in Arms: British Aid to Russia, 1941–1945,* London, Davis-Poynter, 1980, p26.

4. Previously unpublished testimony.

5. Previously unpublished testimony.

6. Previously unpublished testimony.

7. *Halder War Diary,* entry for 3 July 1941, p446.

8. The Chief of Staff of the War Economy and Armaments Office regarding the armament programme of the Air Force, 26 June 1941, BArch RW 19/559, pp43–46 (Der Chef des Stabes des Wehrwirtschaftsund Rüstungsamts betr.

Rüstungsprogramm der Luftwaffe, 26. 6. 1941). Also quoted in: Georg Thomas, *Geschichte der deutschen Wehr-und Rüstungswirtschaft (1918–1943/45)*, Harald Boldt Verlag, Boppard am Rhein, 1966, pp448–451.

9. *Halder War Diary*, entry for 11 August 1941, p506.

10. Ludolf Herbst, *Das nationalsozialistische Deutschland 1933–1945. Die Entfesselung der Gewalt: Rassismus und Krieg*, Suhrkamp Verlag, Frankfurt am Main, 1996, p360ff. Original reference is a chart in Halder's war log, Generaloberst Halder. Kriegstagebuch, Band III: Der Rußlandfeldzug bis zum Marsch auf Stalingrad (22. 6. 1941—24. 9. 1942), bearb. von Hans-Adolf Jacobsen, Stuttgart, 1964, pp199, 213.

11. Walter Warlimont, *Inside Hitler's Headquarters 1939–1941*, Presido, 1964, p189.

12. *Halder War Diary*, entry for 22 August 1941, p514.

13. Heinz Guderian, *Panzer Leader*, Penguin, 2009, p200.

14. Tagebucheintrag vom 19. August 1941, in: Joseph Goebbels, *Die Tagebücher von Joseph Goebbels*. Im Auftrag des Instituts für Zeitgeschichte und mit Unterstützung des Staatlichen Archivdienstes Rußlands hrsg. von Elke Fröhlich. Teil II: Diktate 1941–1945. Band 1: Juli–September 1941, München [u.a.] 1996, pp255–272.

15. *Hitler's Table Talk*, 19–20 August 1941, p28.

16. ibid., 23 September 1941, p38.

17. Ernst Deuerlein (ed.), *Der Aufstieg der NSDAP in Augenzeugenberichten*, Düsseldorf, Karl Rauch Verlag, 1968, pp108–112.

18. *Hitler's Table Talk*, night of 27 January 1942, p257.

19. *Hitler's Table Talk*, night of 25–26 September 1941.

20. Communication from naval office to Army Group North, see Domarus, *Vol. IV*, p2483.

21. Domarus, *Vol. III*, p2491.

22. ibid., p2497.

23. Episode 1, *War of the Century*, written and produced by Laurence Rees, BBC2, 1999.

24. Weber, *Essays*, p248.

25. *Halder War Diary*, pp529–530.

26. *Table Talk*, 17 October 1941, p69.

27. ibid., 17–18 October, p71.

28. ibid., 25 October, p87.

29. ibid., 10 October, p51.

30. ibid., 19 October, p74.

31. ibid., 25 October, p90.

32. Hugh Trevor-Roper, "The Mind of Adolf Hitler," in *Table Talk*, pxxxix.
33. *Table Talk*, 13–14 October, p58.
34. Interview with author for WW2History.com.
35. Interview with author for WW2History.com.
36. Interview with author for WW2History.com.
37. Previously unpublished testimony.
38. War diary, Wehrmacht office of military economics and armaments/staff, 13 October 1941. BArch RW 19/165, pp274, 554.
39. Kershaw, *Nemesis*, pp440–441.
40. *Halder War Diary*, entry for 10 November 1941, p555.
41. Guderian, *Panzer Leader*, p264.
42. ibid., pp265–266.
43. Hitler's directive to Army Group Centre, 12 December 1941 (Weisung Hitlers für die Heeresgruppe Mitte, 20. 12. 1941) quoted by: Wolfgang Michalka (ed.), *Das Dritte Reich. Dokumente zur Innen-und Außenpolitik, Vol. 2: Weltmachtsanspruch und nationaler Zusammenbruch 1939–1945*, Deutscher Taschenbuch Verlag, München, 1985, pp66–67. The Original is in: Institut für Zeitgeschichte (IfZ) Munich, Dok. NOKW-539.
44. A point made by Ribbentrop at his meeting with the American Chargé d'Affaires in Berlin on 11 December 1941. See Documents on German Foreign Policy, Series D, *Vol. XIII*, pp999–1000.
45. Alexander Mitscherlich and Frederick Mielke (eds.), *Medizin ohne Menschlichkeit Dokumente des Nürnberger Ärzteprozesses*, Frankfurt am Main, Fischer Bücherie, 1960, p187.
46. E. Klee, *"Euthanasie" im NS Staat. Die Vernichtung "lebensunwerten Lebens,"* Frankfurt, S. Fischer Verlag, 1983, p51.
47. Handwritten anonymous letter from Ramsau, October 1941, Staatsarchiv München (StAM), LRA 31933.
48. Letter from Maria Aigner to the School Inspector, 17 September 1941, StAM, LRA 48235.
49. *Table Talk*, 14 October 1941, p59.
50. Interview with author for WW2History.com.
51. Longerich, *Unwritten Order*, p60.
52. Previously unpublished testimony.
53. 16 July 1941, Hitler Comments, Conference in Führer Headquarters, in Czesław Madajczyk (ed.), *Generalny Plan Wschodni: Zbiór dokumentów*, Warszawa, Główna Komisja Badania Zbrodni Hitlerowskich w Polsce, 1990, pp61–64. Also in Nuremberg Trial Documents: IMT, Vol. 38, p92 (221-L).

54. For a detailed analysis of *Generalplan Ost* (in English) see Tooze, *Wages of Destruction*, pp466–476.

55. Goebbels' diary, entry for 19 August 1941.

56. Testimony of Uwe Storjohann, in Laurence Rees, *Auschwitz: The Nazis and the "Final Solution,"* BBC Books, 2005, p76.

57. Testimony of Erna Krantz in Rees, *Darkest Hour*, p195.

58. Goebbels' diary, entry for 16 December 1941.

59. Präg and Jacobmeyer (eds.), *Das Diensttagebuch des deutschen Generalgouverneurs in Polen 1939–1945*, pp452–459.

60. Toivi Blatt testimony from interview with the author. See WW2History.com and also Rees, *Auschwitz*, pp208–210.

61. Interview with author for WW2History.com.

62. Longerich, *Unwritten Order*, p109.

63. Goebbels' diary, entry for 27 March 1942.

64. See pp199–200.

65. Rees, *Auschwitz*, p78.

66. David Cesarani, *Eichmann, His Life and Crimes*, London, Heinemann, 2004, p197.

67. Testimony of Hans Friedrich, episode 1, *Auschwitz: The Nazis and the "Final Solution,"* written and produced by Laurence Rees, BBC, January 2005.

68. Ulrich Herbert, *Hitler's Foreign Workers*, Cambridge University Press, 1997, pp389–390.

CHAPTER FIFTEEN

1. Previously unpublished testimony.

2. Goebbels' diary, entry for 20 March 1942, *The Goebbels Diary*, translated and edited by Louis P. Lochner, Hamish Hamilton, 1948, p92.

3. Winston S. Churchill, *The Grand Alliance, The Second World War Vol. III*, Penguin Classics, 2005, p539.

4. Previously unpublished testimony.

5. Previously unpublished testimony.

6. Previously unpublished testimony.

7. Previously unpublished testimony.

8. Kershaw, *The Hitler Myth*, p188.

9. ibid., p187.

10. Hitler speech, 26 April 1942, Domarus, *Vol. IV*, p2623.

11. ibid., p2628.

12. Goebbels' diary, entry for 27 April 1942, p141.

13. ibid., entry for 29 April 1942, p144.

14. *The Ciano Diaries*, Hugh Gibson (ed.), Simon Publications, 2001, entry for 29 April 1942, p477.

15. ibid., entry for 30 April 1942, pp478–9.

16. ibid., entry for 30 April 1942, p478.

17. See p112.

18. *Halder War Diary*, entry for 23 July 1942, p646.

19. Stenographic report of the meeting of Reich Marshal Göring with the Reich Commissioners for the occupied territories and Military Commanders on the food situation; at the Hermann-Göring-hall of the Ministry of Aviation, Thursday, 6 August 1942, 4pm. Léon Poliakov and Joseph Wulf, *Das Dritte Reich und seine Diener*, Frankfurt am Main/Berlin/Wien, Ullstein Verlag, 1983, pp471ff. Also in Document 170-USSR, in: *Der Prozess gegen die Hauptkriegsverbrecher vor dem Internationalen Militärgerichtshof Nürnberg*, 1 November 1945–1 Oktober 1946, Band XXIX, Nürnberg, 1949, pp385ff. (Translation here is the official one used at the Nuremberg trials.)

20. Tooze, *Wages*, pp573–4.

21. As commander of Army Group A, Hitler reported to himself as commander in chief of the army, then himself as supreme commander of the Armed forces, then himself as Chancellor of Germany and then himself as head of state.

22. *Halder War Diary*, entry for 24 September 1942, p670.

23. Tooze, *Wages*, p587.

24. Interview with author for WW2History.com.

25. Previously unpublished testimony.

26. Hitler speech, 30 September 1942, Domarus, *Vol. IV*, p2675.

27. Previously unpublished testimony.

28. Interview with the author for WW2History.com.

29. Rees, *The Nazis, A Warning from History*, p256.

30. Chris Bellamy, *Absolute War, Soviet Russia in the Second World War*, Macmillan, 2007, p533.

31. Previously unpublished testimony.

32. Rees, *The Nazis: A Warning from History*, p276.

33. Situation conference 1 February 1943, Helmut Heiber and David M. Glantz (eds.), *Hitler and His Generals, Military Conferences 1942–1945*, Enigma Books, 2004, p61.

34. ibid., p62.

35. ibid., p66.

36. ibid., p59.

CHAPTER SIXTEEN

1. Göring speech in the Honours Hall of the Reich Ministry of Aviation, 30 January 1943, Domarus, *Vol. IV*, pp2745–2746.
2. Order of the day to the Sixth Army, 24 January 1943, Domarus, *Vol. IV*, p2743.
3. Previously unpublished testimony.
4. Testimony from episode 6, BBC TV, *Nazis: A Warning from History.*
5. Previously unpublished testimony.
6. This and the following paragraph, previously unpublished testimony.
7. Nicolaus von Below, *At Hitler's Side, The Memoirs of Hitler's Luftwaffe Adjutant 1937–1945*, Frontline Books, 2010, pp162–163.
8. Previously unpublished testimony.
9. Previously unpublished testimony.
10. Previously unpublished testimony.
11. 6 October Posen meeting. Heinrich Himmler, *Geheimreden 1933 bis 1945*, Bradley Smith and Agnes F. Peterson (eds.), Frankfurt am Main, Propyläen Verlag, 1974, pp169–170.
12. Previously unpublished testimony.
13. Von Below, *At Hitler's Side*, p189.
14. Testimony from episode 4, BBC TV, *War of the Century.*
15. Michael Balfour, *Withstanding Hitler*, Routledge, 1988, p126.
16. Fabian von Schlabrendorff, *The Secret War against Hitler*, Westview Press, 1994, p231.
17. Used because this was the only liquor that comes in square bottles. See *Secret War*, p233.
18. ibid., p231.
19. Previously unpublished testimony.
20. Schlabrendorff, *Secret War*, p269.
21. ibid., pp268–269.
22. ibid., pp271–272.
23. Kershaw, *Nemesis*, p670.
24. Hans Bernd Gisevius, *Valkyrie, An Insider's Account of the Plot to Kill Hitler*, Da Capo Press, 2009, p67.
25. ibid., p182.
26. ibid., p200.
27. Interview with Major Otto-Ernst Remer for the ITV series *World at War*, published in Richard Holmes, *The World At War, the Landmark Oral History*, Ebury Press, 2007, p419.
28. Previously unpublished testimony.

29. Karl Heinrich Peter, *Spiegelbild einer Verschwörung. Die Kaltenbrunner-Berichte an Bormann und Hitler über das Attentat vom 20. Juli 1944. Geheime Dokumente aus dem ehemaligen Reichssicherheitshauptamt,* Seewald, Stuttgart, 1961, pp1–10, some extracts in Kershaw, *Hitler Myth,* pp215–216.

30. Guderian, *Panzer Leader,* p341.

31. ibid., p342.

32. Interview with author for WW2History.com.

33. Guderian, *Panzer Leader,* p340.

34. As told by Ulrich de Maizière.

35. Ian Kershaw, *The End, Hitler's Germany, 1944–1945,* Allen Lane, 2011, pp111–114. The German military police report, compiled in the aftermath of the Soviet attack, quotes 26 dead.

36. Quoted ibid., p114.

37. Traudl Junge, *Until the Final Hour. Hitler's Last Secretary,* Weidenfeld and Nicolson, 2002, p145.

38. Testimony from episode 4, BBC TV, *War of the Century.*

39. Tooze, *Wages,* p639.

40. ibid., p653.

41. Goebbels' diary, entry for 2 December 1944.

42. Von Below, *Hitler's Luftwaffe Adjutant,* p223.

43. Manfred Messerschmidt, "Deserteure im Zweiten Weltkrieg," in Wolfgang Wette (ed.), *Deserteure der Wehrmacht,* Essen, 1995, p61.

44. Klaus-Dietmar Henke, *Die Amerikanische Besetzung Deutschlands,* Munich, Oldenbourg, 1995, pp806 and n132.

45. Previously unpublished testimony.

46. Speer, *Inside the Third Reich,* p588.

47. Testimony from episode 4, BBC TV, *War of the Century.*

48. Midday Situation Report, 2 March 1945, Helmut Heiber and David M. Glantz, *Hitler and his Generals,* Enigma Books, 2003, p684.

49. Entry for 2 March 1945, Joseph Goebbels, Hugh Trevor-Roper (ed.), *Goebbels Diaries, The Last Days,* Secker and Warburg, 1978, p24.

50. Testimony from *Bombing Germany,* BBC 2001, written and produced by Detlef Siebert, Executive Producer, Laurence Rees.

51. *United States Strategic Bombing Survey, Summary Report (European War),* 30 September 1945, "Some Signposts," p23 point 4. On the web at both http://www.airforce-magazine.com/MagazineArchive/Pages/2009/October/202009/1009keeper.aspx and http://www.anesi.com/ussbs02.htm.

52. Von Below, *Hitler's Luftwaffe Adjutant,* p228.

53. Rudolf Jordan, *Erlebt und erlitten: Weg eines Gauleiters von München bis*

Moskau, Leoni am Starnberger See, 1973, pp251–8. Quoted in Kershaw, *The End*, p245.

54. Yehuda Bauer, *American Jewry and the Holocaust: The American Jewish Joint Distribution Committee, 1939–1945,* Detroit, Wayne State University Press, 1981, pp429–430.

55. Felix Kersten, *The Kersten Memoirs, 1940–1945*, London, Hutchinson, 1956, p286.

56. Professor Sir Ian Kershaw, *What is Hitler's Place in History?* BBC lecture transmitted on BBC 4, 30 April 2005, Executive Producer, Laurence Rees.

57. Testimony from *Himmler, Hitler and the End of the Reich*, BBC TV, 2001, written and produced by Detlef Siebert, Executive Producer, Laurence Rees.

58. Welch, *Propaganda*, p234.

59. Junge, *Last Secretary*, p177.

60. Testimony from BBC TV, *Himmler, Hitler and the End of the Reich.*

61. United States, Office of United States Chief of Counsel for Prosecution of Axis Criminality, *Nazi Conspiracy and Aggression*, 8 vols. and 2 suppl. vols. (Government Printing Office, Washington, 1946–1948), VI, pp259–263, Doc. No. 3569-PS.

62. Junge, *Last Secretary*, p181.

INDEX

Hitler, Adolf:

CHANCELLOR OF GERMANY, ROAD
TO BECOMING, 68–77
  becomes Chancellor, 74–7, 81
  General Election, November, 1932, 70–1
  German elite's overestimation of ability to
    control, 69–70
  Hindenburg and, 68, 70, 71, 74, 75, 76
  intransigent personality and, 68–9, 70–1
  Lippe-Detmold local election, 1933 and, 74
  Schleicher and, 71–2, 74, 75, 76
  Strasser and, 69, 71–3
  Vice-Chancellorship, von Papen offers, 70
  von Papen and, 69–71, 72, 73, 74–5, 76
CHANCELLORSHIP, 1933–39, 81–107
  Cabinet, 81, 84, 89, 91
  charisma transforms opinion, 88
  Christianity, opinion of during, 101–3
  Communists and, 84
  concentration camps, first, 83
  Constitution and, 81, 82, 84
  creation of charismatic aura around during,
    96–107
  economy, 96, 106
  Enabling Law, 85–6
  foreign policy triumphs, 105
  General Election, 1933, 84
  Jewish boycott, 86–7
  Jews, attacks on in days after assuming role
    of Chancellor, 82
  need to transcend party and rule all
    Germans, 81–2
  "The Night of the Long Knives," 94–5
  oath of loyalty, armed forces swear, 96
  SA threat to superiority of army and, 90–6
  use of violence against opponents, 82–4
  Volksgemeinschaft (the idea of a people's
    community), 106
CHARACTER/CHARISMA:
  ability to feel events emotionally and
    demonstrate emotion, 4, 22, 25–6, 58–9,
    156–7, 173, 212, 227, 277
  all-or-nothing gamble, attraction to, 194,
    206
  animal nature of human life, 45–6, 193, 288
  annihilation, wish to practice, 164, 183, 193,
    203, 226–7, 230, 237, 242, 247, 248, 286
  anti-Semitism *see* Jews
  appeal for loyalty, 74, 260–1
  appeal not universal/immunity to charisma,
    4, 28, 68, 69, 70, 73, 76, 88–9, 113, 115, 116,
    119, 124, 148, 155, 207
  appearance, 3, 9, 21, 29
  arrogance, 269

blames others for failure, 259, 293
bravery, 12, 42
capacity to hate, 9, 173
capitalism and, 30
casualties, lack of care over German, 237,
  243, 288–90
central components of character become
  weaknesses, 241–2
certainty, 10, 19, 27, 31, 53, 68, 120, 129, 139,
  152, 174, 175, 179, 193, 196, 239, 241, 287
children, connection to German, 100, 101
Christianity, views on, 23, 45, 85, 101–3, 239,
  245–6, 247
cowardice, 42
daily habits, 118
dealing with subordinates to unsettle and
  destabilise powerful figures, 89
debate, unable to intellectually, 3, 10, 19, 37,
  51, 146–8, 151, 152, 155, 156–7, 171–2
decline and death of charisma/popularity,
  272–93
democracy, contemptuous of, 20, 24, 33, 54,
  56, 60, 77, 81, 82, 105, 241–2
denial, 271
desire to embrace death in defeat, 271
desire to lay waste to cities, 239
distance, 31, 97, 105, 246
"either—or," presents life as, 27, 227
end of war as end of Germany, sees, 288
excitement/chance to make history, offers
  Germans, 179, 183, 195, 239
extra-judicial killings, publicly allies himself
  with, 56–7
faith and, 53, 74, 105, 166, 169, 171, 207, 230,
  265, 267
fantastical quasi-utopian plans, 225, 245–6,
  250
father and, 10
film, on, 5, 56, 65, 92, 98, 103–5, 168
Final Solution, charismatic leadership
  legitimises, 254 *see also* Jews
finances, 10
first political statement, 16
first reference to "charismatic" quality, 19
followers' ambitions, ability to realise his,
  131–44, 179
followers' inability to believe wrongdoing
  of, 52, 246
gathering of Germans into one community,
  100
"General Bloodless," 162
Grösster Feldherr aller Zeiten ("the greatest
  military leader of all time"), 202
grudges and seeking vengeance, on, 239

Hitler, Adolf *(continued)*:
MUNICH, LIFE IN POST-WAR, 15–20
acceptance of Communist revolution in,
15–17
anti-Semitism, 19–20
first signs of charisma, 19–20
first speeches, 18–19, 20
Freikorps units and, 15, 16, 17, 30, 35
German Workers' Party and, 19–20, 29, 31,
36, 271
mission, discovers, 20
re-education agent, 18
repulsion at Socialist state of, 16
NAZI PARTY AND:
Bamberg Nazi conference, Bavaria, 14
February, 1926, 51, 52, 53, 54, 174
Beer Hall Putsch, Munich, 1923 and, 40–3,
50, 73, 142, 157, 190, 216, 264
Chancellorship/rule of Germany, road to,
68–76
Chancellorship/rule, 1933–39, 81–106
consolidates position as leader of on release
from prison, 50–4
Einsatzgruppen and *see Einsatzgruppen*
gains dictatorial power over, 30–1
growth of and, 36–7, 38, 49–54, 56–67,
68–76, 81–106
importance of enemies in bonding, 108
movement not political party, sees as, 22,
30, 35, 37, 49, 50, 53, 69, 71, 72, 73, 101,
106, 142
SA and *see* SA
SS and *see* SS
threat to position in, 1921, 36–7
"twenty-five points" of party programme,
presents to, 1920, 29–30, 101
RACE AND:
brings together German people, 100
citizenship, only those of "German blood"
considered, 29–30
ethnic reorganisation of Poland and, 58, 180,
185, 216, 218
ethnic reorganisation of Soviet Union/
Eastern Europe and, 249–55
ethnic reorganisation of Sudetenland and,
146
Jews and *see* Hitler, Adolf: Jews and
immigration policy, 29
Lebensraum argument and, 46–7
"National Community" idea and, 57–8, 84
purging Germany of degenerate elements,
orders, 132–8, 244–7
quasi-Darwinian view of, 46, 98, 243, 289

requirement for army recruits to prove
Aryan nature policy, 91
superiority of Aryan outlook, 24, 46–7,
106–7
RADICAL NATURE OF, 117–30
allows argument and disagreement, 120,
122–3
Austrian invasion and, 125–6
German Army, relations with, 117–30
hatred of committee meetings, 117
lone decision making, 117–19
refusal to read briefing notes and memos,
117
RHETORICAL SKILL/SPEECHES, 21–32
ability to establish a connection through,
21–32, 129
after-dinner monologues on Barbarossa, 239
anti-Semitism in, 19, 20, 22, 23–4, 29, 139,
164, 247, 250, 251
appearance during, 21–2, 29
broadcasts of, 180
certainty in, 28
charisma and, 21–31
constructed to provoke emotional response,
22–3
desperation of audience and, 22, 27
early, 21–5
emotional sincerity/authenticity of, 25–6, 88
first, 19, 20
footage of, 5, 56, 65, 98, 103, 168
Göring enthused by, 26–7
Hofbräuhaus, Munich, 28
hypnotising effect of, 5, 59, 156
importance of enemies in, 23–4
lack of compassion in, 229
loses rhetorical power in small groups, 31
presents life as "either—or" in, 27
redemption offered in, 99–100
reinforces peoples ideas in, 27–9, 31, 59, 60
religious terms in, 100, 101, 102
simple ideas in, 29
speaking ban lifted, 54
speech, April, 1926, Munich, Goebbels
attends, 52
speech, Nuremberg, 1929, 134
speech, 1932 election, 56
speech, 1932, Kaiserhof hotel, 73–4
speech, 10 March, 1933, on SA, 83
speech, Reichstag, 23 March, 1933, 85, 86
speech to *NS Frauenschaft*, September, 1936,
100
speech to party officials on Jewish question,
1937, 139